�֍ FOURTH EDITION �֍

MENU

Pricing & Strategy

FOURTH EDITION

MENU
Pricing & Strategy

JACK E. MILLER, FMP
St. Louis Community College

and

DAVID V. PAVESIC, Ph.D., FMP
Georgia State University

JOHN WILEY & SONS, INC.
New York • Chichester • Weinheim • Brisbane • Singapore • Toronto

Text design by Tenenbaum Design

This publication is designed to provide accurate and authoritative information in regard to the subject matter covered. It is sold with the understanding that the publisher is not engaged in rendering professional services. If professional advice or other expert assistance is required, the services of a competent professional person should be sought.

Library of Congress Cataloging-in-Publication Data:
Miller, Jack E., 1930–
    Menu pricing & strategy / Jack E. Miller and David V. Pavesic. —
  4th ed.
      p. cm.
    Includes bibliographical references and index.
    ISBN 0-471-28747-4 (pbk.)
    1. Restaurants—Prices. 2. Food service—Prices. 3. Menus.
  I. Pavesic, David V. II. Title.
TX911.3.P7M55 1996
647.95' 0681—dc20   96-17742
                                    CIP

Printed in the United States of America

10 9 8 7 6 5 4

Contents

Preface to the Fourth Edition

When the fourth edition of *Menu Pricing and Strategy* was first considered, my concern was to have a publication that would offer a body of information that had been improved and updated since the third edition. There have been major changes in menus and customer food habits during the time since the publication of the third edition. There are always certain operational principles, rules, and standards that will remain constant in their application to the restaurant industry, but there are supplements within these areas that make the information more clear or more easily understood.

My first consideration of you, the reader, was to provide an improved publication and to expand the views and opinions in the book by selecting a coauthor. I was aware of the writings concerning menus and pricing of Dr. David Pavesic, professor and director of the Cecil B. Day School of Hospitality Administration at Georgia State University. I was anxious to have David included as a contributor to the book and was able to work out an agreement with him as a coauthor. This union has resulted in the implementation of a considerable amount of new and expanded information for the menu and pricing book. David and I share the same views concerning the purpose and content of the book, so we were able to write with the same objective in mind: to have a book available for both owner/operator and student that develops sound mathematical calculations and economic principles for a profit oriented restaurant.

This edition continues to offer alternatives about pricing and strategies for the menu, not solutions with internal copy that says there is only one way to price and design your menu. You will make choices about the menu, sales, marketing, employees, and menu prices based upon your philosophy, operational style, and profit objective. The book will offer guides, concepts, and practical applications in all areas of menu planning, pricing, marketing, layout design, sales, employee training, and development. Your final decision will be based upon what is best for you in your restaurant. If your objective from planning and pricing is to accomplish a profit oriented business, this book, with its menu development and the information and strategies for the menu pricing, marketing, and sales, will offer a plan and guide to assist in attaining your goal.

This book is for the owner/manager to use along with the known marketing concepts, mathematical formulas, and economic principles, combining all to make rational managerial decisions. For the student, this book contains elements that will help you understand the principles of menu design and pricing. It will provide you with new insight that will require you to begin a critical thinking process for finding solutions about menu designs and pricing. After reading this book you will gain the knowledge to make decisions that are most appropriate for your restaurant and that are based upon sound management principles.

Acknowledgments

We want to thank and acknowledge the following individuals and organizations for their help and assistance in the development of the fourth edition. There are always some people in the restaurant industry who are willing to share information, menus, and materials about their operation. The persons we have recognized in this section are some of those fine individuals from our industry who were willing to share their knowledge and expertise.

Our special thanks to: Mike Hurst, 15th Street Fisheries, Ft. Lauderdale, Florida; American Express Publishing Co., New York City; Dick Stubbs, Applewoods, Inc., Oklahoma City; Scott Cobb, Classic Chicken & More, St. Louis; Steve Zimmer, Crusoe's, St. Louis; Michael Grisanti, Grisanti, Inc., Louisville, Kentucky; Sally Hopkins, Hallmark Cards, Inc., Kansas City, Missouri; Tom Kershaw, Cheers, Boston; Dr. David K. Hayes, Educational Institute, AH&MA, John Wiley & Sons, New York City; Tod Burnam, Max & Erma's Restaurant, Cleveland, Ohio; Carl Degen, Missouri Restaurant Association, Kansas City, Missouri; Ralph Brennan, Mr. B's, New Orleans, Louisiana; Joan Long, 9th Street Abbey, St. Louis, Missouri; Gary Leabman, Peerless Restaurant Supplies, St. Louis, Missouri; Rockbridge Publishing Co., Natural Bridge Station, Virginia; The Cornell Hotel and Restaurant Administration Quarterly, Ithaca, New York; Roger Shephard, Tippin's Restaurant & Pie Pantry, Overland Park, Kansas; Vincent Bommarito, Tony's, St. Louis, Missouri; Tom Scheffer, Zeno's, Rolla, Missouri; Jeff Prince, National Restaurant Association, Washington, D.C.; Jeanne Boyce, 13 Coins Restaurant, Seattle, Washington; Fred Hipp, Houlihan's Restaurant Group, Kansas City, Missouri; Lynn Reiner, National Restaurant Association; Donald M. Barickman, Hospitality Management Group, Charleston, South Carolina; Barbara Dudley, Independence Regional Health Center, Independence, Missouri; Laura G. Rozalsky,

The Abbey Restaurant, Atlanta, Georgia; Ted and Pat Kramper, St. Louis, Missouri; Don Schiffman, St. Louis, Missouri; Nancy Gilbert, Simi Winery, Simi Valley, California; Ken Hill, Applebee's International, Overland Park, Kansas; Donna Hood, F&B Business, Ronkonkoma, New York; Wilma Weimer, The Italian Oven Restaurant, Latrobe, Pennsylvania; Red, Hot & Blue, Inc., Arlington, Virginia; Lynn's Paradise Cafe, Louisville, Kentucky; Michael Chollet, The Noonday Club, St. Louis, Missouri; Rich Gorczyca, Cardwell's Restaurant, Clayton, Missouri; David Gilbert, The Rice Planter's Restaurant, Myrtle Beach, South Carolina; Barbara Bode, Council of Better Business Bureaus, Arlington, Virginia; Emil Pozzo, Rich & Charlie's, St. Louis, Missouri; Ron Regan, Regan Corporation, Kansas City, Missouri; D. Goodwin, Malone's Grill and Bar, Norcross, Georgia; Rick Rivera, Longhorn Steaks, Atlanta, Georgia; Ron McDougall, Brinker International, Dallas, Texas; Kathy Sutton, Truckstops of America/Country Pride Restaurants, Cleveland, Ohio; Robert L. Purple, The Spaghetti Warehouse Restaurant, Garland, Texas; David Bedard, East Bay Trading Company, Charleston, South Carolina; Chris Sullivan, Outback Steakhouse, Tampa, Florida; Craig Nickoloff, Claim Jumper Restaurants, Irvine, California; Dr. Richard Pillsbury, Georgia State University, Atlanta, Georgia.

We wish to acknowledge the restaurant associations of California and New York for their information on truth in menus. In addition we are grateful for the statistical data provided by the National Restaurant Association as well as *Nation's Restaurant News* and *Restaurants and Institutions* magazines.

There have been so many students in past classes who have required examples of how the theories work and practical examples of the use of the material in the book. They have required us to show the best and current examples for the book materials for their career future; practical, not academic, use of the formulas. They want to prepare themselves to deal with their future in the restaurant industry. There were also so many people who attended seminars on menu and cost control with a challenge to be current and correct about the material. We offer our thanks and gratitude to all who gave their assistance, attention, and questions to accomplish this fourth edition.

As senior author, I would like to thank my wife, Anita; I want you to know how I appreciate how hard you have worked helping me with the manuscript for the fourth edition, with a tireless dedication to accomplish a better publication than the previous editions. We had occasions where tempers were strained, but you persevered to reach our objective, and as a result we have a finished fourth edition.

Menu Development

The Role of the Menu

Menu is defined by Webster's as "a detailed list of food served at a meal." This definition came out of a kinder, gentler time for the restaurant owner, a time when competition was less fierce, tax laws were less rigid, operation was not measured by yield management, and patrons' knowledge and expectations were lower. Health factors were not as high a concern then as they are today either.

The role of the menu in a food service operation far exceeds the basic dictionary definition. It is an oversimplification to consider the menu to be a mere list of the food items a restaurant or food service operation has to offer. Too often menus have been considered simple bills of fare without any consideration for the way the menu can affect the revenue and operational efficiency of the establishment. We start with the assumption that the menu has been determined by customer preferences, possibly even after a detailed market study has been conducted. Menus driven by factors other than customer preferences, which consider the personal likes and dislikes of an owner, manager, or chef, will not serve the operation well. Consider then that a menu is more than a simple "bill of fare." In this chapter you will discover that the role of the menu is not just to list the food selections, but more importantly, that the menu is a major communication device that projects the personality and concept of a restaurant; it is an important cost control, internal marketing, and merchandising tool.

The nucleus of any food operation is its menu, but other factors may affect sales and customer participation, as discussed in later sections of this text. The principal source of revenue and continued customer preference concerning the restaurant of choice remains your menu. The menu will be the ultimate controlling factor as the profit center, customer attractor, and theme determiner.

The menu should not attempt to be all things to all people. Although you may try, you cannot cater to everyone's tastes. There will never be a restaurant menu that will appeal to every customer because it could not offer every conceivable menu item from breakfast to dinner and fast-food fare to gourmet continental cuisine. Therefore, menus must emphasize what your staff does well and what most of your clientele want to eat.

The menu now becomes the owner's final limitation. It will dictate to the operator the foods that will be necessary to serve the clientele you hope to attract.

As a limiting factor, the menu will provide the basic guidelines that you may have concerning space, equipment, and the personnel required for operation. The menu must provide a clear definition to those you hope to attract as customers and indicate that you may offer a better alternative in dining than do your competitors. This menu concept involves everything that affects the patron's view of what your restaurant is.

When the restaurant menu is built around a predominant menu item (one-concept menu), for example, fried chicken, hamburgers, Italian food, or Chinese food, certain operational aspects of the restaurant are simplified and easier to manage and control. In particular, purchasing and preparation can be standardized fairly easily. Labor costs are reduced because less skilled employees can be trained to follow the procedures and produce a consistent quality product. This is not the case in restaurants with extensive menus.

Most fast-food operations' menus are built around a single menu item. For McDonald's, Wendy's, Burger King, and Hardee's, it is the ubiquitous hamburger. For Outback Steakhouse, Longhorn, Ruth's Chris, and Steak n' Ale, the steak is the main menu item. Other well-known chains that have built their concept around a single menu item are Kentucky Fried Chicken, Pizza Hut, Starbuck's, and Taco Bell, just to name a few. While in all of the aforementioned operations, menus have certainly expanded to include other items, the mainstay of their menu continues to be the single menu item that made them successful. This specialization not only gives these operations an identity, it impacts the cost controls, marketing, purchasing, and management functions.

Your concept of your restaurant and menu must be exciting and innovative. It is not so much new ideas but rather new concepts of food and delivery systems for that food that is important. The point is that with every operation there is someone waiting to modify it to provide the consumer with a more desirable alternative. It may be that your concept is not new but provides a better, more refined alternative and improves upon something that now exists.

The menu is the ultimate profit center and theme control of a restaurant and is always the focal point.

THE HISTORY OF THE RESTAURANT INDUSTRY IN THE UNITED STATES

Although today about 40 percent of us eat at least one meal a day away from home, most colonial Americans never dined in a restaurant even once. They did eat away from home at church socials, funerals, weddings, and other special occasions. As early as the seventeenth century, taverns, inns, and boardinghouses were at one time required by law to offer meals for sale to travelers and workers away from home.

Restaurants in those times were really just stores specializing solely in the selling of food for on-premises consumption. Coffeehouses and oyster houses began appearing in many coastal cities in the late 1700s. The introduction of these single-concept menus is attributed to the European guild traditions. Guilds regulated who prepared food for sale and under what conditions such food could be sold.

The term *restaurant* was coined by the French in the 1760s. Earlier the term had referred simply to fortifying oneself with respect to food. Specifically, it referred to the consumption of bouillon, a dish of boiled chicken with coarse salt, and some types of eggnogs that were often served in refreshment rooms called *bouillons*. The term *restaurant* came into general use in America in the nineteenth century. The term *eating house* was common as late as 1830 in New York City, while *dining room* was also commonly used in various cities. Delmonico's in New York City became the symbol of fine dining in the 1800s and operated for over fifty years until it fell victim to prohibition (see fig. 1-1).

The cities of New York, Philadelphia, and Boston were at the leading edge of restaurant innovation in the mid 1800s. Mass production of food was brought about through the invention of prefabricated restaurant buildings. These prefabricated restaurants were called *diners* because many were retrofitted Pullman dining cars from the railroads. The diner story begins in 1872 when Walter Scott, a street vendor, traded his hand-carried basket of food one night for a horse-drawn wagon. The wagon allowed him to serve a larger number of customers without having to return home to replenish his stock. It also gave him a place to stand protected from the rain and snow.

Scott earned a living for forty-five years, retiring in 1917. On his menu were hard-boiled eggs, bread

FIGURE 1-1
Reputedly One of the First Printed Menus in America. Printed with permission of the New York Public Library, General Research Division, Astor, Lenox and Tilden Foundations.

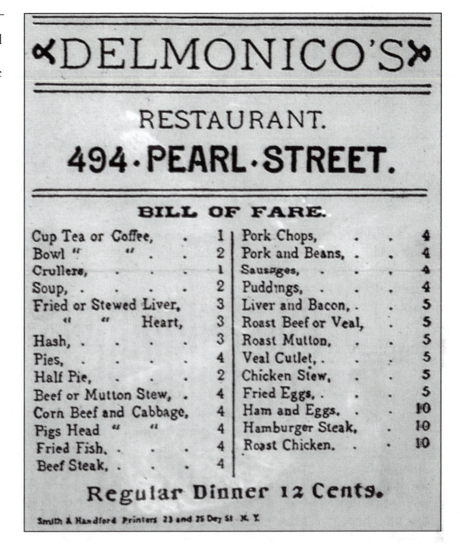

and butter, frankfurters, and chicken-salad sandwiches. Each cost just a nickel. His lunch wagon was an instant success in Providence, Rhode Island, and the concept was quickly copied throughout southern New England.

Lunch wagons evolved into diners during the early 1900s. They quit making their daily journeys through the streets and eventually settled permanently on small parcels of land. Soon trolleys, streetcars, and railroad dining cars were converted into diners. The menus in diners remained simple through time and were one of the factors contributing to their later decline in popularity. The menu offerings were significantly expanded in the 1920s.

During the same period, soda fountains became a much-appreciated part of the away-from-home eating experience. These operations, usually located in drug stores, served beverages made of a mixture of soda water and sweet-cream syrup. Soon the operators of the soda fountains added sandwiches, cakes, and other food items to their menus. This led to the evolution of luncheonettes in 1912 and coffee shops by the 1920s.

Chain restaurants began to appear before the invention of the automobile. Americans were eating in chain restaurants in the late 1800s in Baltimore, New York, and in a series of towns along the western railroad lines. The latter were called *Harvey Houses*, because the chain was started by Fred Harvey.

With the expansion of travel and the boom in factory and office work, more and more Americans left the farms to work in the cities. Fueled by the industrial revolution, urban populations were growing fast, and people found themselves away from home and in need of places to sleep and eat.

Scientific management manifested itself in the restaurant industry with the development of the cafeteria. Essentially, the cafeteria represented the restaurant industry's first attempt at emulating the factory assembly line that followed the recommendations of Frederick W. Taylor and Frank and Lillian Gilbreath.

In 1926 the Restaurant Association of America held its annual convention in Buffalo and published a map of the location and character of the restaurants near the hotels as encouragement for potential conventioneers. Thirty-five restaurants were listed, including ten cafeterias, seven lunchrooms, four sandwich shops, three coffee shops, and eleven full-service restaurants.

Self-service operations in all areas of the retail industry began to emerge in the early 1900s. In Philadelphia, two men by the name of Horn and Hardart ordered the first automat mechanism from a German firm that installed vending machines in European train stations. In an automat, as in a cafeteria, the food was cooked in advance and the customer could see the actual meal he would purchase. The difference between the cafeteria and the automat was that instead of an employee serving the customer, the patron simply stepped up to a wall of refrigerated or heated glass compartments, dropped money into a slot, opened the door, and removed their food.

By the late 1920s the automobile was becoming commonplace and restaurant operators sought to capture the business of motorists. This required driveways and parking to accommodate cars. Drive-up windows were added for convenience. Eventually drive-in restaurants were developed so that people did not have to get out of their cars to order or eat and were served by "car-hops." The finest drive-ins were in California, where the weather allowed them to operate all year. *For detailed information on the evolution of restaurants, we recommend* Orange Roofs, Golden Arches *by Philip Langdon and* Googie: Fifties Coffee Shop Architecture *by Alan Hess.*

Certain restaurant's concepts and certain chains are stronger or more prevalent in certain parts of the country than in others. Menu selections are also distributed geographically. In addition, the customer preference for independents or chain-affiliated restaurants is geographically influenced. Richard Pillsbury, in his wonderful book, *From Boarding House to Bistro,* explains these concepts in detail.

Pillsbury's research shows that the distribution of the top-grossing independent restaurants does not match the nation's population distribution. If there is any pattern, it seems to be tied more to tradition, economic power, ethnicity of residents, and recreation. Not surprisingly, the Pacific Northwest and the South are the largest centers of fish consumption. Chicken consumption is the greatest in the South and Southwest. Preferences for the many fast-food offerings are unevenly distributed. Hamburgers are strongest in the Great Plains, the intermountain West, the Far West, and the growth areas of the South. Pizza is king throughout most of the southern and eastern European immigrant communities of the Northeast and Midwest. Pizza chains are relatively weak in the Northeast and Midwest, where independents are strong. A Pizza Hut or Domino's franchise in New York or Chicago does not do as well as you might expect.

Pillsbury has studied the location of the various restaurant chains and has formed a hypothesis that America is composed of six major and several minor restaurant regions. Figure 1-2 shows American restaurant regions as developed by Richard Pillsbury. Dinerland is characterized by neighborhood independent restaurants; in particular, the pizza parlor. This region has more fine-dining restaurants than any other region, and Italian food is the ethnic food of choice with Chinese right behind. Submarine sandwiches are also popular in Dinerland.

Taverntown is largely confined to the corn and dairy belt agricultural regions of the Midwest. While the number of pizza parlors is less than in Dinerland, Taverntown is the location of the home offices of Pizza Hut, God Father's, Little Caesar's, and Mazzio's. The sale of hamburgers in this region is below the national average in spite of it being the home of McDonald's and White Castle. The family restaurant, not the ethnic restaurants one would expect because of the number of European immigrants who settled in cities like Chicago, Milwaukee, and Detroit, is the favorite dining-out place for Midwesterners.

The Barbecue Pit is the cultural South but is not confined to the eleven confederate states. The family buffet may be the most distinctive of all southern restaurant traditions. Hardee's, which began in the Carolinas, has a stronger presence in this region than McDonald's, Wendy's, or Burger King.

Cajunland is clearly distinguished from the Barbecue Pit in terms of what is eaten and how it is seasoned. Blackened redfish, oyster po'boys, crayfish etouffee, and shrimp creole are examples of this region's unique cuisine.

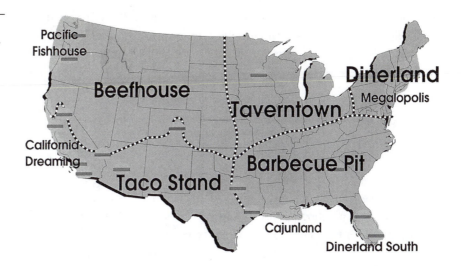

FIGURE 1-2
Regions for American Restaurants.
Reprinted by permission of
Richard Pillsbury.

The Beefhouse is largely the traditional northern section of the West. The steakhouse is king! Within Beefhouse is the Pacific Fishhouse. Salmon, crab, quahogs, and oysters abound in the Pacific Northwest. Also within this vast restaurant market is a small section called California Dreaming. This is a world of chains and concept restaurants, and it has been dubbed "Hamburger Alley."

The much-changed Southwest has been called the Taco Stand, which is somewhat a misnomer that implies pure Mexican cooking. The cuisine is more a Tex-Mex combination characterized by mesquite-smoked flavor and chili powder.

Finally, Chain Alley is a new discontinuous urban region composed of the twentieth-century growth cities. Included are Atlanta, Dallas/Fort Worth, Miami, Houston, San Diego, Portland, and Phoenix because they all have one thing in common: because of their dynamic growth, chains have sought to establish a presence in these cities.

Within these defined areas are sub-areas that seem to cluster restaurants together. The five elements that appear to strongly affect location, character, and structure of the restaurant cluster are demographic characteristics, consumer intent, accessibility, regional effects, and temporal effects. Temporal effects refer to including new cuisines on the menu, presenting new service styles, or reviving old concepts.

Pillsbury's examination of restaurant locations concludes that within cities and municipalities, restaurants can be found within fourteen different general environments. We can only describe a few, to give the general theory behind the cluster concept.

The first cluster is the Central City Cluster. This is the central business district, where the street vendors and lunchrooms of the eighteenth and nineteenth centuries first located in order to be near the factory and office workers. This cluster contains large numbers of low-priced restaurants offering traditional fare. The restaurant types found in this cluster are bar and grills, sandwich shops, office building cafeterias, and a few moderate-priced specialty restaurants. One also finds take-out and delivery services offered. Fast-food chains have also entered the central business district, and urban food courts are common.

The Hotel Convention Zone is another cluster that creates a distinctive restaurant landscape. Hotel coffee shops and restaurants satisfy a large percentage of the demand created by conventioneers. However, there are usually a few quality dinner houses within walking distance that serve as places to take clients in order to get away from the hotel.

Exotic and Ostentatious restaurants cluster nearby the Hotel Convention Zone and are but a short cab ride from the hotels. Some hotels have successfully integrated this kind of restaurant into their property, but local residents infrequently eat at such restaurants. The other zones are Middle City, Ethnic Neighborhood, Upscale Shopping, Residential Suburban, Freeway Interchanges, and Suburban Shopping Mall Food Courts.

Pillsbury's research demonstrates that one needs to understand the impact geographic region and local restaurant cluster locations have on the financial success of the restaurant concept and menu. Specific regions of the country will support certain restaurant concepts and food items more than others. This knowledge can assist owners and managers in improving the odds that their operation will be financially successful.

THE MENU AS A COMMUNICATION TOOL

Menus cannot be written without knowing the customer. It takes considerable insight of customer demographics and psychographics to write an effective menu in terms of the items it lists and the price points it pursues. Clearly today's menu writer must understand the demographics of the customer base they hope to attract and retain.

In the past the independent restaurant operator knew many of his or her customers. The owner greeted, seated, and even personally prepared the food for customers. The menu design was not considered important in projecting the personality of the restaurant; it did not need to because the owner was present in the establishment. This type of personal attention exists today primarily in owner-operated establishments. In Los Angeles the personalities of owner-operators like Wolfgang Puck and Michael McCarthy, who cannot be physically present at all times, are now personified in the menu.

In corporate-owned restaurants the personality of a manager, maitre d', or chef is not the primary vehicle for establishing and maintaining the personality and image of the restaurant concept. The menu plays the most significant role in establishing the public image and personality because managers, chefs, and maitre d's are often transferred. The menu, through the image that it expresses, remains the permanent link between the operation and the dining public.

Some menus communicate relaxed, leisurely dining while others scream "eat and get out!" The very thought of dining at a favorite restaurant raises our expectations of social and recreational releases, not just satisfying our hunger. The menu communicates to the customer the concept, decor, and ambiance. It is therefore fitting and proper that with this book we establish the proper layout and design of the menu.

The menu is always written with the tastes and food preferences of the clientele first and foremost in mind. When an owner or chef puts his or her preferences on the menu without considering the tastes and

wants of the target market, a major mistake can be made with the menu. The customers who will patronize your restaurant should be the major influence on the type of menu and the foods that are listed on the menu. Each type of operation will have identifiable types of customers, for example, businesspeople, families with small children, empty-nesters, retired people, etc. Menu preferences, prices, and portions will be different for each category of customer, and your menu must address these issues accordingly. While no menu can be "all things to all people," it must offer items acceptable to the majority of the clientele who eat there or they will not return. Many of the factors of the marketing plan reflect the demographic and physiographic profiles of the customers in the market.

Menus are made up of food courses served in a sequence from appetizer to dessert. These meals may range from a very elaborate seven-course formal French service to a build-your-own meal from separate a la carte selections. Prevailing cultural and social backgrounds dictate what menu offerings will be popular to the dining public. Management's task in menu development is to constantly monitor trends and customer preferences; these are occurring more rapidly than ever as consumers become more cosmopolitan in their tastes and expectations.

In the final analysis, you will find that the menu in fact belongs not to the owner but to the customer of the restaurant. The menu is a reflection of those people whom you hope to attract into your restaurant and the products you want to serve them—at a profit. Management has to be in constant communication with the customers, because they come to you by choice. The larger the operation, the farther removed management is from the customer. It is vital to talk to customers every day to find out about their likes and dislikes.

RESTAURANT OBJECTIVES

A crucial part of menu development is establishment of your objectives. The objectives for your operation should outline how you want the public in general, and your customers in particular, to perceive your restaurant. These objectives cannot be too specific—they should merely define the general feeling or impression you want to create. These objectives are then expressed in your menu concept.

A sample objective might be stated as follows: the restaurant will serve two limited-menu meals (lunch and dinner) six days per week to a consumer group with an average age of twenty-five to thirty-five in an informal atmosphere. Division of income will be one-third derived from lunch and two-thirds derived from dinner. Income will be split 60 percent food sales and 40 percent bar sales. Such an objective will help you clarify the menu that you develop.

In this sample objective, bar business requires emphasis, since the ratio here of food-to-bar business is lower than average. (According to National Restaurant Association statistics, the normal split is 80 percent food and 20 percent bar.) The informal setting means that service personnel will wear informal uniforms, no table linen will be used, and the decor and furniture will not be elaborate. (The ubiquitous plants and stained glass tend to be the current decor for expressing informality.) To meet the objective, sales will be concentrated at dinner rather than lunch. The number of meals and the number of days the restaurant will be open are also established in this sample objective.

After you have established the objectives, begin to expand on what you have in mind for the menu. Once you have decided exactly what you want to serve, you will know the classification of your restaurant. The classification strata of restaurants is based on the "hierarchy of needs" concept devised by the noted psychologist Abraham Maslow. Maslow theorized that people must satisfy basic needs before they can try to fulfill more esoteric goals. For example, people will make sure that they have food and shelter before they worry about getting a college education. Menu and marketing strategies for restaurants closely parallel Maslow's pyramidal hierarchy of needs. A restaurant can be a place to eat—nothing more—or it can provide a "dining experience," with food, ambiance, and service to match.

Classifications ranking restaurants according to type and amount of service, price range, and type of menu are found in table 1-1. The classification begins with the simplest operation, in which the only objective is to satisfy the physiological need for food. The menu in such an operation will be very basic, without much choice, and prices will be low. A typical example would be a street-corner pushcart that serves only hot dogs and soda. At the opposite end of the scale is the posh restaurant with fancy food, elaborate service, elegant decor, and high prices.

TABLE 1-1
TYPES OF MENUS
• Primarily take-out
• Snack stand
• Limited menu/Low price/Self-service
• Limited menu/Low-moderate price/Self-service
• Limited menu/Moderate price/Service
• Full menu/Low-moderate price/Service
• Full menu/Low-moderate price/Self-service
• Full menu/Moderate price/Service
• Full menu/Moderate-high price/Service
• Luxury menu/High price/Continental service

The *Nation's Restaurant News* chart segments the industry by market share (see fig. 1-3). Our own classification system continues to make use of classifications used by *Restaurant Business* magazine and the NRA. For our purposes let us classify, as the NRA has done, fast-food restaurants, family restaurants (at both ends of the price range—from ones very modest in price, decor, and service to upscale family restaurants), white-tablecloth restaurants (with all the implications of the term), and, the last of the NRA designations, atmospheric restaurants (implying high standards throughout the restaurant). The final classification, a new one not used by other sources, is that of the desti-

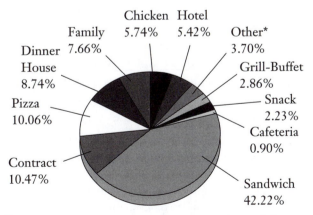

Top 100 Market Shares by Segment
(Of projected $111.7 billion aggregate
sales total for 1995; in percentages)

Family 7.66%
Dinner House 8.74%
Pizza 10.06%
Contract 10.47%
Chicken 5.74%
Hotel 5.42%
Other* 3.70%
Grill-Buffet 2.86%
Snack 2.23%
Cafeteria 0.90%
Sandwich 42.22%

*Includes standard buffet, coffee, C-store, fish, in-store and theme park chains.
Source: NRN research

FIGURE 1-3. Top 100 Market Shares by Segment. Reprinted by permission of *Nation's Restaurant News*.

nation restaurant. Such a restaurant is defined as one of the best, at the top of Maslow's range of the hierarchy, where price is not a consideration, customers are there for the enjoyment of the meal or the occasion, and there are no bounds to its market area. A destination restaurant has a strong enough reputation to draw people when they come into the city where the restaurant is located as well as to attract locals for special occasions or entertaining. There will always be a limited number of destination restaurants, if any, in a given city or area. They may be forced over time to make some market changes, but basically they occupy a niche that is unique to them.

The objectives for your restaurant must indicate the need you hope to satisfy (how your establishment will be classified) and the segment of the population that you hope to attract.

LIMITED VERSUS EXTENSIVE MENUS

A menu can be written on a continuum ranging from what can be described as limited to extensive in the number of selections it offers. This aspect of the menu can be examined from two perspectives: (1) the actual number of items listed on the menu, referred to as *variety*, and (2) the number of ways a product is prepared or presented (see fig. 1-4).

The most simplified and limited menu is best exemplified by the menus of fast-food operations that are typically limited in both number of items offered and preparation methods. These are the one-concept menus mentioned earlier.

From the limited/limited menus of the fast-food operations, one progresses to a limited/extensive menu that is limited in the number of different items but makes up for it in the variety of ways the item is prepared and served. An example of a limited/extensive menu is the menu for Darden Restaurants Inc.'s Red Lobster seafood restaurant; they offer fish, shrimp, and other seafood prepared by frying, broiling, baking, and steaming with a variety of accompaniments such as vegetables, rice, pasta, and potatoes. Italian, Mexican, and Chinese restaurant menus are also very good examples of how many different ways common ingredients can be combined, seasoned, and prepared to form completely different menu offerings.

Contrast the custom preparation of the fine-dining restaurant to the assembly line fast-food or lim-

ited-menu operations. Speed in preparation of menu items is critical in serving many customers in relatively short periods. Whenever check average is low, the number of transactions must be high to achieve revenue objectives. Therefore, the high volume/low check average operations demand an even more efficient kitchen layout than fine-dining restaurants, where speed of service and seat turnover is not as critical.

The next progression in menu-item development is the menu that offers an extensive variety of items prepared or presented in a limited number of ways. The best examples are coffee shops and family restaurants like Denny's, Shoney's, and the International House of Pancakes. Also in this menu category are restaurants like Bennigan's and Ruby Tuesday.

The final menu category consists of those operations with menus that are extensive in both number of items and preparation methods. Usually fine-dining French and continental restaurants with certified chefs and large kitchens are in this category, as are many hotel restaurants and private clubs. However, after reviewing the selections on the menus at restaurants like TGI Friday's and Houlihan's, one would have to categorize their menus as extensive in both the number of items and the preparation and presentation. The number of overall selections on both of these menus has been reduced considerably over the years, as slow selling items have been deleted in greater numbers than new items have been added.

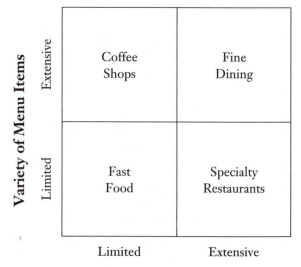

FIGURE 1-4. Matrix for Limited and Extensive Menus

In every city there are a limited number of restaurants that can be classified as destination restaurants. This is a restaurant that defies the normal definition of classification by most standards. A destination restaurant offers food and service that has local, regional, and even national acclaim. Customers are attracted for the "total" restaurant experience. High menu prices and distance traveled are not factors that deter customers from seeking out a destination restaurant. There will be a limited number of these restaurants in any given location and they will occupy a niche that is unique to them. Examples of destination restaurants are The Atlanta Fish Market (Atlanta, Georgia), Joe's Stone Crab (Miami Beach, Florida), Commander's Palace (New Orleans, Louisiana), Tavern on the Green (New York, New York), and Victor's (San Francisco, California).

There are advantages to both the limited and extensive menu. Most operators will try to strike a balance between the two extremes and emphasize the positive aspects of limited and extensive menus.

Extensive menus require more equipment and more kitchen and storage space for ingredients; equipment needs will be more specialized and the skills of kitchen workers need to be at a higher level. The more extensive a menu is in terms of the number of items listed and the preparation methods required, the more difficult the management task will be to maintain quality and cost control. If a menu becomes too extensive, the restaurant runs the risks of doing nothing well and lacking menu items that are identified as house specialties or signature foods.

If a menu is too limited, the customer base becomes limited as well. Limited menus require a convenient location, which will assure high customer counts. Extensive menus have greater overall appeal to a broader segment of the market than limited menus, but they offer a menu that is void of truly unique items that are identified exclusively with them. You must have some signature menu items that build the restaurant's identity and reputation. Remember, you cannot be all things to all people. Ingredients must be used in more than one dish, and daily specials may be needed to use perishable ingredients.

❊ Advantages of a Limited Menu

1. Less equipment is needed.
2. Less kitchen space is needed.
3. Preparation can be simplified and speeded up.
4. Fewer and less-skilled employees are needed.
5. Purchasing is simplified.
6. Inventory and storage space are minimized.
7. Cost controls are simplified.
8. Quality control is simplified.
9. Overall operating costs are lower.
10. Transaction time and seat turnover can be increased.

❊ Advantages of an Extensive Menu

1. Appeals to a broader range of customers
2. Appeals to new customers
3. Regulars find a greater variety and return more often
4. More responsive to changing customer tastes
5. Menu is more flexible
6. Has the advantage of product differentiation
7. Can charge higher prices for unique items

Regardless of the advantages of an extensive menu, an optimum number of entree selections is twenty to twenty-four. This range of selections can provide variety and still be efficiently managed. Studies show that if you count the number of entrees sold for a period of thirty days or more, approximately 60–75 percent of the total number will be concentrated among eight to twelve items, no matter how many choices are available. What this tells us is that *variety* is not defined exclusively by the *number* of choices, but by the number of *acceptable choices*. For example, liver and onions, seafood creole, meatloaf, spaghetti casserole, and smoked ham hocks may offer "variety," but many customers would not find any "acceptable choices" among them. Menus offering forty or more choices are of little benefit to operator or customer. If the majority of items sold are concentrated in twelve or fewer items, you can see that offering more than twenty-four items can complicate operational tasks of purchasing, inventory control, cost control, and training.

MARKET AREA

I once heard a speaker define a restaurant as being a "Three Mile Island," drawing concentric circles out from the restaurant and defining its customer base and competition as it exists within this area. Success and profit appear to await any restaurant that can define its market area and offer products and services appropriate to that area. When the type of demand in the market area changes, for whatever reason, and the restaurant operator does not realize the change and accordingly change the restaurant's products and services, the participation and profit will both begin to decline.

The first step in a feasibility study for a restaurant is the selection of a market (or target) area. Your restaurant's location will be a major factor in the success of the operation. Restaurants are located in all manner of places, and in many unpredictable spots. Some are along major thoroughfares, some are in large shopping centers, some are just off main streets, and some are in areas where they should never have been located. You need to define the market areas from which you hope to attract customers. Market areas vary widely. I have seen plans with market areas that range all the way from a three-block radius up to a thirty-mile radius.

Let's examine how you define your market area. If you are in a congested urban center where most people do not drive and little parking is available, your market area will be a radius of approximately three blocks. In such an area, your market is more or less defined *for* you. If your proposed location is near good public transportation and good parking facilities, the majority of your customers will come from within three to five miles. In a suburban area you are likely to draw customers from a ten-mile radius.

If your restaurant is one of those rare establishments that offer imaginative and unique food, flawless service, and unusually tasteful decor, the market may be unlimited. This type of restaurant, of course, does not draw the same people everyday—the customers come perhaps once a month or once a year. People will travel a longer distance to a restaurant that is defined as a specialty or atmosphere restaurant. Family occasions and celebrations will also draw guests from a greater distance.

The urban market can also be defined by the time it takes patrons to leave their present location and reach the location of the restaurant. This roughly translates into a five- to ten-minute walking distance. For locations near public transportation and good parking facilities, the three- to five-mile radius can be defined as a fifteen-minute distance for the majority of your customers.

The suburban location can be up to thirty minutes in travel time from customer to location. This final classification of restaurants is one I define as a destination type of restaurant, which is so well known by people that it is a *must* on their dining list. It may have regular local customers, but the population base is large enough to support the infrequent participation of the diners.

No matter what your market area, you still must define it and then examine the customer potential within that area.

Population and Consumers

The second consideration in your market survey is the size and characteristics of the population within your market area. It is essential to analyze the local demographics and preferences in order to develop a market profile.

It is important to realize that markets will change and that all the information given here simply indicates trends developing in foodservice markets. Many restaurant and foodservice trade publications periodically contain articles and information about new and changing markets. This information will be of value in keeping you on top of current developments in menus.

Your market survey should delve into consumer behavior in your target area. Today's average customer is more educated about food than ever before. Customers recognize value in food. Many people who will patronize your restaurant believe that the meal is a reward they give themselves. If you provide them with quality service and quality food, they will return to spend their money in your establishment. Customer behavior is critical to success. Your philosophy, policies, and objectives must match the needs and expectations of the people in your area in order to create a compatible situation.

The family unit size and composition is changing. There are more single-parent homes and more households where both spouses work full time. There is also an increase in the desire to do things as a family, so children influence where and what families eat in commercial restaurants. Time is an important consideration to busy people trying to combine careers and family with social and recreational activities.

As the baby boomer generation ages and the total population of persons over fifty continues to increase, the need to address the specific needs of this customer base intensifies as more and more businesses compete for their disposable incomes. The increase in spendable income establishes a market for entertainment and dining within this group and will cause people in this group to seek a high price-value for their dining dollar.

Nutritional and dietary needs of a fitness-conscious public also impacts menu selections. This will be increasingly important to patrons of this age group. According to an NRA study of menus, over 12 percent of all restaurants now offer healthy choices on their menus.

Within all age groups of customers there is also a growing awareness of environmental concerns that are affected by commercial restaurants. These concerns range from air and water pollution to the chemicals used in growing vegetables and the feed used for raising chickens, cattle, and fish. Add to this the concern about recycling and depleting our forests for paper containers used in fast-food restaurants and one can see the number of issues that influence public opinion. The public will boycott those operations that are doing things that are seen as harmful to the environment and support those that demonstrate conservancy.

Italian, Chinese, and Mexican foods continue to be the most popular ethnic foods sought by customers of all ages. By the year 2000 nearly one of every three Americans will be a minority, according to the Population Information Bureau. Ethnic foods will expand and become even more popular with the general public. Regional cooking is also finding its way onto menus. Examples are the Low Country foods of the Carolinas, Cajun foods in Louisiana, and southwest specialties. Regional food choices are much like what ethnic food choices were in years past. The dining public is becoming more interested in trying new food items for the first time.

Bear, Stearns & Co. figures show that in 1995, 85 percent of fast-food revenue came from chains and franchise operations. Full service, casual dining chains are accounting for a major share of the dining dollar. McDonald's continues to be the major player in the hamburger market, but the casual dining segment is increasing its market share with the likes of chains such as Applebee's, Ruby Tuesday, Outback Steakhouse, Longhorn, Chili's, and TGI Friday's. The growth and success of the chain restaurant is creating intense competition for the independent operators, who are finding it increasingly difficult to maintain the market share. As competition increases, independent operators must constantly improve their operational skills and knowledge if they are to remain profitable and stay in business.

In a recent *Nation's Restaurant News* editorial column, Rick Van Warner commented that for any operation to be successful in today's competitive economic times, it must satisfy its customers every day. This may sound simple, but very few operations are able to pull it off. The need to hire, train, and retain good employees who do whatever is necessary to satisfy the customers cannot be overstated. Providing interesting menu selections, prices that offer good value, and attentive and friendly service in an exciting and comfortable atmosphere all work toward providing total guest satisfaction. It is a demonstrated commitment to the *little details* that make and keep a restaurant competitive and successful in the marketplace.

According to Joyce Goldstein, chef/owner of Square One in San Francisco, "American cuisine is best described as schizophrenic: American diners want it all—exotic and ethnic foods—comfort foods that are calorie laden yet nutritious—low fat, low sodium healthful foods—chocolate everything for dessert." (Quoted from an address given at the American Culinary Federation Convention, San Francisco, July 1994.)

The Fifth Annual Marketing War College offers the following marketing facts. Eighty-seven percent of fast-food patrons travel only three to five minutes to restaurant destinations. Sixty percent of fast-food customers are local residents and workers. This points out the importance of convenience to a large customer base within a two- or three-block radius of the location.

Casual diners frequent one particular restaurant 50 percent of the time, while fine-dining customers frequent one destination restaurant 40 percent of the time. This tells us the importance of repeat business. Loyal customers are the best source for word-of-mouth advertising, which brings in new customers.

As the willingness of the public to travel farther from their homes to seek out specific food choices increases, the competition for their business will intensify. The opposite is also true. Busy people with limited time will not be willing to travel long distances to eat. Therefore, the food needs to be brought closer

FIGURE 1-5
Breakdown of Restaurant Types.
Reprinted by permission of the
National Restaurant Association.

Quick-Service Restaurants	Midscale Restaurants	Upscale Restaurants
Sandwich	Family-style	**Moderate Check**
Hamburger	Family steak	
Other sandwich	Other family-style	
Specialty	Specialty	Specialty
Fish/seafood	Fish/seafood	Fish/seafood
Chicken	Sandwich	Steak
Pizza	Barbecue	Barbecue
Mexican	Mexican	Oriental
Oriental	Oriental	Italian
Barbecue	Italian	Other specialty
Ice Cream	Other specialty	Casual dining
Donut		Mexican
Other specialty	Cafeteria	Burger
		Fern bar
Retail stores	Retail stores	
Convenience stores		Varied menu
Food stores	Hotels	
All remaining outlets		
Varied menu	Varied menu	**Higher Check**
		Specialty
		Fish/seafood
		Steak
		Oriental
		Italian
		Other specialty
		Hotels
Lunch $4.34	Lunch $6.89	Lunch $10.81
Dinner $5.21	Dinner $10.90	Dinner $18.19
• Restaurant is perceived as fast-food/takeout if food specialty is pizza, ice cream, chicken, or donut.	• Restaurant may (but is not required to) accept credit cards and serve beer, wine, or alcohol.	• Credit cards are accepted • Full liquor service (beer, wine, liquor) is available.

Source: National Restaurant Association report: *Price/Value Relationship at Restaurants, 1992.*

so it is easy to obtain with minimum inconvenience. Competition for this customer is coming from convenience stores, gas station mini stores, and supermarkets. Prepared foods will be available from nontraditional sources. If the customer will not come to get it, the food will be delivered to his or her home or office.

Providing "good food" is no longer enough. Dining out is becoming more and more a social and enter-tainment experience. The top operations will be leading the way while the slow to react will follow behind.

Many men and women enter the job market for the first time in a foodservice position. The foodservice industry continues to expand as the portion of the food dollar expended outside the home approaches 50 percent. The vast majority of the employees in the foodservice industry are females and minorities under thirty-five years of age.

The value meal has become commonplace to most fast-food chains. In an effort to get customers to purchase more than just a sandwich and drink, they have packaged french fries together with the sandwich and drink and offer it at a price that is less than if the items were purchased separately. This is a form of table d'hôte pricing found in full-service restaurants. This is a marketing strategy that packages items together into attractive bundles for ease of purchase by the customer.

Competition in the industry is becoming more intense because customers are much more sophisticated than they have ever been in the past. In markets in which the number of restaurants is greater than the demand, the amount of the dining dollar captured by each operation shrinks. Those who are followers are the ones who feel the new competition the most. Customer loyalty is a fleeting thing and cannot be taken for granted. Today's customer may defect to the competition tomorrow if he or she becomes dissatisfied.

As much as 72 percent of the meals we eat are still eaten at home. Eating at home continues to be the major competition to restaurants. There are still more restaurants closing than there are opening. People are eating out more often, but it is increasingly difficult for a restaurant to be profitable.

The restaurant industry projects sales of $290 billion for 1995, but it is still dominated in the total number of business establishments by the independent operator. Three out of four operators have only one unit. Forty percent of them have a check average of $4 and generate annual sales less than $500,000. The average American man or woman eats out over two hundred times per year. VISA reported their restaurant charge volume increased 21 percent in one year.

The NRA estimates that the elementary school population will increase by four million to over thirty-six million by the year 2000. The numbers become important because of the influence children have in the choice of restaurant and food. In another NRA survey, one half of adults with preteen youngsters said they are "very influenced" or "influenced" by their children when they eat out. Targeting the children of these adults makes good business sense. Taco Bell, a division of Pepsico, has launched a Meals for Kids program with a $10 million television advertisement promotion. Taco Bell has even reformulated their menu and seasonings especially for kids. They hope to increase their market share of the family business during the dinner hour.

Home-style cooking is being promoted and now includes ethnic taste. The intent is to give the customer new taste experiences using familiar foods to which ethnic seasonings have been added. This is exemplified by ethnic seasonings like curry and filé powder being added to vegetables and rice dishes.

The NRA and the various state restaurant associations are continually revising and updating their statistics, and as they change so must your marketing strategy. Make it your responsibility to read current trade publications to be aware of current trends in food and service. Put yourself in a position of leadership in current foodservice products and trends. Do not sit idly by and let your operation become the restaurant that merely reacts to what others are doing (see fig. 1-5).

Some classic marketing strategies have been developed in the fast-food field. Fast-food restaurants have targeted their market segment carefully and know where they want to be with their products. The ones that are most successful stay with that market and those products, producing what they do best for the clientele they serve best. There is a market segment out there for every level of restaurant.

RESTAURANT CLIENTELE
Eat-Out versus Dine-Out

Customers will classify a restaurant as a place to *eat out* or as a place to *dine out*. An eat-out restaurant is selected primarily based on convenience, price, and speed of service. The primary concern is the satiation of hunger. Many of us eat out during lunch. We frequent the office cafeteria or restaurants within a ten-minute walk. If it is raining outside, we may not leave the building and may call for delivery. After work we may be running late and seek a substitute for cooking at home. On such occasions we will be more price conscious and will check to see if we have any coupons for the pizza or fast-food restaurant that we can stop at on the way home.

When we dine out our expectations and budget expand significantly. We dine out for reasons other than just to satisfy our hunger. If a restaurant is considered a dine-out operation, the visit is regarded more as a social occasion or as entertainment. Price is not as much of a factor as it is for an eat-out restaurant, and we are willing to travel greater distances to get there.

The prices paid to eat out and dine out are defined by the family or individual income bracket. Two adults eating out during the week will likely spend a minimum of $12–$15 if they eat in a restaurant like Denny's, Golden Corral, Applebee's, or Chili's. It would not be out of the ordinary to spend as much as $25 just to eat out. A family of two adults and two children will spend a like amount in fast-food or family restaurants.

A few years ago $25 was considered a rather high check average. Today it is considered at the low end of moderate check averages. More and more, people treat eating out as a substitute for eating at home and will budget for such expenditures. Restaurant operators are responding to more conservative spending habits by switching their concepts and images from dine out to eat out in order to boost the frequency of visits of regular customers.

If the restaurant is considered an eat-out place and local residents come in on weeknights, because they are using money from their food budget, they are likely to be very price conscious and will probably be enticed by discounts or daily specials. Specials are very rarely offered on weekends, since people are usually dining out rather than eating out. The money spent is considered entertainment/recreation and not their food budget. That is why the check average in dine-out restaurants is usually higher than in eat-out restaurants. This is also a reason why people will travel farther to dine out than eat out. Location is not so much a factor for dine-out restaurants, but it may be critical for eat-out restaurants, where convenience, low price, and quick service are important to the purchase decision. In addition, dine-out operations have more ambiance and atmosphere, and food presentation and service are usually more elaborate. These all contribute to the price-value perceptions of the customers.

Spending is more liberal if social, entertainment, or recreational budgets are mentally debited. Therefore, the restaurant operator must price the menu accordingly and offer price differentiation (discounts) selectively. If one can create an atmosphere of a social or entertainment nature, the operation moves from an eat-out to a dine-out restaurant in the minds of the customer.

When an eat-out restaurant is vying for the weeknight family business, use of incentives like "early bird" specials are used to entice eat-out patrons. Have you ever noticed that there are fewer discounts offered on Friday and Saturday nights? Part of the reason is that on weekends, entertainment and social motives are driving the dine-out decision, and budgetary constraints are relaxed. Eat-out operations with dine-out prices will not be frequented by patrons who are seeking price-value. Dine-out operations that offer discounts to attract eat-out clientele may lower their overall image and fail to optimize their sales potential. Further, regular customers who willingly paid full menu price may start redeeming coupons themselves.

Knowing how patrons evaluate a restaurant is important to the pricing decision. Eat-out operations will experience more frequent visits by patrons than dine-out operations, but the average check will be lower per visit. Regular weekday customers may go elsewhere for special celebrations like anniversaries or birthdays. Weekend clientele may differ greatly from weeknight customers. For example, local residents may be the bulk of traffic during the week, while weekends may bring visitors, tourists, or people traveling from outside the restaurant's normal market area. Such patrons categorize the operation as a dine-out or special-occasion restaurant and will not be as price conscious.

Examples of eat-out restaurants are all fast-food chains, Shoney's, Waffle House, and International House of Pancakes. Examples of dine-out (destination) restaurants are Eccentric's (Oprah Winfrey's restaurant in Chicago) and most white-tablecloth restaurants with high check averages. There are others that are a combination of both eat-out and dine-out; examples are Houlihan's, Houston's, Outback Steakhouse, and Olive Garden.

What this means to the restaurant operator when it comes to pricing the menu items is this. The operator must know how the majority of his customers classify his restaurant. To some it may be a dining-out spot while to others it is simply an eat-out restaurant. Rarely will a restaurant be both to the same customer. Weekday regulars may not frequent the same restaurant for special occasions. People who eat there on special occasions will not eat there during the week. In order to get the customer to spend more, we must get them to mentally transfer their expenditure from their food budget to their entertainment budget.

People who eat in restaurants tend to fall into four categories. The first group can be termed *the experi-*

menters. They go to every restaurant opening and pass judgment on whether it is acceptable. Your restaurant had better do it right for them the very first time.

The second group might be called *the experimenters' friends.* Such people try new restaurants only after the experimenters have assured them that it is OK to go there. This is a very fickle group: they may very well try a new restaurant but then never return.

The third group is termed *the majority.* These people go to new places after they have become established. Then they return, and they may become regular customers. Although they do not eat out as the experimenters, they do eat out. You may have been open six months or a year before some of *the majority* come in. They may have heard about the restaurant and want to try it, but it is some time before they do so.

The fourth group might be termed *the seldoms.* These are the people who eat out perhaps once or twice a month—only to celebrate an anniversary, a birthday, or some other special occasion. *The seldoms* require a special occasion to motivate them to dine out. They are not adventuresome in their menu choices and will likely seek out restaurants that offer steaks, chicken, roast beef, and potatoes. They will likely dine with rather large parties, which is why *seldoms* are still worth pursuing as customers.

The clientele you want to attract should consist of the two middle groups. You cannot survive long on all new business—or on infrequent business. You must have a repeat crowd coming into your restaurant. Your sales and marketing efforts need to focus on the largest potential market that you believe is most likely to seek out the food and style of service you provide.

Several years ago, Standard Brands Corporation conducted a survey on why people eat out and why they go to specific restaurants. So complex is the reasoning and so emotional is the thinking of the average customer that it can be very difficult to produce a profile. Therefore, it is essential to collect data on many tangible factors—such as demographics and income—in order to understand your potential clientele. No matter how difficult, it is crucial that you target a specific market and population segment with your restaurant and its menu.

Perceived Value

One of the biggest intangibles in developing a menu for a particular market area and particular clientele is the concept of perceived value. Value may be perceived by the customer in a variety of ways. Many times it is seen in the presentation or the appearance of an item as it is served. Or it may be seen in a method of service or the ambiance of the dining room. It is indeed difficult to measure a perception of value, because so much of it is subjective and based on emotion. A customer's positive reaction can involve factors beyond the menu and the restaurant. When someone recalls "the best meal I ever had," a part of that recollection may be related to the person or persons with whom he or she had the meal. Thus, developing a menu that gives customers perceived value is a major challenge.

Even though measurement of perceived value is difficult, a customer value scale (fig. 1-6) can provide some guidelines. In this illustration, if the customer's perceived cost of your product is 5 and his perceived value (of food, service, and dining surroundings) drops to 3 or lower, it is likely he will not return. The optimum value for both customer and operator lies

FIGURE 1-6

Scale of Perceived Value vs. Perceived Cost

Perceived Value by Consumer		Perceived Cost by Consumer
1		1
2		2
3	*(perceived value too low)*	3
4		4
5	*(optimum value for customer and operator)*	5
6		6
7	*(perceived value too high)*	7
8		8
9		9
10		10

between 4 and 6 on the perceived value scale. As you develop your menu, consider what you and your staff will do to ensure perceived value.

Price-value has become a very important objective of menu pricing because of the competition in the marketplace for the dining-out dollar. Most fast-food operations have responded with bundling accompaniments into a package called a *value meal*. The term *value pricing* is a result of the effort to increase profits by deeply discounting menu prices. Taco Bell and Mc-Donald's have been in the forefront of this practice, and value pricing appears to be a long-term competitive strategy. According to Hayes and Huffman, in its simplest form, value pricing is an attempt to use product price to satisfy customers' increasing demand for value.

Value pricing is basically form of table d'hôte pricing applied to a fast-food operation. The accompaniments are analogous to courses included in the menu price in table-service restaurants. The *combination price*, or the *value meal*, is lower than the price would be if the items were purchased separately.

The value meal is perceived by the customer as a better value and is an inducement for purchase. Two things are accomplished for the operation. First, the average transaction value will increase (this is the fast-food equivalent of average check), and second, it actually simplifies ordering and transaction time. Instead of having to enter a sandwich, drink, and french fries, the salesperson simply presses the preset key for the respective number of the value meal selected.

The perceived value of the entire experience is a combination of the price, food quality and quantity, service, and overall expectations. Leading the priorities of the customer in price-value are food quality, cleanliness of facilities, attentive and service-minded employees, and reasonable prices.

In a study titled "Price-Value Relationships at Restaurants" conducted in 1994 by the NRA, the following attributes were identified as most important to value perception. (The following information is reprinted by permission of the NRA.)

❊ Fast-Food Restaurants

1. Clean dining area
2. Accurately filled order
3. Consistent food quality
4. Correct change
5. Speedy service

❊ Moderately Priced Restaurants

1. Clean dining area
2. Quality of food
3. Fresh ingredients
4. Friendly staff
5. Timely service

❊ Higher-Priced Restaurants

1. Clean dining area
2. Quality of food
3. Fresh ingredients
4. Timely service
5. Comfortable atmosphere

In the study, adult patrons were asked whether the value they received for the price they paid *exceeded*, *met*, or *fell below* their expectations. The results indicate that moderately-priced restaurants are providing the best value for the price paid, with 88 percent of the patrons reporting that the value received met or exceeded their expectations, compared with ratings of 76 percent and 74 percent, respectively, for fast-food and higher-priced restaurants.

Patrons will form their judgement by what they perceive you to be, not necessarily what you think you are. This is why restaurants trying to be dine-out restaurants that are perceived by the customer as eat-out restaurants do poorly. The table-service chains are also advertising using price-value strategies; for example, Applebee's menu has a $10 price ceiling, and Bob Evans restaurants advertise complete meals for under $5.

THE COMPETITION

Hand in hand with a thorough survey of the market area goes an analysis of the competition. Many restaurants open in areas where the owners are totally unaware of the competition. Know what foodservice operations exist in your target area. Your direct competition is any restaurant that is similar to the concept you envision, offers similar service, or is in the immediate area where your restaurant will be located. Identify these competitors by walking around, driving around, looking around—within a circle that has the same radius as your market area.

When it comes to identifying competitors in your market, it is not specific enough to simply say that anyone who sells and serves food is competition. While there are a growing number of indirect competitors who are selling prepared food and meals cooked and eaten at home (e.g., supermarkets, convenience stores, and gas stations), you need to know who your *direct* competitors are. Direct competitors are defined as those operations that offer similar menu items at similar prices and served in a similar atmosphere. For example, Chili's, TGI Friday's, and Applebee's are in direct competition. Indirectly, Fuddrucker's competes with them as well.

Whenever a new restaurant opens, similar operations in the market will experience a drop in market share. Anticipate what impact new restaurant openings will have and develop marketing plans to keep declines to a minimum. Restaurants operating with high standards in food and service will lose fewer customers and recover more quickly than restaurants that are marginal. Competition demands that you be better tomorrow than you were today if you expect to keep your customers from defecting to the competition. You must exceed the competition; just being as good or equal will not attract or keep your customers. Determine who patronizes each restaurant that is competitive. Notice when the establishment is busiest and what special features seem to attract the customers. What can you offer that is better?

The Marketing Plan

Once you have developed your objectives and have a proposed menu in mind, a feasibility study needs to be conducted to ascertain the likelihood of your restaurant's success. When you begin to develop a restaurant concept, your policy decisions and objectives will be only as good as the information that you have available. Collect information in the feasibility study and include it in a marketing plan. You will begin to see the total picture and the realistic likelihood of success or failure.

Figures 1-7 and 1-8 are sample worksheets supplied by the NRA. You can adapt them to your own needs in order to analyze the dining situations and physical attributes of your competition. You are, after all, competing for the same dollars within your market area.

Some feel that the physical menu is a marketing plan in its purest form. The menu may just be the most important internal advertising device used to influence what the customer will ultimately select when they arrive at the restaurant. Not only can it influence what the customer will order but also how much will be spent. It can determine not only the volume of business you will do but also strongly influence the ultimate success of your operation. Management is constantly forecasting business volume and using this knowledge to make decisions on how much food and beverage to buy, store, and prepare and how many employees to schedule. The menu impacts every one of these decisions.

A properly-designed menu can direct the attention of the diner to specific items and increase the likelihood that those items will be ordered more frequently than random chance would dictate. Although the customer's selection cannot be controlled, it can be directed. The profit picture brightens, the food cost improves, and the check average increases when the customer chooses items that contribute positively toward these ends.

While the personality of the owner, manager, or chef may be so unique that this in itself generates demand for the restaurant, most commercial restaurants do not have this drawing card. The rule is know your customer and have a good menu and marketing plan. Businesses don't plan to fail, but many of those that do fail to plan. The menu is a restaurant's most important marketing tool. If properly designed, the menu will have a significant impact on delivering or conveying the image or concept of a restaurant as well as affecting sales.

Most of the popular restaurants of today have gone to what is an adapted form of table d'hôte menu listings and pricing. They have had to in order to keep their prices reasonable and respond to the fact that people just do not want a seven-course meal when they go out; it's simply too much food and too expensive. Dining in such restaurants is limited to special occasions and visits by customers are infrequent. Therefore, such restaurants are primarily found in large metropolitan areas with populations of several million. The marketing plan will identify the dining attributes of the customers who are likely to frequent your restaurant.

All too frequently, restaurateurs fail to produce a written marketing plan. A well-researched and well-designed marketing plan can pinpoint the market segment, suggest the type of sales required, and predict success.

Facility	Menu Orientation	Number of Seats	Meals Served and Price Range ($)	Hours of Operation	Beverage Service	General Comments
Around the Corner 175 First Street	Light fare Sandwiches Salads B	64 café 30 downstairs 32 balcony 16 bar	B,L,D 3.95–6.95	Su 9a–1a M–Th 8a–1a F 8A–31 S 9a–31 (7 days)	Full bar	Live music Thu–Su 9p–12a Popular in neighborhood with culturally oriented people; emphasis on drinks Busy
Glenda's 250 First Street	Appetizers Sandwiches Salads Entrees Specials A	8 bar 80 dining	L,D Lunch: 5.95–10.95 Dinner: 6.95–13.95	M–S 11:30a–2:30p M–Th 5:30p–10:30p F,S 5:30p–11:30p (6 days)	Full bar	Attracts embassy staffers and bureaucrats for lunch Refined decor (Laura Ashley look) Fine dining for dinner Very busy
Ken's Fish & Chips 183 First Street	Fried seafood D	60	L,D 1.95–3.95	11a–11p (7 days)	No	Fast food Seafood take-out Same block as proposed restaurant Slow
Forest Inn 875 Main Street	Appetizers Salads Sandwiches Burgers Entrees B	22 bar 70 dining	L,D 4.25–10.75	M–F 11:30a–2:30a S,Su 10:30–2:30a S,Su 10:30a–3:30p (brunch) (7 days)	Full bar	Neighborhood restaurant Pub style with garden Attracts business people for lunch Clean and organized Moderately busy
Pompeii Pizza 155 First Street	Fast food Pizza Subs D	34	B,L,D 1.15–9.95	M–S 7a–10p Su 12p–10p (7 days)	No	Takeout Popular lunch spot Nonprofessional clientele Busy

Instructions for Completing Restaurant Inventory Worksheet (Dining Attributes)

1. *Facility*—Specify the name and address of each restaurant.
2. *Menu Orientation*—The following are suggested categories.

   A = full menu, table service, upscale menu   B = full menu, table service, moderate-price menu

   C = limited menu, table service   D = fast food   E = bar/lounge only

FIGURE 1-7. Feasibility Worksheet—Dining Attributes. Reprinted by permission of the National Restaurant Association.

In addition to identifying the menu type by assigning the appropriate letter, give a brief description of the general theme (e.g., steakhouse, Oriental, continental) and typical menu items.

3. *Number of Seats*—Specify the approximate number of dining and bar seats.
4. *Meals Served*—Record all meal periods served.
5. *Price Range*—For each meal period served, indicate the menu items that are lowest and highest in price. Also, specify average drink prices.
6. *Hours of Operation*—Indicate the operating periods for each restaurant.
7. *Beverage Service*—Indicate whether or not each operation offers alcoholic beverages.
8. *General Comments*—Briefly note any special features such as Sunday brunch, promotions, menu items, and service style.

FIGURE 1-7. *continued*

FIGURE 1-8
Feasibility Worksheet—
Physical Attributes.
Reprinted by permission
of the National Restau-
rant Association.

Facility	Location Characteristics	ADA & Building Accessibility	Visibility	Exterior Appearance	Interior Appearance	General Comments
Around the Corner 175 First St.	Directly across the street from site; combined with Jewelry Store; backs on 4th Avenue; has outdoor seating	Limited parking Front Access only	Signage poor (on window only)	Well maintained	Dark paneling Neatly kept	Inviting ambiance
Glenda's 150 First St.	One block south from sit on same side	Has parking for 20 cars in adjacent lot with front and side door	Visible sign flat on front of building	Plantings not well cared for; otherwise, neat	Bright and airy, with clean, neat appearance	Attractive decor with new, fresh look
Ken's Fish & Chips 183 First St.	One-half block south and across street	No parking or drive-up Front access	Very brightly lighted sign at night; large with bright colors for daylight	Well maintained	Rustic tables and chairs; well worn but clean	Standard chain package
Forest Inn 875 Main Street	Around corner from site	Off the main street, with no off-street parking	Hanging sign visible from intersection with First Street	Warm-weather patio unappealing in cold weather; not well kept Exterior well maintained	Moderate light, with well-worn booths and furnishings Clean and neat	Conformable ambiance
Pompeii Pizza 155 First St.	One-half block north across street	No off-street parking; people double park for carry-out	Neon sign in window Additional signage above and below	Paint chipped, windows dirty Windowsill plants scraggly	Relatively clean, but dirt in corners and tables not wiped Brightly lit	Generally unappealing appearance

Instructions for Completing Restaurant Inventory Worksheet (Physical Attributes)

1. Facility--Specify the name and address of each restaurant. Other businesses that may create traffic in area.
2. Location Characteristics--Describe the location in relation to your site, information on housing, the residential makeup of the area, income, education and ethnic background. Also include other businesses that would generate area traffic.
3. Accessibility--Document ease or difficulty of entering the restaurant and the location of parking; A.D.A. law requirements; competition's compliance to the law; traffic congestion on the street, parking, speed limits, stoplights or signs in the area, entry access into and out of the restaurant.
4. Visibility--Record comments on the visibility of the restaurant the effectiveness of signs; visual and sound pollution in the area.
5. Exterior appearance--Describe the general appearance of the restaurant from outside; business nature of the area; crime rate; the general neighborhood condition; area visual assets or distractions.
6. Interior Appearance--Record impressions on the interior design, lighting, and degree of cleanliness. Stress cleanliness of the operation if it follows any national or ethnic theme in decor.
7. General Comments--Briefly specify any special features such as location on below-ground level, presence of a nearby transit stop, secondary access from rear of building, types of businesses in the area.

Preparation of the written marketing plan involves five steps: (1) establishing the restaurant objectives, (2) collecting input, (3) making decisions, (4) determining operational procedures, and (5) conducting outcome analysis. Following the guidelines discussed earlier in this chapter, you should have already established your restaurant objectives. Each of the next four steps is covered below.

The second step, collecting input, is the collection of alternatives that you need to reach decisions related to the feasibility of your objectives. There are three parts to the input process: intuition, information, and experience.

Steps in a Marketing Plan

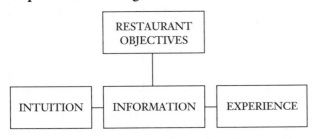

1. **Intuition**—a nonrational area based upon ideas that you believe will work.
2. **Information**—the objective and measurable or observable circumstances that are available to you from personal research or from government data.
3. **Experience**—methods of operation and merchandising practices that have been successful for you or for some other operation in the past.

When you have reviewed and listed these elements, the decision-making process is the third step.

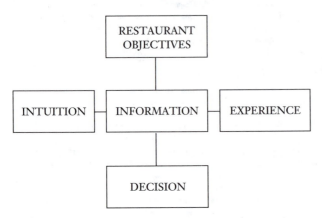

With all the information available from the three input sources, decisions are made as to how best to reach the original objectives—if, indeed, the objectives can be attained with the existing assets, location, and talent. These decisions involve the selection of theme, menu items, and decor.

The fourth step is to determine the operational procedures needed to accomplish the original objectives.

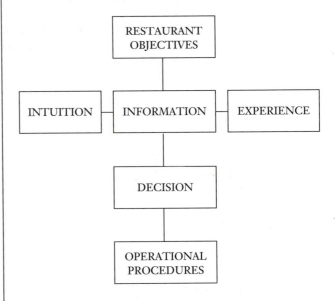

Operational procedures include technical competency of employees, the physical menu, decor, training programs, and sales and advertising programs.

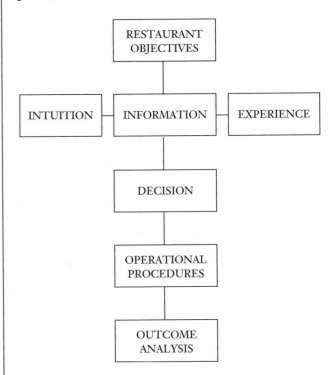

The fifth and final step is conducting outcome analysis of operations for information about success (profit) or failure (loss).

Outcome analysis is based upon operating statements, ratio analysis, and all information and data pertinent to operations. This outcome analysis may show positive feedback (profit) or negative feedback (loss), with each result indicating action to be taken.

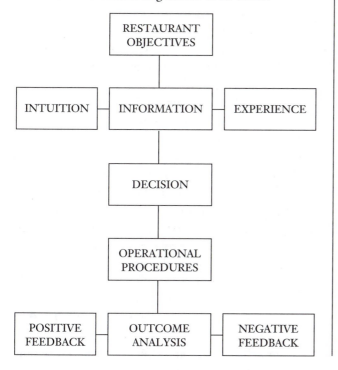

Positive feedback indicates that you should continue your current method of operation, with changes made only to correct or improve minor operating methods. Negative feedback indicates that either the original intent of the operation was misstated or the input was incorrect, resulting in incorrect decisions. A complete revision may be required, or, if specific areas can be pinpointed, you can take remedial action in regard to that specific target.

In the following chart, the three input elements are necessarily simplified. In preparing your marketing plan, you will need to expand on these elements in some detail. Each of the three factors—intuition, information, experience—involves a number of components that assist management in making menu and operational decisions (see fig. 1-9).

These are not the only marketing considerations. You may have other areas and specifics to add to this model. The major goal is to remove as many unknowns as possible and, by research, increase the accuracy of operational decisions.

INTUITION

Identity
Decor
Colors
Uniforms
Logo

Dining Trends
Food habits
Popularity index
Product availability

Interpersonal Influences
Value
Service
Peer groups
Habit

INFORMATION

Consumer
Age
Sex
Income
Occupation
Marital status

Geographic Factors
Population
Location
Climate
Resident status
Area trends
Traffic

Costs
Land
Building
Equipment
Furnishings
Operational costs

Employees
Ethnic
background
Education
Group identity
Schools

EXPERIENCE

Competition
Number of operations
Types of operations
Sales
Failures

Personal History
Employment record
Development operations
Systems technique

Education
Training
Design and layout
Control system

FIGURE 1-9. Components of Menu Operational Decisions

SUMMARY

If there were a magic formula for menu success, some consultant would have written about it, and it would be included in this book. The truth is that it just does not exist. You increase the chance of success by providing the right food and service at a price the customer is willing to pay. The restaurant business has always been a business of attention to detail in every operational phase. Today, you must be aware of happenings and changes occurring locally, regionally, and nationally, or you will fall behind the competition. Take note and be ready to compete with those who seek your customers. There are only so many customers and sales dollars in your market area, and you want to maximize your share of that business. Being aware is to be forewarned and prepared to respond to competitive challenges.

Customer satisfaction with a restaurant and its menu is the foundation for building a successful restaurant. One of the critical elements of success is knowing your customer. If you designed your menu with your customers' wants and needs in mind, offer good value for the price paid, and maintain high standards of service and food quality, you should earn their regular patronage and endorsement.

The menu also has a direct impact on whether the business achieves its sales and profit goals. The physical menu communicates the restaurant's personality and character to the customer and is a significant driving force behind attracting new customers and increasing the frequency of repeat business. It is far more than just a marketing tool, however. It is also a major cost-control tool that helps achieve your desired food cost, contribution margin, and labor cost. It increases the accuracy of forecasting and makes worker scheduling and food purchasing and production easier to predict.

Realize that all restaurant chains that are your competition have marketing and sales departments, and they closely monitor current consumer trends and demographics changes that impact products and services. Their menus are not as quick to react to change as independent operator's are, and that is one advantage the independent operator has over the chain operations. By reading current trade publications, such as *Nation's Restaurant News*, *Restaurant Hospitality*, *Restaurant Business*, and *Restaurants and Institutions*, the independent operator can learn about the sales strategies chain operations are using and can preempt them in their market area.

Changes in customers' tastes will cause menus to be ever evolving and changing to meet the new trends and tastes. Changes will occur in the menu items, ingredients, and preparation methods. Operations must change to get ahead or at least keep up with anticipated customer needs and wants. Demand shifts are causing dramatic changes in menu items and pricing philosophy. In today's market we see the consumer sending a message to the upscale restaurants to lower their prices and to lower-priced restaurants to upgrade on all aspects of their operation. The menu plays such an important role in restaurant profitability that it needs to be given the attention that any major capital investment decision requires. Because of the importance of the menu, we have devoted this book to helping restaurateurs create effective menus for their businesses.

The well-designed and effective menu can be summarized in five statements.

1. It is an effective communication, marketing, and cost-control tool.
2. It emphasizes what the customer wants and what the restaurant prepares and serves best.
3. It obtains the necessary check average needed to realize sales goals and bottom-line return.
4. It utilizes staff and equipment in an efficient manner.
5. It allows for accurate forecasting of sales and menu mix.

The rule is "know your customer and have a good menu and marketing plan." An operation based on guesswork and haphazard decision making is bound to fail. When you use well-tested marketing techniques to develop and finalize your menu, you have laid the groundwork for success in the restaurant industry.

The Physical Menu

MENU COMMUNICATION

The menu may be the most important document you will ever write for your restaurant. It is the one piece of printed matter produced for your restaurant that is *guaranteed* to be read by your customers. Your menu is the strongest and most consistent internal-marketing and sales tool your restaurant employs.

The menu should communicate the personality of the restaurant. Radio, television, newspaper, direct mail, and even word-of-mouth advertising are all *external* communications with the customer that serve primarily to interest the public in coming to your restaurant. Once the customer is inside, the menu takes over as the primary sales tool and should *guide* the customer through the menu selection process.

Author and consultant Nancy Loman-Scanlon led a seminar at a recent National Restaurant Association (NRA) convention. The subject of her seminar was the importance of the menu to a restaurant's overall success. Her message was simply that the menu should be the restaurant's best friend.

The physical menu is in effect a basic model of the communication process, the tool by which you and your customers communicate. As such, the menu must be devised so that all lines of communication are wide open and no misunderstandings can occur. The menu writer must "speak" clearly to the customer, and the customer must "hear" his message and react to it. The model shown in table 2-1 shows that process. It is adapted from *Supervision in the Hospitality Industry*, by Jack E. Miller and Mary Porter (New York: John Wiley & Sons, 1985).

Approaching the menu as a communication device, the menu writer should imagine that he is seated across from the customer and carrying on a conversation. The menu then becomes the conversation piece, logically following the model.

Let's examine the model in more detail to assess the menu's objectives—three principal ones for the menu writer and three principal ones for the customer.

1. The menu writer first thinks about what needs to be said, basing his thoughts on the concept devised for the restaurant. Development of the menu message involves the three types of input described in chapter 1: information, intuition, and experience. As the menu writer, you are deciding here what you want to say and do with your communication tool.

2. Express your policy and philosophy. Tell your customers, via the menu, what you want them to buy and what image you are projecting for the restaurant. Spell out your objectives. Make decisions about the categories of food, the names of dishes, and the number of items to be offered.

TABLE 2-1

COMMUNICATING VIA THE MENU

The Menu Writer

1. Considers meaning of message
   a. Concept
   b. Information
   c. Intuition
   d. Experience
2. Expresses meanings in words or symbols
   a. Objectives
   b. Policy
   c. Philosophy
   d. What and how to say things
3. Transmits message via printed menu
   a. Cover
   b. Copy
   c. Print
   d. Color
   e. Art
   f. Location

The Customer

1. Receives the message
   a. Interprets it
   b. Forms attitudinal concept
2. Translates words and symbols
   a. Decodes
   b. Develops expectations
   c. Sees perceived value
3. Understands and accepts the meaning
   a. Acts
   b. Buys desired items
   c. Buys profitable items
   d. Returns to restaurant

3. Design the physical menu, making decisions about the cover, the descriptions, the art, and the locations of the various food items. The cover makes the all-important first impression, the copy that describes the menu items is a significant part of the communications goal, and placement of the menu items, the art, and color are all critical elements in the message you want to convey to the customer. These elements establish a formal or informal atmosphere for the entire operation. The final product—the menu—should accomplish your objectives with regard to profit, sales, and image.

Now the menu goes to the customer, who communicates in return.

1. The customer reacts first to the physical form of the menu—the shape, the paper quality, and the cover. Then the customer must interpret the message that the menu writer is delivering. This is the first test. Are the items that you want to sell going to sell? Has the menu projected the image that you planned?

2. Now the customer must decode what you have included in the menu. Is the menu compatible with the decor of the interior and exterior of the restaurant? Does the menu tell your story? Does the customer seem to recognize perceived value in the menu? Has it met his expectations?

3. At this point the customer accepts or rejects the various aspects of the menu. Customer reaction is both subjective and objective. Customers respond to the general impression of the menu—and they respond on both levels. If they accept what you have done, obviously you have written a good menu. The customers will then take action, buy the profitable items you want them to buy, and, most important, return to your restaurant as regular guests.

CLASSIFICATION OF MENUS

Static Menu

The static menu is one that does not change the selections except for seasonal changes. When static menus are used week after week, the sales mix remains constant regardless of the customer count and makes forecasting purchasing and preparation quantities more accurate. Static menus are widely used in quick-service and most moderate-priced restaurants like Chili's, Applebee's, TGI Friday's, Outback Steakhouse, and Olive Garden.

Restaurants with static menus do not respond quickly to any fad foods and cannot incorporate leftovers into other menu items. When the menu is reprinted, prices are typically the only thing changed. Static menus allow the restaurant staff to become "specialists" in the preparation and service of the menu items. Preparation can be simplified, allowing employees to quickly and efficiently prepare the items. Skilled culinarians are not needed to put out a static menu. Service is also standardized with a static menu.

The principal drawback for a static menu, if there is one, is menu monotony for regular customers. Customers who eat at a restaurant with a static menu more than twice a week may become tired of the menu selections. For this reason, a static menu can be supplemented with "daily specials" to add variety for frequent customers. Magnolias Uptown-Down South (fig. 2-1) is such a menu. However, it has a kitchen staff with the skills to produce the additional offerings.

Market Menu

Great creativity and variety in the menu can best be accomplished by the use of what is referred to as a *market menu*. Applebee's restaurant is a form of market menu (fig. 2-2). A pure market menu takes advantage of the seasons and harvest times to assure the inclusion of the freshest and most plentiful fruits, vegetables, cuts of meat, and poultry. However, pure market menus are not practical for the simple fact that customer preferences do not necessarily follow the seasons and market availability. Through the use of processed foods and quick freezing, seasonal vegetables and some seafoods can be processed during the peak season and then sold year-round. McDonald's, long known for their great french fries, converted from fresh to frozen potatoes years ago and now has consistent french-fried potatoes all year long.

While seasonality may bring lower prices to certain ingredients, the menu selection needs to be driven by customer preference. Pure market menus may eliminate boredom and provide variety, but the menu sales mix is more difficult to forecast. A market menu allows for the incorporation of leftovers, but restaurants with static menus have virtually eliminated leftovers by cooking to order or by cooking in only small batches.

Cycle Menu

A cycle menu is primarily used in operations with a "captive clientele," for example, institutional foodservices such as high schools and colleges, hospitals, the military, and employee cafeterias in plants and office complexes. By "captive clientele" we mean those customers who have very limited opportunity to eat outside the confines of school, work, or living accommodations. The ultimate "captive clientele" are residents of state and federal prisons. The menu from the Independence Regional Health Center (fig. 2-3) is an example of a cycle menu.

A cycle is written as a reference to the length of time that a particular menu will run until it will repeat the first menu offering. As an example, a cycle for a health center feeding residents three meals a day, seven days a week may be a thirteen-day cycle. The cycle may incorporate certain dietary and nutritional requirements as well as types of foods and preparation methods. For example, if four entrees are to be offered at the dinner meal, the cycle may include one chicken, one beef, one fish, and one extended selection in each daily menu. In addition, preparation methods may be controlled to include one baked, one broiled, one grilled, and one steamed item. Such menu specifications are often written into the agreements with the contract management company operating the facility. Companies like ARAmark, Service America, and PFM (Professional Food Management) operate accounts for schools, sports authorities, and health care agencies.

Forecasting production levels, purchasing, and employee scheduling are more difficult if the competing selections are changed on a daily basis. However, most cycle menus offer the same entree, vegetable, salad, and dessert items each time the menu is repeated. In a thirteen-day cycle menu that starts on a Monday with menu 1, that particular menu will not appear again for fourteen days and not on the same day until seven weeks later. Even with such a wide variety of food offerings, management can still manage production from the sales mix analysis.

Specific selections from a cycle menu can be made to improve the combinations of colors, textures, tastes and shapes and still utilize the same ingredients. The cycle menu can reflect the seasonal foods and holiday specials that occur in the time frame of the cycle. Computer programs are now available that can write cycle menus according to the dietary and nutritional parameters required of the clientele. The nutritional and caloric attributes of each menu, the raw food cost, and even the purchase quantities needed for projected recipes can be done by the computer program. At the end of the month, the program will calculate inventory value based on usage, purchases, and sale records (see "Computerized Nutrient Analysis" in Appendix 1).

EXECUTIVE CHEF DONALD BARICKMAN
CHEFS: CASEY TAYLOR, GERALD MITCHELL, DON DRAKE
MICHAEL DRAGON

Uptown Down South Starters

SKILLET SEARED YELLOW GRITS CAKE
with Tasso Gravy and
Yellow Corn Relish 6.25

SPICY BLACK BEAN CAKES
with a Red and Yellow Tomato Salsa and
Yellow Pepper Oil 5.25

CHILLED ASPARAGUS
with a Wild Berry Vinaigrette and Fresh
Mango 6.95

PAN FRIED CHICKEN LIVERS
with Caramelized Onions, Country
Ham and Madeira Sauce 5.95

SPICY BBQ PORK
with Jalapeño Cheddar
Cornbread and Mustard Slaw 5.25

PARMESAN FRIED OYSTERS
with a Roasted Garlic Remoulade and
Yellow Corn Relish 7.95

BLACKENED GREEN TOMATOES
with Creamy White Grits, White Cheddar
Cheese and Country Ham 5.25

HOUSEMADE PIMIENTO CHEESE
with Charleston Flatbread 4.95

DOWN SOUTH EGGROLL
Stuffed with Collard Greens, Chicken and
Tasso, served with Red Pepper Purée, Spicy
Mustard and Peach Chutney 6.75

HOUSEMADE POTATO CHIPS
with Crumbled Blue Cheese and Scallions.
Enough for two 5.75

Soups and Salads

CREAMY TOMATO BISQUE   Cup 3.50
with Lump Crabmeat and a   Bowl 4.50
Chiffonade of Fresh Basil

WADMALAW FIELD GREENS
with a Lemon Lingonberry Vinaigrette 3.95
with Crumbled Blue Cheese 4.50

GRILLED TUNA FILET
with Roasted Garlic, Sautéed Spinach, Fresh
Tomato, Shaved Red Onion and Lemon Herb
Vinaigrette 9.25

HERB GRILLED CHICKEN BREAST
with Wadmalaw Field Greens,
Caramelized Onions, Lemon Vinaigrette
and Parmesan 7.75

CAJUN CLAM CHOWDER   Cup 3.95
with Fresh Cilantro   Bowl 4.95

ROMAINE LETTUCE
with Caesar Dressing
and Garlic Herb Croutons 4.25
Parmesan Fried Oysters 8.95

CHILLED JOHN'S ISLAND TOMATOES
with a Carolina Goat Cheese Crouton,
Shaved Red Onion and Roasted Garlic and
Herb Vinaigrette 6.75

GRILLED PORTOBELLO MUSHROOM CAP
layered with Fresh Tomato, Shaved Red
Onion, Avocado & Carolina Goat Cheese
with Spicy Tomato Chutney 7.95

Pastas, Grits & Eggs

SPICY SHRIMP AND SAUSAGE
with Tasso Gravy over Creamy White Grits ... 9.50

GRILLED SALMON FILET
over Creamy White Grits with a Dill and
Shallot Butter 9.95
without Butter

POACHED EGGS AND GRILLED
BEEF TENDERLOIN
with Grilled Corn Bread, Creamy White Grits
Bearnaise Sauce and Yellow Corn Relish 8.25

FRESH SALMON AND SPINACH LINGUINI
A Carolina Goat Cheese Cream, Sundried
Tomatoes, Shiitake Mushrooms and Basil ... 13.50

GRILLED DOLPHIN FILET
in a Nest of Fresh Fettuccini
with Asparagus, Yellow Corn
Tomatoes, Garlic and
Herb Olive Oil 14.00

BOW TIE PASTA
with Apple Smoked Bacon,
Fresh Tomatoes, Blue Cheese,
Garlic and a Cracked Pepper
Cream 11.95

GRIDDLED SALMON CAKES
with Poached Eggs,
Country Ham, Sautéed Greens and
Hollandaise Sauce 8.95

Down South Dinners

SMOKED DOUBLE PORK LOIN CHOP
with Herb Butter, Collard Greens and
Buttermilk Mashed Potatoes 15.95

ASSORTED GRILLED VEGETABLES
with Creamy White Grits, Roasted Garlic and
Lemon Herb Vinaigrette 10.95

SEAFOOD SUCCOTASH
with Creamy Shrimp, Sea Scallops, Lobster and
Fresh Butterbeans, Yellow Corn, Roasted Red
Pepper, Herbs and Grilled Cornbread 18.50

GRILLED TUNA FILET
with Fresh Green Beans, Smashed Red
Potatoes and a Warm Tomato Vinaigrette ... 17.95

MAGNOLIAS' VEAL MEATLOAF
with Mushroom Gravy, Buttermilk
Mashed Potatoes and Tobacco Onions 14.25

GRILLED DOLPHIN FILET
with a Honey Mustard Butter, Fresh
Green Beans, Yellow Corn Relish
and Red Rice 15.50

SAUTEED LOCAL BLACK GROUPER FILET
with Creamy Cajun Shrimp and Yellow
Corn over Creamy White Cheddar Grits 18.25

8 OZ. FILET OF BEEF
topped with Homemade Pimiento Cheese,
served with Grilled Roma Tomatoes, Scallions,
Smashed Red Potatoes and Madeira Sauce .. 17.50

CAROLINA CARPETBAGGER FILET
with Parmesan Fried Oysters, Green Beans and
and Madeira and Bernaise Sauces 18.95

GARLIC MARINATED LAMB LOIN
with Spicy Tomato Chutney, Collard Greens,
Buttermilk Mashed Potatoes
and Mushroom Gravy 18.50

SPICY BUTTERMILK FRIED GAME HEN
with Collard Greens, Buttermilk Mashed
Potatoes and Mushroom Gravy 14.95

14 OZ. PEPPERED NEW YORK STRIP STEAK
with Red Potato Sod Busters, Sauteed Greens
and Bearnaise Sauce 18.95

MAGNOLIAS' CHICKEN AND DUMPLINGS
with Shiitake Mushrooms, Green Peas,
Yellow Corn and a Cracked Pepper Gravy . . 14.95

SAUTEED SALMON DIAMOND
with Grilled Jumbo Shrimp, Lobster Butter,
Sauteed Greens and Smashed Red Potatoes ... 17.95

Southern Sweets

Your Server will present our separate Dessert menu.
These selections consist of numerous items prepared fresh daily in our bake shop.

All Seafood may be Steamed, Grilled or Baked with lemon and herbs as Heart Healthy items

Magnolias' Southern Cuisine

Whether through ingredient or recipe, the prevalent theme in all of our dishes is traditional "down south" with a
contemporary "uptown" presentation. Chef **Barickman** and his staff strive not only for originality and diversity,
but constantly focus on quality of prime ingredient, freshness, and use of local products. Every dish is inspired by
Chef **Barickman** and his Associate Chefs.

The Magnolias Suite

The art displayed throughout Magnolias are original monotypes and oil paintings by Taos, New Mexico artist, the late
Rod Goebel. Through our private commission, the "Magnolias Suite" is the result of his 1990 springtime visit,
and represents the largest collection of this celebrated artist's work outside of galleries and museums.

Thank You for Refraining from Pipe and Cigar Smoking

Designates Heart Healthy alternatives on our menu that are lower in fat, cholesterol and sodium.

Please Ask Your Server About Magnolias' T-Shirts, Caps, Wine Tools and Gift Certificates.

FIGURE 2-1. Magnolias Uptown-Down South Menu, Charleston, South Carolina

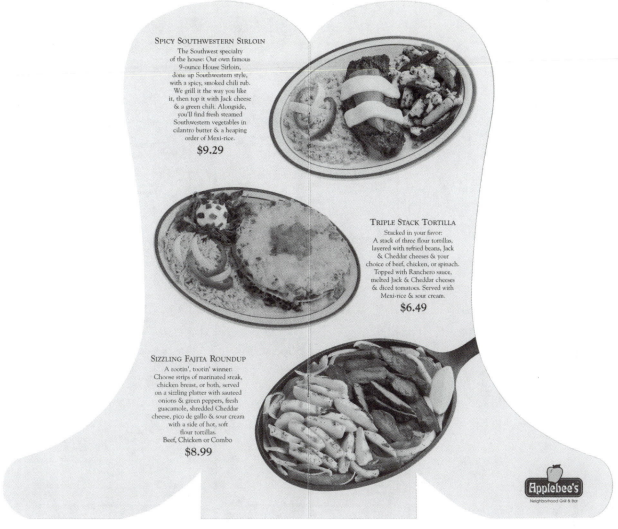

SPICY SOUTHWESTERN SIRLOIN
The Southwest specialty
of the house: Our own famous
9-ounce House Sirloin,
done up Southwestern style,
with a spicy, smoked chili rub.
We grill it the way you like
it, then top it with Jack cheese
& a green chili. Alongside,
you'll find fresh steamed
Southwestern vegetables in
cilantro butter & a heaping
order of Mexi-rice.
$9.29

TRIPLE STACK TORTILLA
Stacked in your favor:
A stack of three flour tortillas,
layered with refried beans, Jack
& Cheddar cheeses & your
choice of beef, chicken, or spinach.
Topped with Ranchero sauce,
melted Jack & Cheddar cheeses
& diced tomatoes. Served with
Mexi-rice & sour cream.
$6.49

SIZZLING FAJITA ROUNDUP
A rootin', tootin' winner:
Choose strips of marinated steak,
chicken breast, or both, served
on a sizzling platter with sauteed
onions & green peppers, fresh
guacamole, shredded Cheddar
cheese, pico de gallo & sour cream
with a side of hot, soft
flour tortillas.
Beef, Chicken or Combo
$8.99

Applebee's
Neighborhood Grill & Bar

FIGURE 2-2. Applebee's Neighborhood Grill & Bar Menu

Verbal Menu

Even with all these classifications of menus, it is also quite common for many restaurants today to have the server present to the guest a verbal menu list of "off the menu" specials. Mike Hurst of the 15th Street Fisheries in Fort Lauderdale, Florida, has carried the verbal presentation to its ultimate form by the use of individually arranged cards in an attractive frame with a built-in light. Hurst gives his servers product knowledge that enables his staff to sell foods on the menu. They are aware of the contents of the various menu items and have sampled the items offered by the restaurant (see fig. 2-4).

As a strong advocate of *word-of-mouth advertising* and *server upselling*, Hurst utilizes personal selling on the part of his service staff to supplement the market-

ing efforts of the printed menu. In the 15th Street Fisheries, there is a house rule that servers cannot memorize the daily specials and simply rattle off a canned sales presentation to the customers. He wants server recommendations to be genuine and personal. A greater responsibility for suggestive selling is placed upon his servers by the fact that the restaurant does not list the daily specials on the printed menu. This system of verbal selling is used to supplement—not replace—the printed menu. The printed menu remains the most consistent sales tool. While the 15th Street Fisheries may have a server staff that can effectively up-sell the menu verbally, it is an exceptional restaurant, and only a select few can do it effectively. Another downside is that verbal menus take time if they are to be done right. A high level of server skill is necessary for positive sales efforts. Exclusive use of

FIGURE 2-3
Independence Regional Health Center Menu, Independence, Missouri

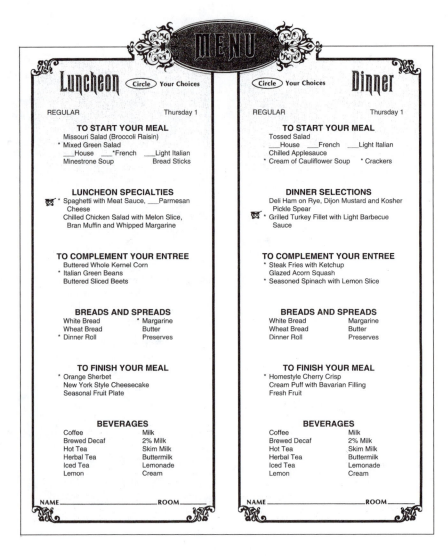

verbal menus is not practical for popular-priced restaurants, where speed of service can be a factor impacting table turnover.

My problem with most verbal presentations is that if there is more than one, I tend to forget what the server has told me. This is especially true if I have had a martini before the server arrives. My remembrance of one verbal presentation, at the Cafe Provençale in Evansville, Illinois, is that after the presentation was made, the waiter had a three-by-five notecard with the specials and their prices written on it. The card was given to the guest, and the waiter said he would be back for the order in just a minute. This system lets a guest review the off-menu items and gives the prices of those special items. It works very well in promoting such items.

If you choose to use a verbal menu, employees must be well trained. The waiters need a strong commitment to the operation. They must be knowledgeable in all phases of the food served in the restaurant.

High levels of communication and sales skills will be required to make a verbal menu successful.

Although the above classifications are the principal ones, they can be modified by combining features of one or more. Many establishments have found that a static menu with a cycle or market special (or specials) is the most advantageous for promoting sales.

Many menus are a combination of static, market, and cycle and offer a broader selection to the customers. Static menus are often supplemented with the addition of clip-on specials, chalkboard specials, and verbal specials to add variety to the menu.

NUMBER OF MENU ITEMS

Statistical studies of menus indicate that regardless of the number of items on a menu, sales will be concentrated in eight to twelve of those items. Limiting the menu permits your employees to become specialists in

FIGURE 2-4
Servers Explaining Menu, 15th Street Fisheries, Ft. Lauderdale, Florida

the items you list and sell, and the restaurant, as a result, is then doing what it does best. You cannot afford to maintain menu items that do not sell. You are in business to sell food, not to store it. The excess will be costly in inventory, and quality declines if a dish is not prepared regularly, or if it is prepared but seldom sold. The ideal menu would have ten entrees, with each accounting for 10 percent of total entree sales. This, however, is very unlikely. Only the most extensively researched menu could possibly come close to that ideal.

In chapter 3 there is a calculation for determining the acceptability of sales of the different menu items. Since we will not be dealing with the perfect sales situation, and we continue to work with a limited menu, the owner must be able to relate sales to an acceptable amount of the sales mix for the various menu items that are offered. The majority of patrons do not wish to struggle making a decision about what they will eat from your menu (and an extensive menu only worsens this situation), so the list should be limited, and items should be arranged in line with the suggestions in this chapter.

MENU TYPES

In addition to menu classifications, there are as many types of menus as there are times or places that food is consumed. Some of the possibilities include menus for:

Breakfast	Supper	Tea
Brunch	Pool parties	Hors d'oeuvres
Lunch	Children	Beverages
Dinner	Catering	Desserts

Such specialized menu types have a number of obvious uses, and many are utilized in large hotel operations.

Special-Function Menus

Special-function menus are written to the specifications of the customer usually for a function such as a wedding reception, banquet, or special occasion. The special-function menu is used when an event or celebration requires service and preparation beyond the normal day-to-day menu. Banquet and special menus are designed to the specific desires of the customer. The menu will be written and will follow a format similar to those forms shown in this section. The special-function menu may also have an effect on the reputation of the foodservice for future and continuing patronage by guests invited to the special event, whether on or off premises.

One method of special-function menu development is to prepare a series of complete menus with accompaniments and have the customers make their choice of menus. Having written the menus, you will know that the items fall within your cost, preparation, and serving parameters. A second method, and one that offers the customer greater latitude in selections, offers a choice of several entrees, salads, vegetables, and desserts that can be combined in a way to respond to the customer's tastes and budget. This method will also add your personal touch to the planning of the function. You are also able to upsell the menu to the customer. By your personal sales efforts, you may market any special or signature items that are trademarks of your establishment.

Before making suggestions, ask the client questions that provide you with insight into their needs and tastes. As with any group function, consider the total number being served when you make your recommendations. For any menu to be successful, the production capacity of your establishment must match the food items being served. Certain selections may have very low food costs but require considerable labor to prepare, plate, and serve (see fig. 2-5).

Another consideration for group functions is the equipment you have for the setup of the facility, the tableware for serving the meal, and the required servers for the style of service. The relative complexity of the menu and methods of presentation and service are critical to a successful function. Do not select menu items that will overextend your equipment or the abilities of your staff. A menu that you served successfully to 250 people may be a disaster when sold to a group of 800.

MENU PSYCHOLOGY

The intense competitive nature of today's business climate demands that every restaurant operator understand the factors of menu development, the various types of menu formats, the proper design and layout of a menu, and the specific customers the menu seeks to please. There are certain practices, when incorporated into the design of the menu, that can *influence* and *guide* the customer in the selection of specific menu items. The techniques used to accomplish this are referred to as *the psychology of menu design*.

Remember, a menu needs to be more than a mere list of what the restaurant has to offer. Menu design techniques can help the restaurant achieve its desired check average, sell the items it most wants to sell, help make service function more smoothly, and balance the workloads between kitchen stations. Achieving these goals does not happen by chance; they are accomplished in part by proper menu design. A menu should

be designed to help the restaurant, whether table-service or quick-service, to achieve its sales, profit, and cost goals.

The psychology of menu design seeks to call the guests' attention to certain menu items the restaurant seeks to sell more than others to achieve targeted food cost, profit, and sales goals. The influence a menu has on a customer is accomplished through the layout and design of the printed menu. Any given menu, no matter how it is printed and presented, will produce a certain sales mix when used over and over. Management uses the menu sales mix information to purchase inventory, set production amounts, and schedule employees. The more consistent the menu sales mix, the more accurate forecasting the future sales mix becomes.

Let us be perfectly clear in stating that menu-psychology techniques will not make customers select items they do not want to purchase in the first place. No system can control the customer selection process. What is offered here are techniques that increase the likelihood that certain items will be selected more often than others. In this way the selection process is not left entirely to chance.

There are three primary menu design formats. They are the single-page menu (no folds), the single-fold two-page menu; and the two-fold three-page menu. These menus are shown in figures 2.10–2.14.

Guiding the Customer

If management were given their druthers of which menu items they could sell more than others, and if they designed the menu to improve the likelihood that those items would sell first, they would employ the very techniques of menu psychology described in this book. If those menu items are randomly placed on the menu without any thought or purpose, their selection is left entirely to chance. The psychology of menu design cannot make unpopular items popular or make liver and onions outsell southern fried chicken. However, it will result in more liver and onions being sold than if it were randomly placed on the menu.

Influencing the Customer Selection

In menu layout and design, it must be noted that eye movement across the menu can be directed to certain parts of the menu. Techniques are employed to attract the readers' attention using many of the same methods found in magazine display ad design. The use of

Noonday Club Banquet Menus
June 7, 1995
Page 6

Noonday Club
SAINT LOUIS

Hors d'Oeuvres Selections For Before-Dinner Cocktail Hour

Before-Dinner Cocktail Selections:

Select:
- 3 Hot items (to be passed)
- 2 Cold Items
- 2 Prepared Trays

Price per person (served for one hour): $10.95
Additional Half-Hours (per person): $3.95

Hot Itmes:

1. Crab Fritters, Creole Tartar Sauce
2. Navajo Bread Stuffed with Texas Boar Sausage & Sonoma Jack Cheese
3. Shrimp & Boursin Cheese filled Croissants
4. Flank Steak Skewers Marinated in Hoisin & Peanut Sauce, Wasabi Mustard Dip
5. Gourmet Pizza Station – Assorted toppings: Smoked Salmon, Saga Cheese, Caviar, Shrimp
6. Fried Sea Scallops – Tartar & Cocktail Sauces
7. Miniature Veal & Mushroom Sausage Strudel
8. Bengal Chicken Skewers, Peanut Sauce & Chutney
9. Blackened Rock Shrimp Cakes – Red Peppper Remoulade
10. Fried Sesame Chicken Strips – Hot Mustard Sauce
11. Cheese Puffs, Honey Mustard
12. Jumbo Mushroom Caps stuffed with Sausage and Prosciutto
13. Oriental Crab Rangoon – Hot Mustard Dip
14. Oriental Pot Stickers & Pearl Balls with Won Ton Crisps

Cold items:

15. Red Grape and Cream Cheese Truffles Grapes covered with Cream Cheese & rolled in Chopped Hazelnuts
16. Brie Truffles – Softened Brie Cheese & rolled in Chopped Black Olives
17. Assorted Chilled Canapes: Crab Salad, Poached Scallops, Herbed Chicken Mousse, Corn Madelines
18. Breast of Chicken Gallatine, Basil Sauce
19. Salmon & Fine Herbs "Mille Feuille" Creamed Salmon in Puff Pastry
20. Duck Pate on French Melba Toast with Lingon Berries

One Metropolitan Square • Suite 4000 • St. Louis, MO 63102 • (314) 231-8452 • FAX (314) 231-0519

FIGURE 2-5. Noonday Club Menu, St. Louis, Missouri

bold uppercase letters, color, graphics, photographs, and font styles can be used to "draw the eye." These "eye magnets" can alter the random eye movement across a menu and actually direct attention to selected areas or items. The areas of emphasis are used to list the items that the operator wishes to promote the most. Since the first grade, we have been conditioned to begin reading in the upper left-hand corner of a page. This is the most natural reflex when one opens a menu and there is nothing to draw the eye anywhere in particular (see fig. 2-14).

A sampling of the owners and managers whose menus are contained in this book reveals that they frequently offered daily or weekly specials to supplement their static menus. These additional items were chosen in relationship to the total menu, with consideration of the labor and equipment available for preparing the menu items. Price points were set and items added to provide price-value to the customer while allowing the operator to keep food costs within standards and return a decent gross profit.

The placement of an item within a list of items can improve the likelihood of that item being selected more often than if it were randomly placed. Items featured on backlighted menu boxes consistently outsell other items, according to restaurant operators who use them. The items you wish to sell most should be placed first or last in a list of items. If you verbally present daily specials, the ones mentioned first and last should be the ones you prefer to sell. The reason for this is that we are all more likely to recall what we read or hear first or last. If the item is more likely to be recalled, it increases the probability that it will be ordered by the guest. This is referred to as the theory of primacy and recency, or the first/last bias.

The concept of the psychology of menu design is similar to the merchandising techniques used by major grocery and department stores when setting up store merchandise displays and counters. If they can get us to stop and look, they increase the possibility that we will make a purchase, and that is exactly what we are attempting to do with the design of the menu.

Since menu psychology techniques are designed to get the patron's attention, it is important to understand the way a customer typically looks and or "sights in" on the menu content. Studies have been undertaken that have monitored the eye movement across a page, referred to in a number of books and articles as *gaze motion* or *eye tracking*. This is put to use in menu

design in the following way: place the items one wishes to sell the most in the spot on the menu that will be seen first or last (see fig. 2-14).

Customers tend to scan the menu rather than read it in detail, so the menu must be designed to draw attention to the items we want to sell the most. By the use of graphics, illustrations, and type fonts, one can draw attention to featured menu items.

Since the average customer will spend only 109 seconds reading a menu, the message of the menu must be quickly discernible to the customer. This knowledge tells us that it is important to draw attention to the items we want to sell in order to increase the likelihood that they will be ordered.

MENU POLICY

At this point in the development of our menu, we have established our restaurant's objectives and determined the classification of the menu that we will offer to guests. The sequence of events now involves formulating a policy statement regarding the restaurant. A *restaurant's menu policy* is defined as a statement and commitment to the number of items and the type of food to be offered for sale to the restaurant's consumers.

To make correct decisions on our menu, we need to evaluate our marketing plan constantly and carefully and anticipate our budgeted sales figures. During operation we need to analyze the sales of all menu items. The decisions that are made will have a major impact upon the success and profit of the restaurant.

The first step in formulating a menu is to select the menu groups that will be offered on it. Normally, a menu will offer six or seven food groups. Some examples of these food groups are appetizers, salads, entrees, vegetables, and desserts. These items may be adjusted to what you think is appropriate for the type of restaurant you hope to create.

The second step in menu development is to choose the group classifications within each large menu group. There are nine standard entree possibilities (beef, pork, veal, fish, shellfish, poultry, lamb game, and non-meat dishes), so you need to make a decision about what entrees you will offer. In addition to making these choices in your group classifications you will also need to decide how many of each of the classifications you will put onto your menu. In effect we could have entrees from eight different groups on our menu, then choose from each of these group classifications the number of each to be offered. The menu might contain, for example, two beef, one poultry, two fish, and two veal dishes.

After having made these decisions, we come to a further group specification as to the types of products that will be used on our menu (see fig. 2-6). Using the beef entree, we can subdivide it into a solid, cubed, ground, roast, or previously cooked beef item to be prepared as an entree on our menu.

The next step breaks down the process even further in that we are now to the point of listing the specifications for the exact item to be on our menu. In figure 2-6 we have selected two solid-beef entrees. We can now name those items, and we have chosen a fillet, hunter-style, and a strip steak with béarnaise sauce. We might also have selected two veal items and then specifically listed a veal piccata and a veal cordon bleu.

This decision-making process must take place for every item on your menu. The choices are based upon your marketing plan and sales analysis. The sales analysis must be carefully monitored for indications of any change, indicating that menu changes are in order. The types of food may vary considerably from one establishment to another, but your menu will always be based upon your clientele and the competency of your employees.

The final consideration in the selection of menu items will involve the four factors shown in the flow chart (see figs. 2-6 and 2-7), and they are menu groups, group classification, group specification, and specific menu item. This flow chart is shown to point out that all factors must be considered in the development of the final menu. No single factor is more or less important than another in the determination of the final item selection; each should be considered in tandem with each other.

MENU FORMATS

The principal duty of the menu writer is to direct the customer's attention to those items that the restaurant

FIGURE 2-6
Menu Policy Flow Chart

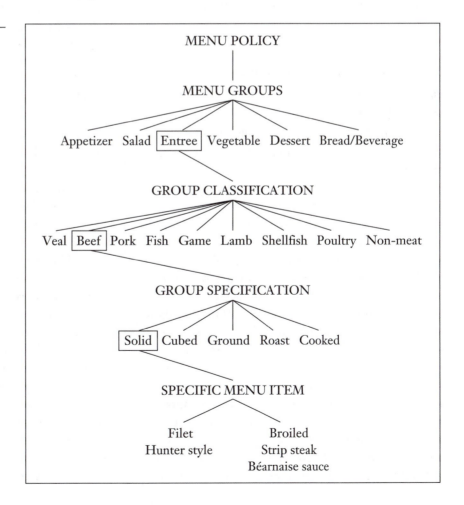

FIGURE 2-7
Flow Chart

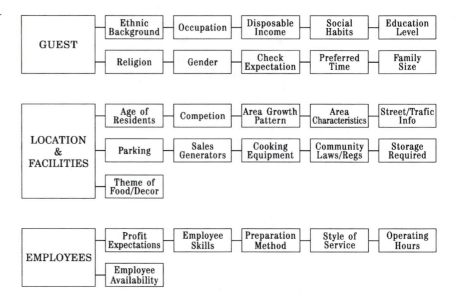

operation wants to sell. The design of the menu is limited only by the imagination of the owner or the designer. As mentioned earlier, the menu must be designed to increase both sales and profit. This section discusses ways to attain this goal.

There are five main types of menu design:

1. Single-page
2. Two-panel
3. Letter-fold (vertical or horizontal)
4. Three-panel
5. Multipage

William Doerfler, a menu consultant and designer, has devised some rules of thumb to assist with the design of the first two types of menus.

On the single-page menu, Doerfler suggests that the area immediately above an imaginary line dividing the menu in half horizontally is the focal point of the menu. This area, therefore, should contain those items that are most profitable (see fig. 2-10).

On the two-panel menu, an imaginary line runs from the upper left-hand corner across the entire menu to approximately three-fourths of the way down the right panel. These two interior sides are the most desirable locations for the items that are most profitable (see fig. 2-11).

The letter-fold menu is folded horizontally or vertically into three equal parts. This design permits you to use six panels—four inside and two outside—for logo identification, advertisement, institutional copy, and food listings and descriptions (see figs. 2-12 and 2-13). One section of this type of menu can even be used for a mailing label so that the menu can be a promotion piece or a souvenir.

The fourth type, the three-panel menu, has right and left panels that are folded to meet at the middle of the center panel. The left panel is one-fourth of the menu, the center panel is one-half, and the right panel is one-fourth. With this menu the eye tends to focus in the center. Concentration of sales, therefore, will be in the items located in this area (see figs. 2-8, 2-9, and 2-14).

The multipage menu is a book-style format used by restaurants with extensive menu offerings. The multipage format has some drawbacks that need to be mentioned. It requires a longer customer decision time and can lower the table turnover rate in the restaurant. Attention can only be drawn to the category of items listed on a single page. The NRA conducted a menu survey that revealed that a customer will spend no more than 109 seconds reading the menu. Unless the customer is a speed-reader, they will not be able to read a multipage menu, which therefore negates its merchandising value. The original TGI Friday's menu was over fifteen pages long. It has subsequently been reduced over the years as slow selling items have been deleted after extensive menu sales mix analysis was conducted.

A six-page menu is considered the maximum number of pages for a menu to be an effective merchandising and cost-control tool. The two-fold, three-panel menu format is perhaps the second most widely used format. Only the single-fold, two-panel menu is used more. The three-panel format provides six separate panels for menu listings. The panels are placed in plastic sleeves for protection. This format offers the advantage of reduced printing costs as each panel can be printed separately, so the entire menu does not have to be reprinted when changes are made. The Malone's Grill and Bar menu is an example of the two-fold three panel menu format (see fig. 2-8). The three-panel look can be accomplished on a single-fold menu with the use of a graphic design as shown in the Regan's Restaurant menu (see fig. 2-9). Other menu designs, shown in figure 2-15, are reproduced from Albin Seaberg's *Menu Design: Merchandising and Marketing.*

The menu has separate components that are each a factor in the overall effectiveness of the menu design. The psychology of menu design addresses each of the following components: menu cover, descriptive copy, placement of price, boilerplate information, type font size and style, color, and institutional copy.

MENU DIMENSIONS AND COVER SIZE

It is critical that the menu cover reflect the atmosphere of the restaurant. It should offer a glimpse of what the restaurant is all about and should begin to presell the rest of the menu. Remember that the menu cover is a major part of your overall advertising program.

The menu cover can be a combination of words and graphics that convey the impression you want and begin the communication process with the customer. The major function of the menu cover is to market and identify the restaurant; examples of this are shown in figures 2-16, 2-17, 2-18, 2-19, and 2-20.

Menu covers have traditionally contained only the name and logo of the restaurant. The cover should introduce the restaurant to the customer. The introduction starts as soon as the menu is handed to the guest. Therefore, the cover must receive special attention in its design.

Elijah McLean's Restaurant in Washington, Missouri, is a classic cover that consists of the basic elements of cover design (fig. 2-16). However, the front cover of many menus is beginning to undergo a significant change. A number of popular national chains using the three-panel, two-fold format are using the front cover to list menu items and give statements about their food and service philosophy. Spaghetti Warehouse, Country Pride, Chili's, and Claim Jumper,

(figs. 2-17, 2-18, 2-19, and 2-20) are prime examples of this growing new trend in menu cover design. The Spaghetti Warehouse states, "Each Day in Our Restaurant . . . We Roll Hundreds of Meatballs By Hand; Sauces Are Prepared Fresh From Scratch; and Fresh Vegetables and Meats Are Purchased From Local Suppliers." Country Pride touts their goal of "complete satisfaction with our quality food, prompt, friendly service and pleasant atmosphere." Chili's front cover is their drink and "Starter" menu and has you checking to see if the menu was folded properly. Note that the Claim Jumper menu cover includes the listings for "Wood Fired Pizza" and "Appetizers." Note how small the logo is on this menu. The rationale must be that the customers know where they are dining. We recommend that if you use the front cover for menu copy or institutional copy, keep your name and logo prominently displayed. Using the front cover to list drinks and appetizers frees up space for menu copy without having to change the overall size and format of a menu. It may also relieve the crowding and clutter sometimes found on interior menu pages.

The Elijah McLean's Restaurant cover contains the statement, "The New Family Tradition." This example of institutional copy attempts to create certain expectations in the minds of the customers as to the food and service they are to receive. The statement implies that families are welcome and traditional menu items are offered. Families are their target market.

Surveys conducted by the NRA indicate that the ideal menu size is 9 inches wide by 12 inches high. This appears to be about as large as is manageable for most people. Although this size is considered ideal, many other sizes and shapes have worked successfully and should not be dismissed. Menus of varying sizes and shapes generally are designed for dramatic effect (see fig. 2-21).

The size of the menu is dictated by the number of menu items and pages. The dimensions should be a manageable size for the guest, table size, and place settings. The page dimensions will decrease as the number of folds or panels increases. The three-panel, two-fold format is recommended, as it provides maximum space for menu copy without crowding or losing merchandising effectiveness.

Text continues on page 43

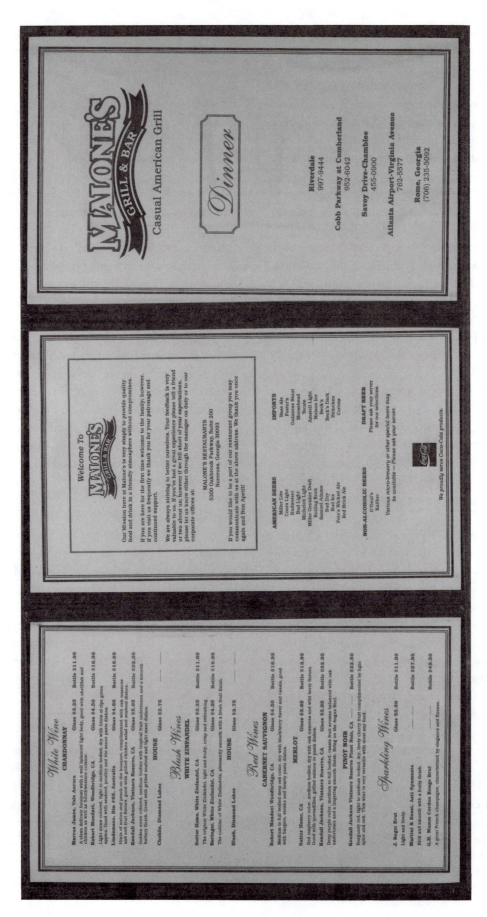

FIGURE 2-8.   Malone's Grill and Bar Menu

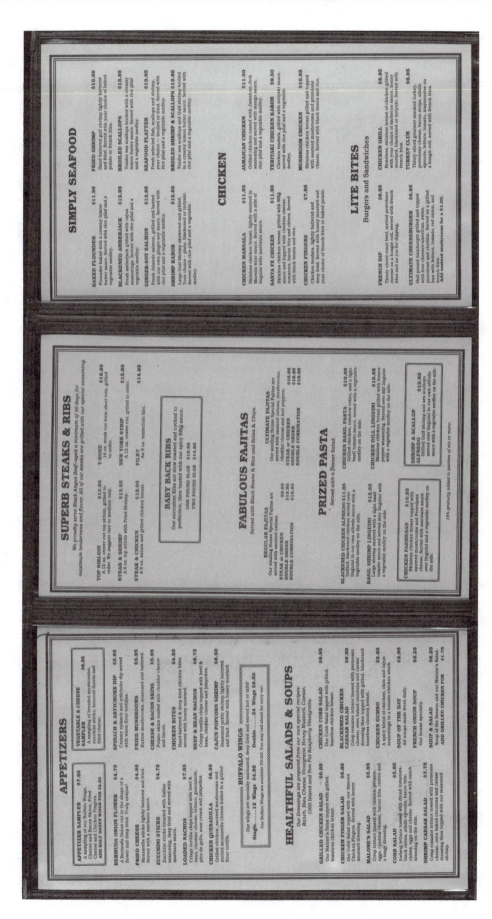

FIGURE 2-8. *continued*

FIGURE 2-9.   Regan's Restaurant Menu, Circa 1979

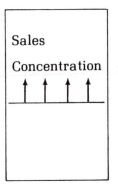

FIGURE 2-10.   Single-page Menu

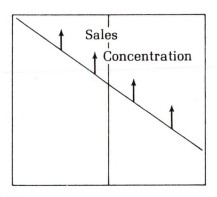

FIGURE 2-11.   Two-panel Menu

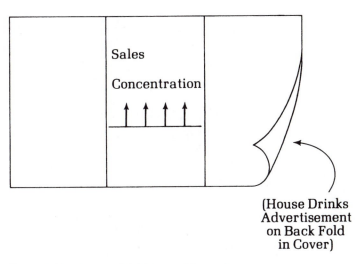

FIGURE 2-12.   Letter-fold Menu, Vertical

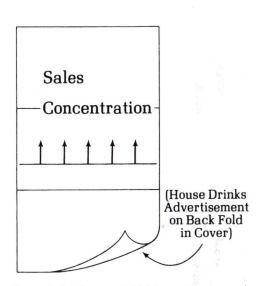

FIGURE 2-13.   Letter-fold Menu, Horizontal

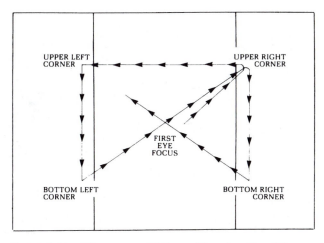

FIGURE 2-14.   Three-panel Menu, Showing Eye Movement

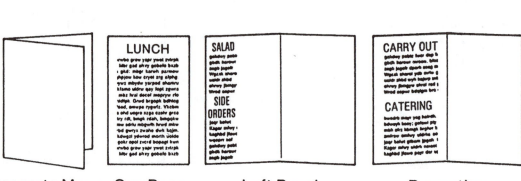

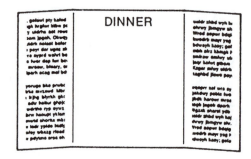

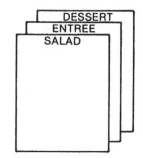

FIGURE 2-15. Menu Design Layouts from Albin G. Seaberg *Menu Design*

FIGURE 2-16.   Elijah McLean's Restaurant Menu, Washington, Missouri

Wine goes with Italian Food

RED

	BOTTLE	GLASS
Chianti, Banfi (Wicker) A robust, dry companion to red sauces.	$13.95	3.65
Valpolicella, Bolla Dry, soft & fruity.	$13.95	3.65
Cabernet Sauvignon, E.J. Gallo Flavorful, full-bodied red from California.	$13.95	3.65
Gamay Beaujolais, Glen Ellen Fruity, fresh, dry and young.	$13.95	3.65
Lambrusco, Riunite Slightly sweet, refreshing taste.	$10.95	3.00

WHITE

	BOTTLE	GLASS
Pinot Grigio, Sartori Crisp and fresh taste with a dry finish.	$14.95	3.95
Soave, Bolla Dry and medium-bodied with a nut-like aftertaste.	$13.95	3.65
Chardonnay, E.J. Gallo Medium-bodied. Fruity taste.	$13.95	3.65
Johannisberg Riesling, E.J. Gallo Light but with full flavor, dry but fruity.	$ 11.95	3.00

BLUSH

	BOTTLE	GLASS
Mateus Rosé Portugal's favorite: light and sweet tasting.	$11.95	3.00
White Zinfandel, E.J. Gallo Light and fruity tasting.	$13.95	3.65

SPARKLING

	BOTTLE	GLASS
Asti Spumante, Tosi A fruity sparkling wine.	$13.95	N/A
California Champagne, Cook's Perfect for any special occasion.	$10.95	N/A

HOUSE WINES

INGLENOOK VINEYARDS

CALIFORNIA **CHIANTI** and **WHITE ZINFANDEL**

Full Carafe $10.95
Half Carafe .... $ 5.95
By The Glass . $ 2.95

BURGUNDY CHABLIS

Full Carafe ..... $ 8.99
Half Carafe .... $ 4.99
By The Glass . $ 2.49

HOUSE SANGRIA

$12.99

*By the Pitcher
Made Fresh at
Your Table*

WAREHOUSE POLICY:
While we want you to enjoy yourself, our alcohol philosophy is consumption in moderation. We have a maximum limit of four drinks per person. We will not knowingly serve someone who is intoxicated. If you feel that you have consumed too much alcohol, let us know and we will make sure that you get home safely. Under no circumstances will minors be served alcohol, including non-alcoholic beers and wines. If you are pregnant or taking medication, we strongly suggest that you not drink alcohol.

U.S. & Imported Beers

Subject to local availability. Please be advised that not all of the beers listed here may be in stock at any given time. This is due, in part, to the complexity of importing and shipping. Thanks.

AUSTRALIA
Foster's

CANADA
Labatt's
Moosehead
Molson Golden

ENGLAND
Bass Ale

GERMANY
Beck's Light
Beck's Dark
St. Pauli Girl

HOLLAND
Amstel Light
Heineken Light
Heineken Dark
Grolsch

IRELAND
Guinness Stout
Irish Harp

ITALY
Moretti

JAPAN
Kirin

MEXICO
Corona
Dos Equis

U.S.
Budweiser
Bud Light
Coors
Coors Light
Michelob
Michelob Light
Miller Genuine Draft
Samuel Adams
Sharp's (NA)
Zima

Draft Beers

Pitcher of Draft ... $ 6.99

Mug of Draft ...... $ 1.99

Pitcher of
Premium Draft ... $ 8.99

Mug of
Premium Draft ... $ 2.49

WICHITA, KS · ©1995 THE SPAGHETTI WAREHOUSE 5/95

NOTICE: There is no connection between The Spaghetti Warehouse Restaurants and the Old Spaghetti Factory Restaurants in the United States.

THE **SPAGHETTI** and **WAREHOUSE** RESTAURANT

Each Day In Our Restaurant

...We Roll Hundreds Of Meatballs By Hand.

Sauces Are Prepared Fresh From Scratch
Following Authentic Old World Recipes.

We Use Real Domestic And Imported
Cheeses In Our Recipes.

Fresh Vegetables And Meats Are
Purchased From Local Suppliers.

Our Lasagne Is Layer After Layer Of Fresh
Meats, Cheeses, Noodles, Spices And Sauce.

We Slice Fresh Eggplants, Use Whole
Boneless Skinless Chicken Breasts
And Premium Veal For Our
Parmigiana Entrees.

We Serve San Francisco Style Sourdough
Bread Hot Out Of The Oven.

Welcome!
We're Glad You're Here.

FIGURE 2-17.   Spaghetti Warehouse Menu

The Malone's Grill and Bar menu is 7.5 inches by 14.25 inches when folded and 22.5 inches when fully opened. A minimum dimension for a three-panel menu is 6.5 inches. However, the Claim Jumper menu utilizes a three-panel plastic cover where each panel is 10 by 18 inches and opens to a full 30 inches. This represents a maximum size. When your menu gets too large, consider putting appetizers and desserts on separate menus or in permanent table tents so the overall dimensions of the menu can be reduced to a more manageable size.

There are literally hundreds of different type font styles to select from when you are ready to print your menu. You will also make decisions on the color of ink and paper on which to put the menu. The assistance of a graphic designer is recommended. The type of food served and the restaurant concept will impact the choice of fonts and graphics or illustrations. Your selections must be in harmony with the restaurant's theme, decor, and the service delivery system. Other critical elements include the size of the fonts used and the density of the print.

Cover Material

Although the menu cover usually is made of some kind of paper, almost any kind of material can be used for the cover or the menu itself. One steakhouse chain, for example, prints its menu on a meat cleaver. One St. Louis restaurant used a leather-covered bottle with the menu burned into the leather. Menus have been printed on wooden spoons and lunch buckets, and cut in the shape of an ice-cream bar. The menu cover or the menu itself can be anything that suits the restaurant's decor and is compatible with the operation.

The cover material needs to be durable and may be separate from the interior pages. Because most menus are used repeatedly, the cover also serves as a protective surface for the interior pages. A cover may be coated paper, a vinyl made to look and feel like leather, or paper laminated with mylar (a heat sealed plastic covering). However, the plastic sleeves used in the Malone's, Claim Jumper, and Country Pride menus remain the most economical way to protect the menu pages from moisture and food soil.

Color is popular on menu covers; it has a psychological impact on the guest and conveys a specific feeling about the restaurant. The color image you choose—whether on the menu cover or in the dining room decor—sets the mood for the meal. If customers enjoy their experience at your restaurant, then each time they see the restaurant's colors or logo, it will evoke a pleasant memory, and they will want to return for another meal.

Remember, however, that the more colors used, the more expensive the menu. Colored ink on colored paper can provide an inexpensive way to put color on the menu cover. Another less expensive yet colorful touch is to attach a ribbon to the menu cover or use multicolored stickers such as are available from most printers.

Cover Art

Many inventive and inexpensive techniques can be used on menu covers to tell customers the story you want them to know and to influence customers' perceptions of the restaurant. A restaurant located in an historic district, for example, might use an old photograph or line drawing of the area. Public libraries and historical societies are good sources of such material. Most are beyond copyright restrictions and can be used at little or no cost. Even contemporary illustrations of local scenes are suitable for identifying a restaurant and/or its location.

One restaurant uses a Hallmark card as the cover for its dessert menu; an attractive, handwritten menu was inserted inside the card (fig. 2-22). The picture on the front of the card presells and makes a favorable first impression on the customer. Remember, of course, if you go this route, to obtain permission to use the picture from the card's publisher.

The artwork done by any menu design company, printer, or artist rightfully belongs to the restaurant that has commissioned it. If you do not anticipate much change in the art for future menu printings, hold onto it for these printings. This saves the cost of redesigning the art or the background, and modest changes can be made at little or no cost.

Text continues on page 50

FIGURE 2-18.   Country Pride Menu

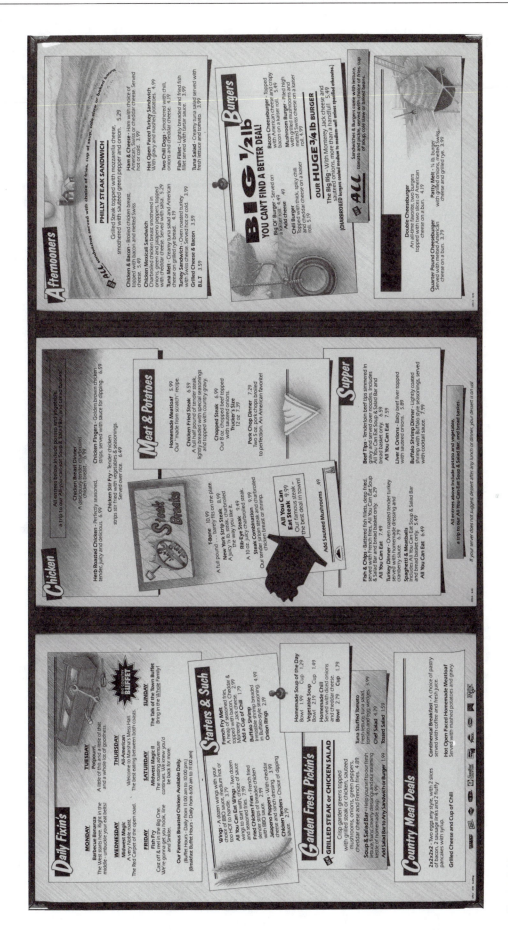

FIGURE 2-18. *continued*

FIGURE 2-19
Chili's Menu

DRINKS

MARGARITAS

PRESIDENTE
Our distinctive margarita made w/Three Generations Tequila, Cointreau® & Presidente Brandy. Hand shaken & served at your table

TOP SHELF
Our own special frozen margarita made with Conmemorativo Tequila & Cointreau®

CHILI'S MELTDOWN™ *NEW*
Our traditional frozen margarita topped w/your choice of Cointreau®, Chambord® or Midori®

BEER & WINE

RUSTY'S ROAD KNIGHT AMBER™ *NEW*
Chili's own beer. This brew boasts three types of hops & is aged longer for better flavor

DRAFT & BOTTLED BEER
Bud, Miller Lite & assorted premium bottled beers

WINE
Premium wines by the glass or by the bottle
Sutter Home® White Zinfandel
Napa Ridge® Chardonnay
Napa Ridge® Cabernet Sauvignon
Beringer® White Zinfandel
Kendall Jackson® Chardonnay

STARTERS

CHEESE FRIES
Fried mozzarella sticks w/marinara sauce 3.99

CHICKEN NACHOS
Sliced chicken breast, cheese, beans, jalapeños, pico de gallo & sour cream 5.29
w/guacamole 5.99

WINGS OVER BUFFALO™
A pound of spicy chicken drummettes w/bleu cheese dressing 3.99

STUFFED JALAPEÑO PEPPERS
Fresh jalapeños stuffed with a blend of cheddar Jack & cream cheese, battered & fried. Served w/our seasoned sauce 4.79

AWESOME BLOSSOM®
Fresh whole onion sliced to blossom, hand battered, fried & served w/our seasoned sauce 4.79

NACHOS
Chili queso nachos, beans, jalapeños, guacamole & sour cream 4.99

TOSTADA CHIPS
w/hot sauce 1.29
w/chili queso 2.29

SOUP OF THE DAY
Bowl 2.69   Cup 1.69
Cup w/any entree .99

QUESADILLAS
Sliced chicken breast, flour tortillas cheese w/pico de gallo & sour cream 4.79
w/guacamole 5.49

CHILI
Bowl of red, red w/beans or pie 2.99

BURGER PLATTERS

OUR ORIGINAL FRESH GROUND 1/2 LB. BURGERS SERVED W/HOMESTYLE FRIES
WHOLE WHEAT BUNS AVAILABLE. ADD BACON TO ANY BURGER .79

OLDTIMER®
Mustard, lettuce, tomato, pickle & onion 4.79

OLDTIMER® W/CHEESE
4.89

TERLINGUA PRIDE®
Oldtimer w/cheese & chili 5.29

VERDE BURGER
Guacamole, lettuce, tomato, Swiss 5.29

BACON BURGER
Bacon, cheddar, mayo, onion, lettuce, tomato & pickle 5.69

ROJO BURGER®
Hickory sauce & cheese 4.89

CHILI'S TRIP®
Chili, cheese & sauteed onions 4.99

MUSHROOM BURGER
Mayo, lettuce, tomato, Swiss & mushrooms 5.29

THE GOBBLER DELUXE™
Fresh ground turkey breast w/honey bbq sauce, bacon, jalapeño Jack cheese, lettuce, tomato & pickle on a toasted bun Served w/homestyle fries 5.49
OUR BURGER PLATTERS AVAILABLE W/TURKEY

OPEN RANGE

CAESAR OR DINNER HOUSE SALAD OR CUP OF SOUP W/ANY ENTREE .99

GRILLED CHICKEN PASTA
Marinated chicken breast served on a bed of linguine w/spicy cream sauce & garlic toast 6.49
Add fresh steamed veggies .99

CALIENTE CATFISH™
Farm raised catfish fillet battered & fried. Served w/homestyle fries & low fat pasta salad 6.49

CHICKEN CRISPERS®
Tender strips of fried chicken breast, curly fries, corn cobbette & honey-mustard sauce 6.29

CHICKEN FRIED STEAK
w/country gravy, mashed potatoes, corn cobbette & garlic toast 6.29

COUNTRY FRIED STEAK
w/country gravy, mashed potatoes, corn cobbette & garlic toast 6.29

SUBSTITUTION OF SIDES AVAILABLE UPON REQUEST

UN/R 5/95

SOUTHWEST GRILL

CAESAR OR DINNER HOUSE SALAD OR CUP OF SOUP W/ANY ENTREE .99

FAJITAS
Half pound of charbroiled steak or chicken on a sizzling skillet 7.99
For Two - a full pound 14.99
PEPPERS AVAILABLE WITH FAJITAS UPON REQUEST

CADILLAC FAJITAS™
Half pound of charbroiled steak or chicken or combination on a sizzling skillet Served w/rice & beans 8.99
Two Seafer - a full pound 16.99

BBQ BABY BACK RIBS
Rack of Danish baby back ribs topped w/bbq sauce & served w/cinnamon apples & homestyle fries 9.99

CHILI'S STRIP STEAK
Fresh USDA Choice 10 oz. strip steak, fresh steamed veggies, garlic toast & mashed potatoes 9.99

MONTEREY CHICKEN®
Grilled, marinated chicken breast w/bbq sauce, bacon & cheese. Served w/mashed potatoes & fresh steamed veggies 7.49

GRILLED CHICKEN
Grilled marinated chicken breast, rice, cinnamon apples & fresh steamed veggies 6.49

GUILTLESS GRILL℠

EACH OF THESE ITEMS HAS BETWEEN 3 & 7 FAT GRAMS AS SHOWN

GUILTLESS CHICKEN SALAD
3 FAT GRAMS
Charbroiled chicken, mixed greens, pico de gallo, kidney beans, sprouts, green onions & our no-fat Southwest dressing 5.79

GUILTLESS VEGGIE PASTA
11 FAT GRAMS
Fresh steamed veggies served on a bed of linguine w/fresh tomato sauce topped w/Parmesan cheese 6.29
Add charbroiled chicken breast 7.49

GUILTLESS FAJITAS
17 FAT GRAMS
Charbroiled chicken & fresh steamed veggies w/Parmesan cheese, pico de gallo. Served w/rice, spicy pinto beans & whole wheat tortillas 7.49

GUILTLESS CHICKEN PLATTER
6 FAT GRAMS
Chicken breast, charbroiled & fresh steamed veggies w/Parmesan cheese 5.99

GUILTLESS CHICKEN SANDWICH
7 FAT GRAMS
Charbroiled chicken w/no-fat honey-mustard, lettuce, pickle & tomato. Served w/low fat pasta salad & fresh steamed veggies w/Parmesan cheese 5.49

DIET BY CHOCOLATE™ CAKE
3 FAT GRAMS
Chocoholics Beware!! Three layers of moist chocolate cake topped with rich fudge & drizzled with warm chocolate sauce 2.99
w/no-fat frozen yogurt 3.29

SALADS

CARIBBEAN SALAD
Grilled, marinated chicken breast, mixed greens, pico de gallo, pineapple chunks, tortilla strips & honey-lime dressing 5.99

GRILLED TUNA SALAD
Seasoned line-caught tuna steak, mixed greens, pico de gallo, sugary walnuts, green onions & Ranch dressing 5.79

DINNER SALAD
Caesar or House 2.49
w/any entree .99

SOUP & DINNER SALAD
Bowl of soup & Caesar or dinner house salad 4.69

CHICKEN CAESAR SALAD
Grilled, marinated chicken breast, romaine tossed w/Caesar dressing, Romano & Parmesan cheese 5.99

CHICKEN FRISCO SALAD®
Smoked chicken, mixed greens, eggs, tomato, sprouts, almonds & honey-mustard dressing 5.99

BLUE RIBBON SALAD®
Fried chicken breast, mixed greens, eggs, tomato, sprouts & honey-mustard dressing 5.99

DRESSINGS: NO-FAT RANCH, NO-FAT HONEY-MUSTARD, NO-FAT VINAIGRETTE, NO-FAT SOUTHWEST, BLEU CHEESE, HONEY-LIME, HERBAL HOUSE, HONEY-MUSTARD, RANCH, CAESAR

SANDWICHES

SERVED W/YOUR CHOICE OF LOW FAT PASTA SALAD OR HOMESTYLE FRIES

TEJAS CHICKEN SANDWICH™
Thinly sliced chicken grilled with onions, bell peppers, guacamole, pico de gallo and topped with jalapeño Jack cheese 5.99

CHICKEN SANDWICH
Charbroiled chicken, bacon, lettuce, tomato, Swiss & dressing on a toasted bun 5.49

TUNA STEAK SANDWICH
Seasoned charbroiled line-caught tuna steak, lettuce, tomato & special dressing on a toasted bun 5.49

CHILI'S CHEESESTEAK SANDWICH
Thinly sliced Philly steak grilled with onions bell peppers, mushrooms and topped with Swiss cheese on a toasted garlic roll 5.99

TURKEY SANDWICH
Smoked turkey, Swiss, mayo, lettuce & tomato on our toasted garlic roll 5.99
Add bacon .99

TURKEY COMBO
Half of a smoked turkey sandwich & your choice of a cup of soup or dinner salad 4.99
Add bacon .59

15% GRATUITY FOR PARTIES OF 8 OR MORE

FIGURE 2-19. *continued*

FIGURE 2-20. Claim Jumper Menu

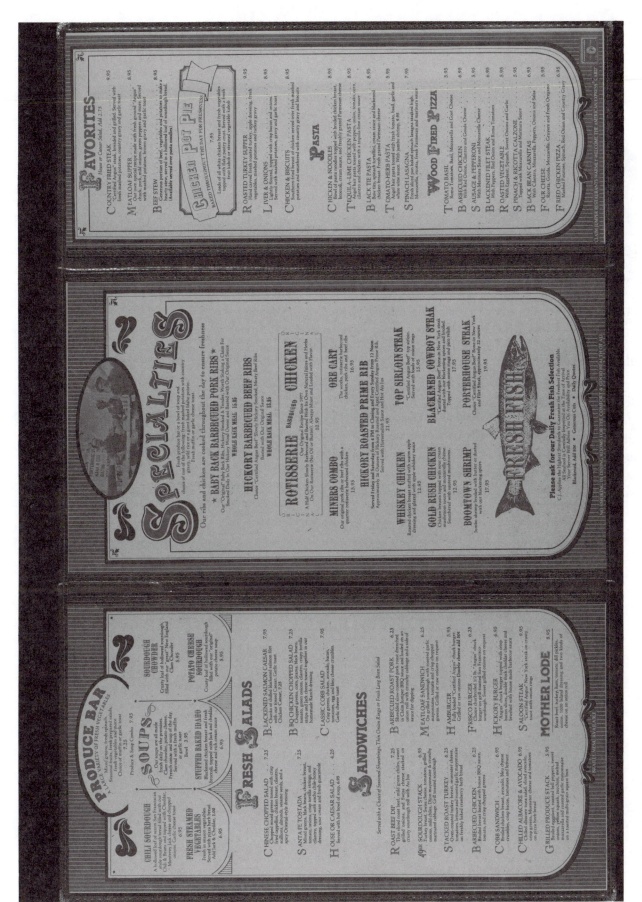

FIGURE 2-20. *continued*

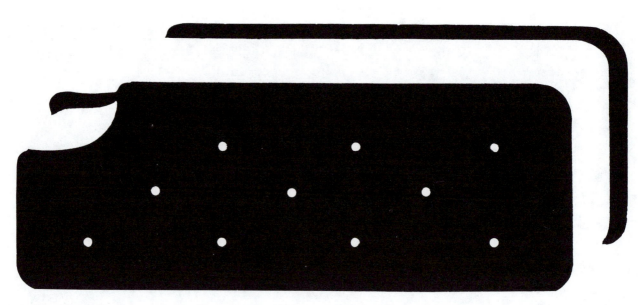

FIGURE 2-21. Ice-Cream Sandwich, Hallmark Cards, Kansas City, Missouri

Boilerplate Information

The menu cover should include what we refer to as boilerplate information. This information refers to institutional copy that tells about the restaurant, for example, address, telephone number, hours of operation, credit cards accepted, and special services such as catering or private parties. Institutional copy also gives historic or idiosyncratic information about the restaurant or location. On the Claim Jumper menu, figure 2-20, the back cover is used for "A Guide To The Miner's Gritty Argot." The Country Pride menu, figure 2-18, contains a map and locations of their other restaurants throughout the country, and Malone's back cover, figure 2-8, gives the corporate mission statement.

If your family has been operating your restaurant for three generations, you want to tell your story. Point

FIGURE 2-22
Notecard from Hallmark Cards, Kansas City, Missouri

The Rice Planters Restaurant Means

We are locally owned and operated by people who live in Myrtle Beach . . . not some out of town chain. We are proud of our restaurant, our employees and our customers.

- Family oriented
- Family owned and operated for 30 years
- We serve foreign and domestic beers
- Homemade cheese spread free with alcoholic drinks
- Thirteen separate dining rooms
- Wedding luncheons and receptions
- Private parties with any special menu desired
- We bake our own breads daily
- Our own salad dressings, we make them from scratch
- Home-baked garlic toast with salad
- We serve fresh boneless chicken breasts
- Unusual seafood dishes served such as panned seafood variety, baked crabmeat au gratin, and shrimp creole
- Brewed decaffeinated coffee
- We serve real sour cream
- We serve real butter
- Cholesterol-free oil used in all our cooking
- No extra charge for broiled foods
- No extra charge for grilling
- No extra charge for blackened
- When available, fresh vegetables are served from our own garden
- Many of our seasonings are fresh herbs from our garden
- Free camellias in season
- Free goodie bags and balloons for children
- Birthdays and anniversaries are special, Let Us Know
- Smoking and non-smoking sections
- Equipped for the handicapped
- Reservations accepted
- Menu items for Heart and Health conscious
- All sauces are made from scratch
- All or our meats are hand trimmed on premises
- All of our fish are hand cut on premises
- The Rice Planters Means Having Fun With Southern Hospitality

We care about

the food we serve, about the people who work here and, most importantly, about you, our guests.

Telephone 803-449-3456

FIGURE 2-23. The Rice Planters Restaurant Menu, Myrtle Beach, South Carolina

FIGURE 2-24. Red Hot & Blue Menu, Arlington, Virginia

out any unique features and how the restaurant has evolved to its present state. Add any historical background of the building or location that may be of interest. If there are any unique collections or artifacts associated with the restaurant, make the facts known in the institutional copy. Any information of this nature can stimulate guest involvement and have patrons discussing events about the restaurant. Recruit guests as ambassadors of the restaurant. (See the Rice Planters and Red Hot & Blue menus, figs. 2-23 and 2-24.) Inclusion of such information on the cover is useful for advertising your establishment (see fig. 2-25).

MENU COPY

The menu is the only piece of advertising copy for your restaurant that you *know* the customer is going to read. No matter how much time, effort, and money you put into advertising in the yellow pages, newspapers, or other forms of advertising, you have no guarantees that potential customers will see any of them. Thus, the menu must be treated as a piece of advertising. If your menu copy follows some of the rules of thumb and techniques used in the advertising business, you can begin to influence your customers in their choices of menu items.

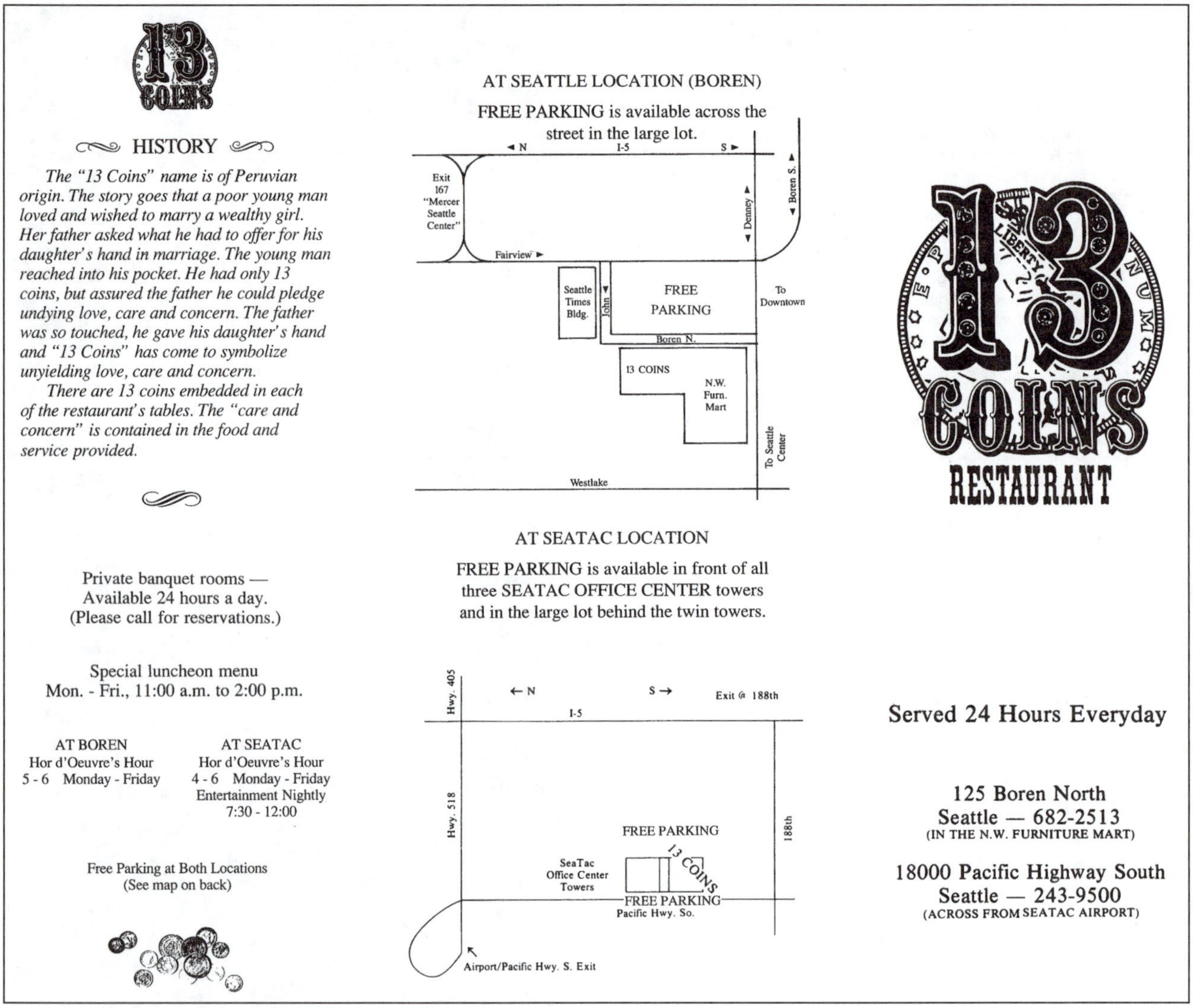

FIGURE 2-25. 13 Coins Restaurant Menu, Seattle, Washington

Categories of Menu Copy

Descriptive Copy

The *descriptive copy* should make it perfectly clear to the customer what they are getting when they order. If a customer has to ask, "What comes with the entree?" the menu is not communicating clearly. The descriptive copy should explain the menu items' preparation methods and the accompaniments included at the price indicated.

The readability of the menu is affected by the size of the type and the contrast between the ink and paper relative to the light level in the restaurant. Small type, poor contrast between print and paper, and low light levels result in difficulty in reading the menu without eye strain.

Well-written descriptive copy presents each menu item in such a way that the customer is encouraged to try the item. Customers will generally respond more favorably to short descriptive phrases about the food items. Try to be personal in your style of menu copy writing, and let the menu reflect the personality of the restaurant. Do not make unrealistic claims that may create expectations that cannot be met. When the ingredient or geographic origin of the item, for example, Nova Scotia salmon, is indicative of quality, it should be used in the description. Other examples of geographic origin useful in menu copy are Vermont maple syrup, Wisconsin cheese, and Virginia ham.

Descriptive copy used on menus and in media advertising is being scrutinized more closely than ever for misrepresentation. The state of California has enacted truth-in-menu statutes that must be followed by licensed restaurants and foodservices. The public must be guaranteed that menu descriptions are accurate and truthful. Truth-in-menu is the obligation of the owner or operator. Typical menu misrepresentations in descriptive copy include the use of the word *fresh* when the product has been previously frozen, listing "imported" ingredients when domestic ingredients were used, listing menu portions as 10–20 percent above the actual amount, and including photographs of menu items that do not resemble the item served to the customer.

The NRA has called for its membership to address this concern before other states and the federal government enact further legislation. If the industry cannot regulate itself, government will step in and enact laws and penalties. Inaccuracies that misinform the public are misrepresentations, and legal action can be taken against the restaurant. The national chains have to be extra careful because watchdog consumer groups are monitoring them. The position statement of the federal government on accuracy and truth in menu descriptions and examples of healthy menu copy for commercial restaurants are given in appendixes 1 and 2.

Food additives and ingredients can cause adverse reactions in some customers, and the restaurant may be held responsible for medical expenses if a customer becomes ill from eating food that was misrepresented in printed or spoken descriptions. If you are using strong or spicy seasonings that are a change from the norm, include this information in the menu descriptions.

Merchandising claims are the gray area for descriptive copy. If there is any place for poetic license, it is with merchandising terms. Statements such as "the best Italian restaurant in town," "our service is second to none," "home-style apple cobbler," and "authentic Oriental cooking" are unsubstantiated and boastful statements that would be difficult to dispute or sustain.

As for composing menu copy, the placing of words and phrases in the mind of the reader to create positive mental images takes special knowledge and ability. Professional copywriters may need to be engaged if one wants to do it right the first time. Provided herein are some guidelines that can help improve menu descriptive copy. Remember, these are not steadfast rules, as one must sometimes go against the normal and conservative schools of thought and risk being criticized for the sake of innovation.

1. Be simple. Describe the item clearly and cleanly using as few words as possible, and use phrases and short sentences.

2. Use "food associated" words. Some menu copy reads as if the writer consulted a thesaurus to find more complicated synonyms to describe the food. Words like *majestic, embraced, sensuous,* and *designed* are not words used to describe sauces and desserts.

3. Avoid the use of superlatives, for example, *mounds, drenched, smothered,* and *cooked to perfection.* Descriptive terms in excess will overexplain the food and can turn off a customer.

Big portions are not always the best selling point when there is a national trend toward eating less and being nutrition conscious. Do not make promises you can not keep; do not oversell. Consider a Reuben sandwich described as a "pile of corned beef smothered with a mound of sauerkraut, covered with a thick layer of melted Swiss cheese and topped with a dollop of thousand island dressing on grilled pumpernickel bread." That might be considered overselling. A more moderate approach might read "Warm and tender sliced corned-beef brisket, a touch of sauerkraut, imported big-eye Swiss cheese, homemade thousand island dressing on dark pumpernickel bread, grilled and served with Kosher pickle spear."

4. Don't confuse the issue. Overdescription can turn a simple menu item into a confusion of sauces and ingredients and can be a turnoff for customers. The descriptive copy does not need to be the recipe.

5. Using foreign words to sell the item is fine, but care must be taken to provide an explanation if the phrase or description is not self-explanatory.

6. Commonly known items do not need long explanations. Copy for a steak may indicate the grade (USDA Choice), geographic origin (Iowa beef), quality (corn fed, black Angus), and preparation (charbroiled over mesquite coals). Adding copy such as "broiled to perfection" and "turned to a degree of doneness that melts in your mouth" are unnecessary.

The following information is generally covered with the descriptive copy.

1. Method of preparation, such as broiled, baked, grilled, sautéed, or deep fried

2. Essential or main ingredients if they are unusual or unique
3. How it is served or what comes with it (accompaniments)
4. Quality claims such as grades or freshness
5. Variety or geographic origin such as Alaskan King Crab, Smithfield ham, or Angus beef

Next is a *listing of the food*. The name of each food item is critical, because everything listed conjures up some mental image for the person who is going to consume the food. A great deal of the satisfaction with a meal comes from food meeting the expectations of customers about the items listed.

Restaurant Business magazine once published a survey on the subject of menu names. Results indicated that most people do not like cutesy names for menu items. Strange or cute names for food are merely fads and fade quickly. Unusual names might be acceptable on the menu of a private club, but a general, public type of restaurant should have familiar and specific names for food items. Some menus have done an excellent job with gimmicky names, but these usually are designed to carry out a restaurant's theme or to serve a specific advertising purpose.

When one uses clever names to merchandise menu items, a detailed description must be used to fully explain the food and its preparation and service to avoid customer dissatisfaction because they did not fully understand what they were ordering. Sports bars will take exception and name items with the owner's name or terms relating to the sports covered in the restaurant's theme. Their hamburger with grilled onions and sautéed mushrooms may be called "The Linebacker," and their cheese steak may be called "The Quarterback." Those names require descriptive copy to explain what the customer is ordering.

Portion Size

On the subject of size, you should never state the ounce size of anything on the menu. The ounce size is generally the raw weight of an item, and one major class-action suit against a fast-food corporation claimed that the product did not weigh what it was advertised to weigh *after* it was cooked. The courts ruled in favor of the plaintiffs on the basis of false advertising. Other words can be used to describe a portion size, a *petite steak*, for example, indicates size.

Although brief descriptions usually are the best, you might, for example, want to describe items that are healthy and nutritious, but you need to be able to validate your claims.

Where and How to List Price and Style of Service

Service style and menu price are two elements the customer uses to assess the price-value of the total dining experience. There is a correlation between service delivery and the prices customers find acceptable. The more attention paid to service, the greater the price-value perception by the customer. The next decision one must make is the determination of which items to price a la carte, table d'hôte, and a combination of both.

Most menus are a combination of a la carte and modified table d'hôte. Luncheon and dinner specials are likely to be priced table d'hôte, while the regular luncheon and dinner entrees will be served with one side dish and bread and butter only. Most commercial restaurants include salad and bread with dinner and charge extra for additional items such as a potato or vegetable.

There is an art to the manner in which the prices of foods are placed on the menu. You want the customer to read the descriptive copy before they look at the price. In reviewing hundreds of menus for this edition, we have noticed a major shift in the manner in which the prices are listed on the menu. The intent of price placement is not to deceive the customer but to have them make their choice of food without primary attention to the price. We found that operators are reducing "price shock" by the placement of the price immediately following the last word in the menu description. The closer you can list the price to the description of the item, the less psychological impact the price will have on the customer.

Figure 2-26 presents illustrations of the methods for printing prices on menus for each of the foods listed. The listings and prices are printed by permission of The Abbey restaurant (Atlanta, Georgia), The Rattlesnake Grill (Denver, Colorado), and Houlihan's Restaurant Group. These are shown as examples of how to best avoid customer shock with menu price listings.

1. The use of leaders and dots and an even right-hand margin will tend to call attention to and emphasize the prices.
2. The price listed in close proximity to the menu description keeps the price from being the main focus of the menu item.

The Abbey

"There is no love sincerer than the love of food."
George Bernard Shaw

Meat Entrees

Roast Rack Of Lamb In Garlic-Herb Crust
Eggplant Tart & Goat Cheese Ravioli   23

Seared Range Chicken Breast
With Sage Sausage, Polenta Cake,
White Bean Cassoulet & Marsala Jus   18

Crisp Magret Duck Breast In Cinnamon-
Honey Glaze, Bourbon Sweet Potato Confit
& Black Currant Sauce   19

Grilled Veal Rib Chop In Black Truffle Sauce
Wild Mushroom Ragout
& Prosciutto Gratin Potatoes   23

Broiled Filet Of Beef With Chili Cilantro Leeks,
White Cheddar Mashed Potatoes
& Poblano-Peppercorn Sauce   23

THE RATTLESNAKE GRILL

SIMPLY FROM THE GRILL

THE "RATTLEBURGER" 8.95
All Beef Burger(No Rattlers), Served With Swami Sauce and Steak Fries
GRILLED CHICKEN "BURGER" 9.95
All Chicken Burger, Served With Swami Sauce and Steak Fries
GRILLED AHI TUNA "BURGER" 9.95
Herb Tuna Burger, Served With Tartar Sauce and Steak Fries
PRIME NEW YORK STEAK (10 Oz.) 18.95
STERLING SALMON (9 Oz.) 19.95
AHI TUNA (9 Oz.)**(4) 22.95
DRY AGED FILET OF BEEF (10 Oz.) 24.95
PRIME PORTERHOUSE STEAK (24 oz. Bone In) 29.95
Grilled Selections Include Choice of Potato or Vegetables

▰ HOULIHAN'S CLASSICS ▰

Add soup or side salad for 2.50.

Barbecued Baby Back Ribs
Baby Back pork ribs, charbroiled and basted in Kansas City-style barbecue sauce. With barbecued baked beans and natural-cut fries. *Full Rack* includes soup or side salad. 13.99 *Half Rack* 8.99

Sizzling Fajitas
Houlihan's award-winning recipe! Char-grilled beef, chicken or both, served in a sizzling hot skillet with bell pepper and onion. With guacamole, sour cream, cheddar cheese, shredded lettuce, warm tortillas and salsa. 9.79

Stuffed Chicken Breast
Tender chicken breast filled with savory herb and garlic cheese, then lightly breaded, sauteed and topped with a delicious dill-butter sauce. Served with Houlihan's Smashed Potatoes and sugar snap peas. 8.99

Jambalaya
Boneless chicken breast, beef sausage, smoked ham and shrimp in a spicy creole sauce with red onion and bell pepper. Served over rice. 8.99 *Lighter Size* 6.99

3-Way Sampler
A collection of flavorful favorites. Barbecued Baby Back Ribs, Teriyaki Grilled Chicken Breast and Spicy Cajun Shrimp served with natural-cut fries and a cajun-mustard sauce. 9.99

FIGURE 2-26. Three Menus: The Abbey, Atlanta, Georgia (top); The Rattlesnake Grill, Denver, Colorado (middle); Houlihan's, Kansas City, Missouri (bottom)

3. The price list on the menu for The Abbey does not use leaders and dots. The system of listing only the dollar digits of the price does not utilize the odd-cents price advantages.
4. Spelling out the dollars and cents rather than using traditional Arabic numbers is being used in fine-dining establishments and is not practical for popular-priced restaurants.

Arrangement of Copy

Although it may sound obvious, it is important to remember that categories of food (or courses) must be arranged in the order in which they are eaten. Even though the menu must take into account the customer's eye focus, the customer needs to be able to know the food categories that are available in the order he wants to eat them.

The location of items on the menu is a critical aspect of the menu as a marketing tool. The marketing principle of *primary and recency* states that what catches your attention first and last will remain uppermost in your mind. If you watch people examining menus in a restaurant, you will see this principle at work. It is important to the properly designed menu. Applying it by featuring those dishes that make the most profit will help you increase sales of items you want to sell.

Surveys and research indicate that in any list of ten menu items, those listed first, second, and last are the ones that will sell best. Do not list menu items in order of their prices—that is, the lowest to the highest, or vice versa. List them in the order in which they are profitable. If your highest-priced item is the one on which you make the most profit, list it either first or last.

White Space

White space is the printing/production term that designates what is *not* printed. Menus need white space. In fact, the printed menu's copy, drawings, and any other material should cover no more than 50 percent of the total space available. Menu copy that is surrounded by white space (it is called that even if you use colored paper) emphasizes the type and makes the menu easier to read, avoiding the cluttered look. If the white space amounts to less than 50 percent, not only will it make the menu look crowded, but also it will hinder the customer in reading the menu and making food decisions.

Margins, the outside edges of the menu, are one form of white space; they should all be consistent. This contributes to the symmetry of the menu and makes it easier to read. On the left-hand side, the type should all be even against the margin, while on the right-hand side, the type can be ragged, or uneven. The right-hand margin begins at the end of the longest ragged line. Columns of copy should be no wider than 3 inches.

Blank space, meaning a space on the menu that seems to demand filling, can be used effectively to advertise other special offerings. Blank space on a breakfast menu, for example, might be well utilized to advertise your Sunday brunch. If the arrangement of copy and drawings on your menu results in blank space, by all means make good use of it. Never just leave it blank.

Color in the Menu

Color may be used in a menu to call attention to specific menu items, but it is also used, as described earlier, on the menu cover to emphasize the restaurant's theme and decor. The amount of color used is determined by the budget; the more colors used, obviously, the higher the cost of the menu.

Only a small amount of color used in the printing or design of a menu results in a considerable effect; excessive amounts of color can distract the patron's attention from the actual menu. Intense colors should normally be avoided on a menu unless they are used for some special effect. Colors are usually most acceptable in headings and for separating items on the menu.

Menu Paper and Ink

For maximum readability, a menu should be printed in black ink on white paper. It is acceptable to use tinted paper or tinted ink compatible with the atmosphere and color scheme of the restaurant, but be warned that it is all too easy to select colors that blend into one another and are then not readable at the light level of the dining room. Test the combinations in a simulated setting before you make your decisions.

Menus usually are printed on paper. Other materials were mentioned earlier in the section on the menu cover, but the standard material for the interior is paper. The quality and type of paper used depends upon the permanency of the menu. The character and type of restaurant dictate the quality of the paper. If the menu is changed daily or relatively often, a lower quality can be used because the menu is quickly obsolete. Fast-food operations, on the other hand, often prefer coated (laminated) paper because of the menu's long-term, constant use. A reusable menu requires durable paper that will stand a great deal of handling by both customers and employees.

The texture and weight of the paper stock upon which the menu is printed are its lasting qualities (see fig. 2-27). Be choosy about your menu material. Once again, remember that it is conveying your restaurant's image. Spend some time examining catalogs from a printer. Evaluate the small samples of papers in various colors, weights, and textures. Make your decisions rationally and economically. Ninety-pound stock is fine for an average restaurant. (Such determinations of weight are based on trade formulas and are best explained by your printer.)

The menu stock should not amount to more than 10 or 15 percent of total menu costs. Purchase stock in sizes that yield the maximum number of menus generally in the 9-inch-by-12-inch size recommended earlier.

Color

Attention now turns to selecting the appropriate colors for the ink and paper. Color in the paper and ink can add much to the design of a menu. More than any other aspect of the menu, color has definite psychological effects on the customer. Colors are used to create a mood, establish a restaurant's image, stimulate the appetite, and call attention to particular items. Color should be used to merchandise specific items the operator wishes to sell. There are some common colors found in restaurants. For example, steakhouses often use black and red, country clubs are partial to

FIGURE 2-27

Types of Menu Papers from Albin G. Seaberg *Menu Design*

TYPES OF PAPER

Antique paper.   Paper with a rough, textured surface.

Bond.   Paper for letterheads, forms, and business uses.

Book paper.   Paper having characteristics suitable for books, magazines, and brochures.

Bristol.   Cardboard that is .006 of an inch or more in thickness (index, mill, and wedding are types of bristol).

Coated.   Refers to the treatment of paper or paperboard with clay or some other pigment.

Cover stock.   A variety of papers used for the outside covers of menus, catalogs, booklets, and magazines.

Deckle edge.   A rough edge on paper formed by pulp flowing against the frame (deckle), creating a feathered, uneven edge when the paper is left untrimmed.

Dull-coated.   A low-gloss coated surface on paper.

Eggshell.   Paper with a semirough surface similar to the surface texture of an egg.

Enameled.   Any coated paper.

English finish.   A machine finish and uniform surface.

Grain.   A weakness along one dimension of the paper (paper should be folded with the grain).

Machine finish.   A medium finish, rougher than English finish but smoother than eggshell.

Offset paper.   Coated or uncoated paper suitable for offset lithography printing.

Vellum finish.   A finish similar to eggshell but from harder stock and with a finer-grained surface.

forest green, and French restaurants frequently use pastel colors and white.

Psychological testing has shown that people react differently to specific colors. Colors and lighting can make people feel cold, hot, happy, depressed, romantic, and so on. Deep red and purple convey richness and opulence and are often used in high check-average restaurants and hotel dining rooms. Beige, pink, light green, and lavender imply a warm, soothing atmosphere. Certain colors are associated with different cuisines: Italian—red, white and green; Mexican—yellow and orange; French—white, gold, silver, or black. Because these color associations are already fixed in the customer's mind, the menu planner should use these color combinations to full advantage.

Paper Stock

The type of paper that is best for your particular menu will be determined by the following criteria.

1. Overall size and shape of the menu
2. The number and types of folds, panels, embossing or die cuts used
3. The inclusion of color photos or illustrations
4. The permanency of the menu desired

Restaurant menus require a paper stock that is versatile. The paper must readily accept a variety of graphic treatments such as gold leaf stamping, die cutting, and embossing. It must be durable and be able to hold up under frequent handling, folding, and unfolding and still appeal to both the eye and touch.

Mechanics of Menu Copy

The smaller the operation, the easier the task of writing the menu copy. When the owner/operator has continuous public contact or is preparing and serving the product, he will know by verbal feedback or visual perceptions what is right and what is wrong with the menu.

MENU PRODUCTION

Following the preparation of the menu copy, the next stage is to choose typeface and size of print—and then produce the physical menu.

The menu's typeface sets the style for the atmosphere of the restaurant and should reflect the estab-lishment's ambiance. Just as corporate logos and trademarks are important elements of corporate images, the menu conveys the image of a restaurant. The colors and logo or trademark of a restaurant should be a part of the menu and should be used as identifiable characteristics for every printed item in the restaurant.

As you make your choices in producing the menu, keep in mind that any type style that is difficult to read or not easily understood destroys all the groundwork you have laid in developing the menu. This pertains also to the size of the print. If the menu print is so small that it cannot be read in the dining room, all your other efforts are useless.

Reading research shows that the average person comprehends and reads better in a line approximately three inches in length. The length or width of the lines in your menu copy will thus affect customers' comprehension of the menu. The eye does not flow evenly across the printed line but grasps and comprehends groups of words, then moves on to a new group of words. There is a chance of the customer's losing his place, then having to refocus and begin the reading process again. Separating different elements by bits of spacing and special kinds of type are methods of giving emphasis to items on the menu.

Typeface Styles and Sizes

Typefaces come in many different styles and sizes. Printers and designers have catalogs with printed samples. Typefaces appropriate for menus fall into three categories—serif, sans serif, and script.

- Serif typefaces—those with tiny lines at the ends of the letters—are graceful, readable, and solid, but nowadays they are considered old-fashioned or traditional. There are hundreds of families of serif type; five samples are shown in figure 2-28.
- Sans serif typefaces—those without the serifs—are generally block-shaped, simpler, and considered more modern. Samples of sans serif type are shown in figure 2-29.
- Script typefaces, while appropriate for menus, should be used sparingly. They can add variety in the printing and highlight the food items you want to merchandise, but they (and italic as well) can cause eyestrain from the slanted angles of the letters (see fig. 2-30).

COFFEE - our own blend 50
COFFEE - our own blend 50
COFFEE - our own blend 50
COFFEE - our own blend 50
COFFEE - our own blend 50

FIGURE 2-28. Serif Typefaces

COFFEE - our own blend 50
COFFEE - our own blend 50
COFFEE - our own blend 50
COFFEE - our own blend 50
COFFEE - our own blend 50

FIGURE 2-29. Sans Serif Typefaces

Coffee - our own blend. 50
Coffee - our own blend. 50
Coffee - our own blend. 50
Coffee - our own blend. 50
COFFEE - our own blend. 50
COFFEE - our own blend. 50
COFFEE - our own blend. 50
COFFEE - our own blend. 50

FIGURE 2-30. Script and Italic-Style Typefaces

The text of the menu should be printed with a combination of uppercase (capital) and lowercase (small) letters. Most menus are printed effectively if they have about twice as many lowercase letters as uppercase letters, since lowercase letters are considered more readable.

Use uppercase letters for categories of food and for proper names, as well as to draw attention to special items on the menu. One restaurant in St. Louis, for example, lists Beef SANDWICH in the center of its luncheon sandwich offerings, to draw attention to that section of the menu. Their sales analysis indicates that this particular sandwich is the best-selling one on the menu. Although it was not their original intention to highlight only this one item, the device has been effective. Such a mixture can be used in other ways to develop customer awareness by design.

Exotic typefaces and offbeat printing styles should be used very sparingly in a menu. They are difficult to decipher and are handicaps to the readability of the material (see fig. 2-31).

The weight or boldness of the typeface is another critical element in the design of the menu. Typefaces come in light, medium, and bold weights (see fig. 2-32).

As mentioned earlier, the menu conveys the restaurant's image, so the printing must be compatible with the decor that you have developed for the restaurant. Thus, the typeface style and the boldness of the letters should be consistent with the mood of the restaurant.

Never use more than three different typefaces on a menu. This confuses the copy, results in a haphazard appearance, and conveys the wrong message to the customer.

Since readability is the ultimate goal in the production of the menu, you will have to select type sizes that fit in the space you have available. The type must be large enough to be legible, but the menu should not be overcrowded and look cluttered.

Type size is measured in points—seventy-two points per inch. Menus should not be printed in sizes smaller than twelve points, which is roughly equivalent to the size of a letter on a pica-style typewriter (see fig. 2-33).

The space between the lines of printing is called leading (pronounced "ledding"). For ease in reading a menu, three-point leading is essential. Anything less

AVOID SETTING SCRIPT STYLES IN ALL CAPS.
Avoid setting Script styles in All Caps.

AVOID SETTING OLD ENGLISH STYLES IN ALL CAPS.
Avoid setting Old English styles in All Caps.

FIGURE 2-31. Examples of Italic and Script Fonts

COFFEE - our own blend. 50
COFFEE - our own blend. 50
COFFEE - our own blend. 50
COFFEE - our own blend. . . . 50

FIGURE 2-32. Type Examples Showing Different Weights and Boldness of Fonts

---

12 point SANS SERIF
12 point SERIF
12 point DECORATIVE

FIGURE 2-33. Examples of Twelve-Point Type

SERIF GOTHIC 12/3

THE GOURMET -with grilled onions,
sauteed mushrooms and swiss cheese. 4.50
    12/0
THE GOURMET - with grilled onions,
sauteed mushrooms and swiss cheese. 4.50

FIGURE 2-34. Type Showing Three-Point Leading Between Lines (top) and No Leading Between Lines (bottom)

reduces readability. In figure 2-34 the copy with three-point leading (indicated as 12/3) is more legible than the copy with no leading (indicated as 12/0). Printing with no leading is said to be *set solid*.

Spacing between the letters is also adjustable, depending on the requirements of your menu copy. A feeling of space can be created by a typesetting process known as *kerning*, which involves the removal of space between letters, or by *letterspacing*, which involves adding space between letters (see fig. 2-35). The following items are recommendations for copy printing.

The combination of black ink on white paper is 33 percent more readable than light ink colors on dark paper.

Using all uppercase (capital) letters in menu descriptions decreases readability by 25 percent compared to the readability of lowercase letters. AS AN EXAMPLE, CONSIDER THE READABILITY OF THIS SENTENCE COMPARED TO THE REST OF THE TEXT.

Serif type in blocks of type is 55 percent more readable than sans serif type.

※ Guidelines for Selecting Type Sizes and Styles

1. Use 12 point type size or larger.
2. Use lowercase letters for menu descriptions.
3. Use uppercase letters for headings and subheadings only.
4. Do not mix more than three different styles of type.
5. Have at least 3 point leading between lines.
6. Script and exotic type should be used sparingly if at all.
7. Leave at least 50 percent white space (unprinted surface) to provide contrast and emphasis.
8. Check for sharp contrast between ink and paper-color for optimum readability under low light conditions.
9. Select colors and type styles that match the character of the restaurant.

Desktop Publishing

One of the most promising new areas of menu publication is in desktop publishing, a system used in the computer world today. All restaurants who are on an advanced system of computer use are now utilizing some system of computer publishing. Computer publishing concepts of menu printing have changed time constraints for menu development and printing. The use of a personal computer with writing and graphics software and a printer to produce finished copy is being used more and more by restaurant operators. The last time you had menus prepared, no doubt considerable time was used up in preparing, proofreading, and printing. Having a desktop-publishing system allows

---

FIGURE 2-35
Examples of Letterspacing and Kerning

12 point HELIOS
12 point HELIOS with letterspacing
12 point HELIOS with letterspacing
12 point HELIOS with letterspacing
12 point HELIOS with kerning
12 point HELIOS with kerning
12 point HELIOS with kerning

you to typeset in your office, see the results immediately, and correct the copy before printing. It saves time and money and becomes a much more affordable system for producing menus.

The advantage of desktop publishing, with the addition of programs containing dozens of type fonts and clip art, is its greatly reduced cost for producing a menu. It is becoming increasingly easy, with your own computer, programs, and printer, to design and produce menus in your own office. However, this will not replace the professional design and printing firms who specialize in menus. They have the same technology and have the staff to advise restaurant operators on menu design, paper stocks, ink colors, type fonts, and the like.

An example of an in-house desktop-published menu is shown in figure 2-36. This menu was printed on a laser printer. Changes in item or price can be made at the convenience of the restaurant.

LUNCH
LIGHTER FARE
PECAN WOOD SMOKED SHRIMP WITH WILD RICE SALAD, SAVORY CHEDDAR
CHEESE-PECAN WAFER.. 8.95
FLASH-FRIED CALAMARI WITH CHILI MAYONNAISE........................ 7.95
A SALAD OF SEASONAL GREENS AND HERBS WITH WALNUT OIL AND
ROASTED GARLIC VINAIGRETTE OR CREAMY MAYTAG BLEU & GRUYERE
CHEESE DRESSING.. 3.75
TODAY'S FRESHLY PREPARED SOUP SELECTIONS........................ 4.25

SANDWICHES * SALADS
SANDWICHES SERVED WITH CHOICE OF FRIES
OR SEASONAL VEGETABLE SLAW
SOUP AND SALAD.. 6.25
SPINACH SALAD WITH MELON, BERRIES, KIWI FRUIT, PICKLED SWEET ONION,
ALMOND CRUSTED GOAT CHEESE, CITRUS POPPY-SEED DRESSING... 7.25
CHINESE BBQ CHICKEN SALAD WITH CRISP VEGETABLES, FRIED NOODLES AND
SPICY PEANUT DRESSING........................ 8.25
CAESAR SALAD WITH ROSEMARY & LEMON PEPPER GRILLED CHICKEN, HARD
COOKED EGG, RAW MUSHROOMS........................ 8.25
CAESAR SALAD HALF PORTION........................ 6.25
GRILLED SIRLOIN BURGER: SERVED WITH TRADITIONAL GARNISHES AND
CHOICE OF CHEESE........................ 6.25
TODAY'S SPECIAL SANDWICH SELECTION........................ QUOTED
SOUP AND HALF SANDWICH........................ 6.95
VEGETABLE SANDWICH WITH LETTUCE, TOMATO, SPROUTS, ROASTED PEPPERS,
CUCUMBER, AVOCADO BUTTER WITH HERB MAYONNAISE, ON
MILLERS FIVE GRAIN........................ 6.50
GRILLED HERBED BREAST OF CHICKEN CLUB WITH ARUGULA, TOMATO, PEPPERED
BACON, SMOKED MOZZARELLA CHEESE ON GRILLED SOURDOUGH BREAD...... 7.50
HOUSE SMOKED BREAST OF TURKEY AND MONTEREY JACK CHEESE ON GRILLED
SOURDOUGH BREAD WITH SIDE OF RED PEPPER MARMALADE........................ 6.50

MAIN COURSES
OUR GRILLED FOODS ARE SEARED AND COOKED OVER
FLAMING HICKORY AND PECAN & CHERRY WOODS
FRESH FISH: YOUR SERVER WILL PRESENT TODAY'S SELECTIONS........................ QUOTED
SEAFOOD STEW: FRESH FISH, SHRIMP, CLAMS & MUSSELS, BRAISED WITH
SAFFRON-TOMATO STOCK, HEIRLOOM BEANS, SWEET PEPPERS & HERBS,
GRILLED OLIVE BREAD & GARLIC AIOLI........................ 8.95
FRUITWOOD SMOKED SALMON, CORNMEAL GRIDDLE CAKES, FRESH
HORSERADISH CREAM........................ 8.95
SAUTÉED CRABMEAT CAKES WITH REMOULADE SAUCE, VEGETABLE SLAW AND FRIES... 9.95
GRILLED PEPPERED TOP SIRLOIN STEAK WITH SAUTÉED MUSHROOMS & MELTED
MONTEREY JACK CHEESE OPEN FACED ON GRILLED SOURDOUGH, FRIES........................ 9.25
GRILLED HERB MARINATED CHICKEN BREAST WITH TOASTED MULTI GRAIN PILAF,
HOUSEMADE BBQ SAUCE & VEGETABLE SLAW........................ 8.25
VIETNAMESE-STYLE CHICKEN OR SHRIMP STIRFRY WITH BROCCOLI, SWEET PEPPERS,
GREEN ONION & MUSHROOMS, STEAMED JASMINE RICE........................ 8.25

SWEET * BEVERAGES
INDIVIDUAL WARM BITTERSWEET CHOCOLATE CAKE WITH ESPRESSO
ICE CREAM, BITTERSWEET AND WHITE CHOCOLATE SAUCES........................ 4.95
MACADAMIA AND WHITE CHOCOLATE SOUFFLÉ CAKE, CARAMEL SAUCE........................ 5.95
LEMON CHEESECAKE WITH CORNMEAL LEMON CRUST, PASSION FRUIT SAUCE........................ 4.95
HOUSEMADE ICE CREAM OR SORBET SELECTIONS........................ 3.50
HOUSE BLEND COFFEE OR DECAFFEINATED FRENCH ROAST........................ 1.50
POT OF TEA: SPICE, ENGLISH BREAKFAST, EARL GREY, SWEET DREAMS
DECAFFEINATED........................ 1.50
ICED TEA........................ 1.50
ILLY CAFE ESPRESSO (REGULAR OR DECAFFE)........................ 2.25
CAPPUCCINO........................ 2.50
6/2/95   GIFT CERTIFICATES AVAILABLE FOR ANY OCCASION

FIGURE 2-36. Cardwell's Restaurant Menu, St. Louis, Missouri

There are several different options for menu publishing with a personal computer. Specific menu-printing software is now on the market, and more is being developed. Hardware and software options can be grouped into three main categories.

1. The high road: very expensive; a polished product produced by high-end typesetting software and equipment

2. The middle road: not so expensive; a high-quality finished product produced by a laser printer

3. The economy road: least expensive; product varies widely in quality

Full-color printers can produce in-house menus of exceptional quality. The same applications for menu printing can be used should you elect to produce a newsletter for your restaurant. The systems described incorporate Apple Macintosh, IBM PCs, and any clone or product compatible with these systems.

Word-processing software permits you to quickly set up dozens of versions of a menu, edit the text any way you choose, and experiment with endless combinations of layouts, type font sizes and styles, and print densities. There are currently packages available for drawing images into your computer text. This is done through using light pens, a drawing pad, or, if you have the skill, freehand drawing. There are also programs with images already prepared. (See fig. 2-37 for examples of different sizes and styles of print and clip art.) Once you have decided the quality and application you want, you will be able to choose the equipment that best suits your needs.

Printing menus by desktop-publishing techniques will give you the flexibility to change menus by adding or deleting items almost at will. Producing your own menus will provide a cost and labor saving from normal printing price changes on your menu that will help the system pay for itself.

As you become more familiar with the computer, you will advance to spreadsheet applications for all manner of cost control and other accounting applications. The computer is one of the most useful of the machines available to us for charting expenses, conducting sales analyses, developing internal controls, practicing accounting procedures, and printing internal documents. In order to survive in today's market, a computer is an essential piece of equipment; information on costs and sales mix is necessary for analyzing operational data, and this task can not be adequately done manually.

Times Roman 48 point size

Courier New 20 point size

Arial   6 point size

This entry is done in Univers 12 point size and none of the examples have been boldfaced or had other printing modifications. They could have been **Boldface** or *Italicized* on the computer. The above and below are simplistic examples of what can be done on your computer.

The above examples have been done in different sizes and styles of print to illustrate the versatility of publishing with the computer.

Who is most likely to consume alcohol in a restaurant?

Beer
According to the National Restaurant Association's beverage preference study, consumers who drank alcohol away from home said they were more likely to order bottled beer (68 percent) than a glass of draft (62 percent) or a draft pitcher of beer (40 percent). Consumers said they are likely to order domestic beer (62 percent) over imported beer (47 percent).

Other beer-drinking facts about consumers who drink alcohol away from home:
□ Men are more likely than women to order beer in a restaurant (with the exception of light beer).
□ About half of both men and women said they would be at least somewhat likely to order light beer.
□ Thirty percent of women and 7 percent of men would never order beer in a restaurant.
□ Preferences for beer decrease with age.
□ Persons 45 years old and older are considerably less likely than younger consumers to order beer in restaurants.

Wine
Two-thirds of those who drink alcoholic beverages away from home said they were likely to order white wine, 51 percent said red wine, 47 percent said champagne and 38 percent said a wine cooler.

With the exception of champagne, women were more likely to order wine than men. The appeal of white and red wines does not appear to differ by age. However, with increasing age, there is decreasing interest in ordering either champagne or wine coolers. A similar trend occurs with rose wine.

Mixed drinks
More than half of those who drink alcohol away from home (51 percent) said they would be likely to order mixed drinks in a restaurant. Men are more likely to order mixed drinks than women (57 percent versus 44 percent). On the other hand, thick, sweet and fruity cocktails appeal more to women than men (53 percent versus 34 percent); and the likelihood of ordering them is negatively correlated with age—66 percent of drinking customers between the ages of 18 and 24 were very likely to order them, compared to 43 percent of 25 to 44-year-olds and only 30 percent of people older than 45. After-dinner liqueurs are equally popular among men and women (38 percent).

Computer applications can be used to calculate the formulas from this book as well as the formulas in the Miller-Hayes cost control book (see bibliography). Recipe programs will adjust quantities, print food purchasing requirements, and list the dietary content of food. There are packaged programs available to yield the answers to most operational problems, but you must define the problem and the input needed to get the correct solution.

Cocktail Menus

Operations that serve alcoholic beverages are unfairly labeled as causes of alcohol-related accidents. Many restaurants have instituted policies and procedures to assure responsible alcoholic-beverage service and are making a conscious effort to monitor guest consumption and underage drinking.

Listing cocktails on the menu has caused a great deal of controversy among restaurateurs. If one elects to print a cocktail menu as a separate menu or as a part of the regular menu offering, keep in mind that this is a very expensive form of advertising and that there must be a proportionate income return for the amount of space given to the cocktail menu. Over the past few years, the per capita consumption of alcohol has been declining, but alcohol still represents a high-profit item in restaurant sales (see fig. 2-38).

If it is your intention to have a drinks menu, your marketing thrust should be directed to high-margin cocktails that are specialties of the house. If you decide to print a drinks menu, note the technique used by Nick's Fish Market in Chicago, which has introduced drinks of the thirties and forties to revive interest in cocktail business. The names of these drinks are new to today's bar crowd and renew interest in them.

Another option is to give less space to the bar and its operation to cut down on the expenses of building and decorating. Bars are now being designed to look more like a home in their atmosphere than a commercial bar in order to induce customers simply to come in and enjoy themselves.

On your drinks menu the best utilization of space and advertising should be given to the drinks that you have developed as your own house specialties. Lists of commonly known drinks are not a good use of menu space. House drinks can be marketed at higher profit margins and help you build your reputation as well.

Having some special drinks on your menu may offer you the option to allow the customer to keep the glass in which the drink is served. The glass is figured in as a part of the price of the drink and reminds the patron of the restaurant where it was obtained. It serves as a conversation piece to bring up the restaurant's name. Giving the names of all the special drinks on the glass would be in keeping with the theme of the restaurant, a classic example of one of the marketing principles covered in this book. With the names of the drinks and a brief description of them, you tend to create a demand for specialty drinks at premium prices (see fig. 2-39).

DRINK IT 'N KEEP IT!

Order one of our Special Drinks or a draught beer and you get to take your glass home as a souvenir of your visit to the world's most famous Pub.

The Beacon Hill BLIZZARD

Made with light rum and an array of fresh fruit juices. Topped with "Bacardi Black" rum and garnished with an orange slice and a cherry. **$9.95**

The World Famous Bull & Finch Pub BLOODY MARY

Multi award winning, this recipe is a trade secret only your bartender knows. Garnished with fresh celery and a wedge of lime. **$9.95**

20 oz. Cheers Beer!

Choose from our entire list of draught beer:

Boston Ale
Moosehead
Bass Ale
Miller Lite
Budweiser
Samuel Adams
Guinness
$9.95
Refills available for $4.50
(add 50¢ for Guinness)

Soda, Too!

Either take home glass is also available with soda or a virgin cocktail
$7.95

FIGURE 2-39. Cheers—The Bull & Finch Pub, Boston, Massachusetts

CHILDREN'S MENUS

The growing importance to parents to do things as a family has an impact on the way restaurants respond to the public. Family values are an important consideration in how a family spends their time and resources. The children in the family have an increased amount of influence as to where parents eat as well as the amount of money spent on meals. The presence of children's influence on restaurant dining is shown in both the choice of location and the amounts of money spent on food away from home. The NRA reports that over 50 percent of parents rate their preteen children as having an influence on the decision of where they go to eat. More mothers are going out to eat with their children than they were fourteen years ago. Children and families capture a larger portion of the total spending for food away from home.

The menu, service, and atmosphere of the restaurant must be family driven to capture the family market. In a proactive manner, restaurants seeking to be "kid friendly" are offering specially-designed menus for children twelve years and under.

One of our associates has always maintained that children should not be permitted to eat in a restaurant until they are at least twenty-two years of age. In today's market we cannot live with this premise, because many parents enjoy having their children join them for a meal at a restaurant, and baby-sitters are expensive if not unavailable, so that there is a market for the family menu (see the discussion on demographics in chapter 1).

There is always controversy among restaurant owners as to whether or not one needs to have a children's menu for these younger patrons. The children's menu has often been an afterthought with an absolute sameness of items from one to another or simply a notation that half-size portions are available for children. From an inventory standpoint, the items on the children's menu should be compatible with the regular menu offerings, only with smaller portions and prices reduced proportionately.

By making known their likes or dislikes, the children of a family can have a tremendous influence upon where the parents eat. Special consideration should thus be given to menu design for children.

Developing a children's menu offers a great deal of room for innovation and creativity in the naming of items. Parents today are more than ever concerned about the nutritional choices available to their children. Even though we offer a meal away from home, we must emphasize the nutritional correctness of the food items we list. Children very much enjoy offbeat types of names, and taking a traditional item and giving it a more exotic name may well give it considerably more appeal to a child. As children's menus are reviewed, it becomes clear that they are fairly predictable in their offerings and can be expanded by way of better nutritional offerings providing lighter more nutritious alternatives.

Factors that are important to customers with children are foods that are popular with children served in smaller portions at a price appropriate to their budget. The child's menu as done by the Italian Oven in Latrobe, Pennsylvania, is an example (see fig. 2-40). Their effort won them the NRA award as the best children's menu in 1995. Their thinking was, who is better qualified to write a child's menu than the ten-year-old son of the owner? The Italian Oven's menu has been designed with artwork drawn by children. This menu follows the food preferences of youngsters and is written in an easily understood style for children to order from themselves.

Central to the children's menu is the idea that it should be a take-home menu. Such a design should permit children to play by using the menu during their time in the restaurant. This time becomes critical in that children have a natural lack of patience, and parents often become nervous when dealing with a hungry child. The waiting staff should thus be forewarned to make every possible effort to serve children as quickly as they can in order to relieve the stress of both the parents and the children.

Young customers may be offered a menu that has a mask design on the cover or games in its interior to occupy them during their wait for food. Several national restaurants are now designing food packages that are a combination of food and activity for the child. This concept is one that is warmly welcomed by many parents. In the instance of providing some sort of reward for the child, everyone must win something, and everyone should leave with an impression of having been at a restaurant where they enjoyed themselves and the food.

Some restaurants have a marketing strategy of offering free meals to children under twelve accompanied by an adult. In an attempt to capture a larger market share of family diners, several restaurants

FIGURE 2-40. The Italian Oven's Kid's Menu, Latrobe, Pennsylvania

have established child-care service for diners. During the week these restaurants have taken a banquet room and offered a child-care service for diners. This service has increased the family visit frequency, and it makes friends of your guests by offering the service. Restaurants like Chuck E. Cheese are basically designed around safe and fun activities that children under twelve can do with minimum adult supervision. The liability issues associated with a child-care service are lessened if you target families with small children as your market because you may create an atmosphere that *only* customers with small children will appreciate.

Is there any one of us who has not witnessed the success of the play areas at the McDonald's restaurants? Keep the child happy and occupied, and you will keep the parents happy. Crayons and stickers are typical favors that will keep children occupied at the table while the food is being prepared.

The purpose of the child's menu is not only to sell food but to influence the child to urge his or her parents to bring them back to a particular restaurant. To the child the value of the restaurant may be in the gift and the physical form of the menu as opposed to the food. The child may consider these factors very important parts of having dinner out.

The child's menu should limit the number of items and stick fairly closely to standard items that children enjoy or standard items taken from the adult menu. The language on the menu should be straightforward and simple for the child. If the child is of a reading age, he should be able to read the menu.

When designing a menu for a hotel years ago, we listed the items as being for those who were "kinda hungry," "pretty hungry," and "real hungry." Things that children are familiar with work better on the menu for them. Consider that the child's menu is a merchandising piece for the restaurant that will cause the child to influence the parent to return. As we expand our market to develop a broader base of customers, we must do whatever is required to win over these young customers in influencing their parents. By using some type of device to call the customer's attention to such specialty items, you can indicate what you want to sell.

SUMMARY

For any restaurant continued growth and profit require a changing menu to capture food trends and customers. At the same time the menu sales mix needs to be forecasted for efficient staffing, purchasing, and preparation decisions. The menu is so important to the overall financial success of any foodservice operation that it warrants significant attention and forethought from ownership and management. It has been said that 80 percent of a restaurant's success is determined before it opens its doors; the menu plays a major role in that success.

At whatever level you are planning a menu, there are some principles that will always apply. Variety is the one menu factor that must be provided on all menus. Variety is demonstrated by offering items that provide different preparations, prices, presentations, tastes, textures, and types of food choices.

A menu must be planned with the specific tastes and preferences of the clientele it hopes to attract in mind. A menu is much more than a list of what the restaurant has to offer. It must communicate to the customer the personality of the restaurant, and through the psychology of menu design help the owners achieve their cost and revenue goals.

The benefits of a well-designed menu are that it will not only please the customer but make management's job more predictable. A well-designed menu will make forecasting more accurate. You will be able to predict which items the customers will order, giving yourself insight into what needs to be purchased, prepared, and what staff levels are required. While there is no perfect menu that can be written or emulated, there are certain menu designs and psychology techniques that can be employed to make any menu a more effective merchandising, communication, and cost-control tool. A well-designed menu can make a successful operation even better.

A well-designed menu will communicate to a customer visually, mentally, and even physically the personality of the restaurant. The size, shape, color, texture, and format of the menu will all create images and expectations in the mind of a customer. A properly designed menu, if shown to a customer who has never been to that restaurant, will accurately communicate to the customer everything from price range to ambiance and service. The menu should produce certain images and expectations in the mind of the customer that closely resemble what the actual restaurant provides.

Marketing Strategies

INTERNAL MARKETING

The material in this chapter is devoted to sales and merchandising strategies and techniques that are employed after the customer is inside the restaurant. This is referred to as internal marketing. Internal marketing is broken down into the factors that impact overall guest satisfaction, their expectations of food and service they will receive, and even the ambiance and decor of the restaurant.

Every restaurant owner knows you cannot keep a customer forever. A past National Institute for the Foodservice Industry (NIFI) study, called "The Spirit of Service," details the reasons why customers quit patronizing a restaurant: 1 percent die, 3 percent move out of the area, 5 percent find new interests or friends, 9 percent change for competitive reasons, 14 percent change because they are dissatisfied with the restaurant, and 68 percent encounter an attitude of indifference or unconcern by one or more employees.

With the help of extensive guest histories, the Disney Corporation has discovered that over 60 percent of their guests had previously visited one of the Disney operations and are coming as a repeat visitor. Disney has also determined that if they are to achieve their sales objectives for the theme park, the percentage of second-time customers must exceed 40 percent. Because of this, as a corporation Disney is committed to satisfying visitors to insure their return. This has fostered the world renowned "Disney philosophy" of *always exceed the expectations of the guest*. This philosophy permeates the entire Disney organization from top to bottom. They live, breathe, and eat this philosophy to the point that it becomes a normal way of doing business, and it becomes ingrained in each employee. They strive to make sure that each visitor to both of the Disney theme parks has a memorable experience. One of the reasons for Disney's success is that they realize they have the systems in place to help their employees deliver service.

As a manager or owner you must do all you can to prevent service indifference; should a breakdown in you service standards occur, make it right immediately. Since you have control over the elements that impact guest satisfaction in your operation, you are in a position to insure they are 100 percent satisfied with all aspects of their visit.

You may be asking, why are we taking space in a book on menu pricing to discuss the importance of service? Well, restaurants rated by their customers as having better than average service charge and receive approximately 9 percent more for their menu items, grow twice as fast, and gain market share at a rate of 6 percent per year (compared to a 2 percent market share loss by those with below average service).

There is approximately a 12 percent return on sales for those restaurants rated in the top half of service compared to only 1 percent for the rest. Only 3 percent of your customers quit eating at your restaurant because they move away. Nine percent leave for competitive reasons, and 14 percent leave because of product dissatisfaction. More than 65 percent of your customers will not do business with your restaurant again just because of indifference displayed toward them by one of your employees, not because they did not like your food, prices, or decor.

The cost of quality is far less than the cost of lost business due to customer dissatisfaction with food or service. There is a saying designated by the letters SOQ NOP: it stands for "Sell on quality, not on price." You cannot build and maintain market share based only on low price. Price will bring in shoppers, not customers. By establishing high quality standards, you can change a commodity into a specialty good. A hamburger is a commodity; so is steak and fried chicken. But any of those items can be a specialty good and command a higher price with a commitment to quality and service.

What it comes down to in these times is that your service reputation can become your most effective weapon against the competition. Customer loyalty is fleeting. Marketing research into customer decisions to return to a restaurant a second time has revealed that service is the most important element in their decision. Think of your service package in two parts. The first is providing quality products fairly priced and courteously and efficiently served in clean and attractive surroundings. This is what a restaurant provides. The second part supports, complements, and adds value to the first part. It is what you do to offer uniqueness and distinctiveness that provides you with a competitive edge.

To paraphrase service guru Peter Glen, good service is just finding out what people want, determining how they want it, and giving it to them just that way. *Good* service is, simply, satisfying your guests. *Exemplary* service is delighting your guests by totally exceeding their expectations. Service is not *what* you do, it is a state of *mind*.

Good service can only be described and understood from the customer's point of view. Even cus-tomer satisfaction is not enough; it only means that the customer got what they expected. Simply meeting expectations is not enough to gain market share. Industry observers note that the distinguishing feature between exemplary operators and the others lies in their absolute belief in mastering the small details. In order to score positive points in service with a guest, you need to exceed their expectations, and in order to exceed their expectations, you need to know a lot about your guests. Leonard Schlesinger, a professor at the Harvard University Graduate School of Business Administration, spoke recently to the Multi-Unit Food Service Operators (MUFSO) conference put on by *Nation's Restaurant News* and admonished the restaurant industry that it was not in touch with its customers. He warned that merely talking about the importance of service is not enough. Service needs to be customer-driven. Service is critical to a restaurant's financial success and ability to establish and maintain customer loyalty. There is a direct link between customer loyalty and profitability.

Customer service is a responsibility of every employee in your organization, especially those employees who come in regular contact with the customer. Employees reflect the service commitment of the organization and must be trained to carry it out. You must empower your employees to do whatever it takes to satisfy the customer.

Treat Customers as Your Guests

Customers begin to assess your operation's customer service attitude upon their first interaction with an employee. That first interaction may come during a telephone call to make a reservation or ask for directions. The manner in which you instruct employees to answer the phone can say a lot about your commitment to service. The tone of voice of the person answering the phone and the greeting creates expectations and signals your customer service attitude. The greeting used to answer the phone, a seemingly small detail, reflects how serious you take customer service. For example, a greeting such as "Good afternoon. Thank you for calling (name of restaurant). How many I help you?" is preferred to an abrupt single-word greeting such as, "Village Diner."

When guests arrive at a restaurant, the first person who greets them once they are inside is often left to an hourly employee and not a member of management.

This we believe is a practice that needs to change. Too often the manager is back in the kitchen expediting the food orders and not managing service in the dining room. In fact, too often the only time a customer has contact with a manager is when there is a problem with their food or service.

We need to train employees to greet customers as soon as they come through the front door. They should see smiling faces and hear cordial greetings. That greeting should not be "It will be about a 45-minute wait" or "Smoking or nonsmoking?" or even "How many in your party?" It should be something along the lines of "Good evening, welcome to the Village Diner." Then you can go into the standard questions.

The visible presence of management is important. Your manager represents the corporation or ownership to the customers and is the messenger for your service attitude. Choose your hosts/greeters with great care as they will be the first employees customers encounter when they enter. We recommend that a member of management be stationed at the front door and not an hourly employee.

Internal marketing continues until the meal is finished and the customer departs the restaurant. Internal marketing seeks the *total* satisfaction of the guest in *all* aspects of the visit including the food, service, management interaction, and even the physical facilities (i.e., lighting, temperature, seating, etc.). Internal marketing is not a program or campaign, descriptions that imply that it is a temporary technique. It should be an extension of the management's service attitude expressed through each and every employee. If management treats customers with casual indifference, it will be reflected in employee attitudes toward the customer.

Restaurant Employees and Internal Marketing

Mike Hurst, former president of the NRA, includes the following standard question when screening applicants for server positions in his 15th Street Fisheries restaurant: "What is the funniest thing that ever happened while you were working in a restaurant?" If servers are too serious, they may dampen the mood of people who are out to have a good time and enjoy themselves. If the servers can create a warm and pleasant atmosphere, there is an improved atmosphere for selling food from the menu and a more pleasant dining experience for the guest.

A required interaction takes place between the server and customer, and this interaction will have much to do with the guest's enjoyment of the meal. It is important to hire employees who are naturally friendly, pleasant, and have what we call a "service-minded attitude." Unhappy or unfriendly employees are not effective in delivering quality service to your customers.

Never underestimate the importance of your employees, because they have direct contact with your customers. They are the sales and marketing representatives for your restaurant. It is generally agreed by marketing people that a dissatisfied customer will tell ten people about their dissatisfaction, and it takes six positive service encounters to cancel out one bad one. Many times a restaurant is never given a second chance to make up for a service blunder, and the customer is lost forever.

Keep in mind that in a commercial restaurant a customer eats with you by choice, not because they are required to. In marketing your restaurant, it is important not to have an attitude that you and your employees are doing the customer a favor by serving them. Fostering a positive attitude among the employees who serve and prepare the food is critical to successful internal marketing.

How many times have you seen a server or dining-room supervisor wander through a dining room asking customers "How was your meal?" If there was a problem, you would probably have heard about it in very definite terms, but the patron usually answers simply, "Fine," and the server or manager moves on to the next table. This is not communicating with your customers. This is almost condescending. Do not expect such casual questioning to substitute for sincere listening to your customers. You must realize that if no one has a constructive comment or minor complaint it is not proof that you are satisfying your customers. Look up the definition of *fine* and you will find the words *average, fair* and *mediocre*. Being described as "fine" may mean problems exist with your food and service.

Employee Training for Quality Service

Employee training should attempt to instill the need to always seek to exceed the expectations of the customer. It was most likely the great hotelier Elsworth Statler who, in responding to a guest who asked if they could ask him a question, said, "The answer is yes. Now what is the question?" The customer is *always* right, even when he is wrong. The customer must always win and the correct response is the response the customer expects first.

Advertising, promotions, give-away coupons, table tents, culinary skills, etc., are of no value without a motivated staff who demonstrate by their actions that the customer comes first and who possess a customer-service attitude. The customer must have a good feeling about spending his or her money in your restaurant. You want to give the customer the opportunity to spend more money by the sale of additional food from the menu. How many times have you finished you entree and been greeted by your server with, "You don't want any dessert do you? Can I bring you your check?" The proper response may be "Yes" to both questions with an added "I've apparently caused you enough trouble. Just bring the check and I'll get out of your way."

The server is in one of the most important positions in the restaurant because servers must interact with the customer and with the other employees of the restaurant as well. If you could buy customer-service attitude, every owner or manager would go out and purchase a share for every employee they hire. Unfortunately, you can't buy positive customer-service attitude and give it to each employee, but your servers must have some if they are to exceed customer expectations for food and service. If your employees do not take pride in their work and do not perform it with enthusiasm, they will never be more than order takers and delivery persons.

The server must focus on the job of pleasing the guest. We know that a customer-service attitude cannot be taught to all employees, and that is why many companies seek out naturally friendly people without previous restaurant experience. They can be trained to wait on tables but they cannot be trained to have a customer-service attitude.

During seminars Jack Miller has conducted all over the country, many people have commented to him that suggestive selling by servers will cause an increase in the sales of specific items they recommend. How many salespeople do you have in your restaurant who effectively assist the customer when they are trying to decide on what to order? When a customer asks a question about a menu item, they are signaling that they want a recommendation on what to purchase.

Too often the response to "What do you personally recommend?" is "I don't know how it tastes. I've never eaten it." If you want your servers to be effective salespersons instead of being ordinary order takers, they need to be able to make personal recommendations to your customers.

You can train employees to be better servers, but if an employee does not possess a customer-service attitude, it will eventually show in the service. Train your servers to be more than just order takers, and give them sales training. A customer-service attitude starts at the top of the organization by example of ownership and management. You can train employees for what they should do, but unless management is unrelenting in its commitment to service, training doesn't mean a thing.

❋ Elements of a Customer-Service Attitude

1. Hire only employees who enjoy serving people.
2. Set high standards for service delivery.
3. Be uncompromising in attaining your standards.
4. Continually listen to your customers; ask them, "How are we doing?"
5. Make it easy for customers to tell you specifically how you are doing; make management and staff easily accessible to customers.
6. Follow up with guests who take the time to make suggestions.
7. Don't just listen, take action; go one step beyond what is necessary to remedy the complaint or service blunder.
8. Pay attention to the little details.
9. Remember the two words *quality* and *pride*.

The characteristics of successful foodservice salespeople are that they:

1. Possess a satisfactory amount of basic ability to sell;
2. Have a positive attitude and are confident in their ability;
3. Are knowledgeable about the menu;
4. Possess the necessary skills of their job.

If you design, build, operate, and maintain your restaurant with quality, your employees will take pride in what they do.

Suggestive Selling—Upselling

My wife and I visited a well-known restaurant in Michigan and asked the waitress what she would recommend from the menu if she were having dinner there. Her immediate response was "Nothing. I'd have a cheese sandwich; I'm a vegetarian." Such a comment from an employee who is there to sell the menu points out the loss of an opportunity to provide a service to the customer and upsell. The negative repercussions of having a server who does not eat the foods the restaurant sells have an enormously negative effect upon the sales effort.

Suggestive selling is the most obvious way to increase total sales. Sales are promoted first and foremost by the menu layout and design, but the merchandising of product by your servers can make your menu an even stronger marketing tool. All servers should be trained in how to make menu suggestions when they approach the table to take an order. Keep in mind that the purpose of suggestive selling is to increase the customer's satisfaction with the entire dining experience. Also, verbal upselling and merchandising are *not* substitutes for the printed menu; they are supplements to the printed menu.

Above all, do not lose focus on the fact that effective suggestive selling must always place the customer's enjoyment and satisfaction first, regardless of whether they purchase add-on or upgraded items. Thus, there are tangible benefits to the customer, the business, and the server. The customer gets greater enjoyment, the business realizes increased sales, and the server realizes increased tips.

Upselling is not manipulation of the customer to get them to purchase something they do not want. Restaurant diners know what they like and dislike and are not going to purchase something they do not want just because it is suggested. The objective of upselling is to satisfy the customer to the level that they will tell their friends and return often. Upselling the customer is marketing the restaurant directly, consistently, and personally. While a well-designed menu can do the first two, only a server can *personalize* it.

Personal selling begins with the first contact with the customer. This may occur over the phone, when the customer is making reservations or simply asking directions, or face-to-face, when the customer enters the restaurant. Upselling is a proactive selling; this means *inviting* the customer to buy rather than *waiting* for them to order.

Upselling is a communication process. The effective salesperson tells the customer about something they would like to buy. The salesperson renders a service. They provide information to help the guest make a selection they will be happy about. There are three objectives in upselling. First, upselling is suggesting something additional to what the customer would normally order, such as an appetizer or dessert. Second, upselling is upgrading their selection, for example, a premium brand of liquor in their cocktail. Third, upselling is selling the customer on returning again.

Product knowledge is critical to turning servers into effective salespeople. When it comes to suggesting menu items and wines, it gives the server credibility when they say they have personally tried the items. Product-knowledge training sessions must be conducted. Include tasting of the wines combined with bite-sized samples of your menu items. The service personnel will be better qualified to make suggestions and recommendations to the customer when they have personally tasted the menu items and are knowledgeable about the ingredients and preparation methods. If the servers can speak with enthusiasm and knowledge about the foods on the menu, the guest is more likely to accept the suggestions and recommendations the server gives. When the server can honestly and truthfully say, "that is one of my favorite foods on our menu," it establishes credibility with the customer.

Suggestive selling is best exemplified with dessert. In Tippin's Restaurant and Pie Pantry (see fig. 3-1), the selling starts before the order is taken. The idea of ordering desserts begins with a table placemat that tells the customer to "Save your fork." The servers actually do a targeted marketing promotion with their suggestions of the pie flavors of the day. From the minute guests are seated they are reminded to save their forks for dessert, and the varieties of all the pies served at Tippin's are listed on the placemat. Descriptions are shown to create desire for one of their desserts. Advertisements of this type may be used for any promotion occurring within the restaurant. One can feature a special celebration, a meal, or special menu items on a placemat. The objective is to reinforce what you want customers to order or to have them become active participants in sales of the item.

Save your fork.

Fruit Pies.
Apple Tart, ripe apples spiced with cinnamon and butter and baked to a golden brown.
Blackberry A light stroke of icing completes this masterpiece.
Boysenberry Lots of big, deep purple Pacific Coast boysenberries with just the right tartness.
Cherry Big, juicy Michigan red cherries cooked in their own juices and swelling with pride.
French Apple The accent is on the apple filling. Lots of it. With a whisper of nutmeg and a butter crumb topping. Perfect a la mode.
Peach Tree-ripened Albertas, a little nutmeg and a golden brown crust make this pie just peachy.
Raspberry Tart, red raspberries sweetened and ripe for the picking.
Strawberry Rhubarb Tart, Pacific Coast rhubarb and sweet 'n' juicy strawberries. Opposites attract.
Sugar Free Fruit Pies: Apple, Wild Berry The only thing missing is the sugar. Delicious fruit fillings in a flaky double crust. Specially designed for those with a dietary restriction of sugar.

Oven Filled Pies.
Custard The freshest eggs, whole milk, half and half, nutmeg and real vanilla. As good as Mom made, bless her heart.
Coconut Custard Rich custard. Angel Flake coconut. Heavenly.
Pecan Pecans, pecans and more pecans. Bathed in creamy caramely butter, then baked moist and crunchy. Just try to pass it up.
Pumpkin Tender pumpkin spiced with cinnamon, nutmeg and ginger. Ask us to decorate your pumpkin with a hearty ladle of whipped cream.

Tippin's Feature Pie.
An original creation every month by Tippin's bakers. Ask your server for this month's special feature.

Baker's Choice.
Black Bottom Cream A layer of French Silk and a layer of rum-laced Bavarian cream capped with whipped cream and chocolate shavings. Delicious from top to bottom.
Chocolate Boston Cream Moist yellow cake layered with French vanilla cream and topped with chocolate fudge icing.
Cream Cheese Cherry Cream cheese, eggs and heavy cream fill a buttery graham cracker crust. Topped with big, juicy cherries and whipped cream.
Dixie Crunchy walnuts, chocolate chips and a gooey caramel filling. Southern hospitality you can taste.
French Silk Real milk chocolate, eggs and butter whipped until they're as light and smooth as silk. Covered with whipped cream and real milk chocolate shavings.
Fresh Strawberry Two full pints of fresh strawberries in every pie. Bathed in a sweet strawberry glaze and crowned with whipped cream. (Made only when fresh strawberries are available.)
German Chocolate For German Chocolate pie lovers there's only one response – surrender.

Lite and Sugar-Free Pies.
If you are on a restricted diet or just looking for a reduction in calories, these special creations are just for you. They are sugar-free, low in cholesterol and fat and are truly calorie conscious. Don't let their taste fool you. (Nutritional information is available from your server.)

Apple*	Chocolate Cream	Lemon Cream
Wild Berry*	Coconut Cream	Banana Cream
Sugar-free only.		

Whipped Cream Pies.
Banana Cream French vanilla cream over banana slices. Topped with whipped cream and walnuts. The cream of the crop.
Chocolate Cream Real chocolate in a rich creamy filling. Resistance is useless.
Coconut Cream Angel Flake coconut in a creamy filling topped with whipped cream and even more coconut.

Meringue Pies.
Chocolate Lots of real milk chocolate and creamy butter go into this delicious filling.
Coconut Creamy French vanilla laced with Angel Flake coconut.
Lemon Tangy lemon with layers of feather-light meringue.

Cakes and Breads by the Slice.
Brownies So rich, so chocolatey, they should be illegal. A chocolate frosting completes the temptation. Served plain or with walnuts.
Coffee Cake A special creamy cake layered with our own crumb topping of brown sugar, cinnamon and walnuts. Laced with white icing. Not just for breakfast any more.
Carrot Cake This moist cake holds lots of secrets – carrots, pineapple, cinnamon, walnuts and more. Topped with our special cream cheese icing.
Banana Nut Bread A sweet, moist bread with popular appeal. Made with fresh bananas and walnuts.
Cornbread A sweet cake-like recipe served with honey butter.

These favorites are also available for carryout.

Toppings.
For just a little extra, these toppings can add a finishing touch to your dessert.
Whipped Cream
A La Mode   **Cheese Slices**

Tippin's
RESTAURANT & PIE PANTRY

Our pie says it all. Take one home. We bake fresh every day in our own bakeries using only the finest ingredients.

FIGURE 3-1. Placemat from Tippin's Restaurant and Pie Pantry, Kansas City, Missouri

Suggestions by the servers should be done in a way that makes it difficult for the guest to respond with "no." For example, "Which one of our delicious fresh-baked pies can I bring you for dessert? Today's specials are chocolate silk pie, apple, and pecan. I will split a piece so you each can have a taste if you like." This is much more likely to get a positive response than, "Can I bring you some pie for dessert?" Have your servers use their own words when recommending the menu items they sell, as they will come across as more honest and believable than if they deliver some memorized sales pitch. Don't let the servers make claims that are not true.

Employees and Promotions

Service personnel can also be helpful in promotion campaigns that are designed to stimulate the customer to ask questions about menu items. An executive who had attended one of Jack Miller's seminars on food cost control and food merchandising once sent him a button from his restaurant that said "Do you know?" This stemmed from a suggestion made at the seminar that servers use buttons to elicit the response from customers, "Do I know what?" The servers used the question as a segue to tell the customer about their current internal sales campaign. However, if the customer does not react to the button, the server will initiate the dialogue by saying, "I bet you're wondering about this button I'm wearing." This same kind of promotion can be accomplished with table tents, menu clip-ons, chalkboards, or signs.

With my own personal encounter with this technique, I immediately asked, "Do I know what?" to which the server responded, "Do you know that we are starting a Sunday brunch?" She then went on with the sales spiel for the brunch.

Service consultant Bill Main recommends that when training service personnel you should have them say "We have *sold* out" rather than "We *ran* out of that menu item." Using the term "sold out" rather than "ran out" says the same thing and has a more positive psychological impact. You can increase your sales by as much as 10 percent if you can get your servers to suggest appetizers and desserts to all their customers. To accomplish this kind of sales increase, the restaurant needs to have a focused sales effort on a specific menu item (e.g., wine, appetizer, dessert) and concentrate the sales effort on those items.

The market will force you to make your menu consumer driven in every way if you expect to capture your market share. Convenience, service, price-value, and well-prepared and good-tasting food will be the factors that satisfy the customer. One must consider all the parts of the environment that are within your control and manage them in a way that will please the majority of the customers. Factors to consider other than food are dining space, sound, light, temperature, and the amenities of the restaurant.

Guest Comfort—Comfort Food

Guest comfort is our goal. Taking a common ingredient and preparing and serving it in a different way presents an improved or updated version of an ordinary item that can sometimes renew customer interest. Presentation may employ the use of colorful serving plates, which can add much to the eye appeal of the food. This presentation changes a customer's whole mental set about the menu item. The food presentation can become a major value-added component that will allow you to charge more, thereby reducing food cost and increasing gross profit.

Featured Menu Items

There may be some instances in which you have a popular item that has a high food cost and requires a significant amount of labor to prepare. It is costing you money to keep it on the menu, but regular customers would complain if it were removed. If you feel that you must keep the item on your menu, design the menu so that you can "hide" the item from the customer. Put it in the center of your list of items so that patrons will have to seek it out. You will be amazed at how much you can decrease the sales of a particular item by placing it where it is not noticeable to the customer. In this way, you retain customer satisfaction and achieve your cost-control objectives at the same time.

As mentioned in chapter 2, the listing and placement of the description of the item is very important in determining which items will be selected more often than if they were just randomly placed on the menu. Chalkboards are another internal sales device that can supplement your menu as a sales tool; they have proven especially successful in presenting luncheon specials (see fig. 3-2).

For optimum effectiveness, the chalkboard must be placed in a prominent location. You should utilize the chalkboard to list only a couple of items to be sure to catch the attention of the customer. Attractiveness and neatness of lettering are also essential for effective

FIGURE 3-2
Chalkboard. Reprinted by permission of the National Restaurant Association.

merchandising of the foods offered. You will probably sell out of the featured item(s) before the meal period is over.

Chalkboards permit you to take advantage of seasonal buys or of special purchases that may be available on a onetime basis and allow you to test-market new items before putting them on the permanent menu. Chalkboards also provide you with the ability to introduce daily specials without the expense of printing clip-ons. Chalkboards also permit instant price changes that a printed menu does not. The chalkboard is a market-type menu and an advertising piece with immediate point-of-sale features. There are currently illuminated menu boards on the market that use felt-tip markers instead of chalk and are very attractive merchandising forms for your menu (see fig. 3-3).

If photography of menu items is used in your menu, you must adhere strictly to accuracy-in-menu guidelines. What you see *must* be what you get. If the picture accurately represents the item that is prepared in the kitchen and served to the customer, the picture is fine. If it does not, expect customers to call discrepancies to your attention.

Since a photograph is an actual depiction of what you are offering for sale, we suggest that you consider the use of line illustration or drawing instead. This can reduce some of the problems in case your cooks do not consistently turn out product that looks like the photographs in the menu. However, the use of photographs leaves no doubt as to how the plate presentation should look.

Remember that photographs for menus are taken under ideal conditions, and that during a busy rush the standards used for the product in the photo may not be upheld. The kitchen's objective may be simply to get the order out, not to match the pictures that are in your menu. However, restaurants employing pho-

tographs of menu items in their menus have found that "a picture is worth a thousand words" when it comes to merchandising menu items. Restaurants such as the International House of Pancakes, Perkins Pancake Houses, Shoney's, and Denny's have effectively used photographs in their menus for years.

If you elect to use a clip-on in your menu to feature items, the clip-on paper should be of the same quality as your printed menu and should use the same colors, type size, and type style (see fig. 3-4). However, some restaurant operators feel that clip-ons need to be totally different from their regular menu to be noticed by the customer. If it is noticed, it will be read, and the chances of the items being ordered are increased significantly. The clip-on is a cycle or a market menu attached to a static menu and is used much like the previously discussed chalkboards or menu boards.

The use of the computer for the development and printing of the menu have greatly lowered the cost of artwork and graphic design used on menus. There are several software programs that contain clip art that can be easily incorporated into your menu design. Samples are shown in the computer section of the text (see chap. 2).

Clip-ons are a good merchandising tactic if they are properly utilized. For the clip-on to be effective, the items offered must be true specials. Relisting items already on the menu but at a different price is not the appropriate way to use clip-on menu supplements.

Take advantage of every holiday and local special event to promote an increase in the volume of business. Promotions of special menu items or special services you are going to give customers during this time are an integral part of menu strategy.

FIGURE 3-3. Tabletop Electric Menuboard. Reprinted by permission of Peerless Hotel Supply, St. Louis, Missouri.

FIGURE 3-4. Clip-on to Match Restaurant's Theme, Print Style, and Menu Paper. Reprinted by permission of Zeno's Steak House, Rolla, Missouri.

Management and Customer Satisfaction

Developing a customer-oriented service staff starts at the top with the owner or manager. If the owner or manager is not customer-oriented, the employees will not be either. The way managers speak about customers when they are out of earshot will be reflected in the way the employees approach customer service. Although it may be true that a service attitude cannot be implanted in every employee, it can be helped along and nurtured by creating the conditions that will encourage employees to be ready, willing, and able to do whatever it takes to satisfy the customer.

In order to ensure the continuing patronage of the customers you currently serve and to build your customer base, management contact with customers is critical. This provides a direct line of communication with your customer and allows you to measure firsthand customer reactions to your food and service. It also provides your customers with a way to communicate with management about any dissatisfaction with the food or service.

Sending a manager or dining-room supervisor into the dining room to talk with customers about the food and service is commonplace today. It is seen as necessary, because too often the management of the dining room has been entrusted to an hourly paid host or hostess who sees their primary responsibility to be seating customers in server stations. An effective host or hostess needs to see the big picture of what is taking place in the dining room at all times; for example, the customers trying to get the attention of their server; the customers seated ten minutes ago who still have not received water or had their order taken; the

server who is "swamped" and needs help; the couple trying to pay their check.

Too often the hostess simply escorts the customer to a table and is oblivious to everything else going on in the dining room. When the restaurant is open for business, a manager needs to be greeting guests when they arrive and supervising the dining room, not expediting guest checks or doing paperwork in his office. Management must realize that a restaurant is established to serve its customers in a manner that will encourage them to return again and again. After listening to customers' comments, management must react accordingly. The age distribution of the population definitely impacts the menu decisions as does gender and income (see fig. 3-5).

Tony's restaurant in St. Louis, Missouri, a previous recipient of both the Mobile Travel Guide Five Star Award and the AAA Five Diamond Award, exemplifies the necessary commitment to customer satisfaction required for these prestigious honors. One of the most important reasons why Tony's has earned these awards is the high standards the Bommarito's have for treatment of the guests, whether they are first-time customers or regular patrons. Each and every customer is welcomed and personally acknowledged as being important among the guests who are dining that evening by Vince Bommarito, the owner. In the event he is not present at the restaurant, a representative will stand in his stead. This individual attention is the difference between Tony's and many other restaurants. There are too many instances where the guest sees a host or manager walking around the dining room asking perfunctory questions about the food and service and rarely

FIGURE 3-5

Population Projections by Age, 1995–2010. Reprinted by permission of *F & B Business* magazine, Ronkonkoma, New York.

Total Population Projections by Age, 1995–2010						
Age Group	Population (1,000)				Percent Distribution	
	1995	2000	2005	2010	2000	2010
18–24 years	24,281	25,231	26,918	27,155	9.4	9.6
25–34 years	40,962	37,149	35,997	37,572	13.8	13.3
35–44 years	42,336	43,911	40,951	37,202	16.4	13.2
45–54 years	31,297	37,223	41,619	43,207	13.9	15.3
55–64 years	21,325	24,158	29,762	35,430	9.0	12.5
65–74 years	18,930	18,243	18,410	21,039	6.8	7.4
75 years and over	14,834	16,639	17,864	18,323	6.2	6.5

Source: *Statistical Abstract of the United States*, 1991

taking the time to welcome or acknowledge any of the customers in a sincere manner. A personal greeting and acknowledgment from the owner or manager is standard operating procedure and one that is most important at Tony's. Each night every guest is treated to this genuine show of welcome and recognition. The restaurant has put a new feeling and meaning into the old restaurant saying "We're glad you're here." These are not hollow words at Tony's.

A most important part of the dining experience at Tony's is that there are people who will go the extra mile to make you feel welcome and appreciated. Every guest wants recognition in the restaurant where they are dining, and they are happiest when the recognition comes from the owner or manager.

The time-tested theme of the NRA of "We're Glad You're Here" that is demonstrated by the ownership of Tony's involves three elements: welcoming the customer, quality food, and quality service. This approach focuses upon having operations redirect their attentions to the customer and what draws them to a restaurant. Mike Hurst, past president of the NRA, is a proponent of the theory that every customer can impact your business by almost one million dollars. By this theory every individual who eats in a restaurant is indeed a one-million-dollar customer when you consider the individuals they can recommend to your restaurant who in turn recommend you to their friends and acquaintances. The point is that when you see a customer in this light, it justifies any extra effort on the part of management or staff to be 100 percent sure that each customer is completely satisfied when they leave your restaurant. The essential goal of customer service is to insure that the customer has a pleasant dining experience. At a time when there are too few customers to go around, good service will augment the customer base. Courteous, friendly service will always be appreciated by the customer.

There are restaurants and owners who continue to prosper and succeed in this overly competitive environment. What has contributed to their continued success and survival, and what is the common attribute they possess? All survivors stress their commitment to customer service and train their employees to demonstrate a genuine customer-service attitude while serving food of high quality and maintaining high service standards. It is the owner's and/or manager's presence in the restaurant that demonstrates the customer-service attitude, and this is missing from so many of the chain operations. Employees at every level in your organization need to make the guest feel welcome.

Breakdowns in the Customer-Service Attitude

Hard as one tries, there will be occasions when a customer is dissatisfied. When a breakdown in service occurs, you need a strategy for service recovery. This is not just empowering the employee; it is a system that notes what happened so that it can be prevented in the future.

The guest may not always be right, but they are always the guest. If a guest is wrong, they need to be wrong with dignity. When a service breakdown occurs, react as follows:

1. Admit you made a mistake.
2. Apologize and assure the customer you will take the necessary action to see that the problem will be corrected immediately.
3. Don't take the customer's money! Always ask yourself, "Would you pay for a service or product that did not meet your expectations?"
4. Employ the R + 1 method; replace the items in question, don't charge the customer, and invite them back for a complimentary meal.

COUPONS AND DISCOUNTS

Couponing

In the beginning a restaurant owner said, "Let there be coupons," and restaurateurs across the land began to use coupon promotions. The coupons offered many different discounts to customers, and those restaurant owners who refused to believe in coupons said, "this too shall pass." But the coupon stayed and stayed. Seriously, we don't know if in the beginning it was the owner of a single restaurant who first used discount coupons to compete with another independent operator or if it was a chain using discount coupons to gain greater market share. What we do know is that discount promotions are now so frequently employed that regular menu prices are rarely charged. The use of coupons has become commonplace in both chain and independent operations as a promotion strategy.

The most recurrent restaurant promotion reported for the year 1993 by the NRA incorporated some form of discounting. Included in discount promotions are: coupons, senior citizen discounts, frequent patron bonuses, early bird discounts, birthday discounts, daily specials, and free menu items. The types of discounts were broken down by the average check size of the restaurants (see fig. 3-6). When sweepstakes, games, premium giveaways, and value meals are included (all of which are forms of discounting), an estimated 90 percent of all commercial restaurants will use some form of discounting. We all have experienced firsthand the growing number of advertisement supplements found stuffed into the Sunday newspaper and the coupons mailed direct to our homes. Rarely will a week go by that coupons from some fast-food operation do not appear in the newspaper or mail.

Profit must be considered a return for risk involved. It doesn't take a person of wide marketing experience to know that you cannot give food away and continue to make a profit by couponing. As operators come to engage in couponing wars and discounting promotions, their profits will fall and their images in the marketplace may be lowered, with the public coming to regard them as of a lower status. The lowering of prices by couponing does not necessarily translate into value for your customers or bargains for them. The practice may instead result in lower status for the restaurant.

Couponing can be considered a methodology that operators use to try to stimulate sales and increase public awareness. Couponing is a form of advertising. But it may be an expensive form of advertising to get the customer into the restaurant unless it accomplishes its principal purpose of getting the customer to come back a second time. If the coupon does not accomplish this, it can be looked at as an excessive cost with no cost-effective value to the restaurant. If coupons are used on a regular, repetitive basis, then yours becomes in effect a discount restaurant. Coupons have the effect of discounting the price of the product that you sell to the customer.

Coupons are a form of advertising used to stimulate sales and increase customer counts by public awareness. The object is to develop business at slow or slack periods. Concentrate on developing business at a time when you need it, not when volume is high.

Restaurateurs work very hard to develop regular customers, and when they begin to offer coupons, regular customers may start to feel that they have been cheated over the years. It is regulars who generate the traffic, and when the restaurant begins to attract what is sometimes referred to as the bargain-seeking diner, the regulars may feel that they are no longer getting the same quality of food and service. Beware of alienating them.

An alternative to the current coupon war is the recent use by Taco Bell of their new "under one dollar" menu feature. In a recent article in *National Restaurant News* John Martin, the president of Taco Bell, suggested that their test market indicated a higher check level than they had previously enjoyed, based on the number of transactions in which average sales went down but also on the number of transactions that had gone up significantly with the new menu prices. This menu will be their marketing strategy in a saturated coupon and game environment. This creative menu is their answer in today's marketplace. It focuses on a perceived value by the customer that has departed from the concept of the traditional discount.

Types of Coupons

There are two types of coupons, the first of which is a free gift coupon or unrestricted coupon. It entitles the customer to buy one of something and get another free. There are no restrictions or qualifications.

The second type is a conditional coupon. With this type there is some condition placed upon the redemption of the coupon.

You *must* specify the redemption conditions *on* the coupon. The customer must buy something or meet some preset requirement. This is not necessarily a two-for-one coupon. The condition may be in the form of a reduction in price so that the customer receives a higher-priced article or more value for the money spent. Such a coupon might, for example, reduce the price of the food for a period of time and under specified conditions, as outlined on the coupon (see fig. 3-7).

If the coupon is not a two-for-one coupon and there is a conditional purchase attached to it, then the coupon is not normally associated with two-for-one pricing but is designed to offer a new product or service that was not available previously. This technique

CUSTOMERS USE COUPONS AT AN INCREASING CLIP

The use of special offers—or "deals"—by consumers at restaurants has grown during the past few years, in part because of a sluggish economy and increased competition. Coupons were the most common type of deal used in summer 1992, used more often than either restaurant specials, combination offers, or senior discounts.

The proportion of transactions involving coupons increased from 7.6 percent in 1988 to 9.1 percent in 1991. In summer 1992, coupons were used on 8.4 percent of restaurant occasions, up from 8.1 percent in summer 1991. Newspaper/magazine coupons were the most popular type of coupon used in summer 1992, just ahead of mailed coupons.

Use of coupons is most popular in the quick-service sector. In summer 1992, 10.3 percent of occasions at quick-service restaurants involved the use of a coupon.

Midscale and Upscale Coupon Use

Although coupons are used most frequently at quick-service restaurants, coupon use has grown in recent years at both midscale and upscale establishments. The use of coupons in the midscale and upscale sectors peaked during 1991, when the proportion of transactions involving a coupon rose to 4.6 percent of midscale occasions and 6.5 percent of upscale occasions. In summer 1992, the proportion of occasions involving a coupon dropped to 3.9 percent of midscale occasions and 5.9 percent of upscale occasions.

Types of Restaurants Where Coupons Are Used Most Frequently, Summer 1992

	Proportion of Occasions on Which Coupons Were Used
Quick-service	
Pizza	26.7%
Frozen yogurt	20.3
Chicken	18.1
Midscale	
Family steak	11.0
Italian	6.3
Sandwich	6.0
Moderate-check upscale	
Fish/seafood	15.9
Barbecue	7.8
Italian	6.9
Higher-check upscale	
Oriental	4.7
Italian	3.8
Steak	3.1

Source: NPD/Crest *Annual Household Report*
Source: CREST, which stands for Consumer Reports on Eating Share Trends, a diary survey by one of the NPD marketing and research companies

—*Renee Iwamuro*

FIGURE 3-7
Crusoe's Coupon. Reprinted by
permission of Crusoe's, St. Louis,
Missouri.

might be used, for example, in an existing restaurant that has been undermarketed and has not completely penetrated the potential of the area where it is located.

A problem with coupons is that it is hard to gauge future sales to persons who were first attracted by the coupons. It is difficult to measure how many people will return because of the incentive that you have offered in the form of the coupon. The only way to measure such response is to use a very sophisticated survey to determine whether they would have visited regardless of the coupon incentive. They might, after all, have come to your restaurant even if they had not had the coupon.

In this instance the coupon is an economic incentive used by a certain group of people for food in a restaurant where they perceive the price to be higher than the value of their normal food habits. If customers will eat only in a particular establishment when they have a coupon, the response to the coupons may indicate that prices are too high for the market.

We have seen coming into play in this type of couponing games in fast-food operations where as a result of purchasing a product and participating in a game, everyone wins something. Although this is perhaps not perceived by some operators to be a form of discount, it is indeed a shallow disguise of a discount. These games serve to offer a discount on many more popular menu items. Such a promotion consists of the sale of a regular-priced item; the customer is then given a reduced price on accompanying or secondary sales items.

Fast-food operations often do conditional-type package promotions. This promotion consists of the sale of a regular-priced item with a reduced price on an accompanying or secondary sales item. From a marketing standpoint, it is used to get the consumer to buy more than he would buy normally. Secondary

sales are essential in coupon promotions, and employees should work to stimulate them.

An example of the cost calculation is shown below. The assumption is for two persons using one coupon to buy one, get one free. We assume each person orders a $14 entree and no alcohol is ordered. The numbers and cost percentages are taken from the statement of income shown in chapter 4. One meal costing $14 is ordered, and a second meal of equal value is also ordered. The second meal is free with the purchase; in other words, a two-for-one discount. Although the meal is free, there are costs associated with serving the free meal. There are variable and fixed costs that reduce the gross profit on the transaction. In a simplified example, there will be income of only $14 for both meals (unless the customer purchases beverages, appetizers, or dessert). In the extreme case we will assume that nothing else is purchased.

Using the percentages shown on the statement of income in chapter 4, the following variable costs will be incurred. (We will assume that the only *additional* cost we will incur from the discount promotion is the cost of the free meal and that fixed and variable costs will not double.) The cost of the discounted transaction would be: food cost $10.36 ($14 × .37 × 2); other variable/controllable expenses $5.18 ($14 × .37); and fixed costs totaling $2.50 ($14 × .1785). Since no liquor was sold, the bar cost has not been included in the variable cost percentage. When costs are deducted from the sales revenue, $14 − $18.04, a net loss of $4.04 occurs.

This illustrates the need for customers to purchase add-on items like appetizers, desserts, and beverages for a discount promotion to be a financial success. There has been some change in couponing in that several owners are now offering coupons with the second meal at one half price, not free. Using this scenario of discounts and substituting the new numbers, there is an additional income of $7.00 and the discount is reduced by $7.00, which yields a small gross profit of $2.96 on the discounted transaction.

✖ The Sale of Discount Meals

Item	Income	Deductions	Discount
Meal #1	$14.00	Food Cost $5.18	None
Meal #2	None	Food Cost $5.18	$14.00
		Var. Cost $5.18	
		Fixed Cost $2.50	
TOTAL	$14.00	($18.04)	
LOSS		($4.04)	

Unless one is involved in a major employee reduction or cost reduction program, coupons will rarely result in financial improvement (see chap. 4, pp. 103–109).

Coupon Objectives

If part of your operational plan is to use coupons, you must establish objectives. Design the coupon: (1) to develop business at a particular time during the day or evening; (2) to increase the sales of specific items on your menu; (3) to generate the type of volume you need; and (4) to generate repeat business. As a manager, you must make every effort to track the activity of the coupon promotion and monitor sales volume. Find out whether the coupon meets your promotion objectives, based upon the number of coupons distributed. Account for both the number of coupons redeemed and the specific purchases made with coupons.

At one MUFSO conference, Joe S. Lewis chaired a panel on coupon merchandising and gave the following objectives for any couponing program:

1. Have specific objectives for the coupons.
2. Increase customer traffic and create interest in the product you are promoting.
3. Reinforce advertising and develop a marketing strategy image.
4. Gain an edge on your competition.
5. Build employee involvement.
6. Give positive reinforcement to your market area that this is *the* place to eat.

Use of the coupon must also promote trust on the part of the customer. The customer should feel that you are advertising for competitive reasons, you offer a quality product, and you guarantee that the offer you make on the coupon will be fulfilled.

No promotion you can devise can in any way overcome ineptness or sloppiness of management. If you do not maintain tight controls in the operation of the restaurant, you will find that couponing or discounting will not generate business. It is an expensive undertaking, and in many instances it tends to increase the speed at which an operation will decline. Any establishment that is not run well will not generate profits and will suffer losses and eventually fail.

Methods of Couponing

A primary technique for couponing is direct mail, which involves the use of a random sampling or complete saturation of a mailing list for a specific neighborhood that you believe to be your market area. People in that market area then receive coupons individually or in a pack with other coupons. This method will accomplish several objectives.

1. It makes a definite positive offer to the customer.
2. It describes a definite product or service that you are promoting.
3. It defines the circumstances under which the coupon can be used.

One of problem with coupons is failure of the holder to follow the restrictions and the restaurant to permit improper use. These violations can cause a problem in public relations for the restaurant.

Selecting the Coupon Audience

When selecting the audience for your coupons, geography is extremely important. I tend to think of a restaurant as a "Three Mile Island," but the demographics of the market area are equally as important as its geography. You must know the audience to whom you are sending the coupons—people you hope will redeem those coupons in your restaurant.

Broadly speaking, two-for-one dinner-club coupon books may be thought of as a form of advertising and nonselective couponing. These coupon books reach a large audience, perhaps larger than any other single piece of advertising you may do. People who buy these books surely will see your "advertisement."

After a recent dinner in a restaurant, upon completion of the meal and payment of the check, the proprietor gave out a coupon entitling guests to 20 percent off on the next meal. This form of couponing is obviously reaching an audience of current customers. Upon completion of a meal, the guest will be issued a certificate for a discount on a future meal purchased in the restaurant. The target is certainly reached by this means of couponing.

Recently, newspapers have carried a discount coupon for a hotel. This coupon offers a discount on food and beverages. The discount is redeemable only by a guest of the hotel on a weekend stay. The purpose of the coupon is to encourage customers to be guests at the hotel during what is normally a slow occupancy period. The coupon is restrictive in that to use it you must be a hotel guest, and it is redeemable only on a Friday, Saturday, or Sunday. The guest is given the option of using the coupon for food or beverages, a choice of mealtime, and any food or beverage facility in the hotel to claim the redemption.

Coupon Audiences

Coupons will always affect the bottom line, and to maintain your profit levels, overall sales must increase to the extent that fixed cost percentages will decline more than variable cost percentages increase. Eventually, prices will have to return to normal. That is another danger of overusing coupon promotions. Customers come to expect a discount and are reluctant to pay regular prices. In making the decision to participate in a coupon promotion, one must consider the number of restaurants currently using discount coupons and the amount of the discounts. The market may be so saturated with discount coupons that it becomes "discount elastic." In other words, the customers will only patronize those operations offering the greatest percentage of discount. When this happens, the market becomes so over subscribed that discounts are no longer a factor in the customers' decision on where to eat, and no new customers are motivated to try your restaurant; the discounts come to an end because no one is gaining a competitive edge, and profits are reduced on every transaction.

In the St. Louis market, a bank recently issued a coupon booklet to select customer groups. By participating in this type of discount coupon, restaurants targeted older, retired customers. This group of customers has a sizable discretionary income but is also more likely to be motivated to purchase when a discount is presented. However, this group is less likely to purchase add-on items to make up for the discount.

The principal profit makers from coupon books are usually the people who print and sell the books. A recent issue of *Nation's Restaurant News* showed the breakdown of costs and profits associated with the use and sale of discount books often used by charitable and civic groups to raise money. Most of the income from the books is returned to the company that issues the book for sale. If you do not lose profits, the coupon will reduce your cash flow. The article further indicated that restaurants in some states are taking steps to restrict the distribution of the discount books. In this instance, the restaurants were considering the publication and distribution of their own books for profit from the sales of the books to compensate for lost profits on the discounts.

Coupon Alternatives

If you decide not to become involved with the two-for-one dinner-club books, you might consider creating a dining club. In such a case, the restaurant establishes a fee for membership. This membership entitles the customer to a free meal after the purchase of a specified number of meals or a discount under specified conditions upon presentation of the membership card. You also may be able to work with theaters, specialty food, or liquor stores in your area to offer discounts with the use of the dinner-club card. This provides an additional incentive for the purchase of the card.

As shown in figure 3-8, even though this is not the purchase of a membership card, it is a coattail effect of the highly popular discount system of today called the frequent flyer or frequent guest promotions. These plans are based upon a predefined number or amount of purchases after which the guest is then granted a reward for having done a certain quantity of business with that particular establishment.

The advantage of the self-operated club is that you receive the money for the club membership up front—before the member derives any benefit. That money enters your cash flow before you incur any obligation. The probability that someone will fulfill the entire membership obligation (for example, the member must consume ten meals within a year and will then receive one free meal) becomes more remote the longer the period of time required to fulfill the

FIGURE 3-8
Houlihan's Frequent Diner Card. Reprinted by permission of Houlihan's, Kansas City, Missouri.

Houlihan's Frequent Diner

Name

Address

City/State

Phone

\#
Expires   Restaurant

• Punches must be completed by date stamped.
• Must be redeemed within 4 months of date stamped.
• Not valid if expired or altered.

BOARDING PASS

How the Frequent Diner Program works

■ You'll accumulate 5 Dining Miles for every $5 spent per visit (alcoholic beverages and gratuity excluded).

■ Accumulate 100 Dining Miles, and on your next visit you'll receive up to a $20 meal. (Alcohol and gratuity excluded). VALID SUNDAYS THROUGH THURSDAYS.

■ Your Boarding Pass may be used at any participating Houlihan's location.*

■ Membership is not transferable to other individuals or other cards. Member must be present at time of purchase. Frequent Diner redemption may not be used in conjunction with any other offer or discount.

■ Your Boarding Pass is the only record of your Dining Miles. Regrettably, we cannot replace lost, destroyed or stolen Boarding Passes.

* Frequent Diner Program may vary in Manhattan locations.

It pays $ to be a regular.

Rack up frequent diner miles and earn a free trip to Houlihan's

Dear Member,

Congratulations! You are now a member of Houlihan's Frequent Diner Program. We developed this program as a unique thank-you gift for our repeat customers...because the more you visit Houlihan's, the more Dining Miles you'll earn. Accumulate just 100 Dining Miles and you'll get a free trip to Houlihan's worth $20!

Again, our warmest appreciation for your continued patronage. Enjoy and have a delicious time earning your free trip to Houlihan's!

It's your ticket to a free meal worth $20!

| 5 | 10 | 15 | 20 | 25 |
| 30 | 35 | 40 | 45 | 50 |

Using your Boarding Pass

■ Print your name and address on your Boarding Pass immediately upon receipt.

■ Submit your Boarding Pass, along with the check, to your server. Your order will be recorded only at the time of purchase and your Boarding Pass returned to you.

■ Once you've accumulated 100 miles, redeem card for up to $20 food credit on your NEXT visit. Alcohol, gratuity and cash refunds excluded. VALID SUNDAYS THROUGH THURSDAYS.

Approval _____
Keep this card with you at all times.
Some restrictions apply.

| 55 | 60 | 65 | 70 | 75 |
| 80 | 85 | 90 | 95 | 100 |

---

conditions. But with the sale of the membership card, you have incurred no cost and have preconditioned the customer to buy in order to take advantage of a free or discounted meal. This method is a cost-effective way of establishing a discount program. You can estimate that 25 to 30 percent of the members will fail to fulfill the conditions.

Why Restaurants Use Discounts

No restaurant that enjoys a high check average and expense-account meals will deal with coupons. It simply does not need the incentives, and coupons do not fit the image of such a restaurant. Coupons normally are synonymous with low check average (under $10) restaurants. This does not necessarily have to be true, but there is a clear perception of a restaurant that uses coupons. If you have a high check average restaurant and use coupons, the customer's reaction is likely to be, "Why should I go there and pay full price? I will wait for the coupon." Then he will go when the meal is discounted.

If you elect to use couponing as a marketing technique, be very specific in defining the conditions of the coupon. One restaurant in St. Louis has been involved with unrestricted couponing (no restriction on date or hours) for a number of years. The coupon specifies, however, that the only items available with the coupon are their special Italian dinners. This has effectively limited their coupon participation factor to 25 percent or less on the busiest nights.

Again, the objective of couponing is to develop business at slow or slack periods of time—you want to concentrate on developing business when you need it, not when volume is high. The example of the coupon effect problem (see PVR problem, chap. 4) was for a discount, Monday through Thursday, 5:30 to 7:00 p.m. You must specify the redemption conditions of the coupon.

One of the specific objectives of a promotion is to have customers focus on what they will receive as a value. If you have ever gone to New Orleans, you may have visited Pat O'Brien's, where in all probability you purchased a Hurricane and also got to keep the glass.

The glass became the value of this promotion. It also functions as a factor in volume and profit for the operator. If the customer perceives value from the gift received, the promotion can include a purchase or free item that is a constant reminder of the restaurant.

As competition becomes ever more keen in the battle for market share, we often feel that in order for our sales and customer base to grow we must steal business from each other by whatever means we find available. Evidence for this very aggressive type of couponing is shown in figure 3-9. For this restaurant to advertise on their coupon that "we will honor competitors' coupons" establishes them as being a restaurant determined to meet whatever standards and discounts there are in their market area. We often see coupons and discounting as the way to attract such additional customers.

Employee Involvement in Couponing

One of the biggest problems with couponing is that employees do not understand the restaurant's objectives and have negative reactions to customers who use coupons. They tend to notice only that the bargain diner has a lower check average and therefore tips on the lowered amount, not the original check. A restaurant's customers must be convinced that the service personnel understand and believe in the promotion and the coupon.

Coupon Popularity

Economic conditions will influence and escalate to almost the level of a price war the numbers of coupons being offered to the public. The result for many will simply be to close their businesses, for no one can exist without a return on capital. Having food away from home is a luxury, and people may not eat out without a coupon. Restaurants work hard to develop regular customers, and when we begin to coupon the food the regular customers may begin to feel cheated.

Regulars generate the traffic. The new coupon customer may make it difficult for the regular customer to feel that he or she is getting the quality of service he or she normally would. The regular coupon restaurant will begin to attract the bargain-seeking diner.

Add-on items as secondary sales are essential in any two-for-one promotion. It is almost impossible for secondary sales to increase your sales up to your desired check average. Many coupon customers will buy what is offered on the coupon, but even in the best of markets fewer than 50 percent will order the additional add-on items from the categories of wine, cocktails, appetizers, and desserts. You cannot rely on such sales to increase your profits and contribution to margin within the coupon sales plan's strategy.

Coupon Use

Most operators insist that they do not approve of the use of coupons or discounts. But discounting is growing evermore popular as one of the promotional tools people are using to increase sales. It is becoming a way of life and a way of operation for the restaurant business.

At the beginning of this section, space was devoted to the financial consequences of discount coupons and methods of how to calculate the income loss incurred by the use of coupons. A recent issue of *Nation's Restaurant News* contains an interview with a long time owner who was asked his solution to the coupon glut in his market. His recommendation was to just quit using discount promotions. Instead of discount-

FIGURE 3-9
Unrestricted Coupon from Classic Chicken & More, St. Louis, Missouri

ing, he provides price-value by serving food that is of premium quality and served by attentive, well-trained servers. By exceeding customer expectations, he demonstrates that the food he serves is priced fairly.

Mass couponing offers one coupon for all customers, and all customers are not the same. These coupons will obviously miss the objective of using coupons in a restaurant. We are working to develop a base of repeat and loyal customers, and coupon customers are neither loyal or repeat customers. They do not have brand name or restaurant loyalties. There may be a marketing situation where one could use a targeted product sales promotion to a greater advantage than blanket couponing. A typical coupon ad is shown in figure 3-10.

Direct mail is a more effective way to distribute discount coupons because you can target specific customers who live in the market area for your restaurant. This is especially useful to fine-dining restaurants, where people are willing to travel longer distances to dine out. *Direct Marketing* magazine has reported that couponing (of all types) has reached a saturation level, with 99 percent of households using them for products and services. Direct mail coupon redemption can be measured more precisely than mass media coupons. Direct mail seems to work best when used to reach potential customers within a three- to five-mile radius of the restaurant.

FIGURE 3-10. Rich & Charlie's Coupon

If part of your operating plan is to use coupons, you must establish objectives for the coupons. Coupons have a place and can aid your volume of business if you set objectives and are selective in the use of coupons. You *cannot* reduce or eliminate the profit of the restaurant and hope to stay in business, so couponing *must* be done in a way to promote business and maintain profits. If it is not possible to do this, then perhaps couponing is not for you.

SIGNATURE ITEMS AND SPECIALTIES

Critical to the success of any restaurant and a criterion for a good menu is the establishment of the house special or signature item.

We need to define and make a distinction between the house special and the signature item. For our purposes a signature item is a menu item that is always served in your restaurant. The menu special is any item that is offered on either a regular or an irregular basis from a product that either is in good supply or needs to be used from inventory, or else it is a seasonal item and an exceptional profit item for you.

A signature item is an item for which you are known. Although signature items normally are food items or preparation methods, they do not have to be. A signature item can be the method of service, a name, or the presentation of the food.

As a restaurant operator, you must devise your specials or signature items and let your customers know through menu listings that they are different. Do not wait for customers to discover signature items on your menu. Develop items for the restaurant that are unusual, unique, and truly superior to what your competition is doing.

Current trends in food preferences would indicate that good items to develop would be either appetizers, soups, breads, or desserts. More people are now consuming these products in restaurants, and such items are easily developed into signature items. These items can easily be merchandised to guests. Some examples might be fritters served as soon as the guest is seated, a loaf of fresh, hot bread at each table, or a demitasse of specialty soup. From the standpoint of merchandising, one may have the dessert cart strategically placed as one enters the dining room, or present the dessert tray to guests at their table when the meal is complete. My criterion for a signature item is that the food, presentation, and service are the best that I have experienced anywhere and result in a positive and memorable dining experience.

A signature item is something that has been promoted and developed specifically by or for the restaurant, for which the restaurant comes to be known as being better than the competition for that item. The best reputation will go beyond a local area to a state or national level. Consider, for example, Senate bean soup, Cincinnati chili, Chicago deep-dish pizza, or other such items that come to mind as the *best*. A signature item is ultimately very hard to define.

A signature specialty item is a menu item that is not easily obtained or easily prepared at home. Such an item gives a diner a unique experience, one that the restaurant has developed as a signature item.

An item may attain this special classification because of its uniqueness or because of the amount of profit derived from its sale. Since it is special, it deserves distinctive recognition on the menu. The menu writer must decide how to draw attention to that item. This can be done in at least five ways:

1. Uppercase (capital) letters
2. A bolder or darker typeface
3. Special boxes
4. Stars or asterisks
5. A different color (if color is used)

A change in the marketing of specialty menu items has been included in the menu of Grisanti's restaurant in Louisville, Kentucky (see fig. 3-11). As the industry has changed to a more customer-driven menu presentation and marketing thrust, Grisanti's menu has listed and marketed their specials as "Customer Favorites," not "Chef's Special," thus giving the emphasis to the customer's choices. As an added feature of the "Customer Favorites," Grisanti's restaurant guarantees of food quality and fresh ingredients for the menu items included in the "Customer Favorites." These items are marked with a special asterisk to call the diner's attention to those items.

A story was once told to me about promotion of a food item in a Chicago restaurant. The chef at this restaurant prepared several items he considered to be signature items. One of the items was a veal dish that he felt he prepared particularly well. When new menus were to be printed, the chef requested that an asterisk be placed next to each of the signature items, with a notation at the bottom of the menu that these

FIGURE 3-11. Grisanti's Menu—Guests' Favorite. Reprinted by permission of Grisanti's, Louisville, Kentucky.

were his specialties. The printer inadvertently left off the asterisk next to the veal dish. When the menus were delivered, the chef purchased gold stars and pasted one on each menu next to the description of the veal dish.

The reaction from customers was, "What's the significance of the gold star?" This forced the service staff to reply that it was the chef's special item and that he took particular pride in that dish. As a result, there was a dramatic increase in the sales of that item. When the menus were next reprinted, the chef made sure the asterisk was printed next to the veal dish. But when the menus were printed that way, the sales dropped dramatically. So the chef again purchased gold stars and pasted them next to the veal dish.

Bring to the attention of the customer a particular item of food to point out that it is your special item—it is what you are famous for serving, and you have developed it specially for your customers. Have the service person promote the item to the customer. This presentation to the customer is critical to the success of the item. To leave it at "Did you enjoy it?" or "How did you like it?" is not enough from the service person. Instead, "Wasn't that the best you have ever eaten?" or "Didn't you enjoy that?" is a more positive approach to the guest to promote the item chosen as a signature item. All of this presentation is part of the development of the signature item, which is equally important.

Specialties listed on the menu should be limited to not more than two or three per meal, over and above the one signature item for which you are nationally or regionally known. A common error in marketing is to try to feature *every* item. This leads to the suspicion that perhaps nothing is special.

Development of Signature and Specialty Items

Every restaurant continually looks for that magic item that can become a specialty that will keep them abreast of current customer-preferred food trends.

One suggestion for developing a signature item is to have an item of conspicuous consumption. When this item is served you want to draw the attention of all the diners in the dining room to it. A classic, simple example is the serving of melted butter with a lobster. In any case, one does something in the dining room that causes the attention of all the diners to fix on that item. This in turn develops a demand from the other diners who have seen the item. Further examples might be a dessert cart, a salad tossed tableside, soup served in a tureen—all well done and well presented. Make this service create a demand from other guests in your dining room for the consumption of the item.

The item is special or unique, an item not easily duplicated by competition and/or home preparation.

Because of this uniqueness and demand, this item may be priced at the upper end of your menu prices. The item creates a competitive distinction for your operation, and this is enhanced by the character of the restaurant and/or the service of the item in the restaurant. The signature item may involve a historical perspective of the area where you are located and be traced back to foods typical of the geographical location. It could involve the preparation and/or product of the signature item. Many signature items develop on the part of the patron a mouth-watering remembrance of foods of the past. Most signature items are basic dishes that have been made classic by your preparation and service of the item.

During one panel at a Missouri Restaurant Association conference, Dick May, then president of Gilbert Robinson in Kansas City, offered insight into how they develop signature items or new items for their menu. They run the special item first for a designated period of time on a chalkboard or as a menu clip-on. During this time it undergoes scrutiny in three areas.

First, are the ingredients available in quality and quantity on a year-round basis? Based on the demand that you would anticipate for a specialty item, you certainly want to have it available on a year-round basis. If you are going to develop it as a specialty item, you don't want to have to curtail the item because of certain ingredients' nonavailability.

Second, do you have personnel available to prepare and serve this item that you are developing? Nothing is more dismal than to find that you have developed something but then do not have the talent available to prepare or serve it. This is an obvious requirement for whatever you do with a specialty item.

Third, will it sell to your guests at a profit? The signature or specialty item does not do a lot of good if it doesn't sell and you can't make a profit on it.

The major considerations for a signature item are to meet these three criteria and abide by them in developing the item.

If the item is to be special, it should be so popular that other restaurateurs will attempt to imitate it in order to capitalize on the sales and profits from the item.

Signature Examples

A restaurant south of St. Louis, Lambert's Cafe in Sikeston, Missouri, features what are known as "throwed rolls." The owner walks around the dining room with a basket of rolls and throws dinner rolls to the customers. This type of service certainly creates an unforgettable impression. The restaurant now advertises statewide on billboards as the home of "throwed rolls." I will not say whether I approve or disapprove of this practice, but merely mention it as a way one restaurant has chosen to create a memorable signature item.

After the publication of the third edition of this book, Lambert's Cafe in Sikeston, Missouri, opened a second unit of their "throwed roll" restaurant in Branson, Missouri. While visiting Branson, television celebrity Jay Leno asked the hotel concierge for a recommendation on where to eat, and he ended up at Lambert's, the home of "throwed rolls." When he returned to California to do his nightly show, he mentioned the "throwed rolls" in his monologue. His stories about what was involved in the "throwed rolls" restaurant was very good national coverage and publicity that one could not begin to afford.

A classic signature item is something positive you have created to give the customer an outstanding remembrance. You can create a signature item in one of three ways.

1. *Quality of product.* It must make the customer feel that it is the best he has ever eaten. There is no substitute for quality in whatever food you prepare and sell. The customer will remember quality forever.

2. *Image.* The dining experience should conjure up a favorable image every time the name of your restaurant is mentioned. I remember, for example, baked alaska at the Oceanbeach Club in Nassau, salad at Regas Restaurant in Knoxville, Tennessee, and the bartender at Henry Africa's in Alexandria, Virginia.

3. *A unique name for a menu item.* Years ago I had dinner at the Magic Time Machine in San Antonio. We ordered the Roman Orgy, a huge roast surrounded by vegetables on a platter so large that it was carried by two waiters. The memorable name and service made this a signature item.

The menu writers' and restaurant owners' charge is to develop food that provokes the customer comment, "I want to eat there for the dining or the food experience." If one remembers back to some of the most memorable dining experiences, they usually were based on food, service, or presentation, an enjoyment that you want to experience again with friends.

Menu Profiles

A survey done by *Restaurants and Institutions* magazine has given us a list of good sellers by market segment. (see fig. 3-12).

CURRENT FOOD TRENDS

In making sure that your marketing strategy puts you ahead of your competition, it is crucial to be aware of current food trends. The food industry is an ever-changing one, and trends come and go relatively quickly.

Defining the difference between a trend and a fad is a very important factor in writing or developing a menu. Food fads will appear and disappear in a short period of time. The development of a trend takes a long time to become a part of the menu, but once it is developed and accepted, it will have a long staying effect and will eventually become a menu standard. One must make a judgment as to what is occurring in the industry concerning foods for the menu. If you believe that what is happening is a fad, then your option is to get into the fad as quickly as you can, and as soon as there is a decline of sales, be just as quick to get out. This is a case of "strike while the iron is hot."

The phrase "back to basics" can be heard frequently in the foodservice industry. The byword this year for the National Restaurant Association is "We're Glad You're Here." The basis of our industry is indeed the customer, and we are truly glad they're here—or is the customer sometimes seen as an interruption of other work we are trying to accomplish? I have seen too many restaurants, managers, and employees for whom "We're glad you're here" is just lip service. The customer is central to our industry at all times, and we must treat them as a valued commodity.

Menus are now becoming more customer driven in an effort to meet the needs and demands of changing customer groups and the spendable income levels of the population today. Milton Bergstein of Pennsylvania State University said in a recent speech at a Chain Operations Executives conference (COEX) that today's customers are in constant flux, and we must target a whole new American public (see the discussion of demographics in chap. 1). For one, the traditional family market profile is quickly changing and losing its dominance. For another, menus are being redesigned and reworded to promote profitable items

TOP GOOD SELLERS BY SEGMENT

Commercial	Fine Dining	Family Restaurant/ Café	Casual Restaurant	QSR	Hotel/Motel	Caterers
Appetizers	Calamari	Calamari	Chicken wings/ nuggets	Hot cheese appetizers	Chicken wings/ nuggets	Crudités
Soups	Clam/seafood chowder	Clam/seafood chowder	Clam/seafood chowder	Chili	French onion	French onion
Salads	Caesar	Grilled chicken	Caesar	Caesar	Caesar	Caesar
Salad dressings	House	Ranch/ buttermilk	Ranch/ buttermilk	Ranch/ buttermilk	Ranch/ buttermilk	Ranch/ buttermilk
Breads	French/Italian	Pizza bread/ focaccia	French/Italian	Soft pretzels	Dinner rolls	Dinner rolls
Meats	Filet mignon	Lamb	Roast beef/ prime rib	Hamburger	Steaks	Flank steak, London broil
Poultry	Grilled chicken breast	Roast turkey	Grilled chicken breast	Roast turkey	Grilled chicken breast	Turkey breast
Fish and seafood	Salmon	Pollock	Crab cakes	Mixed seafood platter	Salmon	Mixed seafood platter, perch
Asian	Stir-fried chicken	Chop suey/ chow mein	Oriental/teriyaki chicken	Oriental/teriyaki chicken	Stir-fried chicken	Hot and sour soup, Oriental/ teriyaki chicken, tempura
Italian	Veal/chicken/ turkey parmigiana	Spaghetti and meatballs	Fettuccine/ linguine	Pizza	Pasta with white sauce	Lasagna with meat
Mexican	Empanadas	Fajitas	Fajitas	Tacos	Quesadillas	Tacos
Vegetables	Asparagus	Green beans	Stir-fried vegetables	Stir-fried vegetables	Green beans	Corn
Pasta and grains	Pasta	Pasta	Seasoned rice/ rice blends	White rice	Pasta	Seasoned rice/ rice blends
Potatoes	Baked	French fries	French fries	Formed, shaped fries	Baked	Stuffed (entree)
Sandwiches	Pita	Hamburger	Hamburger	Hamburger	Hamburger	Chicken patty, sliced turkey
Cakes	Cheesecake	Cheesecake	Specialty/signature	Chocolate	Cheesecake	Cheesecake
Pies	Rhubarb	Apple	Apple	Ice cream	Apple	Apple
Other desserts	Pastry tray	Soft-serve ice cream	Cobblers/crisps	Soft-serve ice cream	Soft-serve ice cream	Soft-serve ice cream, pastry tray
Juices	Orange	Orange	Orange	Orange	Orange	Orange
Other beverages	Coffee	Coffee	Beer	Cola	Coffee	Coffee
Breakfast items	Eggs Benedict	Eggs	Omelets	Breakfast sandwich	Eggs	Eggs Benedict

FIGURE 3-12. Top Good Sellers by Segment. Reprinted by permission of *Restaurants and Institutions* magazine, Chicago, Illinois.

that are easier to prepare and have less-expensive in-gredients. There are also more nontraditional items and methods of preparation on menus now, so that as customers and tastes change, the menu can be changed to accommodate them. Our success will be measured by whether we are willing to make these changes or whether we fail to recognize them and adjust to them.

The NRA surveys its members regularly for changes in menu offerings and customer demands. Recently they analyzed sixty-six menus from 1993 and their counterparts from 1988 to examine the changes that occurred. The findings point to the following changes.

1. Focus on lower-priced items requiring less labor to produce
2. Addition of "meatless" dishes, specifically pasta dishes
3. Variable portions to accommodate quantity and price points
4. Expansion of ethnic entrees and appetizers to include Asian and Japanese cuisine
5. Expansion of offerings in main-dish salads

National Restaurant Association, *Menu Analysis 1993*, Dec 1993.

For over twenty years, *Restaurants and Institutions* magazine has conducted a "menu census" (see fig. 3-12). In their census, they inquire as to which items are currently on the menu, which items were added in the past year, and which items are considered good sellers. Their menu-specific findings support the NRA's report. Look for more vegetarian entrees, such as pasta shells with broccoli and cauliflower, and more salad entrees with protein, such as beef, chicken, seafood, eggs, and cheese. "Sure bets" (you can count on them) include gourmet coffees (e.g., espresso, latte, and cappuccino) and homemade bread (which becomes almost a "signature food"). Microbreweries will also show their presence in the market place.

While limited-menu chains will not fight menu labeling so hard, independents could react by withdrawing all nutritional claims from the menu. *If you cannot back up your nutritional claims, it is best not to make any.* However, as we have stressed in this book, let your menu do most of the talking about your food and beverage.

Take-out and delivery menu items are up by 16 percent and are two of the greatest areas for expanding your market and sales revenue. The increased demand by customers for carry-out and delivery has been fueled by working parents and single parent homes. Take-out has become one of the most convenient ways for busy people to purchase food away from home. Empty-nesters, mature adults whose children no longer live at home, are also users of take-out and delivery because they find it cheaper to eat out than cook at home for just two people. They also have increased their budget for food eaten away from home. They want and will look for an easy and convenient way to obtain food. Take-out has been a concept

tried with some success by Cracker Barrel to capture this rapidly expanding market. A fully cooked meal is prepared and then chilled. Now a meal is sold that only needs to be reheated at home to be ready to eat. It is a market whose time has come.

The evidence of portion-size change was found in another NRA survey. The survey indicated that 50 percent of American restaurants are now offering different-size portions on their menus; sampler and taster sizes with options for petite or grand for entrees. A menu revolution of sorts is taking place. Once upon a time, appetizers were eaten before the main course, salads and soups were eaten only as a course. But in the 90s such strict organization of the menu has been discontinued. Appetizers are now eaten as entrees, salads are entrees, and soup and salad are entrees, too. This has been the rule in restaurants like Bennigan's, Houlihan's, Houston's, and Ruby Tuesday for some time now. But even the classic table-service restaurants are adapting their menus to the customer tastes.

There is a tendency in foodservice today to serve a smaller portion of food. You can always reduce the portion size of any food item. The reduction is made by reducing the total weight of the item and reducing the actual size of the item. Even as the portion is reduced you and the staff must present the food in a manner that makes the plates look more full. This look is accomplished by using salads, relishes, edible garnishes, fruit, and vegetable garnish with dipping sauce, leaving no empty spaces or places on the plate itself. It is a presentation that makes less look like more. The item must never look smaller than it did before when presented on the plate. It is how the total presentation looks to the guest that makes the final impression.

People believe a fresh and wholesome product is a product made from scratch that is prepared on the restaurant premises. Look for data that confirms your food direction and trends that are occurring in your area. Innovation may be your key to profit. Think ethnic, take-out, breads, upscale menu items, healthy and fresh, and always keep in mind the cost/selling price relationship.

Dessert Menus

Desserts are disappearing as items listed on the menu and alternate sales methods are now being used.

Dessert carts and dessert trays are becoming the primary dessert merchandising tool, and operators are relying less on the printed menu to sell desserts. This table side suggestive selling, where customers can actually see the dessert items, is improving dessert sales in restaurants using dessert carts or trays. The server is given greater responsibility in the sales effort.

Contrary to the diet and health factors that are now being stressed in today's menus, dessert sales are increasing. If you want to have your menu capitalize on these sales increases, you need to think in terms of fresh or prepared-on-premise desserts. Today's dessert sales may find strength in the memory of a dessert from the past. Marketing and sales of the desserts occurs to best advantage by using a cart strategically placed at the dining room entrance for early sales decisions or a dessert tray that is displayed at the table.

The desserts must be items that have a visual appeal, and their appearance on the cart or tray must create desire on the part of the guest. Sales of desserts go beyond a menu description and require the extra effort of visual display and oral description to accomplish the sale.

Ethnic Menus

In today's diversified population almost every geographic area has a demand for ethnic foods. This is especially true if there is a large population of residents from a specific country, region, or geographic area. Restaurants specializing in food of a specific culture must have the preparation skills and recipe knowledge for specific foods of the regional or native foods of that country.

The number of ethnic restaurants is closely related to the number of persons who are currently migrating to the United States. Authentic ethnic foods prepared for ethnic customers must be prepared in the traditional manner with traditional ingredients. However, in order to be accepted by the U.S. public, such ethnic foods need to be modified to U.S. tastes. Servers must be knowledgeable about the food from the area you are duplicating so they can answer questions and give advice about ingredients, taste, and preparation of the menu items. As we become more diversified current food trends are becoming an increased mix of cultures in foods, seasonings, and methods of serving.

Barbecue is actually considered a regional U.S. ethnic food offered in many restaurants. The barbecue traces its origin to both city and native regional origin for taste and cooking methods. The food itself will have numerous sauces and dubious methods of cooking, but it's classified as barbecue, an original U.S. ethnic food.

These days customers pronounce service *convenience*. In fine dining that means a more relaxed atmosphere to accompany lower-priced, less-structured menus. With consumer confidence down foodservice is revising its check averages down as well. We have seen how Wendy's "super value" menus have been copied at all levels of operations. More than ever in the past, cost containment is becoming a necessity. Corporations are searching for ways to keep overhead and operational costs down. With the lower prices they are having to charge, there is very little profit margin left over.

Along with the lower prices come smaller portions, which are perfect for the family market. Children's menus are coming back into favor by even the moderately priced theme restaurants if they expect to get parents there eating with their kids. Good food is back in style, and portions are increasing again. Basics are back as plain food captures the public fancy. "Good cooking" is lighter than grandmother's meat and potatoes.

Don't mistake price and portion reduction as downgrading quality or value. On the contrary, we are seeing a return to the modified table d'hôte pricing (prix-fixe menu). High cost ingredients are being paired with less expensive accompaniments, such as rice, pasta, legumes, and vegetables, to offer larger portions at moderate prices.

Price-value will be foremost in the public eye; conspicuous consumption is out. According to the latest social trends as reported in the *Yankelovich Monitor*, the outlook for the higher average check restaurants is guarded. While individuals and families on tight budgets are not eating out less, they are trading down and becoming more price conscious. They are reducing the number of credit cards they own. The high-priced luxury restaurants will be frequented only for special occasions. People will go to a restaurant by choice, not because it is the trendy place to be seen. They will choose a place to eat based on quality of food (78 percent), efficiency of service (64 percent), good value (58 percent), and good variety (43 percent).

The number of franchise acquisition mergers keeps growing. The incentive for such transactions is twofold: it instantly produces increases in overall revenues, and it allows companies to enter new markets without the expense of building and fighting for market share with competitors. Prime sites for restaurants are at a premium in some markets, and the only way to get one is by purchasing an existing operation. Opportunities will grow in the midrange full-service restaurant category. Consumers no longer believe that quality dining out requires them to spend top dollar. Nor do they view luxury restaurants as a centerpiece of the quality of life. There is, therefore, vulnerability at the high-end restaurants. This will be the rule in the purchase of all consumer goods and services.

To attract a broad customer base, you must expand menu offerings to include foods that range from relatively simple to complex and foods that are sophisticated in both preparation and service. Your best operational option may be to develop an expertise in a limited number of exotic foods rather than trying to be an expert in all foods. Developing foods for the menu that your customers will readily accept is critical to your choice for new items.

If quality and value are lacking, consumers will not be swayed by discounts and price promotions. Low price does not replace a desire for quality food and service. There will be few opportunities for second chances if you disappoint a first-time patron. Customers are not so much fickle as they are demanding; consumers want value for their money—after all, there are too many alternatives for their dining dollar. Promotions and strategies that reward customers do not need to be based exclusively on discounts. Price-value will bring in customers without eroding profit margins.

The dining public welcomes and appreciates special event promotions. Promotions need to build a positive image rather than just short-term traffic. Take advantage of opportunities in niche markets.

Dinner might be the trickiest meal to balance because this meal period attracts the widest variety of patrons, such as those out for social events, or entertainment, those seeking quick and convenient meals, and those simply avoiding cooking at home. Americans regard dinner as the most important meal of the day, and many make it their only "square meal." Dinner is also the most expensive meal from both the customers' and operators' points of view. Therefore, the selections must balance variety, value, and profitability.

The evening meal continues to be the meal that has the largest sales and traffic counts. There have been more items added to dinner menus than have been removed from the entire menu in about 50 percent of restaurants surveyed. Friday, Saturday, and Sunday continue to be the highest volume days in terms of number of guests and dollars of sales for the industry.

In "The Editor's Corner" column of *Nation's Restaurant News* (March 16, 1991) Charles Bernstein talked about the "casualization" and personalizing of a restaurant to achieve higher sales and customer counts. He strongly recommended taking a personal approach with local restaurants and suggested that larger restaurants also take this approach, so as to avoid being perceived as a chain. Such restaurants should foster a spirit of family and of friendly gathering. The consumer wants a restaurant where he has a feeling of belonging, someplace that is relaxed and confortable, with a tavern, café, bistro, or grill type of atmosphere. In such a casual atmosphere there is a shift to lighter, healthier cuisines and less alcohol consumption. The spirit of such a restaurant has to be conveyed by the owner and employees. Its menu tends to feature soups, salads, sandwiches, and pastas with a check that averages in the $8–$12 range. The outlook for the 90s is personalized casualization by both independents and chain operations. We are in the age of value.

Convenience, and service, and the need of the consumer to enjoy relaxing with good food away from home have become a part of the motivation of this value-driven consumer (see fig. 3-13). The pleasure of a special or even a simple meal away from home becomes a part of the perceived value for the consumer, who is sensitive to how we will offer food or service that is better than that of our competition. In this regard, consumer perception is nine-tenths of the law. The ultimate question is how are we, our employees, and our product perceived by the customer? Was it worth the money spent?

The presentation of the product being offered to the guest becomes all-important within this context of value perceived. Some restaurants that come to mind where the food presentation made for the success of the meal are La Plume in Chicago and the French Chef in La Jolla, California. The visual appeal of the food served is critical, for if it doesn't look good, that first impression will be hard to overcome.

We Americans go full circle on foods and trends. The menu writer's job is to know when to come and

Busy Lives Mean Busy Restaurants
A lack of time to prepare food at home is the main reason people are eating out more these days, according to foodservice operators surveyed.

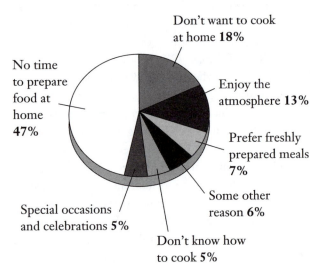

Source: FoodTrends '95 survey

FIGURE 3-13. Pie Chart of Where People Eat. Reprinted by permission of *Restaurants and Institutions* magazine, Chicago, Illinois.

go. At a recent lunch at the Ladle, in St. Louis, the featured item on their menu was chicken pot pie. It was magnificently done. This item had not been seen on an upscale restaurant's menu in a number of years.

Every restaurant owner must go out and study the competition to determine where there is a market gap that has not yet been filled. There are just so many customers, and you have to attract and keep your market share by being different and better, both unique and more unusual.

Examine the menus and service of fast-food operations. If you do not have a fast-food philosophy, you should move out when fast food moves in. When fast-food operators put in salad bars, for example, table-service restaurants began to drop them.

There may come a time in the life of a menu, because of the hyper-competitive nature of this industry, that we must reintroduce the original concepts and basics that made the restaurant successful in the first place. It is time to refocus the effort and message of who we are and what we do best. The industry may be entering the *R* era: many groups are remodeling, reorganizing, revitalizing, reshuffling, repositioning, restructuring, and retraining.

SALES ACCEPTABILITY

Perhaps the most perplexing problem for all restaurants involves the product life cycle; specifically, when to remove an item from the menu. Here we will deal only with the cycle of an item that is in decline. An item in decline is one that is not making a profit, is not selling as well as in the past, or is not maintaining its market share in relation to the other items on your menu. The product itself may have an overall effect on menu sales and thus be required to be held on the menu, but in this instance we will take a hard look at the product to discover when it has reached the point at which it should be removed from the menu. This generally will spur action by the foodservice director or the owner to deal with the item. We may need to act either offensively or defensively with respect to this product to begin to increase its market share or to stop further erosion of the sales of this item as compared to the total offerings on the menu.

The foodservice director must control the cost of the product and its sales, and begin to act aggressively on behalf of this item to develop a strategy to increase its sales. He or she should confirm if it still deserves a place on the menu, where it may take up a very expensive space that could be occupied instead by something more profitable. The decision may also call for a sales blitz by the serving personnel or a promotion of the item to keep it competitive. This calls for careful monitoring of the item to ensure that it achieves a competitive sales level. There will inevitably be some items in the marketplace and on the menu that have truly gone through their decline cycle and perhaps deserve to be taken off the menu. Every item should be judged on its individual merits.

It may be that your consumer group will require you to keep a particular item on the menu forever. However, once demand has been saturated or has matured and sales have begun to decline you will want to closely evaluate the menu item. Regular customers may want it, though, and it may be better marketed as a specialty item for those who demand it. The best strategy is to find an acceptability level of sales for the product to determine the likelihood of whether or not it should remain on or be taken off the menu.

A theory of the perfect menu (one not shared by everyone) would be a ten-item menu, with each item assuming a 10 percent share of the market. Dividing ten into 100 suggests that 10 percent is perfect. Likewise, if we increase to fifteen or twenty total menu items, we will assume an equal percentage of sales for each one. Knowing our market and our population mix of potential customers, which we should know fairly well, we should be able to make a fairly logical assumption about their buying habits, and we should form a statistical pattern of how they might analyze a menu's mix of items. Then we can analyze whether or not there is any likelihood of their buying certain menu items. Because we do not live in a perfect world, we obviously will never attain this 10 percent contribution for each of the menu items.

Based upon this assumption it is necessary to establish a participation factor of sales that is acceptable for the total menu sales. This factor is the amount or percentage of sales deemed acceptable, for example, 80 percent of perfect on the ten-item menu as the requirement for item sales. When realized, the item has an acceptable sales amount based on total sales in the category. The participation percentage is based on the number of selections on the menu.

A participation factor of 80 percent is set up for a menu with ten items. In other words, if one has sales of 80 percent of perfect on a ten-item menu, or 80

TABLE 3-1

Number of Menu Items	Menu(%) Sales on Perfect Menus		Participation Factor		Acceptable Sales Menu Mix(%)
5	20	×	.90	=	.18
10	10	×	.80	=	.08
20	5	×	.70	=	.035
25	4	×	.60	=	.024
30	3	×	.50	=	.015

TABLE 3-2

ITEM ACCEPTABILITY

Menu Item	Number Sold	Percent of Total Sales*	Acceptable Factor	Item Acceptability†
Steak	25	.131	.08	A
Chicken	30	.157	.08	A
Shellfish	15	.078	.08	U
Fin fish	20	.105	.08	A
Chopped beef	10	.052	.08	U
Veal	22	.115	.08	A
Pasta	28	.147	.08	A
Pork	14	.073	.08	U
Sandwiches	18	.094	.08	A
Lamb	8	.042	.08	U
Total Sold	**190**			

*Total no. sold divided by no. of each item sold = percent of total sales
†A = Acceptable   U = Unacceptable
Percent of total sales compared to participation factor = Acceptable (A) or Unacceptable (U)
All menu items and figures are hypothetical.

percent of the 10 percent perfect sales goal, this participation factor of .08 percent sales makes the item acceptable as contributing to its fair share of sales (see tables 3-1 and 3-2 on p. 93). Then we can begin to determine the items that are to be on the menu based on their participation factor rather than on a perfect percentage factor. This application can be used for menu items put on as special items, special-run items, clip-ons, or on chalkboards to determine their acceptability for the menu.

Let us take the menu based on the categories it offers: appetizers, salads, entrees, vegetables, and so on. Or we can break down entrees by their various classifications on the menu to come up with the number of items that are to be on the menu. We must assume that based on an analysis of the menu, the item's participation in a particular percentage range of total sales or menu mix, or its contribution to total sales, is acceptable.

For items that are not acceptable we must begin to make some type of menu adjustment of sales toward an acceptable sales figure, considering whether the item deserves to remain on the menu or whether it has indeed gone through stagnation and decline and is now ready to be removed and replaced by a more salable item. The participation factor is where we look to find our optimal menu mix, to determine whether a specific item is performing in an acceptable or unacceptable manner in regard to sales.

Table 3-1 shows an example of five to thirty menu items with a participation factor for each that is based on work I have done developing menus for various companies.

In all probability, statistically speaking, the more choices one has on a menu, the lower the probability of their being chosen equally. The way random choice works, the more items we have on our menu, the less the probability of each item's being selected, based on the number of choices offered on the menu. So it really is a problem in menu mix as to the number of items to offer. This was recently illustrated by a menu that needed to be redesigned for a company. The number of menu items showed that some of the items were so far below an acceptable factor that the only solution was to restrict greatly the number of items they offered and design a menu that presented a more equal distribution of choices by patrons.

We know from past experience the customer base and past consumption patterns that establish this selection process of random choice for the items in a restaurant. This knowledge can then help to devise a menu giving a much better selection of items and greater equality of the distribution of choices on the menu.

Even with a large number of items, this sales acceptability system can be used to sort out those that are on the decline and to eliminate such items from a menu. This process of deciding the acceptable level of sales of an item can work to your advantage in finding a better item or reducing the number of choices of specific menu items to offer. The numbers of new items to offer can be calculated based upon our expected choices of those items. By carefully monitoring the items that are on our menu, we can have a better opportunity to increase sales and income from the menu by selecting items based on our marketing knowledge. We thus know that our customers' acceptance levels of those items will bring in much better returns from each menu item.

By using participation factors, we can determine the items that are meeting their market share and share of total sales on our menu, based upon the probability of choosing each of the total number of items on the menu. Not everyone agrees with this suggested ten-item base, but using any given number of items we can come up with a participation factor and then determine if our menu is meeting the required market share for each menu item.

The approach to any menu must be that it is the profit center of the operation. To design and develop a menu, equip yourself with all the knowledge possible regarding the standards and rules of menu writing. Through the menu, be a contributor to profit.

You cannot be all things to all people, but you can try. Monitor control, assess the product life cycle, and change periodically, based on item sales. If you adhere strictly to these guidelines, you will have a marketing strategy that will satisfy the needs of all the customers who come into your restaurant.

SUMMARY

The eating-out public has become more food knowledgeable, better traveled, and far more demanding about their food. The most important word in your customer-service vocabulary should be *communication*. How in tune are you with your customers? Are you out there talking to them and getting their comments about your food and service? They will make known their wants if you are there to hear them. The openness between the servers on your staff and yourself is a critical point. The servers are in contact with the guest, and they will hear their comments. If you have a good relationship with the servers, they will relate guest comments about the food, and the comments may be of value to you. Listen to what's happening in your own restaurant. Everyone knows that some of the suggestions will be good and some not so good, but your patrons will make suggestions, and you must weigh them as to their value to your operation.

Don't keep management occupied with back-of-the-house duties when the restaurant is open to the public. Their place is in the dining room, where they can get face-to-face with the customer. They need to be on the floor talking to the guests, working to develop their trust, and asking, "How are we doing?" With the right relationship customers will give you their opinions and some worthwhile operating suggestions.

When new menu items are added or old ones deleted, the portion of sales accounted for by the new or old item will shift to other items on the menu. How much they will affect overall sales will depend on the internal promotion and marketing given to them in your menu design and layout.

Further emphasis can be drawn to the item by price promotions such as discounting, adding or deleting accompaniments, or giving larger portions. In essence you are changing the "package." This is reflected in your decisions as to price a la carte or table d'hôte.

There is always a very big gap between the reality of operations and what you read about trends or fads in the restaurant business. You may say, "Our cus-tomers do not care about the industry trends or statistics on menu items." This is a dangerous assumption in a market with new competitors arriving every month. A restaurant concept and menu can become conceptually obsolete in six months when national chains enter your market. This is the reason all restaurants should be introducing new menu items on a regular basis.

The restaurant concept and menu that best fits the demographics of your market and meets the market plan you have set is the one you should use. If there is a market niche that needs to be filled and your operation fills it, you will be successful.

Today we are seeing a growing number of renowned chefs opening their own restaurants. Their previous successes have given them confidence to expand their menu to include menu items not bound by traditions. Keith Keogh, executive chef for Disney World, spoke at a recent American Culinary Federation convention and remarked that America may now be experiencing what Europe went through 200 to 250 years ago by trying to refine and formulate an American food style into a classic American style. American foods are still evolving and tend to be combinations of regional foods, and cultures are being combined to form multicultural American foods. These chefs use ingredients and products that are indigenous to America or their region of the country. This creativity and imagination creates exciting foods that appeal to the tastes of the American dining public. These menus and foods may appear to be very experimental, but you will find that their backgrounds are well founded in basic food preparation skills. The diversity of food cultures will bring about foods that are a combination of ethnic and regional American cuisines and evolve into classic American cuisine. The public is primed and ready for these different tastes.

Economic Strategies

PROFIT-AND-LOSS OR INCOME STATEMENT

Before devising a plan for economic strategies, you must have an actual or pro forma income or profit-and-loss statement.

The primary financial management statement is the profit-and-loss or statement of income. The latter is the preferred accounting term for this important monthly financial statement detailing income and expense in a format that management can analyze. The line-item descriptions of the income and expense accounts are grouped by sources of revenue and costs of sales. The format of the statement of income reports the different types of costs, for example, cost of sales, controllable expenses, occupancy costs, interest, depreciation, corporate overhead, and income taxes. The format shown in figure 4-1 shows the recommended format for the *Uniform System of Accounts for Restaurants*, sixth edition, National Restaurant Association, 1990, Washington, D.C. *The figures used in this statement are for example only and do not reflect any industry averages or standard costs.* Such a statement matches the revenues against all of the moneys incurred in order to operate the restaurant. The resulting amount is the net profit or net loss.

The profit-and-loss statement is divided into two parts: revenues and costs. The monthly statement of income and retained earnings, a detailed breakdown of income and expenses, is the primary financial report prepared for management to evaluate day-to-day operations. The Uniform System of Accounts for Restaurants was developed and endorsed by the National Restaurant Association (NRA) because it permits a comparison of financial results across the industry and between companies. It also permits industry-wide cost standards to be established for comparison to individual operations. The statement is prepared for a specific time period, and it shows the revenues and expenses with a resulting profit or loss. Control and responsibility for the categories listed on the statement can then be assigned to the managers who are in charge of the various areas of operation. The costs or expenses will be categorized into fixed or variable, controllable or noncontrollable categories. This statement will contain the following information:

Department Revenues: separate food and beverage sales
Less Expenses: food and alcoholic beverages
Gross Profit: sales minus cost of sales
Less Controllable Departmental Expenses: (salaries and wages are the largest expenses in this category).

STATEMENT OF INCOME
UNIFORM SYSTEM OF ACCOUNTS FOR RESTAURANTS, 6TH ED.

	$	%
Sales		
Food	73000	73.0
Beverage	27000	27.0
Total Sales	100,000	100.0%
Cost of Sales		
Food	27010	37.0 vc
Beverage	5940	22.0 vc
Total Cost of Sales	**32950**	**32.95**
Gross Profit	**67050**	67.05
Other Income	NA	NA
Total Income	**67050**	**67.05**
Controllable Expenses		
Direct Labor	26000	26.0 vc
Employee Benefits	2100	2.1 vc
Management Salaries	*2500*	2.5 fc
Employee Meals	250	.25 vc
Accrued Vacation/Holidays	*2150*	2.15 fc
Supplies	1500	1.5 vc
Replacement: China/Flatware	*2000*	2.0 fc
Linen Rental	1200	1.2 vc
Utilities	2100	2.1 vc
Cleaning and Sanitation	1300	1.3 vc
Repairs and Maintenance	1400	1.4 vc
Advertising	*1600*	1.6 fc
Music and Entertainment	1200	1.2 vc
Total Controllable Expenses	45300	45.3
Income Before Rent, Interest, and Occupancy Costs	**21750**	**21.75**
Rent	*5000*	5.0 fc
Insurance	*1000*	1.0 fc
Property Taxes	*2250*	2.25 fc
Total Occupancy Costs	8250	8.25
Income Before Interest, Depreciation, and Corporate Overhead	**13500**	**13.5**
Interest	*500*	.5 fc
Depreciation	*3000*	3.0 fc
Income Before Taxes	**10000**	**10.0**

Fixed Cost = $20,000
Variable Costs = $70,000 or 70%   *fc* = fixed costs
Total Costs = $90,000   vc = variable costs

Authors' Note: The only pure variable costs are food and beverage. Costs are really semivariable having both fixed and variable elements. One of the assumptions of break-even analysis is that one can separate operating costs into fixed and variable components. Variable costs are expressed as percentages and fixed costs in dollars. For the sake of example, we have labeled costs as either fixed or variable.

FIGURE 4-1. Sample Profit-and-Loss Statement. The amounts and percentages are shown for example and calculation of examples in this text and do not represent actual or recommended actual operational numbers.

Income before Occupancy Costs: interest, depreciation, corporate overhead, and income taxes

Occupancy Costs: rent, depreciation, corporate overhead, and income taxes (referred to as "noncontrollable expenses")

Net Operating Profit or (Loss)

All items are assigned a percentage value for income and for cost. This percentage is obtained by dividing the line item expense on the statement by total sales. The only exceptions are food and beverage cost which are divided by food sales and beverage sales respectively. This offers an opportunity to compare one's own restaurant to the average cost of various restaurants throughout the country.

This organization of the statement will show the areas for control and identify the cost responsibility of the manager. The statement of income is management's "report card" and is a direct indication of their performance. Departments and managers who have done well will earn a bonus, and the departments or managers who fall below cost and revenue standards will be able to identify the income and cost areas that need improvement.

Elements of the Profit and Loss

Controllable and Variable Expenses

All of these expenses are under the control and responsibility of management, and these costs are affected by their acts or decisions. These costs are responsive to the volume or income of the operation and fluctuate accordingly.

Fixed or Noncontrollable Expenses

All of these expenses are set or established by company policy or contractual agreement. Management actions will have little influence on changing these costs. These expenses are not responsive to volume of the operation; they remain constant regardless of volume.

Semivariable Expenses

All of these expenses contain elements of both fixed and variable costs, and both are used in the calculation of the total amount of cost. (*Semivariable costs are not used in any of the examples in this text.*)

Total Costs

The combination of fixed costs (noncontrollables) and variable costs (controllables) equals total cost.

$$\frac{\text{Expense}}{\text{Sales}} \times 100 = \% \text{ Cost of Total Sales}$$

ECONOMIC PRINCIPLES

The principles of economics that have been used for many years in manufacturing concerns and other retail establishments have not been applied by restaurant operators in the development of economic strategies.

Appropriate economic theories for hospitality operations are:

Break-even
Daily break-even
Minimum sales point
Price reductions (profit/volume ratio)
Secondary sales
Sales acceptability
Sales profit maximums
Sales mix
Sales variation
Diminishing returns
Market share
Goal value

Break-Even

Break-even is a relationship between profit and volume. The break-even point can be determined by a graph or by arithmetical calculation.

First it is necessary to define the cost factors for establishing the break-even point.

- Fixed costs (F.C.). These are not responsive to the volume of the operation. They remain constant regardless of volume.
- Variable costs (V.C.). These are responsive to the volume of the operation and fluctuate accordingly.
- Total costs (T.C.). Fixed costs plus variable costs equal total costs.

To simplify the construction of a break-even graph, the straight-line relationship is used here, and each cost is classified as fixed or variable (with no semivariables). Use your judgment to specify the category into which each cost should be placed.

A break-even graph covers profits from operations and not such other income as dividends or receipts from the sale of property. Revenues from operations follow the vertical axis and unit sales follow the horizontal axis. You can assume that (1) when unit sales are zero, operating revenues are zero, and (2) when unit sales increase, operating revenues increase.

The graph is constructed by following a sequence of steps (see fig. 4-2).

Total Sales		$100,000
Variable Costs	$70,000	
Fixed Costs	+20,000	
Total (variable and fixed) Costs		−90,000
Net Profit (before taxes)		$10,000

Using the numbers from figure 4-1, the finished break-even graph is represented in figure 4-2. The procedure is outlined in five steps, which are reflected in the graph in figure 4-2. The graph is a quick way to calculate the break-even point (BEP). However, the arithmetic method produces a more realistic number. The calculations for the arithmetic method are given in the material that follows.

Step 1. Construct a vertical axis labeled Cost of Sales and a horizontal axis labeled Unit Sales. Mark off each axis in increments of 10.

Step 2. Plot point A, fixed costs ($20,000), on the left side of the vertical axis. These costs will remain at this level regardless of the volume of unit sales. Therefore, draw a horizontal line across the graph and label the end point B. Line AB now represents the total fixed cost.

Step 3. The profit-and-loss statement in figure 4-1 shows total fixed and variable costs of $90,000. Plot this point (C) on the right-hand vertical axis. Now plot a line from point A to point C. This line represents the total operating costs.

Step 4. Plot point D, total unit sales ($100,000), and an equal amount on the cost-of-sales axis ($100,000). Draw a line from 0 to point D. Line D represents sales income and units of sales. The intersection of the total cost line and the revenue line at point E represents the break-even point. The break-even amount on this graph is $66,666.

FIGURE 4-2
Completed Break-Even Chart
Representing the Placement Lines
and Profit-and-Loss Areas

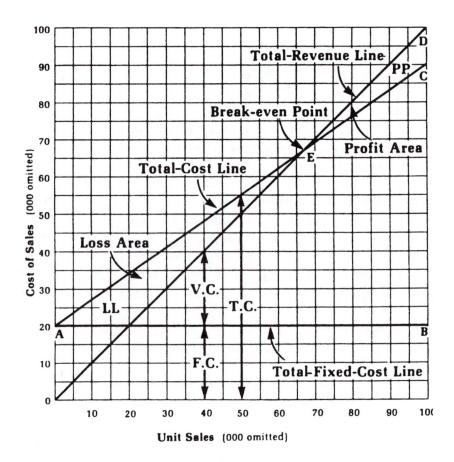

Step 5. Analyze your graph (fig. 4-2). Point E is where total costs and total revenues are equal: the restaurant breaks even. At a lower level of unit sales, total costs exceed revenues and the firm loses money. At a higher level of unit sales, revenues exceed total costs and the firm makes money. The area indicated by LL represents the loss area for the firm; the area indicated by PP represents the profit area for the firm.

The break-even point can be calculated *arithmetically* with the following formula.

$$BEP = \frac{F.C.}{1(100\%) - (V.C./Total\ Sales)}$$

where BEP = Break-even point, F.C. = Fixed costs, and V.C. = Variable costs.

With the same amounts used in figure 4-1, follow these steps:

Step 1 $BEP = \dfrac{\$20,000}{1 - (\$70,000/100,000)}$

Step 2 $BEP = \dfrac{\$20,000}{1 - .70}$

Step 3 $BEP = \dfrac{\$20,000}{.30}$

Step 4 BEP = \$66,666 (rounded to nearest dollar)

In steps 1 and 2 of this break-even calculation, 1 (100%) represents the total sales, even though the example is \$100,000. Sales could be any dollar amount and still be represented by 1 (100%). This determines what percent of total sales the variable costs represent.

In step 3, .30 represents 30%.

This calculation can be more reliable than a graph, because of the difficulty of reading the actual point of intersection of the sales and cost lines. The difference between a broad-tipped pen and a fine-tipped one could cause a fluctuation of more than a hundred dollars at that point.

You can also calculate the break-even point on the basis of the number of customers needed to break even. The formula is:

Q (sales in units) =

$$\frac{Fixed\ Costs}{Contribution\ to\ Margin\ per\ Unit\ (Gross\ Profit)}$$

Using the figures from the previous break-even calculation, follow these steps:

Step 1 $Q = \dfrac{\$20,000}{\$5.50\ (average\ check) - Total\ V.C.}$

Step 2 $Q = \dfrac{\$20,000}{\$5.50 - (70\%\ of\ \$5.50)}$

Step 3 $Q = \dfrac{\$20,000}{\$5.50 - \$3.85}$

Step 4 $Q = \dfrac{\$20,000}{\$1.65}$

Step 5 Q = 12,121 Meals (\$5.50 average check)

The break-even figure calculated by multiplying 12,121 by \$5.50 is \$66,665—a slight difference from the mathematical calculation of the break-even because of rounding off numbers.

This calculation is used to determine the level of sales the menu item must sell to break even. We will know at what point the cost of production and expected volume will give us a profit. This exercise shows the desired volume of guest counts and product sales needed to operate at a profit. Remember that sales do not necessarily equate with profits until the break-even point has been reached.

How to Calculate Daily Break-Even

Using the amounts shown on the statement of income in figure 4-1, you find the annual break-even. The annual break-even is divided by the number of operating days in a year to establish an approximation of the daily break-even point (DBEP). In our example, the annual break-even sales point is \$66,667. Further assume that the operation is open 350 days of the year. This amounts to an approximate daily break-even of \$1905. The calculation is shown below.

$$BEP = \frac{\$20,000\ Fixed\ Costs}{1 - (\$70,000/\$100,000)} = \$66,666$$

$$DBEP = \frac{\$66,666}{350\ days} = \$190.50$$

While this calculation is arithmetically correct based on the numbers used, a more accurate daily figure can be found by calculating daily cost figures rather than using an annual average. Costs are not the same every day of the week. In addition, break-even analysis can be used to study business volume by meal periods, for example, breakfast and lunch, and by hours of the day. You can determine whether it is financially beneficial to close an hour earlier each night or how much it would cost if you stayed open an hour later on weekends. Remember, the break-even is just an approximation and is not an exact sales point at which breaking even occurs. You may use the figures from your profit-and-loss statement (P&L) and determine cost percentages to judge yourself against like operations in your area. These figures help you to evaluate your operation against an industry standard so you can judge whether the costs are comparable to industry standards.

Once a break-even point is estimated, one must determine if there is enough of a customer base and spendable income to support your operation's profit objectives. The break-even will also permit you to do "what if" calculations to determine how changes in cost or income will affect the profit or loss. If you can reduce your fixed or variable costs or anticipate that there will be expense increases, you can factor these changes into the formula and measure the financial impact of changes on your break-even point.

You might think there would be no end to profits if you could greatly increase unit sales. Many restaurants can do this. For some firms, however, the increased costs of advertising will more than offset increased revenues from increased sales. Moreover, large restaurants are difficult to manage. You must balance the inefficiency of management caused by size against the efficiency of lower unit costs due to larger purchases and the requirements of specialized help and equipment. You can use the break-even chart to forecast income, profit, and expenses under non-changing conditions, and you can determine unit costs at various sales level budgets, or you can merchandise the menu for profit to see the effect of volume on profit. At any given level of sales, you can chart the profit or loss based on the volume of sales in relation to cost. The accuracy of the break-even calculation is short range because of changing conditions. The chart is a tool, not a solution.

An understanding of where profit begins and systems to improve the controls, volume, and spending rates can be used by every manager to develop profit-improvement plans. Losses cannot be blamed on circumstances. Good management must adjust to and control the circumstances.

Minimum Sales Point

Operating hours should be established to maximize the profits of the restaurant. The decision of when to open and close must be based on operation statistics, the tool of decision making. Determine the statistical relationship between total sales for a period of time and operating costs during the same period of time. This is your minimum sales point. Your recorded sales and known expenses are used to determine your minimum sales point.

Are early morning or late evening hours profitable for your restaurant? The menu for these time periods may be highly profitable but, because of circumstances or poor merchandising, you may not attain a sufficiently high net sales figure to operate during such a time frame. During "off" or "slow" hours, it may actually cost more to open and operate your restaurant than it would to close it. When hours of operation are set, you may feel reluctant to change the time, but if you are losing money by staying open, why do so?

Students and restaurant managers have suggested the following reasons that may compel a restaurant to remain open.

1. Promotion to increase volume
2. Competition
3. Pre-preparation
4. Sanitation and cleaning
5. Contract or lease agreement
6. Visibility for new operation
7. Corporate policy

Reasons to stay open do exist, and a value judgment must be made about the legitimate, profitable hours to operate.

Paul Forchuk, former owner of the Organ Grinder Pizza and Earthquake Ethel's in Portland, Oregon, adhered to the following policy for closing: there will be no customer-visible sign of closing until the designated closing time. The important part of this statement is "no customer-visible sign." Behind-the-scenes closing procedures can be accomplished. How many times have you been eating in a restaurant when the personnel began closing around you? The manager thinks, "It's slow. I'll cut my labor by getting them out early." But this is a cause-and-effect or effect-and-cause situation. Your patrons will soon learn you begin closing at 11:45 p.m., and will begin coming early. Then the slow period and start-of-cleaning will begin at 11:30 p.m. Imagine where that can lead.

Establish your hours by analyzing your costs and sales. To establish the minimum sales point (MSP), you need the following figures.

Food costs—37% taken from the monthly profit-and-loss statement

Minimum payroll costs—$60 calculated from the hours and rates of the employees required to operate for the time period

Other variable costs—11.05% taken from the monthly profit-and-loss statement

Fixed costs are eliminated from this calculation because if there is zero volume of sales, fixed costs still exist and must be paid. This calculation gives you the amount of volume in dollars over the fixed costs that must be generated to meet labor, food, and other variable costs. It is, in practice, a break-even point for a specified time period. The formula is:

$$MSP = \frac{\text{Min. Operating Cost (in \$)}}{1(100\%) - \text{Min. Operating Cost (\%)}}$$

Use the figures above and substitute them in the formula:

Step 1 $MSP = \dfrac{\$60}{1(100\%) - (37\% + 11.05\%)}$

Step 2 $MSP = \dfrac{\$60}{1(100\%) - .4805}$

Step 3 $MSP = \dfrac{\$60}{.5195}$

Step 4 $MSP = \$115.50$

Therefore, in the specified time the restaurant will need $115.50 to meet a minimum sales point to stay open. By analyzing your own records of costs and sales, you can determine what operating hours are most profitable. This calculation also gives you an indication of the times to develop off- or slow-hours promotions. One promotion involves encouraging people over sixty-five to eat before 6 p.m. (Perhaps you thought these promos were being done because

the owners liked old folks.) For the reasons listed or for your own, you may not be able to close during the off-hours, but promos and special menus for those times may add the needed volume to put the operation above the minimum sales point.

There are other tools you can use in the critical area of timing. Know when to start and when to stop promotions. This is necessary to develop profit. You must time the promotions accurately, for to be too early or too late will make the project ineffective. In many cases, it is not necessarily what you do but when you do it that causes a project or promo to succeed or fail.

Price Reductions

Of all the reasons operators have to believe that it is to their advantage to lower menu prices, the biggest one is to increase customer counts and thereby increase overall sales volume. However, lower menu prices mean smaller profit margins on each sale. If there was no profit with the original price, there will certainly not be any with a price reduction. The amount of reduction and the menu items that are to be reduced will vary from restaurant to restaurant, and the considerations for price reductions will be rationalized by each owner or manager.

The most critical part of any price reduction is accurately forecasting the change in volume or sales that will occur due to the price reduction. The changes in costs and sales will affect all the factors in the cost/volume/profit equation for break-even. One must carefully set the discounts, or there will not be an increase in profit.

The key to a successful discount promotion is increased customer counts. If the price reduction does not bring in more customers than before the discount, it will bring additional financial stress to the operation. The increased traffic will not bring increased profits unless the overall sales volume increases significantly.

It is critical that the manager/owner realize that in all pricing methods there is an established cost-volume-profit (CVP) relationship that has to be maintained to accomplish the desired profit. When any factor in this ratio is changed, the break-even level changes. The break-even point will change in direct relation to changes in costs; in other words, break-even will rise when costs increase. The numbers within this equation must be changed and the break-even point recalculated. The elements of the profit relationship are cost and desired profit. These two elements will impact the sales level required to cover costs and return the desired profit. Sales is in turn affected by the price charged and the number of customers we serve.

Price reductions come in many forms. It may be as a result of an "early bird discount" where prices are reduced from 4–6 p.m. to increase traffic prior to peak dinner periods that are typically very slow. Other price reductions are offered through discounts to members of the American Association of Retired People (AARP), discount coupons placed in the newspaper or direct mail, and birthday promotions that offer a free dinner or dessert when you dine on your birthday. Fast-food restaurants that sell or give away with purchase "premiums" such as logo glasses from a Disney movie or special edition ornaments (such as McDonald's does at Christmas) are basically other forms of discounting or price reduction. Keep in mind the following when you are contemplating using a discount promotion: *in order for discounting or price reduction to be successful in a financial sense, overall sales revenue and customer counts must increase and fixed cost percentages must decline more than variable cost percentages increase from the use of the discount.* This is the only way that the bottom line can improve when a discount promotion is used.

When the cost-volume-profit equation changes, the break-even point will change. Assume the cost reduction in total payroll expense that would result from downsizing your staff by one twenty-hour-per-week minimum-wage employee amounts to a cost savings of $500 a month. Further assume that sales are expected to remain constant. (Labor cost is treated as a variable cost in this example.) The recalculation for a new break-even would be as follows (the reduction of labor is reflected in this calculation; numbers in this example have been rounded to next dollar):

$500/month $\times$ 12 months = $6,000 annual savings in labor

$70,000 Old Annual Variable Cost $-$ $6,000 = $64,000 New AVC

$$\text{BEP} = \frac{\$20,000 \text{ (Fixed Cost)}}{1 - (\$64,000/\$100,000)} = \frac{\$20,000}{.36} = \$55,556$$

With the $500.00 per month reduction in payroll, the annual break-even point drops from $66,666 to $55,556. Even small changes can have a dramatic effect on the bottom line and break-even level of sales.

If you can reduce costs, operating profits will increase considerably if sales volume is unaffected. Remember, there is no profit until you exceed the break-even point for sales revenue.

In addition to the short-term application of price reduction, there is also a long-term application. This calculation is based on the total effect of the happy hour or meal-club membership on total profit. The happy hour and meal-club plans may be offered only specific times during the day or week. Consequently, the reduction is not 50 percent but may amount to only the equivalent of a 20 percent reduction in price. For example, your two-meals-for-one pricing can be available Monday through Thursday between 5 p.m. and 8 p.m. Using the data from the calculation of the break-even graph at the beginning of this chapter, the calculations follow.

Because of the volume/sales relationship, the first calculation establishes the relationship among sales/costs/profit. The formula to determine variable cost is:

$$\frac{\text{Variable Cost}}{\text{Sales}} = \text{Variable Cost Percent}$$

$$\frac{70,000}{100,000} = 70\%$$

The next calculation, with the original numbers in the break-even calculation, uses the following formula, where RSV is the required sales volume.

$$\text{RSV} = \frac{\text{Desired Profit} + \text{Fixed Cost}}{1(100\%) - \left(\frac{\text{Present Variable Cost \%}}{1(100\%) - \text{Proposed reduced \% by meal club}}\right)}$$

Step 1 $\text{RSV} = \dfrac{10,000 + 20,000}{1(100\%) - \left(\dfrac{70\%}{1(100\%) - 20\%}\right)}$

Step 2 $\text{RSV} = \dfrac{30,000}{1(100\%) - \left(\dfrac{70\%}{100\% - 20\%}\right)}$

Step 3 $\text{RSV} = \dfrac{30,000}{1(100\%) - \left(\dfrac{70\%}{80\%}\right)}$

Step 4 $\text{RSV} = \dfrac{30,000}{1(100\%) - .875}$

Step 5 $\text{RSV} = \dfrac{30,000}{.125}$

Step 6 $\text{RSV} = \$240,000$

The required sales volume tells you what volume of sales is necessary to maintain the current profit level. In this example the required *increase* in sales volume would be $140,000 for the year. Now you can use that information to make your decision for reduced-price promotions. You can monitor the effect the reduction will have on gross profits and determine whether the required long-term increase in volume makes the promotions valuable in your operation.

The basic economic theory of the price-reduction principle is that as the price is reduced, more persons will buy and thus increase the volume of sales. Records must be maintained to track and compare customer volume and increased dollar sales, with immediate goal setting by the manager to determine if the project is on target. If the goal of volume increase is not being met, then take immediate corrective action. The promotion should be adjusted or canceled in part or in its entirety.

Another important element of a discount promotion, besides estimating the expected increase in overall traffic, is to use that estimate to calculate the changes in food or beverage costs and the average guest check. We start with the known profit margin, variable and fixed costs without the discount. To estimate how much additional business (traffic) we will need to do with the discount to be no worse off than we were without the discount, use the following simple calculation. All that needs to be done is to divide the current gross profit before the discount (selling price − food or beverage cost) by the gross profit that will result with the discounted price. The resulting figure tells you the number of dinners or drinks you have to sell at the discounted price to achieve the same gross profit without the discount. If the increases needed to be no worse off than without the discount reach numbers that you feel are unattainable (e.g., customer count needs to increase by 50 percent), you will have to lower the discount until the needed increase in customer traffic is realistically attainable given the customer base within your market area. Keep in mind that as you lower the discount, the potential drawing power of the discount is lowered as well (e.g., a two-for-one discount will draw more than a buy-one-get-second-at-half-price).

Another option that can be used to soften the discount's impact on gross profit is to reduce product cost. There a several ways that the product cost might be reduced, but quality should never be compromised.

For example, labor costs can be lowered by increasing worker productivity or by cutting back on scheduled hours. Review the size of food and drink portions and institute portion controls. Accompaniments and product presentation can be changed or modified to present the product in another form at a reduced cost (e.g., cut back on expensive garnishes or eliminate a side dish that previously came with the item). Keep in mind that if you do not provide price-value to the customer, the discount will not be successful. The menu in figure 4-3 is an example of the use of smaller than normal portion size for a discount menu item.

If the calculation after a discount or price reduction indicates an unrealistic or unattainable increase in customer counts and sales revenue, the amount of the discount must be revised downward. If the discount promotion does not result in an increase in business equal to or greater than that indicated in the calculation, the promotion should be suspended.

As a general rule of discount pricing, the greater the percentage of gross profit that is lost from the discount price, the greater the increase in sales and customer counts that must take place to achieve the same prediscount gross profit.

To demonstrate this, an example using a beverage happy hour promotion will be used. (*It is not our intention to promote happy hour or endorse excessive sale of alcohol in restaurants.*) The same calculations can be done for a meal. The objective is to demonstrate how discounting lowers the gross profit. Using the formula that simply divides the gross profit before the discount (GPBD) by the gross profit after the discount (GPAD), you get a number that tells you the number of drinks you need to sell at the discounted price to realize the same gross profit for the sale of a single drink at the regular price.

FIGURE 4-3. Menu Showing Smaller Portion Sizes for Reduced Prices. Reprinted by permission of Rice Planters Restaurant, Myrtle Beach, South Carolina.

	Cost of Liquor	Gross Profit (Price–Cost)
Drink Price W/O Discount	$3.50	$.95	$2.55
Drink Price W/ Discount	$1.95	$.95	$1.00

$$\frac{\text{GPBD } \$2.55}{\text{GPAD } \$1.00} = 2.55$$

This calculation tells us that we will have to sell 2.5 more drinks per person to realize the same gross profit we received when we sold drinks at the regular price. In this example, such a promotion would not be advised as it would not promote responsible alcoholic beverage service. However, the gross profit could be increased and the number of drinks needed to realize the same gross profit reduced by lowering the portion of the liquor used in the drinks. For example, if 1.75 ounces were lowered to 1.25, liquor cost would be reduced and the amount of gross profit increased.

Another option would be to raise the price of the discounted drinks to $2.25, thereby increasing the gross profit from $1 to $1.30, and the number of additional drinks is reduced to two (1.96). This is how a discount promotion needs to be adjusted to be financially beneficial to the operation.

Secondary Sales

One other major consideration of a two-for-one price reduction is a secondary sales effect. When a person enters the restaurant to take advantage of the price reduction, he normally will buy a second item (wine, cocktails, appetizer, dessert, or some menu item not included in the price) with the meal because he is saving the price of one item or meal. The sale of the special item will cause the sale of one or more other items that are currently being offered on the menu at the regular price. This is the secondary sales effect. The decision to establish a happy hour or meal club, therefore, is based on the belief that the increased patronage will bring a sufficient increase in the sale of other items to cause the gross profit to remain at a predetermined level.

Let's consider a hypothetical situation. As a dinner promotion intended to increase sales volume, a restaurant owner decides to give every diner all the wine he cares to drink with his dinner. Based on his experience, forecasts, and "gut feelings," he believes that with a free-wine promotion he can at least double the number of people who will eat in the restaurant.

Past dinner records show the following:

	Meals	Wine	Total
Meal sales (200 persons @ $5.50 average)	$1,100	$200	$1,300
Variable costs (food & beverage)	407	100	507
Contribution to margin	693	100	793
Salaries			250
Income			$ 543

With this information, the owner expects:

1. No income from wine
2. Increase of 200 persons @ $5.50 check average for evening meal
3. Increase of wine consumption of 100 percent
4. Additional service persons @ total cost of $40

His projection for the wine promo would be:

	Meals	Wine	Total
Meal sales (400 persons @ $5.50 average)	$2,200	0	$2,200
Variable costs (food & beverage)	814	200	1,014
Contribution to margin	1,386	(200)	1,186
Salaries			290
Income			$ 896

The projection for this promotion would be an increase of $353 in income. Contingency expenses in the kitchen are not considered here, and they can make the promotion a marginal experiment. A loss leader is needed to stimulate the sale of higher gross items. (For these calculations wine prices were doubled, as opposed to using the profit-and-loss liquor cost percentage.)

A manager who knows in advance that the relative success of a wine giveaway is marginal can emphasize to his employees the critical need for the secondary sales effect. Selling appetizers, desserts, or any other items regularly on the menu will increase the probability of profit. Displays of items in the dining room to raise the check average will also be a factor contributing to profit.

Prior knowledge will better prepare you to make feasibility studies of any price-reduction merchandising plan. You can avoid disastrous consequences if you assemble as many facts as possible. The object of a promotion is increased profit, not just increased volume. Profit does not necessarily correlate with volume. Accurate records of past profit, costs, and sales are required to make correct profit decisions for the future.

Discounts Change the Equation

The discount promotion may bring in additional customers, but there may be no increase in profits if higher sales levels are not realized. There must be an increase in the number of meals sold in order to offset the reduced margin that accompanies each discounted sale. There is evidence that discounts are eroding the profits and earnings of many restaurants trying to compete in a coupon-elastic market.

The higher the rate of discount and the greater the percentage of discounted transactions relative to total transactions, the greater the need for increased customer counts to achieve the same bottom line as without the discount. Sales volume and customer counts must improve just to offset the costs of discounting. Since discounting reduces the profit margin on each discounted transaction, the break-even point is increased because the food and/or beverage cost also increases as a result of the discount.

It is also important to realize that the higher the percentage of the discount or the greater the percentage of customers receiving a discount, the greater the increase in the food-cost percentage and the higher the break-even point.

To show how discounting affects operating costs and profits, the following example is provided. Assume that without a discount, a restaurant is currently averaging 100 covers per meal period and the average check is $10 per person. Table 4-1 presents the break-even point in condensed-statement format without any discount. The figures and tables provided represent a single day, but the theory and principles used are equally valid for longer periods of time.

In this example, assume a discount promotion of buy-one-get-second-at-half-price is run. One must start by estimating the number of discounted meals one expects to serve. This is a largely subjective estimate that is refined after a sales history is recorded. The redemption rates are controlled to an extent by the conditions of the discount, that is, restricted to certain items, meal periods, days of the week, etc. If we assume that 10 percent of the meals will be discounted, we can estimate that our food cost will increase by 2 percent. The discount is equivalent to a 5

TABLE 4-1		
BREAK-EVEN WITHOUT DISCOUNTING		
	Amount	**Percent**
Sales	$1000	100
Less Variable Costs		
Food Cost	(380)	(38)
Direct Operating Expense	(160)	(16)
Total Variable Costs	(540)	(54)
Contribution Margin	460	46
Less Fixed Costs		
Labor	(280)	(28)
Occupational Expenses	(180)	(18)
Total	(460)	(46)
Net Profit (Loss)	0	0

$$\text{Break-Even Sales} = \frac{\$460}{.46} = \$1000$$

$$\text{Formula}: \frac{\text{Fixed Cost } \$}{\text{Contribution Margin (100\% - variable cost \%)}}$$

percent reduction in sale revenue and is derived with the following calculations: 10% of meals @ 50% discount + 90% of meals @ 100% (no discount) = .95 (.10 (.50) + .90 (1.00) = .95). Using the figures from table 4-1, we take 95 percent of the $1,000 sales and recalculate the food cost percentage, $380/$950 = 40 percent. The average check would drop to $9.50 ($950/100 customers). The check average without the discount is $10 per person ($1000/100). If 10 percent of the meals were discounted by 50 percent, the new check average would be approximately $9.50 [(.10 × .50) + (.90 × 1.00) = .95 ($1000) = $950/100 covers = $9.50)]. Assume further that although customer counts increase slightly, total sales do not increase. The advertising costs of the promotion add an additional $50 per day to operating expense.

If all other costs remain constant, the operating figures for the day would resemble those shown in table 4-2. A loss is incurred of $70 or 7 percent as a result of the promotion.

A loss was incurred because food-cost percentage increased from 38 to 40 percent, and direct operating expenses increased from 16 to 21 percent due to the $50 increase in promotional expenses. Total variable costs increased from 54 to 61 percent, an increase of 7 percent. Because total sales did not increase, the percentage of fixed costs remained the same. Sales must increase a minimum of 18 percent just to break even.

Table 4-3 shows the new break-even point with the discount promotion. The 7 percent increase in variable costs will be covered only if the sales increase by 17.92 percent. This sales increase will reduce fixed cost percentages by 7 percent. This can be expressed in terms of total customers (124) by dividing the new sales figure by the average check with the discount ($1179.20/$9.50 = 124 covers).

These examples demonstrate how significantly the financial situation and break-even point changes when a discount promotion is run. The discount is buy-one-get-second-at-half-price. If 10 percent of the meals are sold at the discount, the total revenue from two meals will be $15. Out of every one hundred dinners served, 10 will return $5, while 90 will return $10. The overall check will be approximately $9.50. Total food expense is the same for both meals, $3.80 each. The operating costs reflect the cost of the promotion (the addition $50 per day) and increases in operating costs from $1.60 to $2.10 per person. Therefore, $3.60 out of every $9.50 will be the allowance to cover fixed costs and profit.

It has been very difficult for operators to see the impact discounts have on their operating costs and profit. Today there are mathematical models being used to estimate the likely effects of price changes and discount promotions before they are put into practice. Such models have shown that over discounting can

TABLE 4-3

BREAK-EVEN WITH DISCOUNT*

	Amount	Percent
Sales	$1,179	100.0
Less Variable Costs:		
Food Cost	(472)	(40.0)
Operating Expenses	(248)	(21.0)
Total	(720)	(61.0)
Contribution Margin**	$460	39.0
Less Fixed Costs		
Labor Cost	(280)	(23.3)
Occupational Expenses	(180)	(15.0)
Total	(460)	(39.0)
Net Profit (Loss)	$0	0

* Numbers rounded to next dollar amount

** Promotion expense is treated as a variable cost since the amount budgeted can be controlled by management.

cause profits to be reduced, even with increased traffic and sales. The calculations for changes are obtained by the use of formulas found in this chapter for break even in dollars, or quantity, and required sales volume to maintain current profit. The figures, either actual or forecasted, are used in the formulas, and a new calculation is made for the new required sales figure.

Break-Even Point

The traditional break-even formula must be modified when a discount is offered. The new formula is as follows:

$$BEP = 100\% - \frac{\dfrac{\text{Fixed Cost \$}}{\text{Variable Cost \% with Advertising Exp.}}}{100\% - \text{overall price reduction due to discount}}$$

Using the figures from Table 4-1, fixed costs are $460 and the *total* variable cost percentage *with the additional advertising* expense is 59 percent ($160 + $50 = $210/$1000 = 21%; + 38% food cost = 59%). A discount promotion of buy-one-get-second-at-half-price, where 10 percent of the meals are discounted, has the same effect on the cost percentages as a 5 percent reduction in sales. Substituting the numbers into the revised break-even formula,

TABLE 4-2

LOSS AFTER DISCOUNT WITHOUT SALES INCREASE

	Amount	Percent
Sales	$1000	100
Less Variable Costs		
Food Cost	(400)	(40)
Direct Operating Expense	(210)	(21)
Total Variable Costs	(610)	(61)
Contribution Margin	390	39
Less Fixed Costs		
Labor	(280)	(28)
Occupational Expenses	(180)	(18)
Total Variable Costs	(460)	(46)
Net Loss	(70)	(7)

$$BEP = \frac{\$460}{100\% - \frac{.59}{100\% - 5\%}} = \frac{\$460}{100\% - \frac{.59}{.95}}$$

$$\frac{\$460}{100\% - .621} = \frac{\$460}{.379} = \$1214$$

The break-even point is just an *approximation* and is not an exact sales point. The $2 difference in the two estimates of break-even are essentially identical. The actual break-even point may be a figure that ranges plus or minus 10 percent from the theoretical calculation. The break-even point is also subject to fluctuation because of what is referred to as *secondary sales effect.* The operator offering the discount hopes that many of the customers will purchase undiscounted add-on items such as cocktails, appetizers, and desserts. The sale of these items will soften the overall cost of discounting. However, some operators using discount promotions have not found this to be the case. In fact, some customers just order entrees and drink water.

The operator and manager must examine the impact of any given discount on profit margins and average check. Each discount promotion has a "trigger point" of increased volume (customer counts and sales revenue) that must be reached to offset the reduced margins of each discounted sale. A rather simple calculation, which is a modification of the traditional break-even formula, is used to estimate the increase in sales and customer counts required to reach this "trigger point."

The calculation allows the operator or manager to estimate the increase in sales the discount promotion must achieve to be successful in the financial sense. With this "trigger point" identified, the discount can be set at an amount in line with existing competitive conditions, historical sales records, and realistic redemption rates.

If the calculation indicates an unrealistic or unattainable increase in customer counts and sales revenue, the amount of the discount must be revised downward. If the discount promotion does not result in an increase in business equal to or greater than that indicated in the calculation, the promotion should be suspended. The following examples show how discounting affects operating costs and bottom line profits.

The formula for this calculation is simply

$$\frac{1}{1 - VC \% \text{ with Discount}}(\text{Change in Var. Cost \%})$$

The formula reads one over one minus the variable cost percentage *with the discount* multiplied by the increase in variable cost due to the discount (or the difference between the variable cost percentages *before* and *after* the discount). Given the numbers in tables 4-1 and 4-2, substituting in the formula one would have the following:

The variable cost with the discount: 61%
The variable cost before the discount: 54%
The increase in variable cost percentage: 7%

$$\frac{1}{1 - .61}(7) = \frac{1}{.39}(7) = 2.56\% (7) = 17.92\%$$

$.1792 \times \$1000 = \$179.20; \ \$1000 + \$179.20 = \$1179.20$

The operator must determine whether the number of additional covers needed can be achieved given the dynamics of the market and competition. Realizing an increase of twenty-four additional customers does not seem to be unreasonable. However, for the promotion to be successful in a financial sense, more than twenty-four additional covers will be needed.

Variations Sales or Income/Positive or Negative

The keeping of historical sales records will allow a manager to more accurately forecast customer counts and menu sales mix. The sales history records become the basis for future projections. With this knowledge a manager is better prepared to plan work schedules and preparation amounts on any given day. Recording menu mix and customer counts by meal period, day, week, and month is the recommended format.

A very basic use of past sales history is to measure the variance in sales from one period to another. For example, if the total sales for the month to date last year were $456,000 and the sales for the same period this year were $463,000, there was a positive variance of $7,000. This represents a 1.5 percent increase. ($7000/$456,000). By computing variances in sales or customer counts, management can detect positive or negative changes in business volume.

Accurate forecasts of business volume are needed to purchase inventory, schedule employees, and determine production needs. Variances provide advance notice of changes in menu item popularity, meal periods, sales trends, and daily sales volumes. You cannot forecast the future without referring to historical activity and the conditions that may have contributed to the variances. You can elect to check for variances on a daily, weekly, or monthly basis to monitor positive and negative changes.

Diminishing Returns

The last economic consideration is the U-shaped curve. Simply stated, a graph is constructed to determine the average cost or expense per unit served (see fig. 4-4). This is important in pricing because, as has been mentioned, there is a point in every operation where profits are maximized, and an increase in volume beyond that point will require an increase in expenses. This all has profound effects on the restaurant operation.

The law of diminishing returns enters in here. If equal increments of one input are added and the quantities of other inputs are held constant, the resultant increments of product will decrease. Thus, keeping constant a specified area of kitchen, dining space, and equipment, the operator can add labor in increasing amounts to the point of minimum average cost and maximum profits. If the volume then increases, space and equipment must be added to compensate for it.

Figure 4-4 is best illustrated by the experience of a local restaurant whose primary income is derived from wedding receptions. Past experience indicated to this owner that he could offer a complete package for a fixed price. Over a number of years, he served an average of two hundred people per reception. This operation was very profitable and successful. During a recent year, the average attendance decreased by approximately fifteen people per event. Food quantities were decreased to reduce that variable cost, but or-

FIGURE 4-4
Graph Showing Point of Maximum Profit per Sales Unit

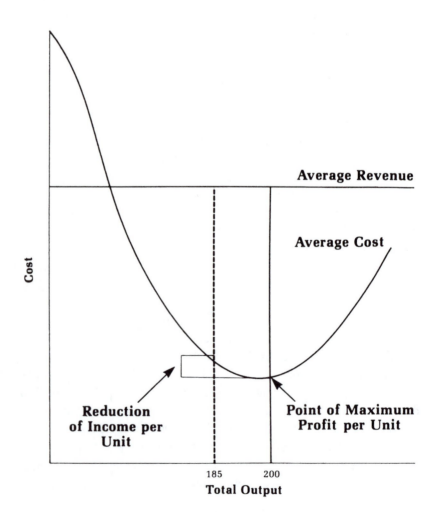

chestra, labor, and building fixed costs were not affected substantially by the smaller number of people. The total effect was a reduction in income that was not proportionate to a possible reduction in cost. The solution for the catered events was a sliding-scale fixed price based on total attendance.

Market Share

The question most often asked in the restaurant industry is "How's business?"

A true response to this question is based upon an analysis of the market share of your restaurant in relation to the total market segment of similar operations.

Market share is a percentage that indicates the relative strength of your restaurant versus that of your competition. It is determined by dividing the sales of your establishment by the total activity or sales of all similar operations. The resulting percentage is your individual market share.

$$\frac{\text{Your Sales Activity}}{\text{Total Industry Activity}} = \text{Individual Market Share}$$

Market share can also be calculated on the basis of volume in units, number of customers served, or any other measurement standard being used within the restaurant industry.

It can be difficult to determine the total sales figures of your area because of the many categories of restaurants and the variety of restaurants that are attempting to capture a part of the market, but it is important to make the effort. The major consideration in defining your market share is to identify your competition and the population base in which you are operating (see fig. 4-5).

MENU ITEM LIFE CYCLE

The menu design and individual menu items have life cycles common to retail products and concepts purchased by the consumer. They are born, they grow, they mature, and they eventually decline. As a menu item passes through each of these phases, the marketing strategy used must also change to reflect the changing stages in the life cycle. Using the factors that cover sales history of menu items and customer demographics, a restaurant can chart specific menu items over time. This information enables the manager or owner to apply the most appropriate marketing strategy for each individual menu item.

External advertising, internal promotion, pricing decisions, menu item additions and deletions, or just overall changes in the menu design can be evaluated and refined at appropriate times to insure the accep-

FIGURE 4-5
Table Showing Frequency of Eating Out. Reprinted by permission of *Restaurants and Institutions* magazine.

FAST TIMES FOR FAST FOOD

Fast-food restaurants continue to capture the lion's share of restaurant business. Fully 47% of young singles, 41% of working couples with children 13 to 17, and 37% of young couples eat at fast-food restaurants more than once a week. Of respondents who spend more than $75 a week at restaurants, 17% eat at fine-dining establishments once a week.

How often do you eat out?

Frequency	Fast Food	Casual/ Family	Fine Dining
More than once a week	27.4%	15.3%	1.0%
Once a week	18.1	20.1	3.2
2 to 3 times per month	19.2	24.1	7.5
Once a month	10.3	16.8	14.4
Less than once a month	13.3	18.5	45.3
Never	4.4	1.5	14.2

Source: 1994 *R&I* Tastes of America

tance and sales of the item. The operator or manager must decide the best course of action that reflects the stage in the life cycle. Only a few menu items remain strong over time, such as hamburgers, fried chicken, steak, and pasta. The majority of menu items will be changed when sales indicate a decline. Menu changes will likely impact sales totals and the income of other menu items, and these changes must be anticipated because of their ultimate impact on the sales and profit objectives of the restaurant.

The information that follows lists the product life stages and suggests the methodology for selling and marketing the menu items at any specific stage. Some of the items may need considerable change to stay competitive in your market. There may need to be adjustments made to the location of the items on the menu, the prominence they present on the printed menu, their written descriptions, and their prices in order to stay competitive.

Stages of the Product Life Cycle

There are five stages in a menu item's life cycle, which will be discussed in detail.

1. Concept
2. Growth
3. Maintenance
4. Maturity
5. Decline

Concept. The process for determining a new product is based upon the following:

1. Idea
2. Opportunity
3. Venture risk
4. Product development
5. Market strategy

Ideas for new products should not present a major problem. Product ideas may be obtained both internally and externally. You can observe innovations in cooking magazines and advertising campaigns, and you can listen to comments from customers. Your employees may offer you suggestions for new products or product modifications. Encourage them to do so. Determine whether the product has enough merit for further investigation and/or development. Be sure, early on, that the product fits your image. Any new

product involves risk and the expenditure of money, but the risk and cost are associated with investment for the future.

Once the decision has been made to introduce a product as a new item on your menu, you must estimate its profit potential. You will need to estimate the amount of investment required in equipment, training, and inventory as well as the amount of time that will be required to develop acceptable market penetration. Will this product have any advantages over a product of the competition? Will it be unique and unusual enough to create customer demand? Will the price level of the competition and the amount of competition restrict the volume and use of the product?

Growth. In the beginning, you can attempt a limited introduction of the new item. This can be done with a chalkboard, a menu clip-on, or a verbal presentation by a service person. This will help you measure your customers' reception of your menu item. Unfortunately, not many restaurants are doing this with new items.

During this period you must monitor the product for improvement, test the price level before making a commitment to the cost of the new product, and determine the sales impact. If growth is evident, there is acceptance of the product. If you make the decision to go forward, focus on high visibility for the item.

The growth period may require higher than normal advertising costs to create a perceived need. Also, quality control and the maintenance of quality standards are essential during the introductory phase. If customers try the product and it does not meet the quality standards they expect, it will not continue to be accepted. You can also encourage acceptance and product awareness if you price the product lower than normal during the introductory period. The success of a new item will also require considerable personal selling by your staff.

Maintenance. In this phase, customers have accepted the new product and there is a steady—perhaps even increasing—demand for the product. Adjustments should have been completed prior to this level, and only minor changes should now have to be made.

The objective at this phase is to build a strong market for the new product. As a manager you now need to refine your production schedule, attempt to lower product cost by improved control, and increase the profit on the menu item.

If you can maintain sales of the new item, there may be an opportunity to increase the price. In any event, you will not need to discount the item in any way. All the advertising will be at the point of sale in an attempt to maximize the exposure of the product to customers.

Maturity. The first indication of the maturity of a product is turbulence in its sales volume and an absolute flattening, with no growth. Another indication may be a saturation of the market, when every restaurant you see has adopted your new item. This is the "trickle-down effect" of menus. The inventive do and others copy, as witness chicken wings, nachos, and potato skins. Customers may then back off because of product overexposure.

Critical to your success at this point is to build and maintain loyalty to your restaurant and your menu. Your ultimate objective is to hold your share of the market.

Decline. Decline does not necessarily mean that an item is unprofitable; it just is not selling as well as it did previously. But if a product cannot make it on its own and has an overall bad effect on menu sales and profit, remove it from the menu. It has reached the end of its life cycle. Do not let your ego get in the way of making the decision to drop a product that is a real loser.

Decline in a product's sales generally spurs either a defensive strategy or an offensive one. A defensive strategy requires that you simply hold your market share to stop any further erosion in sales. Management must control the overall costs, cut production costs of the item involved, and be a little better in every way in order to reverse the decline.

An offensive strategy requires considerable internal sales and promotion to modify the product and to look for alternatives in its presentation.

Continue the offensive strategy by returning to the beginning of the product life cycle and starting again with a new product. This will help you remain competitive in the marketplace.

Careful monitoring is required during every phase of the product life cycle to determine what products should be added and what removed from the menu. Some items may be so accepted by your consumer group that they do not go through a product life cycle and stay on the menu forever. Such an operation is usually a white-tablecloth dinner house with a high check average, where the demand remains despite saturation and product maturity.

Over time, a menu must change just to include the latest trendy foods and to delete the slow selling items. The key factor in such decisions is customer demand. If an item does not sell, it should be removed. When changes are made, the new sales mix and cost figures will affect the break-even level of established operational ratios of the restaurant.

GOAL VALUE ANALYSIS

David K. Hayes and Lynn Huffman titled their February 1985 *Cornell Hotel and Restaurant Administration Quarterly* article "Menu Analysis: A Better Way," but I think it more logical to say simply "a way" of doing menu sales analysis. For theirs is only one of many ways, including the matrix method (described in chap. 6), a method developed by Mike Hurst (a break-even method of analysis), and Smith-Kasavana's Menu Engineering system, plus other less-known methods.

The technique of developing goal values is a useful method of analysis. As with most all methods of analysis, we are here still dealing with assumptions and averages. The basic assumption behind goal-value analysis is that sales and costs will remain unchanged and that the owner-operator will be satisfied with current profit levels and not attempt to make any improvements.

In developing this system of analysis, you will need to create a profit-and-loss (P&L) statement for every item on your menu. Figure 4-6 is a typical example of a P&L statement. In this statement every item is assigned a share of the total variable costs of operation. The percentage of variable costs is arrived at from the P&L statement itself. The example in figure 4-6 also assigns a share of fixed costs to every menu item. Assigning these shares of fixed and variable costs is necessary to develop the goal value. The total fixed cost is divided by the number of menu items. Here the fixed cost was $400, with the ten items resulting in a cost of $40 per item.

All items on the menu are then ranked and summarized by their total contribution to profit or loss (see fig. 4-7). This calculation, to determine an aggregate profit percentage for the entire menu, is similar to that used to determine attainable food costs (shown

	Half-Chicken		Steak		Shrimp		Veal		Pasta	
Sales ($)	166.80		239.00		136.00		62.65		192.50	
Cost of food	41.76	.25%	95.60	.40%	50.72	.37%	21.07	.34%	44.50	.23%
Fixed cost	40.00	.24	40.00	.17	40.00	.29	40.00	.64	40.00	.21
Variable costs	58.38	.35	83.65	.35	47.60	.35	21.93	.35	67.38	.35
Total cost	140.14	.84%	219.25	.92%	138.32	1.02%	83.00	1.32%	152.18	.79%
Net profit [loss]	$26.66	.16%	$19.75	.08%	[$2.32]	[.02]	[$20.35]	[.32]	$40.32	.21%

	Swordfish		Lobster		Beef Burgundy		Fried Chicken		Lamb	
Sales ($)	98.55		319.00		180.70		195.75		107.40	
Cost of food	41.80	.42%	150.70	.47%	56.42	.31%	51.62	.26%	39.96	.37%
Fixed cost	40.00	.41	40.00	.13	40.00	.22	40.00	.20	40.00	.37
Variable costs	34.49	.35	111.65	.35	63.25	.35	68.51	.35	37.59	.35
Total cost	116.29	1.18%	302.35	.95%	159.67	.88%	160.13	.82%	117.55	1.09%
Net profit [loss]	[$17.74]	[.18%]	$16.65	.05%	$21.03	.12%	$35.62	.18%	[$10.15]	[.09%]

FIGURE 4-6. Hypothetical Menu—Individual Profit-and-Loss Statement. Reprinted by permission of the *Cornell Hotel and Restaurant Administration Quarterly.*

later in this chapter), based upon sales and total income. The aggregate-profit percentage would be the total sales of all items divided by the net contribution of all items.

You must also have a targeted food cost. This figure is taken from your P&L statement, arrived at based upon the results of the operation for a given time period. Then you need an average check figure, based upon total sales divided by the number of items sold. For the hypothetical restaurant here it would be $8.50.

Some items on a menu will be selling at a profit, others at a loss. Should we immediately attempt to replace those selling at a loss? Not necessarily—loss

Rank	Item	Net Contribution
1	Pasta	+$ 40.32
2	Fried chicken	+ 35.62
3	Half-chicken	+ 26.66
4	Beef Burgundy	+ 21.03
5	Steak	+ 19.75
6	Lobster	+ 16.65
7	Shrimp	− 2.32
8	Lamb	− 10.15
9	Swordfish	− 17.74
10	Veal	− 20.35
Total		**+$110.00**

FIGURE 4-7. Net Dollar Contribution of Ten Items on Hypothetical Menu. Reprinted by permission of the *Cornell Hotel and Restaurant Administration Quarterly.*

items may contribute to the overall success of a restaurant, and the purpose of goal-value analysis is to determine if our overall operation is meeting the criterion we have set of 6.5 percent net profit. After we have done a goal-value analysis of each item, we can determine its contribution and achievement in light of the total menu.

The formula to determine the goal-value for each menu item and to analyze our pricing decisions will be based on an index that includes food cost, contribution to margin, volume, and fixed and variable costs. The goal-value is expressed as a number, not a percentage or dollar volume; it is simply the goal of our menu's cost and profit breakdown.

The goal value is determined by the following formula:

$$A \times B \times C \times D = \text{Goal Value}$$

A = (1 − Food cost percentage)
B = No. of covers
C = Selling price
D = 1 − (variable cost percentage + food cost percentage)

To calculate a goal value based upon the numbers acquired so far (from the hypothetical operation statements and sales analysis), we know food costs are .35, variable costs .35, average sales per item 20, average check $8.50, and the formula is

$$1 - .35 \times 20 \times [8.50 \times (1 - .35 + .35)] = 33.15$$

	Rank	Item	$A \times B \times (C \times D)$ = Formula Value
Above Goal Value	1	Pasta	$.77 \times 35 \times [5.50 \times (1 - .58)] = 62.25$
	2	Fried chicken	$.74 \times 29 \times [6.75 \times (1 - .61)] = 56.49$
	3	Half-chicken	$.75 \times 24 \times [6.95 \times (1 - .60)] = 50.04$
	4	Beef Burgundy	$.69 \times 26 \times [6.95 \times (1 - .66)] = 42.39$
	5	Steak	$.60 \times 20 \times [11.95 \times (1 - .75)] = 35.95$
	6	Lobster	$.53 \times 22 \times [14.50 \times (1 - .82)] = 30.43$
Below Goal Value	7	Shrimp	$.63 \times 16 \times [8.50 \times (1 - .72)] = 23.99$
	8	Lamb	$.63 \times 12 \times [8.95 \times (1 - .72)] = 18.94$
	9	Swordfish	$.58 \times 9 \times [10.95 \times (1 - .77)] = 13.14$
	10	Veal	$.66 \times 7 \times [8.95 \times (1 - .69)] = 12.82$

FIGURE 4-8. Profitability of Ten Items on Hypothetical Menu. Reprinted by permission of the *Cornell Hotel and Restaurant Administration Quarterly.*

In this restaurant any menu items that exceed the goal value of 33.15 will contribute at least 6.5 percent of its sales to profit. Those that fall below this goal value will not meet the profit criteria (see fig. 4-8).

This method of analysis shows the relationship between profitability and sales for each menu item. No items are penalized, because we are dealing only in average sales and average profit, so one item may in some way redeem itself. All items do not need to meet the minimum goal value for a menu to be profitable.

The following application of goal value analysis is particularly useful to restaurant managers. For one thing, it permits us to access an item before it is ever introduced onto a menu. Every manager has found an item that seemed excellent for his or her menu. Now, with goal-value calculations, we can determine how many of the item must be sold, even before listing the item on the menu. Then when we find an item we want to use as a special, a regular menu item, or on the chalkboard, we can, by using goal-value formula, calculate the sales needed for the item to make its required contribution.

Let us assume that we have found an item we think will sell very well in our restaurant. As in the case of the Hayes/Huffman article, we believe we can sell the menu item for $6.95. The raw food cost will be $2.00, so we will have a food cost of 28.7 percent. An algebraic formula can now be used to determine the goal value of the operation. It uses the following information:

A = 1 − food cost percentage of new item

B = unknown

C = menu price of new item

D = 1 − (food cost percentage of new item + known variable cost of operation)

We now have

A = 1 − .287

B = Unknown

C = 6.95

D = 1 − (.287 + .35).

The formula is now

$$1 - .287 \times B \times [6.95 \times (1 - .287 + .35)] = 33.15$$

Therefore,

$$B \times .713 \times 2.52 = 33.15$$
$$B \times 1.8 = 33.15$$
$$B = 33.15 \div 108$$
$$B = 18.4$$

We have now established that the item will have to sell at least 19 times to meet its profitability goal and be successful. If it sells less than this, you must manipulate its cost, price, or location on the menu for the item to be successful and make its contribution.

There is no one absolute quantitative approach to menu analysis because there are so many psychological factors involved in restaurant and menu choices that ultimately determine both choice and price. It is necessary for you as an owner-operator to have as much information as possible to make your business decisions about the menu. Even so, making up a menu will always involve some informed guesswork about how to write and develop one.

SUMMARY

Economic principles on which all businesses operate will form a basic foundation for marketing and sales of the menu items that are offered for sale at the restaurant. The restaurant industry is essentially a retail-sales enterprise, and many of the sales principles of the retail sector are applicable to the restaurant industry. The concepts and applications of the variability of sales in the retail industry, when properly modified and computed, are appropriate for the restaurant sales and marketing plan. Managers today must be able to think and function in the marketing areas to remain competitive in the restaurant industry. Marketing has become as much of an art as it is a science.

Adaptation of a quantitative application of the principles discussed in this chapter must always be tempered with the manager's or owner's value judgment of the anticipated customers' reactions to changes. This is the "art" part of the science of marketing. We must offer menu items that our customers want, utilize external advertising to get them to come in, and then utilize the marketing power of a well-designed menu to influence them to buy the items that optimize sales revenue while lowering food costs and improving the contribution margin on each sale.

Marketing in the restaurant industry today must identify the consumer's wants, the value they are willing to exchange for the product, and the ability to satisfy their wants at an acceptable price. Market demand and total cost of the product will dictate the final price that must be charged for a menu item to attain a targeted profit objective.

A very difficult accomplishment for the individual restaurant is to develop menu items that are basically "name brands." Such items are "house specialties" or "signature foods" for which the particular restaurant is known. Such items are only available at a particular restaurant, and a monopoly of sorts is created, which brings with it the same pricing and competitive advantages that accompany such a product. Every manager and/or owner will be responsible for making decisions and value judgments. Prepare yourself, for you will be held accountable for the consequences of your decisions.

Pricing Support Systems

In the foodservice area, success is based on developing the right menu-pricing system. But before deciding on one of the seven or so methods of pricing (see chap. 6), it is crucial to establish support systems so that you will be able to document your pricing procedures and make profitable decisions based on them.

THE FOOD-COST BREAKDOWN

Food cost is one of the three most significant costs incurred in the operation of a restaurant. The others are labor and beverage costs. Over the life of a restaurant, these three expenses will exceed the capital costs of the land, building, furnishings, and equipment. Calculation of food cost must be accurate and consistent because it is an important barometer of a major expense category. Menu items are often priced to achieve a *desired* food-cost percentage and month-end financial statements reveal how well management controlled portioning, waste, and theft.

Typically, food cost is expressed as a percentage of the menu price or total food sales, if on a monthly financial statement. Food cost of a given menu item is calculated by dividing the cost of the entree and accompaniments, such as salad, bread, and potato, plus cost of condiments, such as butter, sour cream,

ketchup, and mustard, as determined from a standardized recipe and portion size, by the menu price. The resulting figure is expressed as a percentage of the selling price. For example, if the cost of a steak dinner including salad, potato, and bread condiments amounts to $4.85 and the menu price is $11.95, the food cost percentage is 40.58 percent ($4.85/$11.95).

The food cost shown on the monthly statement of income is based on total cost and food sales. Depending on whether the operation reports cost of food *consumed* or *sold*, the amount is divided by only *food* sales to get the food cost percentage. Many of management's operating decisions take food cost into account, such as menu pricing, manager bonuses, operational efficiency, and expense projections. Depending on how you arrive at your month-end food cost, the resulting percentage is a clue to how well operational procedures are being followed. We believe that the food cost of any given menu item is the best starting point for making a pricing decision.

The basic calculation for food cost is raw food cost divided by menu price (for individual menu items) and total cost of goods *sold* by total food sales. One can tell from looking at the makeup of the monthly statement of income whether the accounting system being used follows the Uniform System of Accounts for Restaurants (USAFR) and whether the food cost shown is food consumed or food sold. Look to see if there is a separate line item for employee meals. If it is indicated, they are following the USAFR and the food cost shown is food sold. If employees' meals are not deducted, the food cost is total food consumed. Food cost will always be a higher percentage of food sales if food consumed is used.

In order to properly analyze changes in food cost percentages from month to month, the food cost dollar is often broken down by major food categories. The USAFR identifies twenty such categories, but typical categories might be produce, dairy, dry and canned goods, fresh meats, fish and seafood, and bakery products. Each of these categories can be further defined; for example, under produce, fruits and vegetables can be divided; under fresh meats, poultry, pork, and beef can be separate categories. The more detailed the breakdown of food costs, the easier it is to locate the exact cause of problems.

You may find it useful to calculate the percentage of your total food cost for each of the food cost categories. You will find that over 50 percent of your food dollar is spent on fresh meats and seafood. This knowledge will help you set controls and procedures to monitor foods that have the biggest impact on your overall food cost. The more expensive the food item, the more control management must place over that category.

$$\frac{\text{Total Fresh Meat Cost}}{\text{Total Food Expense}} = \text{Percentage of Total Food Cost}$$

For example, if the monthly cost of food consumed is $16,800 and the total amount of fresh meat used that month came to $9,875, that particular food category accounted for almost 59 percent of the food expense. In other words, out of every dollar spent on food, $.59 went for fresh meats. When this is tracked over several months, management can see a trend or discover variances that will signal where costs may be out of line.

By comparing monthly figures, one can quickly identify unacceptable variances. If there is a problem in the fresh meat category, costs can be broken down into poultry, pork, and beef to discover which category is contributing to the variance. This kind of cost analysis is critical to so many of managements' decisions.

ATTAINABLE FOOD COST

A formulation for determining an attainable food cost must be devised by the restaurant manager/owner. You can frustrate yourself by trying to meet an objective that is impossible or impractical. The only accurate way to determine what your food cost should be is to do a calculation on attainable food cost. This is something of a chicken-and-egg situation.

The calculation is done by using the form shown in figure 5-1. The form should list all the items offered on the menu. Next you will need to determine a raw cost for each item. To do this, you will need to use an accurate cost based on a standardized recipe. (More on how to devise a standardized recipe and prepare a cost sheet appears later in this chapter. The cost sheet includes no labor or overhead only the per-portion raw food cost and the cost of garnish or accompanying items.) You can then establish a menu price according to one of the methods outlined in chapter 6. Then you take an accurate count of the sales of the items. This can be a manual count or a computer printout from a point-of-sale register.

Using the raw cost, the menu price, and the item sales (number sold), you can determine the income from the sale of the item. The income is just the number sold multiplied by the menu price. The cost of the item is determined by multiplying the number sold by the raw cost. The total for these two columns will give the total income and total cost for all items sold from the menu. By dividing the total income from sales into the total cost of the item, you can determine an attainable food cost for a given operating period.

THE STANDARDIZED RECIPE

As mentioned previously, an essential pricing support system is based on the standardized recipe (S.R.). A standardized recipe is one that has been checked and rechecked for all factors and will consistently produce a known quantity of food at a desired quality. The S.R. is a tool for managers of every type of foodservice establishment. I can envision no food establishment where this is not required. If the operator does not know what goes into a food item and the cost of its ingredients, then the item cannot be priced realistically on the menu.

Management control requires the use of the S.R. For production control, known quantities of food are

Item	Raw Cost	Menu Price	Number Sold	Total Cost	Total Income

Raw cost = Standardized recipe cost

Menu price = Method used (see chap. 6 for menu pricing methods)

Number sold = Manual count or computer printout

Total cost = Item sales × raw cost

Total income = Item sales × menu price

Attainable food cost is determined by dividing total cost by total income.

FIGURE 5-1. Form for Calculating Attainable Food Cost

assigned to the manager and controlled by the manager's use of the S.R. Having the recipe takes the guesswork out of food production. The S.R. is the manager's production blueprint. It improves a manager's planning skill because it specifies portion size, so that amounts can be correlated to the forecast.

The obvious advantages of standardized recipes are

1. Consistency of product
2. A system of operation rather than dependency upon an individual
3. Improved cost control by forecasting and portion control
4. Recognition of deviation from the standard and an opportunity for immediate correction
5. Predetermined item cost
6. Provision of a plan of preparation and elimination of employee preparation decisions
7. An inventory list and purchase control of nonusable items

To develop your S.R. file, start with whatever recipes you are now using or beginning to write. Sources for recipes are offered continually by trade publications, food-manufacturing firms, quantity cookbooks, and your employees. Obtain your recipes from a reliable source and then adapt them to your operation. A recipe, regardless of its source, cannot be considered standardized until it has been tested in your kitchen. Recipe-testing procedures are as follows:

1. Check the recipe for proper ingredient ratios.
2. Check the preparation procedure for clarity.
3. Check the sequence of work.
4. Check your equipment to make sure it is appropriate for preparation.
5. Give measurements of dry ingredients by weight and liquid ingredients by volume.
6. Have a supervisor work with the production person and record any changes.

7. Prepare a small amount of the item for testing for standard.
8. Increase the amounts and retest for standard if the food is satisfactory.

When a recipe is accepted, implement it as you would in any training program.

1. Explain to the employees why the new recipe has been developed and the advantage of it.
2. Stress and detail any part of the recipe that may affect the final quality or a part where a problem may occur in the preparation process.
3. Work with and assist the employees in preparing the item.
4. Follow up on the item when it appears on the menu prepared without your assistance.

For evaluation of the product in the standardization test, use a panel of male and female employees of various ages. This procedure will stimulate the interest of the employees in the recipe program and will make them part of the program. Have the panel refrain from eating prior to the taste test; midday is an acceptable time for testing. Nonsmokers will have a finer sense of taste. Judgment of the final product should be based on the texture and temperature. Odor, visual impact, and size of portion will have an impact on the final rating.

If the item is accepted, write the recipe on a standardized recipe form (see fig. 5-2) and place it in the standardized recipe file. The file consists of one master copy of all recipes in the owner's or manager's office, and individual recipes that are used in specific departments of the kitchen (such as pantry, range, pastry). A suggested file system is a three-digit number for each recipe. The first digit indicates the food group (such as entree, dessert, salad), the second digit the classification within the group, and the third digit the specific food item on the menu. For example, recipe 1-2-21 indicates entree—1, beef—2, Swiss steak—21; recipe 1-2-5 indicates entree—1, beef—2, meat loaf—5. The form in which you present the recipe should be selected on the basis of what is most adaptable to your restaurant. Each form has its advantages and disadvantages. More important than the form is the actual information listed on the recipe. The information recorded should be detailed enough so that the person preparing the item needs to make no decisions.

Recipe Information

Below is the specific information that should be listed on a standardized recipe form.

- *Name of product*
- *File number*
- *Yield.* The yield should specify a total quantity by weight, volume, or specific pan size after final preparation, as well as the number of individual servings.
- *Portion size.* The actual size served to the patron is given by weight, volume, or number of pieces. The portion may also be given by serving utensil size or by the number of portions to be obtained from a specific pan size.
- *Garnish.* For a buffet or cafeteria operation, an amount of garnish per pan size should be specified. For individual serving operations, an amount should be specified per portion. Plate size and type should be specified for individual orders.
- *Ingredients.* Ingredients are always listed in the order used. Any pre-preparation should be specified as the first step of the recipe. Quantities should be expressed in volume for liquids and weight for dry ingredients when more than one ounce is used. Less than one ounce may be expressed by volume, such as 1/4 tsp. All quantity abbreviations must be standardized on all recipes. Quantities must be listed in amounts that can be measured in standard measuring devices. For example, do not list 2/5 cup; use ounces or another standard measure. If the recipe can be standardized to current manufacturers' can sizes, these may be used as a measure, such as one no. 10 can. Give the physical state of the ingredient when added to the recipe: one cup flour sifted, or one cup flour unsifted; one cup nuts chopped, or one cup nuts whole. If the quality of the finished product is dependent upon a specific brand or pack of product, such as whole, peeled tomatoes in puree, state this in the ingredients.
- *Preparation.* List first any preparation for ingredients and preheating of equipment for the item. In the procedure section, list by groups of ingredients the method of combining them. Use the correct terminology: for combining, mix, blend, fold, or cream; for cooking, until

Name of Product		Weight of Ingredients		Mat'l Cost	Total Mat'l Cost	
	Formula No. _____					
Method of Mixing and Comments	Ingredients Used in Order of Mixing	Lb.	Oz.	$	$	$
Scaling Instructions		Lb.	Oz.	Batch Cost		
	Finished Weight of Mix					
	Approx. Cost per Lb. of Mix. $					
	Approx. Cost per Oz. of Mix. $					
Baking Instructions		Handling after Baking:				
Batch Information:						

FIGURE 5-2. Standardized Recipe Form

reduced by one-half, or until thickened to syrupy consistency. List time and speed for mixing if applicable. Emphasize any special directions or precautions for the product.

♦ *Cooking*. Any special preparation of the cooking utensils should be written in the first part of the cooking section. The cooking temperature and length of cooking time should be specifically stated. Indications of doneness other than time may also be given, such as internal temperature or until a knife inserted comes out clean. Instructions for panning are also given in this section, such as the number of pieces, volume, or weight for specific-sized pans.

♦ *Handling*. State any finish that is to be given to the product after cooking, such as brushing with butter or cooling on a rack, as well as where, how, and at what temperature the product is to be held or stored until served.

♦ *Cost*. For accuracy in your menu pricing, every ingredient, including garnish, must be priced to obtain a total cost. A unit price for each ingredient is obtained from the purchase invoice. The unit price is converted into a recipe ingredient cost. When a product is purchased at a price per unit that is different from the unit of measure in the recipe, the product must be converted into the recipe units. The recipe ingredient cost is multiplied by the amount required in the recipe to obtain a total cost per ingredient. Then the costs of all ingredients are totaled to obtain a total product cost. The total product cost is then divided by the number of portions obtained from the recipe to get the cost per portion. Sample forms appear in Kotschevar and Knight's *Quantity Food Production* and Shugart, Molt, and Wilson's *Food for Fifty* (see bibliography), or recipes can be written in measures that are the normal measuring units of purchase.

The standardized recipe file is not static. Changing eating habits, equipment, product development, and product cost, as well as many other factors, will require constant revision of the recipes. Change is required, even desired, but no changes should be made unless the item is reevaluated. No changes should be made to any recipe unless the change is made to all copies in the file. Every restaurant will have a different requirement for the amount of product to be prepared. The recipe should be standardized for the amount that best meets the quantity requirement.

Recipe Adjustment

There will always come a time in your operation when you will find it necessary to adjust the yields in your standardized recipe files and will need to have a formula to adjust these yields. You will frequently have to convert these recipes to different amounts and different portions. There is no best method, there are various ones that work well. Whatever method you use, there are certain factors that must be kept in mind.

One factor is the measurement standards to be used. Weighing is the most accurate method of measuring any ingredient. Use of this technique is fairly well restricted to the solid ingredients in a recipe. We must distinguish weight as purchased, before any trimming or preparation is done that results in loss of

waste, and the weight of the edible portion, which is the weight after all the nonedible or nonservable parts have been trimmed away.

The second method of measurement is by volume. This technique is usually employed for liquid ingredients, for which it is excellent to determine the accuracy.

Adjustments for weight are usually accomplished in one of two ways. The first is the factoring method—dividing the new yield by the old to arrive at a conversion factor. Then every ingredient in the recipe is multiplied by this factor. An example of this is shown in figure 5-3.

In the first example, we currently have a recipe that yields 20 portions, and we need to make an adjustment for a yield of 35 portions. Based on the formula, the known yield is divided into the desired yield, to give us our factor for the increase. Thus, 20 divided into 35 equals 1.75, which is our change factor.

The second method of adjusting yield is the percentage technique. This is the baker's method of recipe adjustment. Since it deals with the total weight of the formula, it is considerably more accurate than the factoring method. The calculation is done by figuring the percentage of each ingredient in respect to the total weight required.

In this procedure, the original recipe must be converted to an edible portion (EP) weight of each ingredient and a percentage then established for each ingredient. When adjusting the recipe you must establish a new weight for each ingredient for the desired amount to be prepared, which is calculated as the portion size times the desired number of servings. This conversion percentage factor is now multiplied times the old quantity in your recipe to give the new quantity required for the adjusted recipe (see fig. 5-4).

In our second example, we currently have a recipe that requires 220 ounces of the ingredient for the total quantity and portion size. We wish to adjust this recipe to the desired amount of 95 3-ounce portions. By the formula, 95 times 3 will require 285 ounces of

FIGURE 5-3
Recipe Adjustment by Factoring
Method

Ingredient	Amount		Factor		New Amount
A	7 1/2 lbs.	×	1.75	=	13.125 lbs.
B	3 qts.	×	1.75	=	5.25 qts.
C	4 tbs.	×	1.75	=	7 tbs.
D	10 oz.	×	1.75	=	17.5 oz.

FIGURE 5-4
Recipe Adjustment by Percentage
Method

Ingredient	Amount		Percentage		New Amount
A	6 lbs., 4 oz.	×	1.295	=	129.5 oz.
B	1 lb., 2 oz.	×	1.295	=	23.3 oz.
C	2 lbs., 6 oz.	×	1.295	=	49.2 oz.
D	4 lbs.	×	1.295	=	82.8 oz.

the ingredient for the new amount. By the formula, the known quantity of the ingredient divided into the desired quantity of the ingredient will give us our percentage factor to effect the change in the recipe. Thus, 285 (the desired amount) divided by 220 (the current amount) equals 1.295, the factor to be used to effect the change in the recipe.

The new amounts, which are given in ounces, should be converted to full pounds and fractional pounds before the actual preparation of the item is done. There is some variation in the total amount required and the total amount shown in this recipe because of rounding off to three decimal points in the percentage column during multiplication.

In all recipe adjustments, a ratio of ingredients should be checked to determine that the recipe will now work as written. Critical to this adjustment is the judgment of the recipe writer for values and the knowledge that some spices do not lend themselves well to such mathematical adjustment. Therefore, human taste becomes critical to making a proper adjustment for consumer tastes and the recipe's consequent acceptance.

Rapidly changing food prices require a review of recipe prices at least once every three months. Restaurant operators whose recipes are computerized will enjoy the advantage of instant reviews of any price change and, with the correct menu strategies, can reflect increases or decreases in menu prices within twenty-four hours.

The standardized recipe must be consistent in all factors of taste, quantity, quality, appearance, garnish, method of preparation, ingredients, style of service, and, most important, specific portions served at specific prices.

The preparation of costed standardized recipes is recommended, although this is a complex matter. It is a very long, involved process, but it is worth the money, time, and effort required. One establishment where I helped to prepare such recipes moved from a position of operating at about $50,000 in the red to profitable

operation when we combined the use of standardized recipes and careful portion control. Figure 5-5 shows a cost form, and figure 5-6 is a hypothetical example.

An operation cannot do an accurate pricing of items on its menus unless costed recipes are available that will tell the portion costs and portion sizes of the items. However, with the forced food cost pricing system, you do not even have to update your recipes because you can calculate a percentage factor and use that factor to update each recipe rather than having to recost the recipes completely. However, every six months you will have to evaluate your recipes to measure your profit.

INDIRECT COST FACTORS

The restaurant's menu prices must be in line with the price category in which the majority of its customers place the operation. The latest pricing trends indicate an overall lowering of menu price ranges. The ultra-priced destination operations are moderating their prices in an attempt to increase customer counts.

If you have ever had a discussion with a customer who thought your prices were too high, and you tried to explain about how much it costs you to put out a particular item, you realize that customers are not concerned with the restaurant's costs and overhead. They are very conscious of the price they pay for meals, and they do comparison shop. They are aware of your competitor's prices and will be quick to change restaurants when they can get what they believe to be a comparable product (quantity and quality) and service at another restaurant at a cheaper price.

Psychological Aspects of Menu Pricing

While we have stated that food cost is the logical starting point in the menu pricing decision, there is more to setting the price than simply marking up raw food cost. We suggest that there are several factors

Item _____ Code _____				

Item _____ Code_____
No. Portions_____
Portion Size _____
Garnish _____
Serving Piece _____

Ingredients	Quantities	Cost Unit	Total	Method
(Ingredients are listed by groups or item, as used, separated by spaces.)				(The methods of preparation and/or procedure for each group or item are separated by spaces. This form shows the method for each group of ingredients or single ingredient and then the method for combining with the following ingredients.)

Total Cost _____
Cost per Portion_____

FIGURE 5-5. Form for a Costed Standardized Recipe

that need to be considered along with raw food cost that can be reflected in the prices you charge. These are referred to as *indirect cost factors*. These indirect cost factors must be taken into consideration when setting the price of menu items. They are

1. Market standing
2. Service commitment
3. Ambiance
4. Customer demographics
5. Location
6. Amenities
7. Product presentation
8. Desired check average
9. Price elasticity

Market Standing

This consideration relates to the operation's position in a particular market segment, that is, whether it is a "leader" or a "follower." If a restaurant is considered the number one operation in its concept category, it can price more aggressively than it could if it were just marginally competitive. Usually the first one into the marketplace has an advantage over others that follow and can set higher prices.

Ambiance

The atmosphere and decor of a restaurant will add much to the enjoyment of any meal. The room can turn the dining experience into an enjoyable social oc-

		Item:	Chicken-Fried Steak
		Portion:	50
			4 oz. raw weight
		Garnish:	Parsley/1 oz. sauce
		Serving Piece:	12 by 20 pan—serve on 8-in. plate

Recipe: 4-1-32
St. Louis Community College
Hospitality—Restaurant Operations

	Quantities	Cost	
Ingredients	**Amount Served:** 50	**Unit**	**Total**
Cube steak (4/1 lb.)	12½ lbs.	$2.00/lb.	$25.00
Flour	1½ lbs.	$0.25/lb.	$ 0.376
Egg mixture	4 cups	$0.15/cup	$ 0.60
Bread crumbs	2 lbs.	$0.35/lb.	$ 0.70

Method

1. Dip steaks into flour, then into egg mixture, then into bread crumbs. Make sure steak is completely covered with crumbs.
2. Lay steaks on a sheet pan until ready to cook.
3. Cook steaks in 375°F deep-fat fryer for 7 min. or until breading is golden brown.
4. Remove steaks from fryer baskets and place in 12 × 20 serving pans (25 per pan), overlapping steaks in pan.
5. Keep hot in warmer or low (200°F) oven for service.
6. Garnish pan with four sprigs of parsley before sending to serving line.
7. Portion sauce when serving.

NOTE: Do not bread steaks more than one hour prior to cooking.

Total Cost $26.675
Per 50 4-oz. portions
Per Portion $0.533

FIGURE 5-6. Sample of Costed Standardized Recipe

casion. People want quality food, and the perception of value is enhanced when the customer eats in a beautifully decorated restaurant. The atmosphere can be informal or formal, casual or elegant, but it should be tastefully done in its style. The customer does not usually object to paying a little more to dine in pleasant surroundings.

Service Commitment

The service element can be just as important as the actual food being served in the customer's decision of which restaurant to patronize. This is especially true when the differences in product quality, quantity, and price are difficult for the customer to distinguish.

The "invisible product"—the service component—is becoming an important measure of competitive distinctiveness. Truly personalized service, that is, service that is driven by the needs of the customer, becomes an intangible that is recognized as an added value by the customer and can be reflected in the prices charged.

Customer Demographics

Although the type of clientele that regularly frequents a restaurant is influenced to a great degree by all of the factors listed, the pricing structure can dictate the status or economic class of clientele a restaurant will attract. The higher the average check or price range, the more selective and limited your customer base will be.

Location

Where the restaurant is located (place) has a significant influence on the prices the customer will be willing to pay and whether the operator should price at "what the market will bear" or at relatively competitive levels. Usually, restaurants with lower check averages and prices must be located in areas of dense population and high traffic. Destination restaurants can be located greater distances from the homes and workplaces of patrons than can eat-out restaurants.

Product Presentation

This is the marketing concept that proclaims, "Sell the sizzle, not the steak." The product presentation is very important in the value perception of the patron. It is often said that "we eat with our eyes." If it looks good, the guests are likely to enjoy it. The presentation can be enhanced by visual or audio accents in the dining room, and a higher price can sometimes be charged.

Desired Check Average

One cannot rely on what is referred to as the secondary sales effect to reach a desired check average if entrees are priced too low. (The secondary sales effect is the sale of accompanying food items, e.g., appetizers, desserts, wine, etc., at a la carte prices in order to build check averages.) The reason for this is that although every customer will buy one entree, fewer than 50 percent are likely to order an appetizer or dessert. The addition of such add-ons cannot be relied upon to achieve the desired check average of $10 if the majority of entrees are priced at or around $6.95. The menu-pricing structure should be designed to make it impossible for a customer to spend less than the amount that will achieve the desired check average. The majority of items in this example need to be priced in the $9.95 range, plus or minus one dollar.

Price Elasticity

Economic theory explains the principle of price elasticity in relation to establishing menu price. Elasticity of demand refers to how sensitive the demand factor is for a menu item when there is a price increase or decrease. Price elasticity means that the demand for the item will vary inversely with the change in price. If an increase in price results in a decrease of sales or demand for the item, and a decrease in price results in an increase of sales or demand for the item, the item is said to be price elastic and have price sensitivity. If demand remains constant when prices are increased or decreased, the demand is price inelastic.

Although related to market standing, price elasticity for a product or service is a key element in the pricing decision. Whenever demand is high the approach to pricing can be more aggressive. In a situation where supply is greater than demand, the sales volume may be very sensitive to the prices changed. Some items on the menu can be priced higher because of their uniqueness. Signature items or house specialties can be priced at the higher end of your price range because they are only available at your operation. This type of aggressive pricing cannot be employed on highly competitive or common menu items. This pricing will be limited to unique appetizers, entrees, and desserts on the menu.

In past years, operators set menu price points to cover food costs and achieve a certain profit margin. The decision on pricing specific menu items is tempered according to what the competition is charging and whether the menu item is a commodity or a specialty good. If we are selling generic steak or chicken, we cannot price at the high end of the pricing continuum. However, if the item is a specialty good or one of our signature items, then we can price it at what the market will bear. In addition, customer demographics and market trends must be considered as well.

Odd-Cents Pricing

A restaurant that draws customers from a market area, such as those located in large metropolitan cities, may find demand can be increased by a form of odd-cents pricing. Odd-cents pricing is a technique used in retail pricing that says if you end the price in a nine or a five, psychologically it will be seen as a lower price than if it ended in a zero. For example, $9.95 is preferred over $10. Even high-ticket items like cars and houses are priced with the odd-cents technique; for example, a new Lexus is $39,999 and a new home is $149,500.

The element of customer perception of price is an important determinant of buyer behavior. We recommend that you set your menu prices in digits ending in 25, 50, 75, and 95. Price increases by these four increments are rarely detected by customers.

Another explanation for odd-cents pricing is that the price creates an illusion of a discount and reduces the buyer's resistance. Odd-cents pricing appeals to a customer group that is price conscious.

Another consideration in the psychology of pricing is that the consumer regards the first digit as the most significant. The number of digits in the price creates an image of the expense of the item. A customer attracted by psychological pricing has a tendency to round off to the nearest dollar, up or down: 39 cents is generally rounded down, 40 to 79 cents is rounded to 50 cents, and 80 cents or above goes to the next full dollar.

Customer Mental Accounting

A psychological theory on pricing is that the customer uses a process of mental accounting when deciding on where to eat. This theory suggests that as consumers we mentally code purchases into budget categories such as food, housing, and entertainment, and that each category is controlled to some degree by a budget constraint. Consequently, the amount spent on a meal away from home will vary depending on whether the expenditure is debited to food or entertainment expense.

How does this apply to menu pricing? If consumers code their expenditures by categories such as groceries, shelter, entertainment, etc., each category is controlled to some degree by a budget constraint. In general there is freer spending in recreation and entertainment, and we need to know what state of mind the customer is in when he or she visits our restaurant. We know that there is more constraint when purchases exceed budgetary limits in each category; for example, using the food (grocery) budget to eat out during the week vis-à-vis using the entertainment budget to dine out on the weekend or for a special occasion. With this knowledge we can more effectively price our menus.

As operators we must determine how the customers categorize our restaurants (e.g., eat-out or dine-out). For example, a meal at a fast-food restaurant is likely to be considered as a food/grocery expenditure and not entertainment. However, dining at a restaurant that provides elegant table service and entertainment would be considered too expensive to deplete the food/grocery budget and would need to be classified as entertainment or recreation in order to justify the spending.

If we can assume that restaurant expenditures can be assigned to the budget categories of food, entertainment, or recreation, we can approach the pricing decision from the consumer's perspective. The objective is to have the expenditure classified into a higher budget category or combine categories together. There is likely to be freer spending from an entertainment budget than from a food budget. The mental budget category can change depending on the occasion and the day of the week. Such considerations may prompt promotions such as early bird specials and discount coupons to entice weeknight diners using their food budgets to eat out instead of at home. Such strategy may not be necessary on weekends, when dining out is done more for entertainment or social purposes and when budget restraints are relaxed.

Reference Pricing

Most customers do some kind of price comparison when they shop for clothing and household appliances. It is not surprising that we also mentally record prices we pay at restaurants. Measure your value perception when you are in a new restaurant for the first time by comparing the prices they charge to those of the restaurant you normally frequent for similar items. If the prices of the new restaurant are lower than your "reference prices," you perceive a good price-value. However, if the prices are higher than you expected to pay, the positive price-value perception is missing. The more we pay, the more critical and demanding we are of food quality and service. We seek to get our money's worth. If you charge at the high end of the pricing continuum, your operation needs to be ready to deal with customers who are more critical about even the little things.

Time and Place Factors

Another psychological aspect of menu pricing has to do with the time and place of the purchase. While at a football or baseball game, the price we are willing to pay for a Coke and a hot dog is going to be higher than the price we would be willing to pay in a neighborhood sandwich shop. This is analogous to eating out while on vacation versus eating out on a weeknight in a neighborhood restaurant; spending is going to be more liberal while on vacation. Such knowledge is providing retailers and restaurants with insight on how to present and market their goods and services to be the most appealing to their customers.

Psychological pricing is common in the restaurant industry. It is just assumed that everyone is looking for a bargain. The validity of such an assumption is questionable, but there certainly is a relationship between an item chosen and its purchase price.

Salad and Food Bar Pricing

One factor in overall menu pricing is the cost incurred by the operation of a salad bar. Salad bar prices normally are based upon a competitor's price and adjusted when there is a general profit decline in the restaurant. The pricing of the salad bar is based upon several considerations.

A principal consideration is the cost of the items in the salad bar and their ingredients. This cost is related to the ABC inventory principle. The A items are expensive and should comprise 20 percent of the total number of items offered; B items are moderately priced and should comprise about 30 percent of the total number of items offered; and the C items are inexpensive and constitute roughly 50 percent of the items offered on the salad bar.

You should prepare a written menu for the selections on the salad bar so that the cost ratios of the offerings remain in the correct proportion. The specific items are not important, but the ratios are.

Pricing By-the-Person and By-the-Ounce

Today's foodservice operations are offering self-service salad and food bars. These restaurants are pricing their food by-the-ounce as well as the traditional all-you-can-eat at one-price-per-person. The problem is how does one arrive at a price-per-ounce or total price when items offered on the salad and food bars have a range of value and price. How can you arrive at a price when you initially decide to offer all-you can-eat at one price or at a single price-per-ounce without any sales history to guide you? The prices must be high enough to achieve your desired profit and allow you to meet your food cost percentage goals.

The most prevalent method of pricing all-you-can-eat salad/food bars has been to arrive at one price for the entire meal. The final price must be a price that is acceptable to both the customer in terms of price-value and the operator in terms of covering costs and returning the needed profit margin. The

pricing is a combination of several factors, including the cost of the food consumed, the cost of an average portion, and the average food cost per customer.

The first step is to cost out all food that is prepared for the salad or food bar. This includes not only the actual food needed to set up the bar in the first place but all the backup stock used to replenish the supply during the meal period. Include the costs of condiments that are placed on the guest table. When the salad/food bar is closed, all food is returned to the kitchen and refrigerated storage. Any food that is discarded is subtracted from the ending inventory and the value of the usable food is calculated. The cost of food consumed is the difference between the opening and ending inventories. The number of persons going through the bar that day is divided into the cost of food consumed. This procedure is followed for each meal period and day of the week for several weeks. This provides the basis for the ultimate pricing decision. You know the food cost for each customer who goes through the bar. Markup is then applied to this average cost per cover (see fig. 5-7).

The mix of customers may change the cost per cover on a daily basis, but overall you should be able to see an average food cost figure emerge. Management must watch the food cost of key menu items. If there are increases in price of food items, management may have to adjust the price it charges. With self-service food bars, other methods can be used in lieu of raising prices. One may cut down on the amount of expensive items that are put on the bar. In addition, one can place the expensive items in places that are difficult to reach and use different serving utensils that do not allow the guest to take large quantities with a single scoop or spoon. Also, less expensive substitute items are introduced to reduce the demand for the expensive item.

The size of the containers, their placement on the bar, the serving utensils, and the speed in which items are replenished are all ways of reducing the overall food cost of food bars. Psychologically, customers go lighter on items in small bowls than they do when the item is served in a large container.

When there is only one price for adults and one price for children, both the customer and the operator are often put at a disadvantage. The light eater pays just as much as the customer who goes back for third and fourth helpings. The answer to this dilemma is pricing by the ounce. In this way, the all-you-can-eat

Item	Original Amount	Table Condiments	Additions	Ending Inventory	Discarded Food	Total Consumed	Cost per Unit/wt.	Total

FIGURE 5-7. A Cost-and-Use Form for Monitoring Salad and Food Bar Pricing

pricing attracts both the diet conscious and the big eaters: each is charged according to their selection of items from the salad and food bar. This is basically a way to charge a single price-per-ounce for whatever items and quantity the customer selects.

The two most common problems in all-you-can-eat food and salad bars are the customers who share with another member of their party who did not pay for the food or salad bar and the problem of wanting to take home what was not eaten. A standard practice in all-you-can-eat bars is that sharing and doggy bags are not permitted.

With the per-ounce pricing method, doggy bags are allowed because the customer is charged according to what they take. In addition, carry-out meals can be sold at the same price-per-ounce; people pay only for what they take, and concern over waste is now the responsibility of the customer, not the operator. When one uses the multiple pricing system, they are often challenged by the customer, and in all likelihood the standards are not consistently applied when the servers must classify the customer in a particular price range.

The process of arriving at a price-per-ounce is not difficult. Consider the extremes in weight and volume of the items served. Items usually cost out by liquid measure or count must now be cost out based on weight. It cannot be assumed that two liquid ounces will weigh two ounces on a portion scale. The ultimate determination to charge single price or per ounce is in fact a pricing decision.

The first step in any pricing decision is the determination of one's cost. Since pricing by the ounce allows the guest to fill their plate with items with a wide range of prices, customers will soon discover the real bargains on a food or salad bar and will not hesitate to take advantage of your pricing blunders. One must calculate the averages out over the day, week, or month. The averages will occur as long as there are light eaters subsidizing the heavy eaters. The portion size is completely out of the owner's control. An owner cannot just charge a price based on the highest cost items because this would not be a competitive price and would most likely overprice to the point were customers would question the value received. This is perhaps the most important consideration in setting a menu price. If the customer does not feel that they receive value for their money, they will not return.

Pricing by the ounce requires you to take the customer's perspective on quality, quantity, and price of your food bar. Set your sales goals based on customer counts for each meal period and the desired average check you need from each customer to realize your sales goals. Know what price the market will bear for your concept, location, and clientele. There is a definite price point for each particular concept, menu, and service delivery system that must be identified before setting the price-per-ounce.

Discriminating clientele look to more than just low price. How well your price-per-ounce is viewed by your clientele will be influenced by the selection of items in your food/salad bar. If the competitor uses primarily canned products and you use all fresh ingredients, that is a premium that allows you to charge a higher price and still provide value to the customer.

If your bar has both hot and cold items, it will be perceived as a better value than one with only cold items. Even the quality of your salad dressing can impact price-value perceptions of the customer. Specialty items like anchovy filets, stuffed manzanilla olives, and pickled corn are premium items, too.

Remember, you don't have to have the lowest price to gain acceptance by your customers—price-value combination is the key. Being the cheapest doesn't guarantee that you will bring in customers. Discriminating customers recognize quality when they see it and are willing to pay a little more for it.

Commercial operations with salad bars are likely to remain with the one price, all-you-can-eat, while the institutional foodservices experiment with pricing by-the-ounce. The pricing by-the-ounce method does provide a way for commercial operations to offer take-home and carry-out heretofore not allowed at the dine-in price.

Commercial restaurants wanting to use a cost-per-ounce pricing system will find it necessary to have all portions weighed before customers arrive at their table, much the way it is done in traditional cafeterias, where a food checker rings up the items on your tray and presents you with a cash register receipt that is later presented to the cashier on the way out.

It would appear that the one price for all-you-can-eat is preferred to pricing by the ounce. Only a small percentage of the dining public is adamant about diet and calorie count, and it is these patrons who are not moved to purchase all-you-can-eat food bars. It appears that the vast majority of the dining public sees one all inclusive price as a bargain price, and they control the amount they receive and believe it to be a value for their dining dollar.

The costs of the ingredients on the salad bar are determined by the actual costs of the amount of ready-to-eat foods. Determine the cost per servable pound or an actual cost by weight for foods that need to be cleaned and trimmed. This calculation is the original weight minus the waste, shrinkage, and trim to determine a usable (edible portion, or EP) weight. Divide the original weight into the usable weight to determine the ratio of the usable product.

> 2 lb. carrots (original weight)
> 1/2 lb. trim
> 1.5 lb. edible product
> 1.5 divided by 2 = ratio of 75 percent for usable product

Once the ratio is determined, the next step is to divide the market price by the ratio to determine the cost per servable pound.

> Ratio = 75 percent
> Cost per lb. = 50 cents (as purchased, or AP)
> .50 divided by 75 percent = .666 cost per servable lb.

This formula can be used to calculate actual cost, or you can use a food-purchasing book that lists product waste.

The costs of all items on a salad bar should be established on the basis of a standardized recipe that has been accurately costed according to the guidelines discussed earlier in this chapter. Once the cost has been established, the pricing of the salad bar is a matter of inventory and monitoring.

The salad bar cost is determined and monitored with calculations on a cost-and-use form (see fig. 5-7). The form consists of a beginning weight or count and any additions that are made during the mealtime minus an ending inventory, which will equal the total consumed. This total consumed, multiplied by a cost per unit or weight, will equal a total cost for each salad bar item. This total cost of all items, divided by the number of customers participating in the salad bar, will produce an average cost per customer. All calculations are simplified if the item can be determined and calculated on a weight rather than a count basis. Customer participation data are determined by a manual count or a computerized system.

PRICE AND PORTION

Something that we found to be effective during the time we were in restaurant operations was a price and portion book. This book listed every item that appeared on the menu of the operation. The information contained in the book gave a stated portion size, price, and recipe number, and provided space for price revision (see fig. 5-8). The portion that appeared in the price and portion book was also the portion shown at the top of the standardized recipe in the space for portion size of that particular item.

The critical points of cost control and menu pricing are the measurement of the ingredients going into the product and of the ingredients served to the customer. Careful measuring is a most important part of preparation in the serving of food.

Restaurant income is achieved through the sale of product to customers, and all profits are derived from the amount of money that is made by the sale of each item on a menu. From my time in operations I think there has never been a cook who has not said at one time or another to himself that if one measurement is good, two must be better, and then done just that. Or consider the server who says, "That just doesn't look like enough," and adds more to the portion.

According to the National Restaurant Association, 4 percent is the average profit in a restaurant, a percentage that must come from the sale of some food product. Losses are incurred by not receiving the amount paid for on invoices, overportioning, wasting food, or incompletely utilizing a product.

The following formula demonstrates the disaster that can arise in this area. Servers have been observed pouring out coffee left in a pot when there is no place to serve it or hold it until additional coffee is needed. If the price of coffee per cup on the menu is $1, these two cups of coffee are equal to $2 in sales. The mathematical formula for profit is X times $.04 = \$2.00$. Thus, $X = \$2.00$ divided by $.04$, or $X = \$50.00$, meaning that you would have to have $50 in sales to make up for these two cups of coffee thrown out. The same formula can be used for inventory shortages in receiving or excessive amounts of food included into the preparation of menu items.

Making changes that the improve a recipe are necessary. However, costs are based upon knowing the ingredients in a recipe, and if any change is to be made by the kitchen, it will require management to recalculate the cost of the menu item.

Taken to the extreme, portion control is simply the process of ensuring that there is enough food in equal portions to serve all the possible customers. Portion control involves everyone; all the staff must

| Item | Recipe Number | Portion | Price | | Cost Extension |
			Date		
Beef Croquettes, sauce or gravy	56	2 2-oz. croquettes, 1 oz. sauce/gravy			
Swedish Meat Balls	72	4 1-oz. (raw) meat balls			

FIGURE 5-8. Sample Page from Price and Portion Book

be aware of portioning. The portions can be determined in several different ways, depending on what is most applicable to the item being served.

Count. The number of items per order.

Weight. May require a portion scale at the serving station.

Volume. Done with scoops or ladles, using the exact size of the scoop or ladle as the portion size.

Division of container or item. Pies or cakes are cut into equal sections as portions, or a specified size of pan is cut into equal portions.

Standard fill. Dishes, cups, or glasses may be filled to a given level, as judged by the eye.

This information on portioning can be usefully incorporated into a price and portion book to give consistency to the quantities served within your restaurant. Doing so fulfills a major part of the profit requirement for the service of food.

Listing each menu item's portion size and price serves two purposes. The first is to document the price and portion of all items served. The second is to provide a convenience to the management staff. Invariably employees will approach any manager with the question, "How much do we serve, and what do we charge for it?" The price and portion book is a ready reference for individual employees as well as management.

Portion control is the absolute responsibility of the management. Any device that you can develop and use to help you and your staff to control portions better is an obvious advantage. The price and portion book is an essential element of portion control.

SUMMARY

One cannot arrive at a selling price without considering some highly subjective factors that have refined the interpretation of traditional economic theory on consumer buying behavior. Psychologists are teaming up with marketing analysts and economists to provide some new perspectives on pricing.

Every restaurant will be categorized by its customers according to the prices it charges. The customer will place the restaurant into one of the following price categories: low-priced, moderate-priced, high-priced, and ultra-high-priced. Generally speaking, as a reference point low check average means un-der $10 per person; moderate, $10–$20, and high, over $20. In addition to socio-economic classification, the area of the country will also affect the perception of the exact dollar amount associated with each level.

When doing a sales analysis of the menu, it is recommended that you use the sales records for a representative period of business activity. A month's worth of sales and cost data is preferred over just a week's. It should be conducted prior to making changes in menu prices or design and a minimum of twice a year when static menus are used.

The right price to charge is the one the customer is willing to pay; this is largely a perception of price-value. Implicit in this theoretical pricing perspective is that customer expectations are directly linked to the circumstances surrounding the visit (eat-out versus dine-out) and the position of the operation in the marketplace (trendsetter versus follower). In addition the customers' subjective perceptions of your operation may not be aligned with where you believe your operation to be positioned, and this can impact your price-value image. This perspective points out the importance of knowing how customers perceive your operation and the circumstances leading up to a visit. Visits during the week may find the customer more price consciousness than on weekends, when social and entertainment motives drive the purchase decisions.

The challenge in menu offerings today is to offer exceptional value for the price paid. This philosophy has spawned the introduction of lower priced menus and the addition of low-cost food items on many menus. Menus are showing upgraded a la carte offerings and an increase in variety. When prices are lowered, check averages decline, but the hope is that traffic will increase and build a higher volume of customers. Portions in high-cost items are being reduced and combined with inexpensive food accompaniments because patrons are balking at paying higher prices for what they believe is less food. Today's guests seem inclined not to eat so much food at one sitting, but they are still value conscious. One marketing strategy is to use a la carte pricing as a way to offer low priced items and still allow the opportunity to build check averages by suggestive selling of accompaniments and side dishes. However, price-value perception does not evolve solely from low price; it is a feeling that the customers have about receiving their money's worth when they pay their check.

Menu Pricing Strategies

PRICING STRATEGY

The pricing of a menu may at first seem a very quantitatively based process. Once we know the cost of the menu item, we mark it up to cover our cost and return a profit. The established prices will actually determine the amount of business that a restaurant will draw and influence the type of clientele attracted to the establishment. When considered in this light, the difference between making the proper pricing decision and making the wrong decision is significant. The optimum price must not only include some contribution to profit; it must also be deemed fair and reasonable by the public.

Pricing decisions are critical because price does impact a customer's selection process. Pricing can skew the menu sales mix, food cost, average check, gross profit, customer counts, and revenue. Costs must be known in order to measure profit contribution on each sale. Some costs can be accurately calculated and assigned to specific menu items, while other costs must be subjectively allocated. Costs serve as a reference to begin developing a pricing strategy. Many operators are experiencing intense competition, rising operating costs, labor shortages, and falling customer counts. Such factors will definitely impact on

profits. Therefore, pricing policy is a major factor in developing a strategic plan to meet such obstacles.

Most businesspersons seek logical and objective criteria on which to base their pricing strategy. This is the main reason we start with determining the cost of a product or service. There is a tendency to rationalize price as a means of returning an amount that will reflect a fair profit for the time, effort, and materials consumed. Of all the business decisions a restaurateur has to make, one that causes considerable anxiety is pricing the menu.

The task of menu pricing is beset with misgivings and uncertainty. Prices that are too high will drive customers away, and prices that are too low will sacrifice profit. The main reason for this anxiety may well be the highly subjective methodology used to price menus in the first place. Anxiety also results over the decision as to which approach to pricing is best or right given the respective menu items, existing market conditions, and the operational concept.

Prices partially influence which menu items will sell, and therefore they impact the overall profitability of the sales mix. Menu items will differ widely in cost, popularity, and profitability. Thus, pricing is not a simple matter of cost markup but an intricate combination of factors that involve both financial and competitive elements. Since rising costs are a fact of life, prices will always need to be adjusted when ingredients and other operating costs increase and cut into needed profit margins. The United States Department of Agriculture (USDA) projects that menu prices will increase an average of 4.1 percent each year through the turn of the century.

In the past, operators set menu prices primarily to cover food costs or to achieve certain gross profit margins. The decision was also tempered with what the competition was doing. However, today's operators must study customer demographics, market trends, and the wants and needs of their customers.

One thing that must be understood by the operator when pricing the menu is that customers are not concerned with the restaurant's costs and overhead, but they are conscious of the price they pay for meals eaten away from home. They are aware of your competitor's prices and will be quick to change restaurants when they can get a comparable product or service elsewhere at a cheaper price. The objective is to arrive at a price the customer is willing to pay and that will produce the desired profit for the restaurant.

Today's economy imposes on the owner-operator the highest cost of doing business that we have had in the recent past. It becomes increasingly difficult to pass these costs on to the customer. Seemingly, the times of plenty from the eighties, with customers' strong needs to reward themselves, have dissipated. We now have instead creative compromise on menus and pricing. The dining experience must offer new ingredients and food presented at reasonable prices that are attractive to the customer.

Pricing is, in fact, an art. The amount of money that is charged and received for the food sold is the sole source of revenue for the restaurant, so the price of the items on the menu will ultimately determine the success or failure of the restaurant.

The pricing of the menu is a profit-planning procedure. How much profit do you expect to make? An optimum price for any menu item depends on its value to all concerned. The value to the operator is a matter of how it contributes to the profit. The value to the consumer is that the price be fair and reasonable. As an owner or manager you must establish objectives for profit in your pricing policies. Both economic and strategic objectives should be pursued when prices are set.

Restaurant owner-operators' philosophies of the right way to price is as diversified as their opinions on the best training methods for waiters or their views on politics or religion. Each believes their own pricing method to be the best.

As discussed in chapter 5, the cost of a product limits what you can charge for it and also indicates whether or not you can profitably sell the product in the price range that you set.

The pricing methods shown in this book are procedures widely used in the industry in one form or another. Pricing is always based on a markup of cost. Some operators will even include overhead when arriving at cost while others will use only raw food cost (the most common method). In some instances where the preparation labor is significant, direct preparation labor will be added to raw food cost. The combination of raw food cost and direct preparation labor is referred to as *prime cost* and will be covered in detail later in this chapter.

Exclusive reliance on a cost approach to pricing can create a menu with an improper balance of prices that is insensitive to market conditions. While costs must be recovered in the price charged, basing prices upon cost alone will not communicate value to the customer. Pricing is a function of demand, competition, and cost. Whenever demand is greater than supply, pricing methodologies that favor higher prices will increase gross profits and average checks, which can be effective in maximizing revenue. On the other hand, if customer counts are flat and strong competition exists for the products and services, such pricing could be disastrous.

The market ultimately determines the price one can charge. If you charge too much, your customers will go somewhere else. However, it is important to interject a warning at this point. Lower prices do not automatically translate into *value* and *bargain* in the minds of customers. Having the lowest prices in your market may not bring customers or profits. Too often operators engage in price wars through discount promotions and find that their market image falls along with their profit on each sale.

Demand and Market-Driven Pricing

What it basically comes down to is that prices can be either market driven or demand driven, and depending upon the uniqueness or monopolistic aspects of the menu item and operational concept, the approach to pricing will differ. Prices that are market driven must be more responsive to competition. Menu items that are relatively common, such as those found on most restaurant menus (e.g., hamburgers, steaks, fried chicken, prime rib, etc.), in markets where customers have a wide choice of where to go for such items must be priced rather competitively. This approach must also be used on new items being introduced or tested, before any substantial demand has been established. Prices that are market driven tend to be on the low to moderate side.

This is contrasted to those prices that are demand driven, where the customers openly ask for the item and where there are little if any alternatives in the market. Perhaps it is a specialty item or signature food item that can only be obtained at one particular restaurant. Consequently, a monopoly of sorts is created, and along with the monopoly comes pricing advantages. Thus prices that are demand driven will be higher, at least until the demand starts to wane due to competitors offering the product or changes in customer tastes. Prices will eventually stabilize and become more competitive.

Cost Markup Theory

Costing out an entree and accompaniments is a relatively objective and logical process. Establishing a price for it is more of an art and is more subjective and intuitive. Whatever the pricing methodology, there is no single method that can be used to mark up every item on any given menu. One must employ a combination of methodologies and theories.

When properly carried out, prices will reflect food cost percentages, individual and/or weighted contribution margins, price-points, and desired check averages as well as factors driven by intuition, competition, demand, and consumer price perceptions. One has to price appetizers, entrees, desserts, and side orders differently, depending on a number of indirect

cost considerations and the market. In other words, quantitative approaches to pricing that do not consider the qualitative factors may be inappropriate for the market.

What, then, is the proper price to charge? From the customers' point of view, it is the price that makes them buy. From the sellers' perspective, the best price is the one that moves the product and produces a profit. Prices can reflect such factors as atmosphere, service, entertainment, and unique product presentation. Customers sense an additional value in being able to receive additional amenities.

With pricing being examined on a continuum (see fig. 6-1) from the lowest price that will still return a minimum profit to the highest price the market will bear, demand sets the ceiling, cost sets the floor, and competition determines where on the pricing continuum the actual price will fall (Pavesic, 1989; Shaw, 1992). Finding the ideal price-point is not easy. One perspective is to charge the highest price you think the customer is willing to pay. When you take this approach, your operation must be on the cutting edge of food, service, and ambiance. The concern is that if you price the product too high, you will drive potential customers away, and if you price too low, you will not earn the additional profit that you could have, and you will not gain additional customers.

When you chose to price at the high end, customers will be more critical of the food and service they receive. Think about your own dining experience. If you go to one of the budget family steakhouses and order a steak priced at $5.69 and it is a little tough and chewy, you might not say anything to your server or cashier when you leave. You filled up on the salad and food bar and felt you got your money's worth. On another occasion you go to an expensive steakhouse and order a steak that costs $19.95, and you have a few bites that you cannot swallow. Will you say anything? Most certainly.

If your operation has a "monopoly" in the marketplace and demand exceeds supply, pricing at the high-

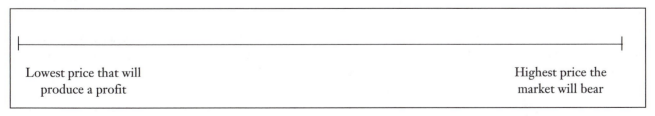

Lowest price that will
    produce a profit

Highest price the
    market will bear

FIGURE 6-1. Pricing Continuum

est price the customer is willing to pay will not result in a reduced demand, and if prices were lowered, demand would not increase enough to make up for the reduced profits.

The extreme opposite approach is to charge the lowest price at which you can still make a reasonable profit. When this approach is taken, customers almost always will comment on the reasonableness of the prices, the large portions, and the high quality of the ingredients. However, the operator does not optimize the revenue or profit with such prices. Perhaps they can charge more and still have the customer feel that they received a great value for their money.

The two pricing extremes, the highest the customer is willing to pay and the lowest that can be charged and still return a reasonable profit, both have their negative aspects. If you price too high for your market, sales may be lowered due to reduced demand. If prices are lower than customers are used to paying, demand may be high, but lower prices may result in less than expected profit levels.

Should one start off high and then reduce prices the way many department stores and auto dealers merchandise "sales"? Are we better off starting low and gradually increasing prices? Precise answers depend on the nature of the operation and the products themselves. What is the market position of the restaurant? Is it a leader or a follower? What about the customer counts: are they flat or increasing faster than supply? What stage of the marketing cycle is the concept or menu item in, that is, new, maturing, or declining?

Obviously trendy, new, and popular operations can charge more than outdated or conceptually obsolete operations. One of the main causes of conceptual obsolescence is failure to change with the times. The new places put the old ones out of business.

Menu Additions and Deletions

Separate and distinct from menu pricing decisions are decisions having to do with the addition or deletion of items from the menu. How often is a manager or owner required to make changes in the printed menu? There is no standard answer that will fit every situation, as timing and sales circumstances will vary from restaurant to restaurant. The years 1994 and 1995 have seen change and revival for the restaurant industry. Changes have come to pass in both menus and

decor. The most frequent menu changes will occur in restaurants that are small, upscale, have higher menu prices, and are frequented by food-wise customers. New items are regularly added and slow sellers are removed. An evaluation of the menu sales mix is regularly conducted to identify sales trends. Demand will be the critical factor for any menu change. Any item must sell its fair share to remain a part of the menu. With the careful recording and tabulation of sales and production records, you can determine the menu items that are selling. With this knowledge, you adjust your menu offerings and sales efforts accordingly.

Retention or deletion of the menu item can be judged by the factors listed in chapter 3 concerning menu acceptability. Some menu changes may be dictated by availability of foods and the prices of these menu items in the local market. The original concept of the restaurant and menu may have been created for one market but must be changed with the times to attract a changing customer base. The classification chart at the end of the chapter will aid in the determination of menu treatment, sales analysis, and pricing of food items (see fig. 6-9).

MENU PRICING METHODS

The methods described here are those currently in use throughout the foodservice industry. Only you, as the owner or manager of a restaurant, can make a judgment as to which is best. You can adapt, combine, or modify as your situation requires. If it works—use it.

Method 1—Nonstructured

This system is probably the simplest menu-pricing method in the world. You simply go to someone else's foodservice operation, take his menu away with you, and copy his prices. This may sound strange, but it has been done, probably by the same people who are advertising restaurants for sale in Sunday's paper, since conditions in any two types of foodservice operation will always be different.

This method is inadequate because it assumes that the customers make their purchase decisions based on price alone and it does not recognize the cost differences in ingredients, labor, and operating expenses incurred by different restaurants. It also fails to account for the many other factors that influence the purchase decision, such as product quality perceptions, ambiance, service, and even location.

This method is also inadequate because it does not take cost into account. Every independent operation has different costs, and unless each one is buying the exact same products and paying the exact same prices for them, they will not realize the same profit by selling menu items at the same price.

If, for example, we wanted to go into the hamburger business and copied McDonald's in every way but their name and logo, including offering the same menu at the same prices, we would not end up with the same operating profits even if were able to match them in sales dollar for dollar. The reason is that our costs would be much higher. Their corporate buying power and economies of scale allow McDonald's to purchase food and paper supplies at much lower costs than any signal unit operator could ever achieve.

Do not be tempted to follow another operator's method of menu pricing, no matter how successful his operation seems. There may be operational factors of which you are not aware. The owner may own his own building and may not be paying any rent. The owner may have fourteen children who work in the dining room and receive no pay except room and board. If you do not know the internal aspects of the operation, the system will not work for you. You must tailor your system to your own operation.

Method 2—Factoring

The factoring system has been in use a long time. To determine a menu sales price, the raw food cost is multiplied by an established pricing factor. You first establish the food cost you would like to have, say 37 percent; then you divide this into 100, and come up with 2.7 as your factor. The percentage you establish as your food cost standard divided into 100 will always equal the multiplying factor. By multiplying the raw food cost by the multiplying factor, you will establish a menu price. The formula is

Raw Food Cost × Pricing Factor = Menu Sales Price

A second way to compute this is to divide the known or desired food cost percentage into the actual cost (taken from a standardized recipe) to determine a selling price.

$$\frac{.533}{.37} = \$1.44$$

Obviously, if you are satisfied with this profit, you can set prices by this method.

The factoring system is popular in foodservice operations because most owner-operators are not mathematicians. It is probably also the easiest way to price a menu. However, there is a serious flaw in this conventional pricing methodology: not every item can be marked up to achieve the same food cost percentage. There are a number of reasons why this is true. First, factoring overprices high food cost items, such as steaks and seafood, and underprices low food cost items, such as soups, pasta, and chicken. Since prices are not exclusively based on cost of ingredients, factors such as competition, uniqueness of product, and plate presentation will enter into the pricing decision. In addition, costs are not equally divided across all menu items. Labor and overhead costs will differ on each item. A single markup to achieve a 37 percent food cost assumes incorrectly that a gross profit of 63 percent will cover remaining costs and leave the desired profit percentage. Some menu items require little or no labor to produce while others require extensive labor. Prices must be adjusted up or down according to the indirect factors and psychological pricing considerations covered in chapter 5. This is why pricing cannot be reduced to a simple formula or markup over cost.

Method 3—Prime Cost

The prime cost method was introduced by Harry Pope, who operated Pope's Cafeterias (and later Forum Cafeterias) in St. Louis and Kansas City, Missouri. He noted that certain items on his menu had very low food costs and considerable labor involved in their preparation. Examples of items that incur more labor costs than raw food costs are homemade soups, pastries, decorative garnishes, canapes, and hors d'oeuvres. He also observed main entrees requiring cleaning, peeling, cutting, breading, partial cooking or other time-consuming pre-preparation and processing. He felt the added labor element needed to be reflected in the total cost of the item. On items to which he added direct labor, the conventional method of marking up only raw food cost omitted a significant part of the cost incurred in making these items.

Direct labor is defined as that labor which is being incurred as a result of making an item from scratch on the premises. Direct labor is that labor involved in the pre-preparation of menu items. Examples include butchering meats, cutting vegetables, baking pies and cakes, peeling and deveining shrimp, etc. The operator incurs the direct labor charge of the meat cutter, salad maker, and baker because the restaurant manufactures its own products in-house. If the operation were to purchase the ingredients in convenience form, such as precut steaks, precut vegetables, premade salads and dressings, and baked goods from suppliers, it would not incur the labor expense to prepare such items from scratch. However, the precut steaks and frozen or ready-to-eat pies and cakes will cost the operator more per pound or per unit of purchase, because the price will reflect both raw food cost and labor for processing. Therefore, items prepared on premises should also reflect both the raw food cost and direct labor.

In order to assign direct labor costs to the specific menu items causing the labor to be incurred in the first place, you must divide your menu into two categories: those menu items needing direct preparation labor and those that have little or no direct labor. Labor that cannot be charged directly to specific menu items is designated as indirect labor, and its cost is allocated evenly across all menu items (just like overhead expenses). Wait staff, line servers, and cooks used to "finish cook" items are examples of indirect labor. Remember, direct labor is essentially initial preparation labor, not the final cooking to order for the customer.

The cost of direct labor can be determined by having management and employees note the time periods they are involved in direct preparation activities each day. What you are actually conducting is a time-and-motion study. Not all of a kitchen worker's time will be classified as direct labor. For example, the head cook may cut steaks only 20 percent of the time. The rest of the time he or she may be working on the serving line plating food or finish cooking entrees. Only the time used to cut steaks is considered in the prime costing method.

By noting the amount of time an employee needs in the preparation of a recipe, the labor cost per unit can be determined. Monitor employees, noting the time it takes to assemble ingredients, utensils, and equipment. This is referred to as the "get ready stage." Washing, peeling, cutting, trimming, weighing, mixing, breading, and preliminary cooking such as parboiling and blanching could be considered direct labor. Do not forget to include the cleanup process that concludes the task. Once the time has been determined, the labor cost can be easily calculated by multiplying the hours by the hourly wage. This labor cost is then divided by the number of pies, salads, or steaks produced to determine the labor cost per unit. When this is added to the raw food cost, prime food cost has been determined.

If one elects not to recognize the direct labor aspect of menu pricing, the cost of steak cutting, baking, or salad preparation will be charged to menu items that do not benefit from the labor. Spaghetti, baked chicken, prime rib, and other items with little or no direct labor must carry an unfair burden of recovering the expense of the meat cutter or baker. Prime cost methodology allocates the direct labor *only* to the items that caused the labor to be incurred in the first place.

Those that argue against prime cost say that direct labor will be covered by spreading the cost throughout the entire menu sales mix. However, smart operators quickly realize that they are not assured of selling one spaghetti for every steak sold. They recognize the benefit of a method that equitably costs out each item to obtain the necessary return.

To demonstrate this pricing methodology, we offer the example of a steak cut on premises (direct labor). The raw food cost is inclusive of salad, potato, and bread.

Top Sirloin Steak: Raw Food Cost $4.50

We further assume the following:

Food Cost Percentage: 37%
Total Labor Cost Percentage: 25%
　Direct Labor: 25% of Total Labor or 6.25%
　Indirect Labor: 18.75% (25% −6.25%)
　Direct Labor Cost Per Steak: $.25
Overhead Expense Percentage: 28%
Profit Percentage: 10%

The prime cost method for pricing the steak would be as follows:

Raw Food Cost of Steak and Accompaniments: $4.50
Direct Labor Cost Per Steak: $.25
Prime Food Cost: $4.75 ($4.50 + $.25)
Prime Food Cost Percentage: 43.25% (37% + 6.25%)

Prime Food Cost Menu Price: $10.98
($4.75/.4325)

In summary, the steps in determining the prime cost markup are:

1. Determine the percentage of Total Labor that is Direct Labor. (.25 × .25 = 6.25%)
2. Add the percentage of Direct Labor to the desired Food Cost Percentage to get the Prime Food Cost Percentage. (.37 + 6.25 = 43.25%)
3. Add the Direct Labor per unit to the Raw Food Cost of menu items requiring Direct Labor and divide by the Prime Food Cost Percentage to get the Suggested Menu Price. ($.25 + $4.50/.4325 = $10.98)

The 10 percent profit is still achieved with a price of $10.98.

Prime Cost @ .4325 × $10.98 = $4.75
   Indirect Labor @ .1875 × $10.98 = $2.06
   Overhead @ .28 × $10.98 = $3.07
   Total = $9.88
   Profit = $10.98 − $9.88 = $1.10 or 10%

Pope's system is essentially the factor system with a built-in direct labor factor. This methodology is used *only* on menu items with high amounts of direct labor.

Method 4—Actual Cost

The actual pricing method (see table 6-1) accomplishes the goal of any menu-pricing system: to include profit as part of every price on the menu. A menu-pricing system always develops to a point where all the cost factors and profit have been established and covered. Using the actual pricing method you are beginning to develop a complete system, but you are not doing it to the degree that it *should* be done.

In setting up an actual pricing system, the first step, once more, is to establish a food cost; we will use $0.37. For this example we will use a total labor cost of $0.26; this is not direct labor, but the total labor cost, including management. This then gives us a total food and labor cost of $0.63. You can arrive at this labor cost by a time-and-motion study or by determining the percentage of the labor cost from your profit-and-loss statement.

Next, use the profit-and-loss statement to get the variable cost, fixed cost, and profit (see table 6-2). The two principal variable costs, food and labor, have been covered by the food and labor amounts used above. Any other variable costs are picked up as percentages from the profit-and-loss statement and are used in the formula. Now we add our fixed cost percentage and, finally, a profit percentage.

We calculate the dollar amount of $0.63 by costing the standardized recipe and calculating a percentage per dollar of the cost of each menu item for total labor. Then we determine a percentage for all other costs and profit by dividing sales into the recorded costs of each additional profit-and-loss cost item and profit. When these figures have been established, we can set up an equation.

The two parts of the procedure are as follows. In the calculations in table 6-3, the menu price is established as 100 percent or X; the fixed and variable costs

---

TABLE 6-1

ACTUAL COST METHOD

Raw Food Cost (dollars)
+ Labor (dollars)
+ Variable Cost (percentage of sales)
+ Fixed Cost (percentage of sales)
+ Profit (percentage of sales)
= Menu Price

TABLE 6-2

PART 1. DETERMINATION OF COST

Costs from P&L Statement

Food Cost	.37	Variable Cost*	=	11.05% of sales
Labor Cost	.26	Fixed Cost	=	20% of sales
		Profit	=	10% of sales
Total Food & Labor	.63	Total	=	41.05%

*Other variable costs not including food and labor

TABLE 6-3

PART 2. CALCULATION

1. Selling Price = X or 100%
2. Fixed and Variable Costs and Profit = 41.05%
3. Food and Labor = .63
4. Food and Labor = 100% − 41.05% = 58.95%
5. .5895 X = .63
6. X = .63 ÷ .5895
7. X = $1.069 Menu Price

plus profit are 41.05 percent; food and labor total $0.63. So the menu selling price equals 100 percent minus 41.05 percent, giving us a percentage of 58.95, representing food and labor. In other words, 58.95 percent of our selling price is equal to $0.63.

Method 5—Gross Profit

The gross profit method of menu pricing is designed to determine a specific amount of money that should be made from each customer who comes into the operation. It is based primarily on past financial statements, customer counts, and guest check analyses. Here is how it works.

A foodservice operation has:

$100,000	Sales (Food)
− 40,000	Food Cost
$ 60,000	Gross Profit Serving 20,000 Covers (Customers)

These figures are based on a one-year operating period. A careful customer count has been kept, which makes it easy to determine the gross profit per check or an average gross profit per customer. The gross profit is divided by the number of customers, and an average gross profit of $3 is established. Keep in mind that this is not net profit. It is profit after the raw product was paid for, but nothing else.

Having established this figure, this system requires adding any extra meal items and the gross profit to the price of the food to arrive at a selling price for each menu item. Referring to the menu, we determine the extra items that will be served and price these to find out their total cost.

A complication may occur in using this system if the owner-operator runs a salad bar, whether it is a large salad bar or a limited one. Probably the best so-

lution is to use the highest cost on the salad bar per person rather than to try to find out an average cost (see table 6-4). (See chap. 5 to calculate the price per person for the salad bar.)

All the extra menu items that are included in the total meal should also be included in the menu price. The next procedure is to determine the cost of the entree item from the standardized recipe. In our sample problem we will use chicken, steak, and lobster. The cost of each entree item is calculated as follows: half-chicken, $0.75; steak, $2.50; lobster, $3.50. List the entree cost and then add the cost for the extra menu items, previously determined as $0.50; then add the average gross profit of $3.00 from the previous year.

It is interesting to compare this with selling prices based on a 40 percent food cost shown in table 6-6 to see the difference in menu prices shown in table 6-5.

With the gross profit method of menu pricing, the higher-priced entree items are brought down to a lower price. This system largely benefits the customer who tends to choose from the expensive menu items and penalizes the customer who is looking for the less expensive items. This system uses figures based on past financial records and a pro forma budget or budget forecast, and it assures the owner-operator that he is going to make a predetermined sum of money on every customer.

This system is currently in use in a steakhouse with a predetermined gross profit factor for appetizers, entrees, desserts, and accompanying items. The gross profit factor for each of the menu categories is worked out. This system has predetermined that for each item sold on the menu the restaurant will receive a specified gross profit. The individual items are priced according to a required gross profit figure.

TABLE 6-4

EXTRA MENU ITEMS

$0.20	Salad Bar
0.10	Baked Potato
0.10	Bread and Butter
0.05	Plate Garnish
0.05	Coffee
$0.50	Total Cost of the Nonentree Items

TABLE 6-5

	Entree Cost	Extra Menu Items	Gross Profit	Menu Price
Half-Chicken	$0.75	$0.50	$3.00	$4.25
Steak	2.50	0.50	3.00	6.00
Lobster	3.50	0.50	3.00	7.00

A principal consideration in the gross profit pricing method is that each customer will share equally in all of the costs associated with the serving of the meal. This method assigns a portion of all fixed and operational costs to the pricing system. The costs are assigned a share; the determination of a share is based upon the history of the operation, taken from the profit-and-loss statement. The system is easily adapted and can be used advantageously to price banquets or other catered events. The gross profit system lends itself well to the costing and determination of a sales price where known customer counts are predetermined.

The gross profit method is probably more adaptable to an institutional operation, such as a hospital foodservice, where it is essential to ensure a certain return for each participant every time a meal is served. The costs of operating change less rapidly in the institutional area, and records are more accessible. In some commercial operations, where the profit could easily be worked out for each category of item and where these categories are not presented as part of an inclusive menu, this method is also applicable. A gross profit would have to be set up on each of the categories of items.

The problem with this system is that it is hard to adjust for any serious decline in business or for major price fluctuations. It breaks down unless the operation runs at a pretty steady level, because it must be based on a projection of total number of customers if the operator is to get the amount of money he is going to need in income.

The gross profit method is a good system; it will work except where rapid and drastic price and/or customer changes are encountered. These distort the actual costs or expenses, since food cost is not the important concern in this system. Gross profit is the important factor; it assures continued net profit for the operation.

Method 6—Base Price

The base price method is a system in which, as the first step, the base price establishing the entree cost is developed from a customer-check distribution graph. This is a system in which the menu items are priced at a certain level to satisfy the market. For example, the "beef and beverage" specialty operations frequently find their market to be the $10 check group.

The first question then becomes, "What can be served for $10?" This system starts with the menu price and then works backward to the profit. It is very much like the actual pricing method but done in reverse; the amount that can be spent on raw product is established last.

The $10 figure simplifies the example; whatever other figure represents the desired price to be paid by the customer can easily be substituted. The figure used should be what is actually spent per customer in the operation. A distribution curve of all checks must be made to determine the average check; then a statistical analysis is made to find out what that check is (see fig. 6-2).

The answer can also be obtained from a forecast or a projection of the preferred type of customer. How much income or how many dollars should be spent by the customer? Whether it is established by check distribution, the statistical analysis of checks, or by predetermining the desired type of customer, the average or the median can be established. In our example it is the customer who will pay $10 for his meal. This customer will have to be provided with an entree or a meal that is going to run about $10.

With this method there must be a known market, because the selling price is designed for that market. Using this information, the owner-operator can go from the selling price to the point where he knows how much he can spend on the raw product and still

TABLE 6-6

SELLING PRICE BASED ON 40 PERCENT MARKUP	
Half-Chicken	$ 3.15
Steak	7.50
Lobster	10.00

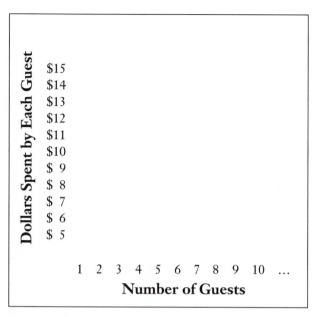

FIGURE 6-2. Chart for Determining Distribution of Check Averages

maintain his required net profit. Price value relationship and customer perceived value are critical points to the success of this pricing system.

The profit-and-loss statement or pro forma budget will establish average percentages of the desired profit, and, using a projection, forecast, or the information from the profit-and-loss statement, the percentage of profit can be set. In this example it is a 10 percent profit. Since 10 percent of $10 is $1, that becomes the profit goal. The overhead figure is established next. If the rate is 27 percent (of $10), the overhead figure is $2.70. If labor is running at 26 percent (of $10), labor cost is $2.60. These figures, derived from the profit-and-loss statement, provide a total of the amount of money to be spent for items other than food.

From the profit-and-loss statement, calculate the following:

$$\text{Profit} = 10\% \times \$10, \text{ or } \$1.00$$
$$\text{Overhead} = 27\% \times \$10, \text{ or } \$2.70$$
$$\text{Labor} = 26\% \times \$10, \text{ or } \$2.60$$

The same percentage requirements for profit, overhead, and labor as previously stated can also be derived from the forecast, budget projection, or actual records of past operation. Subtracting $6.30 ($1 + $2.70 + $2.60) from $10 shows that $3.70 could be spent on raw product.

In other words, any costed standardized recipe with a raw product that costs less than $3.70 can be served and will provide a standard profit while meeting the necessary overhead and labor costs. Information from the check distribution chart will show what price level the operator should not go above or below. Also, he can determine the number or percent of each price range for entrees by dividing the total in each range by the total number of guests.

Method 7—Forced Food Cost

The final pricing method to be considered is an extension of a system first developed by the Texas Restaurant Association. This system seemed impressive at the beginning, but it became clear, after a considerable period of use, that it did not provide some of the essential information needed to price the menu. After further study and use of this system, it was established that the amount set forth as the menu price is really determined by the market.

This system is based, first of all, on the following consideration: operators have to charge enough to stay in business. They must also, as the risk of loss or spoilage increases, make sure they are making a reasonable profit. As the risk goes up, it is only right to charge more for the product. The increase in risk may be, for example, spoilage or no sale for an item, but whatever it is, be sure you have provided for enough profit to cover it.

Volume takes care of a lot of ills and a lot of operating errors as well. However, the opposite is also true. The lower the volume, the higher the markup needed. The pricing system markup is based on some elementary laws of economics.

1. The amount set for any price is determined by the market.
2. To charge more than the price acceptable to the market will cause customers to go elsewhere for the product.
3. To charge less than the price acceptable to the market will cause a loss to the enterprise.
4. As the risk of loss or spoilage increases, the more essential it is for the foodservice operator to take a higher markup.
5. As the risk of loss or spoilage decreases, the foodservice operator may take a lower markup.
6. The higher the volume, the lower the markup can be.

1 Medium Markup	2 Low Markup
– & +	– & –
High Volume High Cost or Risk	High Volume Low Cost or Risk
3 High Markup	4 Medium Markup
+ & +	+ & –
Low Volume High Cost or Risk	Low Volume Low Cost or Risk

FIGURE 6-3. Sales Matrix Graph

7. The lower the volume, the higher the markup needs to be.

Taking the Texas Restaurant Association method outlined here one step further requires an analysis of the menu. Every item on a menu can be fitted into one of the four categories that make up the following matrix (see fig. 6-3).

High Volume—High Cost
High Volume—Low Cost
Low Volume—High Cost
Low Volume—Low Cost

Or, stated another way:

Popular—Not Profitable
Popular—Profitable
Not Popular—Not Profitable
Not Popular—Profitable

Ideally, every item on a menu would be a high volume/low cost or popular/profitable item, but real menus do not work out that way. However, the proper category should be determined for each menu item (see fig. 6-4).

We have elected to classify the categorizations of menu items as winners, marginal (by either sales or profit), and losers. Each one of these categories may require a different strategy on the part of the operator.

A *winner* is best dealt with by a strategy of maintaining very high standards of preparation and service for this item. Have a high presence in the operation for dealing with customers and getting feedback from them about this item. Make the item highly visible through the written menu or by verbal presentations by the service staff. Try to direct the sales of this item to people you believe to be your good customers who would do verbal advertising for you. Recognize immediately any market change in the sale of this product as reflected in customer demand. This item may require its own written standards, as well as constant supervision and immediate retraining of personnel when any variation is seen in the product's standard. Do not add any item to the menu that may cause a significant variation of sales in one of your winners.

The *marginal by sales* items can be relocated on the menu for greater visibility. Or take them off the menu and run them only as specialty items on a selected basis. Keep your regular patrons aware of this item and ask if they are satisfied by it, in the hope of increasing sales. Reduce the price of the item to attract new patrons to that particular item and increase its popularity. Check your competition to ensure that you are giving more value and quality and better dining experience on the same item. Do not permit substandard service or food to cause a decline in sales. Eliminate other unpopular menu items in an effort to increase the demand for this one. As above, use strict enforcement of standards to reinforce the market demand for this product.

FIGURE 6-4
Sales Matrix Form

Menu Item	Cost/Risk		Sales		Markup or Profit
	High	Low	High	Low	

Marginal by profit items can all be tested by increasing their price and determining the change in sales that results. Such an item can be hidden on the menu to cause fewer orders to be placed for it. If a marginal by profit item is one that has been made famous by the restaurant, it must be left on the menu, and the menu must be adapted to the item. To lower costs and improve profit margins, adapt your systems of preparation and service for increased operational efficiency. Monitor the decline of your profits and attempt to draw from competitive markets for increased sales and profits. Consider reducing the sizes of portions or modifying your recipe for a better profit margin. Combine items that are now on your menu that may offer better value in the eyes of your customers—and better profit to you. Rename the items on your menu when they are relocated, and repackage them in an effort to maximize profits.

The most obvious way to deal with the **losers** is to remove them from the menu, but look at other considerations. Could the cause be obsolescence of this item, where old customers are tired of it but new customers not yet attracted by it? Have you failed to monitor current trends in foodservice so that the competition has come in and offered what is currently popular? And the physical maintenance of a restaurant may cause trends in decreasing numbers of people and profit. Renovation and menu revision may be needed to stop decline.

These are all factors submitted for your consideration in adapting your menu based upon the four classifications given above for menu items. Our obvious goal is that of the profitable-popular.

The Texas Restaurant Association has used computers to develop certain percentages of markup for all the items on a menu. They are based on a consensus of the state's leading operators as to what their average markups are. However, their classifications do not permit you to take advantage in your pricing of such basic economic rules as the higher the risk, the more right the operator has to a profit; the lower the sales, the higher the markup should be.

After further work with this system, it was concluded that this system of pricing required a range of percentages rather than a standard, static percentage for an item. It is only by using such a range that the system will work. The range was developed as follows.

Basing the pricing approach on the previously stated economic laws, the matrix of the items and a range of percentages turned out to be a most workable variation of the forced food cost system. It is reasonably simple to apply this system in an operation.

The forced food cost system bases the sales price of an item on the required profit of individual menu items. It permits the food cost percentage to float to the level required for the right profit on each item.

The basics of this system of menu pricing are a well-planned budget broken down into operating (overhead) costs, raw food costs, labor costs, and the markup that gives the desired percentage.

This food cost formula is developed in just six easy steps.

1. Determine your operating (overhead) cost per dollar volume.
2. Budget your labor cost.
3. Determine the desired profit (markup) percentage per dollar of business.
4. Add operating (overhead), labor, and profit-wanted percentages to arrive at your cost without food percentage.
5. Subtract your cost without food from 100 points, the value of the dollar in cents.
6. Determine the raw food cost from the standardized recipe and add the raw cost of extra trimmings. Divide the answer by your raw food cost to find the value of each food point. Then multiply the 100 points by the value of each food point, and you have your menu (selling) price.

Using the costed standardized recipe example given in figure 5-6, we can do the following calculations to determine raw food cost and menu price.

TABLE 6-7	
Menu Categories	**Profit Markup Range Percentage**
Appetizers	20%–50%
Salads	10%–40%
Entrees	10%–25%
Vegetables	25%–50%
Beverages and breads	10%–20%
Desserts	15%–35%

TABLE 6-8

	Percentage of Dollar
Operating (overhead) Cost	27%
Labor Cost	26%
Desired Profit (markup)	+15%
Total Cost without Food	68%
Value of Dollar in Points	100 points
Total Cost without Food	−68
True Raw Food Cost	32 points

TABLE 6-9

Chicken-Fried Steak

Meat	$0.500
Flour	.007
Egg	.012
Bread crumbs	.014
	$0.533

$$\frac{\$0.0167}{32 \text{ points} \,|\, \$0.533}$$

$0.0167 per point × 100 points = $1.67

Menu Price: $1.67

There may be other factors involved in a particular operation that would keep the markup percentage from coming out even. Based on the conditions of operation, your discretionary decisions may indicate that a specific menu item could fall at *any point on the continuum* for a profit markup range; you may have a mid-high or a mid-low rather than an absolute high, medium, or low. While a medium reading is acceptable, the high end, or near it, is preferable (see fig. 6-5).

You have to work this out for your menu items in your own foodservice operation. You determine what markup is needed based on the cost/risk factor and on volume. In a recent exploration of this method, ice cream was used as an example. Ordinarily, ice cream, since it is kept frozen, does not involve a risk. However, one operator was having so much trouble because of the potential for pilferage in his ice cream service that it was one of the highest risk items on his menu.

MENU SALES MIX ANALYSIS

The value of a well designed and priced menu to a restaurant trying to achieve its cost and profit objectives cannot be overstated. Over the past fifteen years, three principal methodologies for menu sales analysis have served to inspire others to offer new interpretations in their efforts to come up with an even better way to analyze the menu sales mix. The holy grail of this methodology is to discover a method of menu analysis that will ensure the identification of items

FIGURE 6-5
Profit Markup Form

	Sales		Cost/Risk		Item	Markup or Profit
	High	Low	High	Low		
1		X	X		Apple Pie	H
2	X		X		Shrimp Cocktail	M
3		X		X	Strip Steak	M
4		X	X		Lobster Tail	H
5	X			X	French Fries	L
6	X		X		Hamburger	M
7		X	X		Club Sandwich	H
8	X			X	Milk Shake	L
9		X		X	Fried Chicken	M
10	X		X		Rib of Beef	M

that should be priced or positioned differently in order to achieve necessary check averages, a lower overall food cost percentage, and an adequate gross profit.

In this section we present a comparison of the three principal methodologies, referred to as the Miller Matrix, Menu Engineering, and Cost/Margin analysis. While more recent methodologies have built upon the components used by these three principal menu sales analysis methodologies, the elements of food cost, menu item popularity, and contribution margin remain the most important elements of the menu sales mix, and for that reason they are presented here. The sales mix data is presented in spreadsheet format and is shown in table 6-10.

The Miller Matrix was the first recognized attempt to identify menu items that are both popular and low in food cost. In the Miller Matrix, every item on the menu is placed into one of four categories: popular and low in food cost; popular and high in food cost; unpopular and low in food cost; unpopular and high in food cost. The categories are later given names that correspond to the aforementioned order, which are, respectively, winners, high volume/high cost marginals, unpopular low cost marginals, and

losers (see fig. 6-6). The sales mix sought is to have at least 60 percent of the sales mix made up of items in the low food cost categories. If less than 60 percent of the items sold are in food cost, the overall food cost percentage shown on the monthly income statement will be higher, and profit will be reduced.

The methodology developed by Michael Kasavana and Don Smith in their book *Menu Engineering*, completely ignores food cost in their analysis. The problem they saw with the Miller methodology is that "you bank dollars, not percentages." In their analysis, it really doesn't matter what the food cost percentage is; what matters is the contribution margin of each menu item. The contribution margin is the difference between the menu price and the food cost. For example, a steak dinner with a food cost of 48 percent and selling for $14.95 brings in $7.77 in gross profit, whereas half a broiled chicken selling for $8.95 with a 40 percent food cost only brings in $5.37.

The Miller methodology identified the low food cost items as the ones to sell. However, Kasavana and Smith discovered that for the most part, low food cost items are typically the lowest priced items on the menu. Consequently, the overall average check will be

TABLE 6-10

LUNCH WORKSHEET

	Raw Food Cost	Menu Price	Number Sold	Weighted Food Cost	Weighted Sales	Weighted Contribution Margin	Food Cost(%)	Sales Volume	Food Cost(%)	Contribution Margin Dollars	Category
1. Cup Soup	$0.10	$0.65	33	$3.30	$21.45	$18.15	15.4	H	L	L	sleeper
2. Bowl Soup	0.18	0.80	36	6.48	28.80	22.32	22.5	H	L	L	sleeper
3. Low-Cal Plate	0.98	2.95	22	21.56	64.90	43.34	33.2	L	L	L	sleeper
4. Chef Salad	1.42	3.25	25	35.50	81.25	45.75	43.7	H	H	L	problem
5. Dieter's Plate	0.86	2.50	22	18.92	55.00	36.08	34.4	L	H	L	problem
6. Turkey Sandwich	0.58	2.10	30	17.40	63.00	45.60	27.6	H	L	L	sleeper
7. Grilled Ham & Cheese	0.61	2.45	23	14.03	56.35	42.32	24.9	L	L	L	sleeper
8. Grilled Cheese	0.46	1.45	51	23.46	73.95	50.49	31.7	H	L	H	prime
9. BLT	0.73	1.95	69	50.37	134.55	84.18	37.4	H	H	H	standard
10. Fish Sandwich	0.95	2.25	28	26.60	63.00	36.40	42.2	H	H	L	problem
11. Ham Sandwich	0.57	2.25	18	10.26	40.50	30.24	25.3	L	L	L	sleeper
12. Patty Melt	0.95	2.25	38	36.10	85.50	49.40	42.2	H	H	H	standard
13. Turkey Club	0.91	3.45	35	31.85	120.75	88.90	26.4	H	L	H	prime
14. Chicken Sandwich	0.76	2.65	25	19.00	66.25	47.25	28.7	H	L	H	prime
15. Hamburger Platter	0.94	2.65	62	58.28	164.30	106.02	35.5	H	H	H	standard
16. Deluxe Hamburger	0.82	2.25	32	26.24	72.00	45.76	36.4	H	H	L	problem
17. Deluxe Cheeseburger	0.94	2.45	26	24.44	63.70	39.26	38.4	H	H	L	problem
18. Deluxe Mushroom Burger	1.02	2.65	7	7.14	18.55	11.41	38.5	L	H	L	sleeper
			582	$430.93	$1273.80	$842.87	33.8%				

H—high   L—low

FIGURE 6-6
Miller Matrix

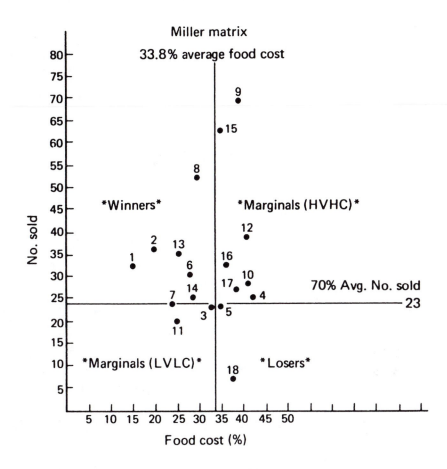

lowered and optimum total sales revenues, needed to reduce fixed cost percentages, may not be achieved if you adopt this strategy. The only way you can make up for it is by increasing the customer count for each meal period.

The Menu Engineering methodology was developed and tested at a supper club restaurant with a high average check and where management sought to optimize the average check for each customer. The restaurant was a special occasion destination restaurant, and customers were less price-conscious than when eating out during the week. In country clubs, where price inelasticity is present, Menu Engineering is the preferred method for optimizing the menu sales mix.

Menu Engineering borrows from the Boston Consulting Group's Portfolio Analysis Methodology and classifies each menu item into one of four categories according to popularity and individual contribution margin or gross profit. An item is either popular with high contribution margin, popular with low contribution margin, unpopular with high contribution margin, or unpopular with low contribution margin. They also gave the categories names; respectively, stars, plowhorses, puzzles, and dogs (see fig. 6-7).

While Menu Engineering seems appropriate in operations where demand is inelastic, such as supper clubs and country clubs, the majority of commercial restaurants could not effectively compete by promoting items with high contribution margins, because these items typically are the most expensive items on the menu (e.g., steaks, seafood, prime rib). Not only would their customer counts fall, they would also see an increase in their overall food cost percentage. Similarly, the Miller methodology was effective for the fast-food and low average check operations, but not for higher priced restaurants in markets where customer counts are flat or declining.

The Miller Matrix sales analysis methodology concentrates on items with low food cost, while Menu Engineering focuses on items with high individual contribution margins. Both methodologies treat food cost and contribution margin as mutually exclusive, when in fact both need to be considered simultaneously. The omission of one or the other contributes to a biased and incomplete interpretation of the menu sales mix.

Subsequently, Pavesic introduced a methodology that combines the elements of Miller and Menu Engineering and calls it Cost/Margin. The name is derived

FIGURE 6-7
Menu Engineering Matrix

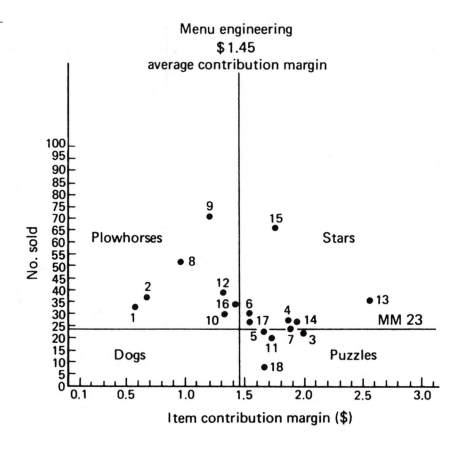

Menu engineering
$1.45
average contribution margin

Plowhorses — Stars
Dogs — Puzzles

No. sold

Item contribution margin ($)

from food *cost* and contribution *margin*. Both of the previous methodologies are extremely biased to either food cost percentage or individual contribution margin. The premise of cost/margin is that the optimum sales mix is the one that simultaneously optimizes dollar contribution margin relative to achieving the lowest overall food cost percentage while optimizing total sales revenues. Note that the word *optimize* is used and not *maximize*. One cannot simply ignore food cost percentage, because if total sales do not increase enough to offset the increase in food cost, there will be no improvement at the bottom line.

All three methodologies use the same data to develop their spreadsheets and graphs. The three elements are sales volume or number sold for each menu item, raw food costs, and menu prices. For purposes of replication and comparison from one period to another, the cutoff points for food cost percentage, popularity, and weighted contribution margin are standardized with formulas.

The food cost percentage cutoff point for high/low is total weighted food cost ($430.93) divided by total weighted sales ($1273.80), giving us a figure of 33.8 percent. Any menu item with a food cost equal to or less than 33.8 percent is classified as low food

cost. The "weight" is given by the number sold for each menu item, which is multiplied by the respective raw food cost and menu price. The weighted food cost and sales for the total menu sales mix are summed for the numerator and denominator in the formula. The weighted food cost percentage is sometimes referred to as "potential food cost" or "standard food cost" by different authors of cost control books.

For purposes of comparison, we will also establish the cutoff point for popularity of menu items and use a variation of the formula used in Menu Engineering. The formula is:

$$\frac{1}{\text{No. of Menu Items}} = \times.70 \times \text{Total Items Sold}$$

$$\frac{1}{18} = \times.70 \times 582$$

$$.0555 \times .70 = .0388 \times 582 = 22.6 \text{ or } 23$$

Any menu item selling 23 or fewer is classified as being unpopular or having low sales volume, and any selling more than 23 is classified as popular or having high sales volume.

Cost/Margin analysis uses the weighted contribution margin rather than the individual contribution margin used in Menu Engineering. By using the weighted contribution margin, both popularity and contribution margin can be combined and provide three discreet elements for the analysis as opposed to two. The contribution margin cutoff point is calculated by dividing the total weighted contribution margin ($842.87) by the total number of menu items (18) giving us the cutoff of $46.83. This is saying that any menu item that contributes more than $46.83 has a *high* contribution margin.

Cost/Margin recognizes food cost percentage, popularity or number sold, and contribution margin in its analysis of the sales mix. Each menu item can be classified into four categories according to its food cost percentage and weighted contribution margin. A menu item is either low cost/high contribution margin, low cost/low contribution margin, high cost/high contribution margin, or high cost/low contribution margin. These are referred to respectively as Primes, Sleepers, Standards, and Problems (see fig. 6-8).

It should also be pointed out that a popular selling menu item with a moderate individual contribution margin will contribute more dollars to the overall contribution margin than an unpopular item with a high individual contribution margin. A popular item already has an established demand with the customers and will be more easily merchandised than an unpopular item.

Cost/Margin analysis is the least biased of the three methods and combines the key elements of both the Miller and menu engineering methodologies. This is not to say that cost/margin analysis is the end all and one best method for menu sales analysis. It is simply offered as an alternative for those commercial restaurants who position their operations between the fast-food/low average check operations using the Miller methodology effectively and the high average check operations and country clubs with price inelastic demand using Menu Engineering for their menu items.

When competition is great in a particular market segment and price becomes important to the marketing strategy, Cost/Margin offers a good middle-of-the-road alternative. When the data is transferred from the spreadsheet to a graph, greater analysis can be conducted. By starting with the menu items plotted closest to the cutoff lines, one can quickly identify the best candidates for change and the best strategy (e.g., changing portions, changing prices, changing menu positioning, etc.).

When performing this analysis, every item on the menu must be counted. However, it is recommended

FIGURE 6-8
Cost/Margin Graph

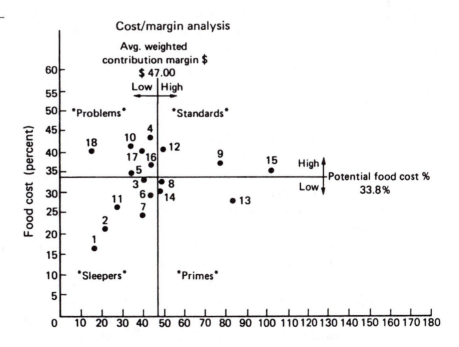

that one analyze appetizers, desserts, salads, and entrees separately. The popularity of the menu items will significantly impact their positioning and ranking. For example, while every customer who enters the restaurant will purchase an entree, fewer than 40 percent will purchase an appetizer or dessert. Therefore, appetizers should be judged against other appetizers and desserts against other desserts. Decisions on positioning and pricing items within the dessert category is done relative to other desserts offered and which ones you prefer to sell.

The quadrant in which the menu items fall will give some indication as to the pricing and positioning strategy one would likely find successful. Those items falling into the Prime quadrant are the items we want to sell the most because they are both low in food cost and high in weighted contribution margin. Note that with either the Miller methodology or Menu Engineering, one is biased to either low food cost or high individual contribution margin.

Cost/Margin seeks to find the items that have both low cost and high contribution margins. Primes are likely items that are "specialties of the house" and can be priced more like specialty goods than common commodities. Because they are signature items in the restaurant, the closest thing to a monopoly we will experience is created. These items can be priced at whatever the market will bear. Every successful restaurant needs to have two or more prime items to lower food cost and increase the contribution margin.

Items that are high in food cost and bring in a sizable contribution margin are referred to as Standards. Steaks, prime rib, and seafood platters are examples. Because these items are popular and usually offered by competitors, prices are kept moderate to encourage sales. The items usually possess high food cost percentages but are also some of the highest priced menu items and therefore return sizable dollars in contribution margin. An operation wants to have a portion of its sales mix in this category, but it must be held to less than 40 percent of the total sales, or the food cost percentage will increase.

An operator who is a leader and not just a follower in menu development will always have a few items in the Sleeper category. These are likely to be new items being test-marketed to see how the clientele responds to them. Hopefully, some of these items will develop into Primes or Standards. These items are characterized by both low food cost and low contribution mar-

gin. The low contribution margin is due to the lack of popularity of these items. These items are likely to have inexpensive ingredients and small markups because there is little demand for these items. They can be new fad foods or ethnic dishes with limited appeal. Together with the Primes, at least 60 percent of the items sold should be generated from these items. Sleepers also serve to soften the high cost standards that are offered on the menu. The innovative operator uses Sleepers to diversify the menu, to keep regular customers from becoming bored, and to broaden the customer base.

Although sales volume (popularity) is not directly plotted on the cost/margin graph (as it is in Menu Engineering and Miller), by virtue of the fact that weighted contribution margin is plotted, many of the more popular items will fall to the right of the vertical average weighted contribution margin line, while the poor and marginal sellers will usually fall to the left. Menu items falling closest to the average lines are the easiest items to move in the sales mix with small price changes and menu repositioning.

The fourth quadrant identifies the Problems. These items have little or no positive impact on the sales mix. They are high in food cost and low in contribution margin. An operation would like to have as few of these items as possible. However, while Problem entrees should be eliminated if possible, some items will not be dropped from the menu. Consider children's meals, where quite often children's items are offered at or below cost. Holiday Inn is running a promotion where children traveling with adults will eat free. In other restaurants, birthday cakes or free desserts are offered to those celebrating their birthday at the restaurant.

Decisions regarding which items to eliminate, reposition, or raise prices on cannot be made exclusively on quantitative data. Marketing policy dictates that children's menu items will never qualify as Primes. Optimum contribution margins and lower food costs will be achieved when the predominant sales mix is made up from primes and standards.

The plotting of each menu item on the graph shows the majority of items falling to the left of the average weighted contribution margin line (AWCM) and concentrated in the Problem and Sleeper quadrants. The numbers adjacent to the plotted points identity the individual menu items. The items closest to the intersecting lines indicate the items to be examined first for improvement. For example, the hamburger platter (15) is a candidate for a price increase that will allow it to move closer to the food cost line and the primes quadrant. Other variables that will influence food costs and contribution margin, such as portions, accompaniments, and ingredient costs, should also be considered for some adjustment. Suggestive selling and table tents could also be employed to achieve some improvement in financial contribution to the overall menu sales mix.

Items in the Problems quadrant need to be adjusted as well by altering many of the same variables mentioned previously. Removal from the menu can be considered if the item is not popular and has a high food cost. The grilled cheese (8) and the chicken sandwich (14) are borderline Primes and can be strengthened through a combination of pricing, accompaniment changes, and merchandising. The graphing of the data makes it much easier to see such close relationships that are not evident from the spreadsheet.

A significant benefit of this kind of quantitative analysis is that it can demonstrate unequivocally that changes made in menu positioning, price, and marketing strategy either work or do not work. Opinion is replaced by empirical proof. One can calculate the number of menu items in the prime quadrant and whether the weighted food cost percentage and weighted contribution margin increased or decreased from one period to the next.

When doing this analysis, it is recommended that you use the sales records for a representative period of business activity. A month's worth of sales and cost data is preferred over just a week's. It should be conducted prior to making changes in menu prices or design, or a minimum of twice a year when static menus are used.

Cost/Margin menu sales mix analysis combines the three key elements of sales volume (popularity), food cost percentage, and contribution margin to provide an unbiased perspective for making menu pricing and positioning decisions. Management can therefore make more precise and measurable changes in menu pricing, product presentation, and positioning on the menu to improve the overall sales mix and to achieve the lowest food cost percentage and the optimum dollar contribution margin.

Whatever method you elect to use as the option for menu sales mix analysis the following criteria should be considered: the sales history for every item on the menu (number sold), the menu price of each item, and the food cost for each item. With these three pieces of information, any of the three methods described can be used. Item popularity and contribution to margin are the critical factors of analysis and choice menu decisions. The systems, when in place, will aid in menu analysis for item replacement, relocation on menu, repricing, or redoing the recipe.

All of the three methods will assign a rank and category to menu items, and the way of dealing with the items is based upon this ranking. All three methodologies use the same data to develop their spreadsheets or graphs and ranking assignments.

Strategies for Dealing with Primes, Stars, Winners, etc.

Once an item has been classified in one of the four categories and plotted on the graph, one can develop a number of strategies to improve the status of the item. The best strategy is to determine which strategy will be the most effective and the least objectionable and noticeable to the customer.

※ Primes, Stars, and Winners

1. Maintain its high menu visibility.
2. Test it for price elasticity and increased price.
3. Keep its quality high and its portions adequate.
4. Monitor its quality and presentation to insure high standards.
5. Promote it internally with table tents and suggestive selling.

※ Standards, HVHC Marginals, and Plowhorses

1. Test it for price elasticity by raising prices.
2. If its portions are large, consider reducing portions.
3. Move it to a less noticeable position on the menu.
4. If it is a signature item, consider raising the price.
5. Promote low cost, high contribution margin items.
6. Reduce its accompaniments.
7. Shop for better prices from purveyors to lower cost.
8. Develop and offer substitute items that are similar and lower in cost.
9. Combine it with low cost ingredients to lower cost.

※ Sleepers, LVLC Marginals, and Puzzles

1. Prominently display it on the menu.
2. Promote it internally through suggestive selling, sales incentives, table tents, displays, and menu boards.

3. Lower prices; e.g., discount it for "early birds."
4. Increase its portions, add to its accompaniments, and increase its quality.
5. Rename it and heavily merchandise it; turn it into a signature item.

✳ Dogs, Losers, and Problems

1. Raise its price.
2. Lower its ingredient costs.
3. Hide it on the menu.
4. Develop substitute items and promote them.
5. Combine it with less expensive ingredients.
6. If all else fails, remove it from the menu.

PRICING DECISION

As mentioned, there are no absolutes and no shortcuts in menu pricing, but one valuable aid to making decisions is a pricing system comparison chart (see fig. 6-9).

On this form you list the pricing system used on each of the menu items. (The example shows three of the methods just discussed.) There is also space to make comparisons with the competitors you consider most likely to share the same market. A check of the competition should include prices, food quality, and dining circumstances to give you some idea of the range of prices that can be charged. The assumption is that the quality of product, service, and ambiance is the same in your restaurant as that of the competition.

The next to last column covers what I refer to as "gut feelings." This is the value judgment that you make about the price, related to sales and profit. We all use such nebulous elements in pricing a menu, no matter how unscientific this may be.

The Best Method for Pricing

The pricing of the menu item by the operator at some point on the pricing continuum is a strategic pricing decision. The actual price determination is a tactical pricing decision. The right price of a product in the mind of the customer is largely an extrinsic indicator of perceived quality and value. Implicit in this theoretical pricing perspective is that perceived quality and value are directly linked to the circumstances surrounding the visit (eat-out versus dine-out) and the position of the operation in the marketplace (trendsetter versus follower). In addition, the customer's subjective perceptions of your operation may not be aligned with your own, which can impact your price-value image. This perspective points out the importance of knowing how customers perceive your operation and the circumstances leading up to the visit. Visits during the week may find the customer more price consciousness than on weekends, when social and entertainment motives drive purchase decisions.

The price set by the operator positions the operation at a certain price-point in the market. If the position is at the higher end of the market, a discounted price can sometimes enhance a customer's perceived

Menu Item	Factor	Gross Profit	Menu Engineering	Gross Margin	Forced Food Cost	Competitor Highest Price	Competitor Lowest Price	Value Judgment	Final Menu Price

FIGURE 6-9.   Chart for Comparing Menu Prices

value. However, while this tactical pricing is effective in the hotel industry, high average check restaurants rarely employ discounted prices. Management must choose a pricing strategy that is consistent with the overall positioning of their operation and the menu item.

Operators are more comfortable with a pricing method that is driven by some quantifiable formula. Keep in mind that the success of any pricing methodology is influenced by many indirect cost factors including, among others, location, competition, clientele, and the restaurant concept. What works for one may not work for another (see chap. 5).

The sales strategy should be to get the customer to focus on positive intangibles of the menu item rather than its price. Concentrate on value and not price. Granted, customers will have a budget in mind when they are dining or eating out. Your restaurant provides a complete dining experience that includes personal service, ambiance, and amenities. Intangibles are very important in the purchase decision. These are factors other than the food and beverage you provide and for which you can create value.

Price becomes an issue in the purchase decision only in relation to the value received by the customer. Therefore, whether budget or luxury restaurant or catered event, what the customer perceives in the way of value is far more important than price.

By using a desktop publishing system, current technology allows you to make instant changes in prices and menu items. We are no longer limited by time in modifying menus. Changing a printed menu has become as easy as changing the price and lettering on a cafeteria menu.

Try to maintain price ranges that are generally within what you normally expect, and that, by check analysis, you have found your customers are willing to pay. There are instances where the owners have taken the attitude of charging as high a price as the market will bear and customers have been willing to pay this price. Conversely, other owners have elected to charge as little as possible, as long as they can make their margin, which makes them highly competitive. Some restaurateurs suggest a price range in which the most expensive item on the menu would be no more than twice the amount of the lowest-priced item. Others suggest a price differential of $5 to $8 between the highest and lowest items. The price range must take into consideration the type of restaurant and make exceptions of daily high-priced items, such as live lobster. The price range may be determined by a chart that analyzes check distribution or a pro forma budget of anticipated check averages.

Price Increases

Some restaurant goers equate high prices with higher quality and better service, although this is not necessarily true. Thus, there are certain destination restaurants where price is not a factor. Such operations are known for the quality of their product and the excellence of their service. People will go to such establishments and pay any price.

Continued maintenance of quality standards is essential after any price increase. The slightest decline in quality will instantly alter the customer's attitude. There is no substitute for food quality, there are no shortcuts for specified preparation methods, and there is no excuse for poorly presented foods. As a manager, be careful to pay attention to the smallest details, to ease the shock of price increases.

Taking the Anxiety out of Menu Price Increases

Of all the business decisions a restaurateur has to make, one that brings on considerable anxiety is having to raise menu prices. When to raise prices and how to do it is just as critical as the amount of the price increase itself. Whenever price increases are made, the operator mentally prepares for some adverse customer responses. The feedback not only comes in the form of spoken complaints but also in the form of the dreaded dropping customer counts. Regardless, the operator must occasionally adjust prices to maintain an adequate profit contribution. However, especially in highly competitive markets, noticeable price increases will drive some customers away.

Increases in menu prices should always be carried out in as subtle and inconspicuous manner as possible. The less attention called to price increases, the less chance there will be of adverse customer reactions. The following suggestions are offered as ways to disguise menu price increases.

1. Use odd-cents increments in prices, such as 25, 50, 75, and 95 for the digits to the right of the decimal point. When an item is increased within this

range, for example, from $7.50 to $7.75, it is less likely to be noticed by the customer. Some operators will price to the next exact penny, for example, $7.72 or $7.86; however, the two most popular terminal digits are 5 and 9, for example, $7.95 or $7.99.

2. Never raise prices when you change the design of your menu. If you are going to a new menu format and design, raise prices on the last reprint of the old menu. Regular customers are more likely to expect price increases when they see a new menu and will scrutinize prices. You will be able to point out that the new menu has old prices.

3. Never cross out old prices and write over with a pen or put stickers over old prices. This will call more attention to price increases, and you are better off reprinting the menu.

4. Hold off as long as possible when price increases require you to go to the next higher dollar amount, for example, $8.95 to $9.25, as these changes are more likely to be noticed.

5. Position items that have been increased to less visible locations on the menu, and emphasize lower priced substitutes in their place.

6. When a price increase cannot be delayed, consider increasing the portions or accompaniments and creating a "new" and "improved" version of the item. In this way, you are providing added value and not just raising the price.

7. If portions and accompaniments are already substantial, consider reducing portion size or eliminating an accompaniment in lieu of a price increase. This may be the appropriate strategy in a highly competitive market that is price elastic. Many operators have dropped either the potato or the salad on dinners and lunches as an alternative to increasing prices.

8. Never raise prices across-the-board. It is rarely warranted and it is much better to raise only a few items at a time with each reprinting of the menu. Start by increasing the most popular items a small amount instead of the slow selling items. A $.25 increase on items that account for 60 percent of the items sold will return more than a $.95 increase on items accounting for less than 10–15 percent of the items sold.

9. Items that fluctuate in cost should not be priced at all and should be listed on the menu as "market priced." Have the server quote the current price on a daily basis.

10. Do not align prices in a straight line down the right side of the menu. Doing so makes prices stand out from descriptive copy and influences the customer's selection decision (see figs. 2-6, 6-10 and 6-11). Never list items in order from low to high, either. Place them in mixed order with more expensive items at the beginning and end of the list. To make the prices less prominent, place the price immediately after the last word in the descriptive copy. Menu price increases should only be made once or twice a year, because today's customer is more likely to notice when it is done and a proportion of cus-

---

FIGURE 6-10
Recommended Placement of Prices

POISSONS ET CRUSTACÉS

NORWEGIAN SALMON STEAK BARBECUED ORIENTAL STYLE
With Sesame Seeds, Ginger, and Garlic   17.75

DOVER SOLE FILLETS POACHED IN SAUVIGNON BLANC
With Shrimp, Mussels, and Mushrooms   20.00

GULF SNAPPER FILLET
*In Romaine Lettuce with Beaujolais Sauce
and Mediterranean Eggplant*   18.00

DOVER SOLE FILLETS SAUTÉED GOLDEN BROWN
"Noisette Butter" and Lemon   20.00

Swordfish Piccata
With Linguini, Spinach, and Tomato Concasse   17.75

SEA SCALLOPS WITH LEEK SAUCE
In Phyllo Crust   18.00

FIGURE 6-11
Traditional Alignment of Prices

SPECIALTIES	
Veal Francese	20.95
A Trotters tradition with lemon-butter sauce	
Veal and Mushrooms	19.95
Tender milk-fed veal sautéed in fresh cream with mushrooms and herbs and served with fettuccine	
Sautéed Medallions of Veal	19.95
With tomato and basil cream sauce	
Calves Liver	13.95
Thinly cut and sautéed with bacon and raspberry-vinegar sauce	
Long Island Duckling	15.95
Roasted and grilled with thin pancakes; served with a black currant sauce	
Rack of Spring Lamb	20.95
Roasted with an herb breading and served with a rich brown sauce	

tomers will reduce the frequency of their visits or go to a competitor.

SUMMARY

It has been said of most retail products and services that the buyer, not the seller, determines the price. Therefore, restaurant owners must be able to make a reasonable profit selling their products and services at the price customers are willing to pay. Regardless of the methodology used to mark up food and beverages, the prices charged by commercial foodservices must not only cover all product costs but must also meet a profit objective that has been established by management. The established prices will actually determine the amount of business that a restaurant will draw, and price will influence the type of clientele who are attracted to the establishment. When considered in this light, the difference between making the proper pricing decision and making the wrong decision is critical. The optimum price must include some contribution to the organization's profit, and the price must be deemed fair and reasonable by the public.

Pricing decisions are critical because price will impact the customer's selection process in the choice of a restaurant and the menu choice. Menu prices will affect the sales mix of the menu and can change the food cost, average check, gross profit, customer counts, and overall revenue. Costs of the menu items must be known in order to measure profit contribution on each sale. Some costs can be accurately calculated and assigned to specific menu items, while other costs must be subjectively allocated. Costs serve as a reference to begin developing a pricing strategy. Many restaurants are experiencing intense competition, rising operating costs, labor shortages, and falling customer counts. Such factors will definitely have an impact on profits. Therefore, the pricing policy is a major factor in developing a strategic plan to meet such obstacles.

The prices listed on the menu will influence which menu items will sell, and therefore, they impact the overall profitability as well as the sales mix. Menu items will differ widely in cost, popularity, and profitability. Thus, pricing is not a simple matter of cost markup but an intricate combination of factors that involve both financial and competitive elements.

Pricing cannot be reduced to a purely quantitative exercise, although we try; in menu pricing one must consider the subjective and psychological aspects of the customer's purchase decision. The considerations for the price will include price-value perceptions of customers, and this price-value consideration will include whether they have received their money's worth when they pay their check. Their consideration will also involve combinations of price, quality, portion size, ambiance, service, and psychological factors, which makes the pricing of a menu both a science and an art.

The objective of any pricing system or method is to arrive at that combination of prices that maximizes customer counts (demand), improves the average check, and improves contribution to margin while achieving the lowest overall food cost percentage relative to optimizing revenue and profit. Whenever someone says that your prices are on the high side compared to the other restaurants they have called, think of John Ruskin, the British writer, art critic, and reformer of the nineteenth century, who said, "There is always someone willing to make something a little worse and sell it a little cheaper, and those who consider price only are this man's lawful prey."

References

Henderson, B.D. "The Experience Curve Reviewed: The Growth Share Matrix of the Product Portfolio." *Perspectives*, no. 135 (1973).

Kasavana, Michael L., and Donald J. Smith. *Menu Engineering: A Practical Guide to Menu Analysis*. Rev. ed. Lansing, Mich.: Hospitality Publications, 1990.

Miller, Jack E. *Menu Pricing and Strategy*. Boston: CBI Publishers, 1980.

Pavesic, David V. "Cost/Margin Analysis: A Third Approach to Menu Pricing and Design." In The Practice of Hospitality Management, 291–305. Westport, Conn: AVI, 1986.

Guidelines for Success

MENU EVALUATION

A profitable operation hinges on a successful menu, but every operation is different. What works in one restaurant may not work in another. As I have said before, "If it works, use it." Menu self-evaluation is a continuing procedure that you can use to compare your menu with the theories behind menu development. The form that follows will help you perform such an evaluation. (Some of the points may not be applicable to your operation.)

The influence of the computer is beginning to be felt in the restaurant industry in the selection of menu items, in their costing, and in the analysis of sales. Consumer dining trends are now being charted on the computer. The design of menus ultimately will be affected by the computer. As a result, the menu is in a state of transition along with the continuously changing habits of a mobile society. Be prepared for change—it is the key to your restaurant's success.

Menu Evaluation Checklist

We are suggesting the forms at the end of the chapter be used for self evaluation of your menu. The evaluation form is self-explanatory, and the scoring will indicate any need you may have for menu revisions.

Input on Menu Design

The menu is such an important part of a restaurant's cost control and marketing plan, it needs to be planned with the same care and attention given any major capital expenditure. Input from owners, managers, chefs, and customers must be part of the planning process.

Number of Menus

The number of menus used will reflect the type of food, time, and place food is served or consumed. All menus need to be designed and planned with the same care and attention given to marketing, cost control, and communication objectives.

Price Spread

Generally, the highest priced complete dinner or a la carte entree should be not greater than 2.5 times the price of the lowest priced dinner. This does not mean that you cannot have entrees priced at higher than 2.5 times the lowest priced entree, but 90 percent of your entrees should be priced within this range. In addition, the prices you place on at least 75 percent of your appetizers and desserts must be compatible with entree prices. The appetizers should be approximately 35 percent of the entree price, and the majority of desserts should be priced within 25 percent of the entree prices.

The prices of wines by the bottle, carafe, and glass need to be similarly priced to reflect the average check sought and the cost of a single entree. The majority of wine selections need to be priced within a range that gives them price-value relative to entree prices.

Recipe Costs

There is no question about it, you must have accurate and up-to-date cost records on all menu items and accompaniments to effectively price the menu.

Menu Pricing Factors

Pricing cannot be reduced to a simple markup of cost or to an arbitrary check average. Other factors, such as competition, uniqueness of the item, and demand, all impact the price you can charge and the price the customer is willing to pay.

Sales Analysis

Menu sales mix analysis is a key function for cost control and marketing. If you are doing it less than four times a year, your menu may contain unpopular items. A minimum period of four weeks should be used to get an unbiased picture of customer preferences and your menu's strengths and weaknesses.

The Cover

The cover makes the all-important first impression, and it should be distinctive. Basic information contained on the cover includes the name of the restaurant or club and a logo.

Type Styles and Sizes

The text of the menu should be printed using two-thirds lowercase type. Exotic typefaces and italics should be used sparingly. Keep the number of type styles to three or less, and do not use fonts smaller than 12 point.

Menu Clip-Ons

If a clip-on menu supplement is used, design a specific area of the menu for it so it does not cover other menu copy. Generally, it is recommended to design clip-ons to be compatible with the regular menu in terms of paper color and type fonts. However, some menu consultants argue that if it is too familiar, it may not be noticed by the customer.

Menu Descriptive Copy

Copy must accurately describe the menu item. The more expensive the menu item, the more important it is for the copy to "sell" that item.

Eye Movement

The "gaze motion" one follows when reading the menu can be directed by the use of color, type style and size, graphics, illustrations, and photographs. Recognizing the value of the theory of primacy and recency, place the items you want to sell more in the places they are likely to be seen first or last. If a menu does not use "eye magnets" to call attention to certain sections or items on the menu, it is not fully utilizing the techniques of menu psychology in its design.

Use of Color

Colors used for the ink and paper can help in overall readability and with the ability to draw the reader's attention to certain menu items.

Paper

Paper texture, weight, and finish are also used to communicate to the customer as well as provide functional utility. The paper used can be coated or laminated to be moisture, oil, and wear resistant.

Pages/Folds

The three-panel, two-fold menu is growing in popularity. The three-panel menu offers up to six pages for menu copy. Even the front cover is being used to list menu items. A menu with extensive copy will often appear crowded when a single-fold, four-page menu is employed. If more than 50 percent of the paper surface is covered with print, graphics, and illustrations, the menu will appear crowded.

Signature Foods

Every restaurant or club needs to have a "house specialty." These items should be given special emphasis on the menu.

Wine Lists, Children's Menus, and Dessert Menus

If one tries to include these items all on a single menu, the menu grows in size and declines in merchandising effectiveness. Wines are best merchandised with their own menu. If you want to attract families with small children, a separate menu needs to be designed especially for kids. If dessert sales are important and you are proud of your desserts, a separate menu may be warranted.

No score levels are established for the rating forms. It will be obvious from your scores if you have a low score. The low score will indicate menu revisions are in order.

MENU EVALUATION CHECKLIST

1. Rate by percentages the input of the following individuals for the most recent menu revision.

	Design and Visual Appearance	**Menu Items**
Management	% _____	_____ %
Chef	% _____	_____ %
Printer	% _____	_____ %
Advertising Agency	% _____	_____ %
Artist/Graphic Designer	% _____	_____ %
Other _____	% _____	_____ %

2. How many separate and different menus are printed? Check all that apply.

Breakfast _____	Lunch _____	Dinner_____	Wine _____
Children's _____	Desserts _____	Banquet_____	Pool _____
Grill _____	Drinks_____	Other _____	

3. The price spread between the lowest and highest priced items in each of the menu categories is examined here. Please indicate the high and low price for the following items:

Appetizers	High _____	Low _____	_____
Salads	High _____	Low _____	_____
Entrees	High _____	Low _____	_____
Desserts	High _____	Low _____	_____
Sandwiches	High _____	Low _____	_____

Divide the lowest price into the highest price for each category above and write the number you get to the right. The value represents a ratio that indicates the difference between the highest and lowest priced items. For example, if the highest priced entree is $23.50 and the lowest is $9.95, the ratio is 2.3. This is saying the most expensive entree is 2.3 times more expensive than the lowest priced entree.

What is the per person average check for:

Breakfast _____   Lunch _____   Dinner_____

4. Indicate the number of menu items priced in each dollar range from the lowest to the highest price on each menu printed. For example, if the lowest complete dinner is $7.95 and the highest is $14.95, the range will start at $7.00–$7.99 and conclude with $14–$14.99.

Price Range	**No. of Items**	
_____to	_____	_____
_____to	_____	_____
_____to	_____	_____
_____to	_____	_____

checklist continues on next page

MENU EVALUATION CHECKLIST

checklist continued from previous page

Price Range   **No. of Items**

_____to _____   _____

_____to _____   _____

_____to _____   _____

_____to _____   _____

_____to _____   _____

_____to _____   _____

_____to _____   _____

_____to _____   _____

Menu Cost Factors

5. (a) Do you have up-to-date recipe and portion costs for every item on the menu? Yes _____ No _____

    (b) If you answered "no," what percentage of the items do you have current cost figures for? _____ %

    (c) How often are cost records updated? _____

Menu Pricing Factors

6. Which of the following is the most important consideration in determining the prices of your menu items? CHECK ONE RESPONSE ONLY.

    Gross Profit Return   _____   Competition   _____

    Food Cost Percentage   _____   Desired Check Average   _____

    Other_____   _____

Sales Analysis Factors

7. Do you monitor the popularity (sales mix) of your menu? Yes _____ No _____

    If yes, how often? By Meal Period _____ Daily _____

    Weekly _____ Monthly _____ Other _____

Menu Mechanics

8. (a) Does the menu have a separate and detachable cover? _____

    (b) Is the menu cover moisture and grease resistant? _____

    (c) Is the cover designed to complement the decor and style of the restaurant?_____

    (d) The length and width of the closed menu: _____ by _____

    (e) The length and width of the open menu: _____ by _____

9. (a) How many different fonts (styles) are used? _____

    (b) What is the smallest size type used? _____

    (c) What is the largest size type used? _____

10. Does the menu utilize clip-on menu cards for specials or luncheon items?_____

    If No, go to question 11

    (a) If Yes, is there a special location designated for the clip-on that does not cover up other menu items?

    _____

MENU EVALUATION CHECKLIST

(b) If the clip-on does cover menu copy, indicate which items are covered.

_____

(c) Is the clip-on professionally printed to coordinate with the regular menu? _____ Yes _____ No

Menu Copy

11. (a) Does the menu utilize descriptive copy on the majority of menu items? _____ Yes _____ No

(b) If descriptive copy is not generally used, indicate why.

_____ Space limitations _____ Items are common knowledge

_____ No one on staff to write copy

_____ Do not feel it is a factor in customer selection

_____ Other _____

(c) If descriptive copy is used, how would you rate the "sell power" of the copy?

_____ Original and unique style

_____ Somewhat ordinary and standard

(d) Does copy accurately describe the items?

_____ Yes _____ No

(e) Can the customer easily ascertain from the copy what accompanies the entree? _____ Yes _____ No

(f) Does the copy explain special ingredients and preparation methods? _____ Yes _____ No

(g) Is the menu organized into categories or sections, i.e., Appetizers, Sandwiches, Salads, Entrees, etc.?

_____ Yes _____ No

(h) Are the menu categories presented in the order the food and beverages are typically served/consumed?

_____ Yes _____ No

Artwork and Graphics

12. (a) When you first open or look at the menu listings, are your eyes drawn to any specific part of the menu?

_____ Yes _____ No _If yes, where? Indicate the page/panel and location on the page, e.g., "To the top right of the right-hand page."_ _____

(b) Are you aware of what caused you to focus on that part of the menu? If yes, what?

_____

(c) Does the menu contain any of the following (check all that apply):

_____ Artwork or Illustrations

_____ Photographs

_____ Graphic Design

(d) What techniques are used to draw your attention and catch your eye?

_____ Use of Color

_____ Use of Graphic Design (Boxes, Lines)

_____ Use of Artwork or Illustrations

_____ The Style of the Typeface

_____ The Size of the Typeface

_____ The Use of Color Screens

_____ Other _____ _checklist continues on next page_

MENU EVALUATION CHECKLIST

checklist continued from previous page

13. Comment on the colors used on the menu for the cover, the ink, or the paper.

    _____

    _____

14. Comment on the weight, finish, and color of the paper or material used in the menu cover and interior.

    _____

    _____

15. How many printed pages or panels does the menu use? _____

    How many folds does the menu have? _____

Signature Foods

16. Which item(s) on the menu would be considered signature foods for the operation? *Signature foods are those items which could be called "specialties of the house." They are usually so good or unique that customers will come specifically to partake in these items. In some instances, the item is so unique that the restaurant has a monopoly of sorts on the item.*

    _____

    _____

    Do these items receive any specific and noticeable emphasis on the menu?

    _____ Yes _____ No

    If Yes, what emphasis (e.g., larger or bolder type, different typeface, graphics, illustrations, contrasting ink color, placement on page, descriptive copy, clip-on, table tent, etc.)?

17. If you identified items that are signature foods and that are given special consideration in their placement on the menu, indicate as to which of the following earmarked the item for special treatment.

    _____ Low Food Cost   _____ High Gross Profit

    _____ High Check Average   _____ Easy to Prepare

    _____ Provides Competitive Distinctiveness   _____ Other

Wine List

18. (a) Is there a separate wine list? _____ Yes _____ No

    (b) How many different wines are offered?_____

    (c) Is wine also available by the glass? _____ Yes _____ No

    If Yes, indicate prices: _____

    Indicate the price range of bottled wines. Divide the highest-priced wine by the lowest-priced wine and indicate that number to the right. The number represents a ratio between the highest- and lowest-priced wines. For example, if the lowest is $12.94 and the highest is $125.00, the ratio is 9.65. This says that the most expensive wine is almost ten times the price of the least expensive wine.

    Bottled Wine   High _____   Low _____   _____

FIFTY TIPS FOR A SUCCESSFUL MENU

In the operational cost control and menu-development seminars I have led over the years, the following fifty ideas have been discussed as techniques for increasing sales and profit through the menu.

1. Establish budgets for comparison of forecasted sales to actual sales. Deviation of sales mix and costs at the end of an accounting period may cause a significant variation in the month-end totals. The budget is really a scorecard, so you can compare where you are to where you should be.

2. Increased prices are inevitable. There is a point, however, when customers will not accept the increase if it is not properly timed. The government is constantly announcing cost-of-living price increases or specific-product price climbs. Time a menu-price increase to national or regional publicity about raw-product price increases.

3. Determine what you are doing that is different or better. Many restaurants are serving less-than-spectacular food but in an environment and with service that make them very successful. Many others are serving well-prepared, quality food in a less-than-spectacular environment and with mediocre service, and they are successful. Price may not be a major customer consideration for food that is unique, food that has high quality standards, or for an environment that is unusual.

4. Keep records as your road map for the future. The details of your recordkeeping should enable you to isolate specific areas that are exceptions to your established standards. A high food cost percentage provides you with little information, but records indicating high cost for a specific commodity zero in on the target.

5. You may classify yourself in any price range you choose, but too wide a price range will tend to make your clientele stereotype you. Provide a range, but establish it by the clientele you hope to attract—high-, medium-, or low-priced. The wide range will tend to increase volume at the lower menu prices and will not give an equitable price spread. Range the prices within each of the classifications.

6. To control profit, establish systems for continuous monitoring of sales mix and recipe cost. The fluctuation of product cost makes it important to review prices and pricing methods a minimum of once per quarter. Any deviation from the forecasted sales mix is to be analyzed as quickly as this on the basis of the total cost/sales/profit relationship.

7. Your prices need not necessarily relate to the prices of restaurants surrounding you. The costs of overhead, labor, and product may vary considerably, and prices must be based upon what you need to charge for a profit.

8. Consider an a la carte pricing system. Many restaurants have gone to such a system. A number of customers surveyed have indicated that excessive amounts of food are served by restaurants. A la carte menus permit the individual to order the amount of food he wants and reduce waste.

9. Today's patron is more sophisticated than in the past and recognizes items of value on the menu. Failure to change prices as product and labor costs change may encourage patrons to take advantage of prices advantageous to them or to avoid high-priced menu items that they consider to be a poor value.

10. It is foolish to maintain the listing of any item that is not profitable to the operation only to increase volume. The loss-leader item must stimulate the additional sales of profitable items or the theory of the loss leader is destroyed and the item becomes a loss-of-profit item. Analyze secondary sales to validate the original intent of using a loss leader.

11. Some less profitable items will always be on the menu. Do not list or arrange the menu in any way that will assist in the sale of these items. Hide them to decrease sales. Make no effort to advertise such items, and recommend a policy of "no suggestion" of the item by service persons.

12. Investigate purchasing procedures and policies. After thorough analysis, be positive that your restaurant is obtaining the best-quality product at the lowest available price for the intended use of the product. Make price comparisons, do some specification-bid buying, and check prices for contract purchases.

13. Write a menu that offers a value concept to the guest using reduced portions, a variety of spices, and new methods of preparation.

14. Written preparation methods should be periodically reviewed; intended preparation methods and actual methods may vary considerably. Yields on many menu items are dependent upon cooking and preparation methods. Improper procedures often cause food waste and higher costs. The portion may be intentionally or unintentionally large.

15. Serving personnel will not usually do suggestive selling. However, if you can use table tents, buttons, or menu copy to cause the patron to ask the service person a specific question requiring a direct answer, suggestive selling may result. Get serving people to recommend high-profit items. Customers welcome suggestions.

16. Modify current recipes by the use of extenders or less-expensive ingredients—more potatoes, more crumbs, more pasta—but do not misrepresent the item as it is listed on the menu.

17. If yours is a cycle or combination static–cycle menu, use expensive, low-profit items less frequently on the menu. Such an item may become a once-every-two-weeks item instead of a weekly one.

18. By combining a lower-cost item with higher-priced items, you may decrease the portion of the high-cost product. The customer perception of value will be there because of additional food, but the actual cost will decrease. In some instances a price increase can be made because more food is being served.

19. Redesign the menu to increase the sales of high-profit items. Use primacy and recency in the list of menu items offered for sale. (If you are operating a cafeteria, relocate items so the most profitable ones are in the first two entree openings.)

20. A natural tendency on the part of an employee is to overgarnish a plate. Write a specification for garnishes and garnishment of every item. Calculate the cost of garnish into the menu price. Food must look attractive, but cost must be considered in total pricing. As the manager, you control the cost.

21. Eliminate holdover food on expensive or low-profit items. Forecast for a run-out time of holdover foods that are not cooked to order. Preparing food a second time is expensive. The second preparation and second-cooking shrinkage will almost double the cost per portion.

22. Instead of adding new items, emphasize a new method of preparation of an entree so that your pricing can effectively incorporate the change. The product cost of the ingredients of the new method is minimized and the total cost slightly increased. Emphasizing the preparation of the entree adds value perception by the patron and improves sales of high-profit entrees. Sales at a slightly higher price will greatly increase the contribution to margin.

23. Take advantage of other services that the restaurant offers to the guest. Through the menu or by communication from the server, merchandise carryouts or product that is manufactured for home use. See that all patrons are aware of any meeting facilities and catering operations at the restaurant.

24. Restaurant managers in every section of the country have indicated that any item listed on a chalkboard as the daily special will sell. Take advantage of holdover food, banquet overproduction, or special purchases to promote high-profit food items as chalkboard specials.

25. When a price increase is effected, the impact on your customers may be reduced by a change in the appearance or packaging of the product. Cutting sandwiches into three pieces instead of the current two-cut method, serving them open-faced, placing the food on the plate differently, or using a different-sized plate may all help reduce the impact on your customers.

26. A contradiction to two other methods previously mentioned is the fixed-price (or *prix fixe*) meal. For this, calculate a price that includes appetizer through dessert. Analysis of customer eating habits can determine the refusal percentage of categories of foods offered. The advantage is that, although the item is included in the price, it is not consumed by the guest.

27. An obvious way to increase profit is to sell more mixed drinks. Actually, to sell more beverages of any type will increase profits. If alcoholic beverages are going to be merchandised, develop special house drinks. Fruity limited-alcohol drinks have tremendous appeal to many drinkers. Wine is an excellent promotion because of the national publicity given wines. Promote nonalcoholic beverages as well.

28. The concept of one-stop shopping is not new to restaurants, but the thought is frightening to most persons in the industry. Vendors are willing to bid lower on the guarantee of a known volume of purchasing for a specified time period. Concentration of dollar volume creates considerable price leverage.

29. Inventory items can be segregated into three groups. Group A, sometimes called the critical few, will comprise about 20 percent of the total inventory items but will amount to approximately 70 percent of the dollar value of the inventory. Focus attention on where the money is being spent. Consider overproduction, overportioning, decline of quality by aging, and pilferage. Isolate items where you have your large dollar usage and control the purchase of these items.

30. Preparation waste control is a major factor of total cost. Conduct a study to decide whether to make or buy an item. In many instances, buying prepared or partially prepared products may substantially reduce total cost. Specific trim loss for products should be determined and spot checked on a random basis.

31. Conduct tests of yield amounts based on grade comparison. Often, lower-grade and lower-priced items will test to a higher plate cost per portion than a high-quality item with a smaller amount of trim. The final profit hinges on what it costs to put the item on the plate.

32. Continually explore for new products to improve labor and/or food cost. Utilize salespeople, employees, and your own eating experiences to explore new products or improved methods of preparation and presentation. Never let your past experience limit your vision for improvement.

33. Eliminate from your menu items that are not selling. These items require dollars of investment and will deteriorate from age to an unusable state because of lack of sales. Establish a sales standard or goal for each menu item and, if there is no justification for below-standard sales, delete the items that are nonsellers.

34. Provide all production employees with the equipment for correct preparation of the food item according to the recipe procedure. Calibrate on a specific time interval the temperature setting on all cooking equipment. Purchase and install timing devices wherever practical in the cooking or preparation process. Use mechanical devices and automation to assist in cooking.

35. Make portioning equipment available and train employees to use it. Standardize the utensils and serving pieces to the specified portion size. Standardize bowl and plate size or capacity to no more than the specified portion size.

36. Use a price and portion book. Every item on the menu should have a specified amount to be served for a specified price. The amount of the portion served should be cross-checked against the stated portion size on the standardized recipe. Conduct random audits on the accuracy of portions being served by your employees.

37. Staying within the bounds of prevailing sanitation and health regulations, you may be able to salvage some items from the table. Any food product that would be reasonable to rescue should be rescued and reused in the same or different form. Individual foil-wrapped butter pats, for instance, can be removed from the table, rechilled, and used again.

38. Until the manager takes command of production forecasting, the cooks will set their own production requirements. This usually means cooking all that is available. Decide and enforce the production schedules and amounts to be prepared, based on past sales records and anticipated increases or decreases in sales.

39. Determine how much food is wasted, destroyed, or unacceptable because of bad timing by your employees. Cold, overcooked, unattractive, or undercooked food will not be accepted, consumed, and paid for by your customers. Customize and systematize the timing of preparation and service to lessen the loss factor of improper timing.

40. Spoilage is a major cost factor for many operations. Have each department supervisor or head person complete a weekly report of loss from spoilage. Careful investigation and follow-up should indicate the responsibility for the loss. Take action to correct the cause and prevent a repeat of the loss.

41. High-risk and high-cost items should be on a continuous-count inventory system. Use visual checks or a physical count. High-cost merchandise needs a daily accounting to permit immediate action to be taken.

42. Poverty may be one of the best production-utilization teachers there is. Ask some of your employees how they would use some of the things you are throwing away. Survey your garbage for trim and underutilization of raw product.

43. Determine how much you are paying for the packaging of your product. A major cost factor of all products is the wrapper or container. The national average of labor productivity is 40 percent. Are there products that you are using that could be purchased in bulk and repackaged for better labor utilization and lower product cost?

44. If you do not receive merchandise, you cannot sell it. Set up a system of auditing and cross-checking for invoice payment. Require approval from two or more persons or systems before an invoice is paid.

45. Use a system of guest-check and cash-register recording devices that is self-auditing. Every food product that leaves the kitchen should be recorded and balanced against a cash/charge sales record and be balanced or audited on a regular basis.

46. Control free food to employees and guests. The authority to void checks should be vested in the manager on duty. Employees are entitled to specified food benefits, but the benefits should be controlled by a recording system. Surveillance of your food give-away should be monitored carefully.

47. When you increase the menu price of an item, determine the point where the customer says no. But remember that there is also a point when all that is humanly, physically, and mentally possible has been done to control the price, yet the price still must be increased.

48. If an item is in an unfavorable corner of the sales matrix and if the situation cannot be corrected, remove the item from the menu.

49. Close the restaurant entirely. This is the ultimate solution to cost control.

50. If you are unwilling to close, fire the manager. Somehow, owners always think this will increase profit and boost the volume.

Obviously, the last two suggestions are facetious. The object of these fifty menu strategies is to make suggestions that will enable you to have every menu item in the high sales–low cost corner of the pricing matrix. Some suggestions may be impractical or invalid for your specific operation. Creativity and flexibility are certainly criteria for successful business operation. These ideas on menu management are offered to stimulate your own creativity for adapting any one of them to increase the profitability of your menu.

Sample Menus and Comments

This chapter consists of menus selected from restaurants that best exemplify the theories and principles outlined in the preceding chapters. These menus all have one or more features of well-designed, well-developed menus. No single menu perfectly exemplifies all the principles given in this book. No one can copy and use someone else's menu, of course, but the samples here show features that can be adapted in designing your own menu. The menus shown in this section are not an endorsement of these menus but examples of the features that can be incorporated into your menu to improve it.

Certain menus illustrate the use of institutional copy and are a pledge of quality to the customer. They may trace the historical significance of their location or describe a family's involvement in the restaurant's operation. Certain of the menus in this section also include advertising, which can be used either on the interior or exterior of the menu to promote anything offered for sale by the restaurant.

Other menus demonstrate good principles of layout and design for promoting their signature items or special products. Some of the following menus show methods of listing or emphasizing menu items that have proven particularly profitable to them. There are also menus that have classic descriptive copy, and menus where an item's name follows a theme the owner is trying to establish for the overall operation.

Although none of the menus here follow every theory offered in this book, they are included to show what can be done in the marketing, merchandising, and layout and design of a menu, and they offer hints and suggestions of what you can do with your own. The menus shown in this chapter offer many adaptable ideas that any restaurant owner can use to better market and merchandise his or her menu.

Tony's

Tony's restaurant in St. Louis is definitely an upscale high check restaurant that can be classified as a destination restaurant (see chap. 1). The restaurant has won the Mobile five star award repeatedly through the years. This menu is an example of a static menu, but the menu is augmented by offering seasonal specialties and daily specialty items (see fig. 8-1). Servers make verbal presentations of individual food items as recommendations to the guests. A management team is used to develop the menu items that are offered on the printed menu. Sales, costs, and income for food and wine are recorded on computer programs, and the records are analyzed with computer calculations and management imput, so that any required changes can be made quickly. Both the food and wine lists for the restaurant are computer driven, so that changes in the printed menu and price can be made quickly if needed.

Primi Piatti

Fresh Ravioli 7.50
Agnollotti 7.50
Cannelloni, Tomato or Cream Sauce 8.00
Fettucine, Romano 7.50
Cappellini Carbonnara 7.50
Cappellini Primavera 7.50
Cavatelli Broccoli 7.50
Capelli d'Angelo, Marinara 7.50
Penne, Fresh Tomatoes - Basil, Arugula 7.75
Linguine, Fresh Clams 8.75

Soups 5.50

Risotto, Fresh White Truffles 15.00
Tonights Risotto see your waiter 9.00

Insalata

Tony's Salad 6.50
Tomato, Red Onions, & Anchovies 6.50
Tomato with Gorgonzola, Balsamic dressing 6.50
Bibb Lettuce, Artichokes, Hearts of Palm 6.50
Spinach, Avocado, Crumbled Roquefort 6.50
Baby Asparagus, Belgian Endive 9.00

Secondi Piatti

Seafood

Grilled Filet of Fresh Halibut 25.50
Fresh Dover Sole 28.50
Filet Mignon of Fresh Swordfish 26.00
Poached Fresh Salmon 24.25
Lobster Albanello 24.50
Grilled Scampi and Lobster Tail, Mustard Sauce 28.25
Linguine with Lobster, Shrimp and Crabmeat 24.00

Entrees

Veal & Beef Buonarotti 24.75
Veal Rib Chop, with
    Eggplant, alla Parmigiano 24.75
Veal Marsala, Wild Mushrooms 24.75
Veal, Lemon and Capers 24.75
Veal, Garlic Cream Sauce 24.75
Veal Cutlet Alla Milanese 24.75
Ossobuco, Risotto Milanese 24.75
Stuffed Quail / Beef Tenderloin Marsalla 24.50
Stuffed Breast of Quail, 22.75
Boneless Chicken Breast, Artichoke & Peas 18.75
Boneless Chicken Breast, Fresh Fruit Sauce 18.75
Risotto Milanese with Chicken 21.50

From the Grill

Veal Loin Chop Truffle Sauce 28.95
Prime Sirloin Steak 28.75
Prime Sirloin Steak, Sicilian Style 28.75
Prime Sirloin Steak Diavola 28.75
Filet Mignon, Chianti Sauce 28.25
Beef Tenderloin with Peppers and
    Onions, Brochette 19.95
Lamb Chops 27.00
Prime Rack of Lamb, per service 28.50
Chateaubriand 58.00

see back

FIGURE 8-1

As we witnessed the demise of the white table cloth, service oriented, high check average restaurant in the late 80s, Tony's continues to maintain its position as a destination restaurant on both a local and national level. Checking the *Ivy* and *Nation's Restaurant News* award winners, the number of such restaurants has decreased considerably. Reasons for the closings of these restaurants range from tax law changes, business downsizing, and changes in dining habits. However, Tony's remains strong in its operation at this level. Some internal changes have been made, but basically the ownership has never compromised the standards of the restaurant's food and service. Food and service are the standards that maintain the respected level of Tony's. See the comments of Vince Bommarito in chapter 3 concerning management duties to operations and guests.

Antipasti

Freddi

Vitello Tonnato 8.50
Smoked Salmon, Mascarpone Filling 8.50
Roasted Peppers, Fresh Mozzarella, Basil 7.50
Prosciutto with the Season's Melon 7.50
Pate of the house 7.50
Carpaccio, Truffle Oil 8.50
Tenderloin Tartare 7.50
Iced Shrimp 8.75
Fresh Beluga Caviar 40.00 per service

Caldi

Mussels our style 8.50
Shrimp in Garlic Butter & Wine 8.50
Snails, in a Fresh Artichoke Bottom 9.50
Stuffed Calamari 7.75
Sea Scallops, Black Truffles 10.50
Manicotti of Eggplant, Four Cheeses 7.50

Tonight's Antipasto   see your waiter

Pipe and Cigar smoking permitted in living room only.

Italian Dinner

Antipasto

Capelli d'Angelo Marinara

Veal with Wild Mushrooms
Arancini

Cannoli
Espresso
45.00

Italian Dinner for Two

Vernaccia   Cappellini Primavera

Swordfish Fra Diablo

Fontodi Chianti   Tenderloin Marsala
Classico   Italian Spinach

Tonight's Cheese - Fresh Fruit

Sambuca,   Tonight's Dessert
Molonari   Espresso
                   120.00

FIGURE 8-1.   *continued*

Applebee's Neighborhood Grill & Bar

This restaurant chain ranked forty-fifth in 1994, and in 1995 climbed to thirty-seventh in the *Restaurants and Institutions* top five hundred. Starting in 1988 the chain has grown tenfold to about 570 restaurants and is still growing.

Applebee's came to the market with a defined customer profile and entered the market with product and price to fit their market group. They have value, convenience, variety, and a relaxed family atmosphere. The restaurants are located near where their customers live. Taking advantage of the customer profile and casual dining group with an all day $8 to $8.50 per person check average, the company has established what they refer to as the ten dollar ceiling. They avoid breaking this dollar amount on the menu.

The corporation has gained strength through their cooperation with their franchisers for growth and sales. The menus have been varied by having at least four-per-year market menus that focus on different menu offerings (see chap. 2). As we have stressed in this book, know your market and cater to that market with foods and prices. The menu identifies the specialty foods as well as the healthy items that are featured on the menu for sales and marketing promotions. The menu is an example of knowing your market and knowing what you do well and then doing it (see fig. 8-2).

FIGURE 8-2

SUPER SALADS

Grilled Chicken Caesar Salad...$5.99
The classic combination of crisp romaine, garlic croutons & fresh grated Parmesan, all tossed in a tangy Caesar dressing. Topped with a char-broiled chicken breast.

Classic Caesar without chicken...$4.49

🦴 **Blackened Chicken Salad...$5.99**
A spicy combination of blackened chicken breast on a bed of mixed greens with eggs, tomatoes & Cheddar served with hot bacon mustard dressing & garlic bread.

Santa Fe Chicken Salad...$5.79
Strips of char-broiled Fajita chicken breast with guacamole & sour cream on a bed of greens tossed with two cheeses, pico de gallo, tortilla strips & our Mexi-Ranch dressing.

🌀 **Low-Fat Blackened Chicken Salad...$6.29**
Our new non-fat Honey Mustard dressing & non-fat Cheddar/Mozzarella blend give this Blackened Chicken Salad the same great taste as our original & less than 5 grams of fat.

Oriental Chicken Salad...$6.29
Crisp Oriental greens topped with chunks of crunchy Chicken Fingers, toasted almonds & crispy rice noodles tossed in a light Oriental vinaigrette.

Fried Chicken Salad...$5.99
Bite-sized chicken fingers on a bed of salad greens surrounded by Cheddar, diced tomatoes & eggs. Great with honey mustard dressing. Served with garlic bread.

COMBOS

Salad & Steamed Vegetables Plate...$5.99
Our dinner salad or small Caesar salad followed by a plate of fresh steamed broccoli, carrots, cauliflower, new potatoes & zucchini.

Soup & Salad Combo...$4.79
Our soup of the day with a dinner salad or small Caesar salad.

Chili & Half Sandwich...$4.99
A mildly spicy mix of ground beef & sautéed onions topped with Cheddar & jalapeños, served with your choice of a half Club Sub or a half Chicken Walnut Salad Sandwich.

Soup & Half Sandwich...$4.99
Our soup of the day & your choice of a half Club Sub or a half Chicken Walnut Salad Sandwich.

Salad & Half Sandwich...$4.99
Our dinner salad or small Caesar salad with your choice of a half Club Sub or a half Chicken Walnut Salad Sandwich.

🦴 Applebee's Signature Items

ENJOY
Applebee's Fantastic

FOOD and DRINK SPECIALS

SANDWICHES

Add Fries to any Sandwich...$.99

🦴 **Club House Grille...$5.49**
Applebee's signature hot club sandwich with warm sliced ham & turkey, Cheddar, tomatoes, mayonnaise & Bar-B-Que sauce on thick-sliced grilled French bread. Served with a side of cole slaw.

Bacon Cheese Chicken Grill...$5.59
A char-broiled, marinated chicken breast with bacon strips & Monterey Jack on a multi-grain bun with lettuce, tomato & onion.
Without bacon & cheese...$4.99

Gyro Sandwich...$4.69
Thin slices of Gyro beef grilled with sautéed onions & rolled in Pita bread with shredded lettuce & tomatoes.

Club Croissant...$5.89
Smoked ham & turkey breast, Monterey Jack & American cheeses & crisp bacon strips, served warm with your choice of French fries, onion rings or cole slaw.

🦴 **"Riblet Style" Bar-B-Que Sandwich...$5.49**
Lean pork shoulder, cooked "Riblet" style, chopped & piled high on a toasted roll. Served with sides of Bar-B-Que sauce & cole slaw.

Tijuana "Philly" Steak Sandwich...$5.49
Lean shaved "Philly" steak rolled into a grilled tortilla roll with Monterey Jack & Cheddar, sautéed mushrooms, onions, tomatoes, bacon & jalapeños.

Salsa Club Rollup...$5.29
Sliced smoked turkey breast & ham rolled in a large flour tortilla. Topped with slices of Monterey Jack & American cheeses & served with salsa, sour cream, fries & a pickle.

Blackened Chicken Sandwich...$5.79
A boneless chicken breast coated with authentic Cajun spices. Char-broiled & served with our Hot Bacon Mustard sauce.

We use cholesterol-free oil in all our frying.

NEIGHBORHOOD SPECIALTIES

Enjoy one of the following: a bowl of Today's Soup, House Salad or Small Caesar Salad with any food item for only...$1.99

Steak or Chicken Fajitas...$8.29
Strips of marinated steak or chicken breast char-broiled, & served on a sizzling platter with sautéed onions & green peppers; fresh guacamole, pico de gallo & sour cream with soft hot flour tortillas served on the side.

Chicken Fingers Platter...$7.29
A hearty portion of breaded chicken tenderloins, fried & served with French fries, cole slaw & honey mustard sauce.

Smothered Chicken...$7.69
Our char-broiled, marinated chicken breast topped with Monterey Jack, sautéed mushrooms, green peppers & onions & served with your choice of potato & vegetable.
Without cheese, mushrooms, green peppers & onions...$7.29

Applebee's House Sirloin...$8.99
A 9 oz. choice sirloin steak served with your choice of potato & vegetable.
Smothered with sautéed onions, mushrooms & green peppers...$9.49

Riblet Platter...$8.79
Over a pound of slow hickory-roasted rib tips in our spicy Bar-B-Que sauce served with French fries & cole slaw.

Char-Broiled Whitefish Filet...$6.99 (Subject to Availability)
Whitefish filet, char-broiled & served in your choice of 2 different styles: broiled with a touch of lemon pepper or Cajun broiled. Served on a bed of rice pilaf with fresh steamed vegetables.

Sizzling Stir-Fry
Beef or Chicken...$6.89 Combo...$7.29
Your choice of teriyaki chicken breast or spicy sirloin steak served on a bed of sizzling rice & stir-fry vegetables with our special stir-fry sauce. Choose both for a Combo.

Tequila Lime Chicken...$6.29
A char-broiled chicken breast marinated in non-alcoholic tequila & lime juice served on a bed of crisp tortilla strips, smothered in a mild sour cream & Jack Cheddar sauce. Served with a side of Mexican rice & pico de gallo.

🌀 **Bourbon Street Steak...$8.99**
A 10 oz. sirloin steak marinated in Cajun spices, char-broiled with sautéed mushrooms & onions & served with fried new potatoes.

🌀 Low-Fat & Fabulous

SIDES

Beer Battered Onion Rings	$2.99
Soup, House Salad or Small Caesar Salad with Meal	$1.99
Basket of French Fries	$1.59
Basket of Garlic Toast	$.99
Bowl of Chili	$2.99 Bowl of Today's Soup	$2.59
Applebee's House Salad	$2.79

LOW-FAT IS FABULOUS

Chicken Fajita Quesadillas...$6.29
Char-broiled chicken fajita breast, non-fat shredded Cheddar/Mozzarella blend, mushrooms, tomatoes, red onions & jalapeños grilled in a whole-wheat tortilla with picante sauce & non-fat sour cream. Only 11 grams of fat.

Blackened Chicken Salad...$6.29
Our new non-fat Honey Mustard dressing & non-fat Cheddar/Mozzarella blend give this Blackened Chicken Salad the same great taste as our original & less than 5 grams of fat.

Lemon Chicken Pasta...$6.79
Thin slices of grilled lemon-marinated chicken breast, fresh cauliflower, broccoli, carrots & zucchini over angel hair pasta tossed with a light lemon herb sauce. Just 12 fat grams.

Bikini Banana Strawberry Shortcake...$3.29
Fat-free banana shortcake on a bed of pureed strawberries with fresh strawberry slices topped with fresh banana & Yoplait® banana yogurt. 99% fat-free & 1 gram of fat.

JUST RIGHT BITES

Riblet Basket...$6.49
A hearty portion of slow hickory-roasted rib tips basted in our spicy Bar-B-Que sauce & served with fries.

Chicken Fingers Basket...$5.79
Breaded chicken tenderloins, fried & served with French fries & honey mustard sauce.

🦴 **Riblet & Chicken Fingers Basket...$6.29**

🦴 **Fajita Quesadillas...$5.99**
Your choice of our famous beef or chicken fajita meat folded into crisp cheese, tomato & bacon quesadillas. Served with guacamole, sour cream & picante sauce.

🌀 **Low-Fat Chicken Fajita Quesadillas...$6.29**
Char-broiled chicken fajita breast, non-fat shredded Cheddar/Mozzarella blend, mushrooms, tomatoes, red onions & jalapeños grilled in a whole-wheat tortilla with picante sauce & non-fat sour cream. Only 11 grams of fat.

Chicken Pesto Primavera...$6.99
Char-broiled Italian chicken breast & fresh garden vegetables steamed with garlic on a bed of fettuccine tossed with basil, tomatoes, walnuts, Parmesan & olive oil.

🌀 **Low-Fat Lemon Chicken Pasta...$6.79**
Thin slices of grilled lemon-marinated chicken breast, fresh cauliflower, broccoli, carrots & zucchini over angel hair pasta tossed with a light lemon herb sauce. Just 12 fat grams.

DESSERTS HAVE MOVED!
Your Server will tempt you with our new DESSERT MENU or look on the back of this menu.

🦴 Applebee's Signature Items

KM#595

FIGURE 8-2. *continued*

Houlihan's Restaurant Group

Houlihan's has over sixty restaurants located throughout the United States. The chain offers a mid price menu level for the items on their menu. The customer base is younger customers as the primary market group.

Houlihan's is one of the first restaurant groups to start menu printing on three panels. Their menus are printed only on one side, and the panels are placed into plastic covered folders for presentation to the guest. Houlihan's is a static menu, but through the use of panels, when changes or menu modifications need to be made, there is less cost.

The corporate objective is to make menu changes at least once a year. The menu is a moderate priced menu with a choice of items that have a broad appeal to their customer base. Houlihan's offers a broad level of preparation skills and tastes (see menu matrix, chap. 1). Managers have the option to offer off-menu specials at their discretion throughout the year. They can use them for holidays, special events, and seasonal foods of their region. The sections of the menu are printed in a manner to merchandise the marketing effort of the restaurant. The menu layout takes advantage of today's customer desire for special and flavored coffees. Note that some of the listings are designated as a specialty of the restaurant for marketing to increased sales. Special beers are listed in a special section of the menu (see fig. 8-3).

Houlihan's includes the restaurant's guarantee of food quality and service and their desire to correct any dissatisfaction as quickly as possible. In this section of the menu, they market their gift certificates and promote their food to go (food to go being a growth area in the restaurant industry). The three-fold menu or three-panel printed menu allows more space to market food, service, and guarantees than other forms of menu presentations.

The menu has marked the healthy items for the guests to make their choices. The menu has a number of house specialties. On the center panel of the menu are the first items the guest sees when the menu is opened. The two-fold, three-panel sales representation is done by showing the desired sales items in the center of the panels when the menu is presented and the other items folding out to the right and left. A number of their signature items are indicated on the menu by blocking the entire item for printing. The number of items on the menu and the diverse methods of preparation give the menu a broad appeal to their market group.

WINES

RED

Nathanson Creek Cabernet Sauvignon
The full fruit and toasty-vanilla flavors of this medium-bodied Cabernet from the California coast make it the perfect match for everything from our juicy burger to our generous New York Strip Steak.
Bottle 11.95 Glass 3.75

Walnut Crest Merlot
Its full body and fruity aroma make this a great companion for chicken as well as beef dishes.
Bottle 12.95 Glass 4.25

Hess Select Cabernet Sauvignon
The flavors of blackberries and cedar combined with the smooth finish of this outstanding Napa Valley Cabernet make it the perfect partner for our Black Angus Filet Mignon or any of our steaks.
Bottle 16.95 Glass 4.95

CHAMPAGNE

Korbel Extra Dry California Champagne
This semi-sweet, fruity sparkling wine is perfect for any celebration and is an exquisite accompaniment to our delectable chocolate desserts.
Bottle 19.75

WHITE

Emerald Bay Chardonnay
This light chardonnay comes to you from Monterey, Ca and is an excellent accompaniment to our Crisp-Fried Calamari or any of our signature chicken dishes.
Bottle 11.95 Glass 3.75

Rosemount Estate Chardonnay
Hints of vanilla, fruit and oak all come through in this medium-bodied Chardonnay from New South Wales Australia. It is the perfect match for either of our fish entrees.
Bottle 12.95 Glass 4.25

Kendall-Jackson Chardonnay
Rich, oak flavors and light body make this California wine the perfect companion for Chicken Fettuccine or any Houlihan's chicken entree.
Bottle 16.95 Glass 4.95

BLUSH

Sutter Home White Zinfandel
Because of its light, fruity character, this California blush is well suited to any dish.
Bottle 10.95 Glass 3.50

SPECIALTY BEERS

Pete's Wicked Lager
Palo Alto, Ca. Light-bodied and full-flavored, you'd never think anything this wicked could be this good!

Sierra Nevada Pale Ale
Chico, Ca. The amber color and exceptionally full body make this an excellent example of the classic pale ale style. Gold medal winner (1989, 1990, 1997) for classic pale ale at the Great American Beer Festival.

Samuel Adams Boston Lager
Boston, Ma. This lager, from the father of all micro-breweries, is known for its full aroma and dry finish. These combine to make this an excellent beer to accompany any meal.

Black Dog Ale
Bozeman, Mt. Number one brown ale in the 11th annual Great International Beer Tasting

Guinness Stout
Dublin, Ireland. Characterized by its ruby black appearance and rich creamy head. A favorite among Irish beer drinkers since it was first poured in 1759. Try a pint and we are sure you will agree. It is the world's finest stout.

Bass Ale
Burton-on-Trent, England. The rich amber color and light flavor make Bass a favorite among import draught drinkers. Brewed since 1777, this is the classic British Ale.

Black & Tan
We start with a half pint of our fine Bass Ale and top it with creamy Guinness Stout. This results in a unique satisfying flavor that we are sure you will enjoy.

O'DOUL's® and Sharps®
Non-alcoholic brew, by the bottle

BEVERAGES

Water served upon request

Gourmet Italian Coffee Flavors
Irish cream, raspberry, vanilla, hazelnut available with any coffee.

Cappuccino
Traditional cappuccino made with low-fat steamed milk.

Signature Cappuccino
Try your own recipe made with "sweet milk" The creamy texture and robust coffee flavor are definitely unique.

Latte
Steamed milk with a shot of espresso.
Regular or Decaffeinated

Espresso
Regular or Decaffeinated

Freshly-Brewed Coffee
Folgers Gourmet Supreme Coffee.
Regular or Decaffeinated Free refills.

Arizona Iced Tea
A big 20 oz. bottle. Available in regular, diet or raspberry

Houli Fruit Fizz
Houlihan's own blend of Ocean Spray Cranberry Juice Cocktail, orange juice, pineapple juice and Sprite.

Calistoga Sparkling Water
Natural, Berry, Lemonade or Peach/Passion

IBC Root Beer
By the bottle. Regular or Diet

Lemonade
A refreshing thirst quencher.

Freshly-Brewed Hot or Iced Tea
Celestial Seasonings. Free refills.

Coca-Cola Classic, diet Coke, Sprite.
Free refills

HOULIHAN'S MAKES IT RIGHT

We're so committed to providing great food and outstanding service that if you're ever dissatisfied we'll do our best to make it right - right now!
And if we can't, you won't pay.
We welcome your comments and suggestions at 1-800-467-4521
Monday through Friday, 8 am - 5 pm CST.

SANDWICHES & BURGERS

Add soup or side salad for 2.50.

Cajun Chicken Grille
Boneless chicken breast blackened in cajun spices and topped with bell peppers, onions and melted mozzarella cheese. Served with natural-cut fries and cajun-mustard sauce on the side. 6.59

Chicken Salad Sandwich
Creamy and light. Chunks of chicken with low-fat mayonnaise and seasonings, topped with lettuce and tomato. Served on freshly baked pan bread with fresh fruit salad. 5.99

Brentwood Chicken Sandwich
Char-grilled, marinated, boneless breast on a freshly baked focaccia bun with melted provolone cheese, lettuce and tomato. Served with natural-cut fries and honey-mustard sauce on the side. 6.59

Hot Stacked Beef & Cheese
A classic. Thinly sliced roast beef, piled high on a toasted hoagie roll. Topped with sauteed mushrooms and melted provolone cheese. Served au jus with natural-cut fries. 6.59

Plaza Club
Sliced turkey breast with bacon, shredded iceberg lettuce, tomato and mayonnaise. Served on freshly baked pan bread with natural-cut fries. 5.99

Sandwich Combinations
Half Chicken Salad Sandwich or half Plaza Club with your choice of soup or side salad. 5.99

Mushroom, Bacon & Swiss Burger
Charbroiled lean ground beef topped with melted big-eye swiss cheese, bacon and sauteed mushrooms. Served with natural-cut fries. 6.29

Old English Burger
Served with melted old english cheese, tomato, lettuce and natural-cut fries. 5.79 With bacon, add .50

SALADS & QUICHE

Houlihan's original recipe dressings: Honey-Citrus Vinaigrette, Country Club Bleu and Creamy Bleu Cheese.
Also available: Italian, French, Ranch, Fat-Free Honey-Dijon and Low Fat Ranch.

Grilled Chinese Chicken Salad
Char-grilled, marinated breast with bell peppers, red cabbage, snow peas, cilantro, sweet mandarin oranges, fried-rice noodles and peanuts on crisp greens with Houlihan's Original Chinese-Peanut dressing. 6.99

Heartland Chicken Salad
Incredibly delicious and always popular - lightly battered, fried, tender chicken atop crisp greens. Tossed with spicy pecans, fresh bell pepper, red onion, avocado and tomato. Choice of dressing. 6.79

Chicken Caesar Salad
Char-grilled strips of chicken breast over crisp romaine lettuce with seasoned croutons, shredded parmesan and Creamy Caesar dressing. 6.49

Acapulco Chicken Salad
A mountain of greens topped with spicy Mexican chicken, tomato, scallions, crisp tortilla straws, grated monterey jack and colby cheeses with guacamole dressing. 6.99

Club Salad
Crisp greens topped with ham, smoked turkey, monterey jack and colby cheeses, chopped egg, tomato, bacon and baked, seasoned croutons. Choice of dressing. 6.59

Freshly-Baked Quiche
Today's featured quiche served with your choice of soup or side salad. 6.99

Soup & Salad
Your choice of Baked Potato Soup or French Onion Soup and either of our side salads. 5.79

SIDE ITEMS

Substitute any of these side items for any entree side dish.

Houlihan's Smashed Potatoes 1.69	**Fettuccine Alfredo** 2.59
Barbecued Baked Beans 1.69	♡ **Fresh Fruit Salad** 2.29 (Seasonal availability)
♡ Steamed Fresh Vegetables 1.69	Spicy Black Beans & Rice 1.69
♡ Seasoned Brown Rice 1.29	Natural-Cut Fries 1.69
♡ Baked Potato 1.99 with choice of toppings	♡ Sugar Snap Peas 1.29

DESSERTS

Kamikaze Brownie 3.79	**Chocolate Cappuccino Cake** 3.79
New York-Style Cheesecake 3.59	Hot Apple Strudel Pie 3.59
Caramel Nut Crunch Pie 3.79	Ice Cream Sundae 2.09

FIGURE 8-3

Lynn's Paradise Cafe

1994 Great Menu Contest Winner

This menu is all hand lettered. It is intended to lend to the feeling of Lynn's that she intends to be herself in preparing food and offering service. The entire menu is designed to create an atmosphere for the food. House menus are used for all the menu items, and the cuisine is defined as "Fine Home Cooking with a Twist," with a notation on the menu that the herbs used in the food prepared at Lynn's are from the garden at the front of the restaurant. The menu reflects the eclecticism of the restaurant and decor, and Lynn's memorabilia collections add to the spirit of the operation. A local artist assisted in the decorating of the restaurant and design for the menus, which are literally handmade (see fig. 8-4). The personal collections of Lynn Winter, the chef/owner, make up a great deal of the decor in the restaurant.

FIGURE 8-4

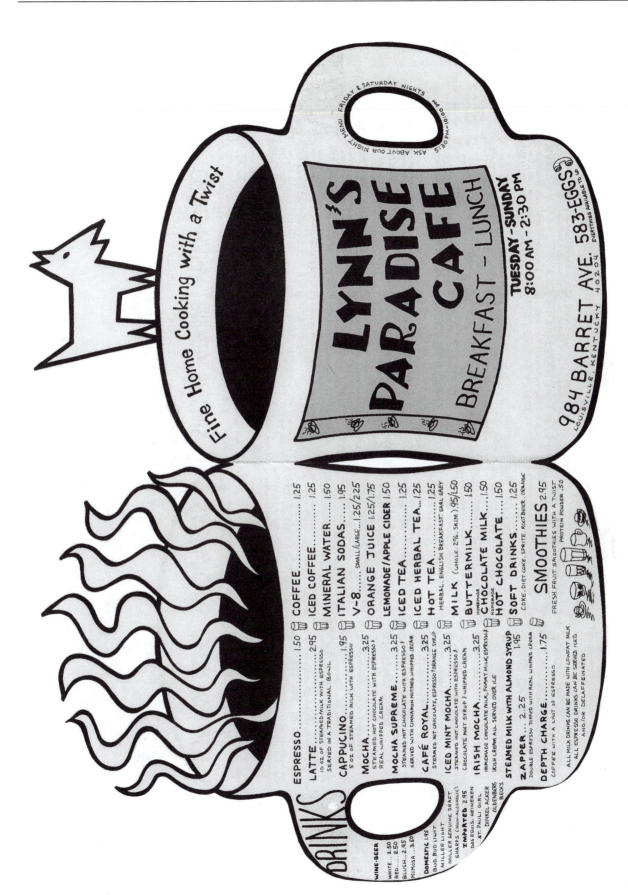

FIGURE 8-4. *continued*

East Bay Trading Company

The East Bay Trading Company in Charleston, South Carolina, is located in an historic building and is full of tradition. The menu is printed on uncoated stock and in the two-fold, three-panel format. The back cover is used to tell the patrons the history of the building, such as the year it was built and the restoration process that has followed the original construc-

tion motif. The menu also contains the restaurant's wine list. The type font has been reduced to 10 point, which is difficult to read under low light conditions. Note the use of clip-art illustrations to break up the monotony of straight print. The only special graphics are the rectangles used to highlight the *East Bay bouillabaisse* and the *beef Wellington* (see fig. 8-5).

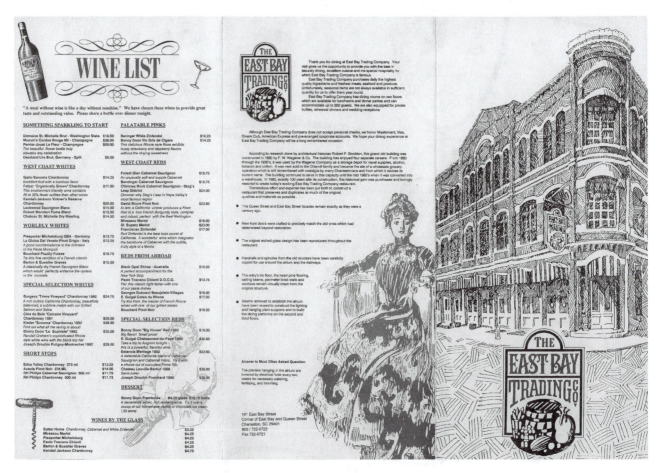

FIGURE 8-5

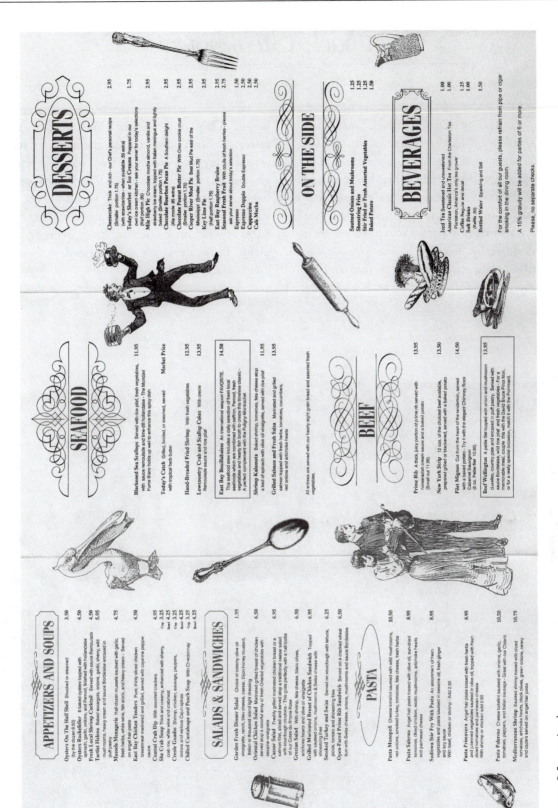

DESSERTS

Cheesecake Thick and rich - our Chef's personal recipe 2.95
(Smaller portion 1.75)
(with strawberries - when available .50 extra)

Today's Sherbet or Ice Creams Prepared in our 1.75
own ice cream kitchen - ask your server for today's selections
(Half portion .95)

Mile High Pie Chocolate mocha almond, vanilla and 2.95
strawberry ice cream, topped with Italian meringue and lightly
baked (Smaller portion 1.75)

Chocolate Bourbon Pecan Pie A Southern delight 2.95
(A la mode .95 extra)

Chocolate Peanut Butter Pie With Oreo cookie crust 2.95
(Smaller portion 1.75)

Cooper River Mud Pie Best Mud Pie east of the 2.95
Mississippi (Smaller portion 1.75)

Key Lime Pie 2.95
(Half portion 1.75)

East Bay Raspberry Brulee 2.95

Seasonal Fresh Fruit With coulis of fresh berries - please 2.75
ask your server about today's selection

Espresso 1.50
Espresso Doppio Double Espresso 2.50
Cappuccino 2.50
Cafe Mocha 2.50

ON THE SIDE

Sauteed Onions and Mushrooms 1.25
Shoestring Fries 1.25
Stir Fried or Fresh Assorted Vegetables 1.25
Baked Potato 1.50

BEVERAGES

Iced Tea Sweetened and unsweetened 1.00
American Classic Hot Tea From the Charleston Tea 1.00
Plantation, America's only tea "grown"
Coffee Regular and decaf 1.25
Soft Drinks 1.00
(Refills .50)
Bottled Water Sparkling and Still 1.50

For the comfort of all our guests, please refrain from pipe or cigar
smoking in the dining room.

A 15% gratuity will be added for parties of 6 or more.

Please, no separate checks.

SEAFOOD

Blackened Sea Scallops Served with rice pilaf, fresh vegetables, 11.95
with sauce remoulade and time-till hollandaise - The Mondavi
Fume Blanc holds up well to enhance this spicy dish

Today's Catch Grilled, broiled, or steamed, served Market Price
with tropical herb butter

Hand-Breaded Fried Shrimp With fresh vegetables 12.95

Lowcountry Crab and Scallop Cakes With creole 13.95
Remoulade sauce and rice pilaf

East Bay Bouillabaisse An international seaport FAVORITE. 14.50
This seafood stew includes a daily selection of fresh local
seafoods which are combined with saffron, Pernod, fresh
vegetables and hearty fish broth to create this timeless classic -
A perfect complement with the Puligny-Montrachet

Shrimp Kalamata Baked shrimp, tomatoes, feta cheese atop 11.95
a bed of spinach with olive oil vinaigrette, served with rice pilaf

Grilled Salmon and Fresh Salsa Marinated and grilled 13.95
salmon topped with fresh herbs, tomatoes, cucumbers,
red onions and artichoke hearts

All entrees are served with our hearty eight grain bread and assorted fresh
vegetables.

BEEF

Prime Rib A thick, juicy portion of prime rib served with 13.95
horseradish cream sauce and a baked potato
(Small cut 11.95)

New York Strip 12 ozs. of the choicest beef available, 13.50
prepared grilled or blackened, served with a baked potato

Filet Mignon Cut from the heart of the tenderloin, served 14.50
with a baked potato - Try it with the elegant Chimney Rock
Cabernet Sauvignon
(5 oz. Petite filet 10.95)

Beef Wellington A petite filet topped with onion and mushroom 13.95
duxelles, country pate and encased in puff pastry. Served with
sauce Bordelaise, wild rice pilaf and fresh vegetables - For a
memorable meal, couple this with the David Bruce Pinot Noir,
or for a really special occasion, match it with the Pommard.

APPETIZERS AND SOUPS

Oysters On The Half Shell Shucked or steamed 3.50
(by the dozen 6.50)

Oysters Rockefeller 6 baked oysters topped with 4.50
spinach, garlic, onions, and Pernod, finished with hollandaise

Fresh Local Shrimp Cocktail Served with sauce Remoulade 4.50
Tartlet Helena Baked escargots, onions, garlic, sherry, wild 5.95
mushrooms, heavy cream and sauce Bordelaise encased in
puff pastry

Mussels Menagerie Half-dozen mussels sauteed with garlic, 4.75
fresh herbs, white wine, fish stock, and heavy cream - Served
on angel hair pasta

East Bay Chicken Tenders Pure, thinly sliced chicken 4.50
breast meat marinated and grilled, served with cayenne pepper
sauce

Coastal Crab Dip With assorted crackers 4.95
She Crab Soup Thick and creamy, enhanced with sherry, Cup 3.25
crab roe, white wine and crabmeat Bowl 4.25
Creole Gumbo Shrimp, chicken, sausage, peppers, Cup 3.25
onions and various Cajun spices Bowl 4.25
Chilled Cantaloupe and Peach Soup With Chardonnay Cup 3.25
Bowl 4.25

SALADS & SANDWICHES

Garden Fresh Dinner Salad Choice of creamy olive oil 1.95
vinaigrette, ranch, bleu cheese, caesar, Dijon-honey mustard,
Italian or thousand island light dressing

Oriental Chicken Salad Marinated grilled breast of chicken 6.50
served atop a colorful array of fresh Oriental vegetables with
sesame vinaigrette

Caesar Salad Freshly grilled marinated chicken breast or a 6.95
salmon fillet, sliced and served atop a traditional caesar salad
with sourdough croutons - This goes perfectly with a half-bottle
of our Cotes du Rhone Rose

Grecian Salad With shrimp, feta cheese, black olives, 6.50
artichoke hearts and olive oil vinaigrette

Grilled Marinated Breast of Chicken Sandwich Topped 6.95
with sauteed onions, mushrooms & Swiss cheese with
shoestring fries

Smoked Turkey and Swiss Served on sourdough with lettuce, 6.25
pickle, tomato and shoestring fries

Open-Faced Prime Rib Sandwich Served on a cracked wheat 6.50
bun with Swiss cheese, onions, mushrooms and sauce Bordelaise

PASTA

Pasta Monopoli Cheese tortellini sauteed with wild mushrooms, 10.50
red onions, smoked turkey, tomatoes, feta cheese, fresh herbs

Pasta Salerno Angel hair pasta tossed with olive oil, sun-dried 8.95
tomatoes, diced chicken, exotic mushrooms, artichoke hearts
and parmesan cheese

Sudiswa Stir Fry With Pasta An assortment of fresh 8.95
vegetables and pasta sauteed in sesame oil, fresh ginger
and soy sauce
With beef, chicken or shrimp - Add 2.50

Pasta Primavera Angel hair pasta tossed with fresh hearts 8.95
and julienned vegetables sauteed in olive oil, topped with fresh
diced tomatoes and parmesan cheese
With shrimp or chicken add 2.50

Pasta Palermo Cheese tortellini sauteed with onions, garlic, 10.50
tomatoes, peppers, and Italian sausage - Great with our Chianti

Mediterranean Shrimp Sauteed shrimp tossed with diced 10.75
tomatoes, artichoke hearts, black olives, green onions, celery
and capers served on angel hair pasta

FIGURE 8-5. *continued*

Outback Steakhouse

The very popular and successful Outback Steakhouse chain uses a small two-fold, three-panel menu printed on uncoated paper that fits their operation. The menus are kept at the tables rather than being passed out by the host or hostess. It uses several colored inks that make the graphics and illustrations stand out (see fig. 8-6). They also use a separate menu, called their Billabong Menu (see fig. 8-7).

Most Outbacks are only open for dinner and reportedly run about a $15 average check including liquor. They rely on very high volume and table turnover. Since the regular menu is so reasonably priced (they have eleven entrees out of seventeen that are priced at or below $10.95), if patrons ordered burgers, "cut lunches," and salads, check averages would fall, since the Billabong items are priced at $6.95 and below. By putting those items on a separate menu, those items are not ordered as frequently as their steaks and ribs.

FIGURE 8-6

Aussie-Tizers

G'day mate! Start your tucker off with one o' these wonders from down under!

Bloomin' Onion°
An Outback Ab-original from
Russell's Marina Bay $4.95

Kookaburra Wings°
Known as Buffalo chicken wings here
in the States. Mild, medium, or hot $3.95

Grilled Shrimp On The Barbie
Seasoned and served with Outback's
own Remoulade sauce $5.95

Aussie Cheese Fries
Aussie chips topped with Monterey
Jack and Cheddar cheeses, bacon
and served with spicy ranch dressing... $4.95

Walkabout Soup°
A unique presentation of an Australian
favorite. Reckon! ... Bowl/Cup ..$2.95/$1.95

Gold Coast Coconut Shrimp
Six colossal shrimp dipped in
beer batter, rolled in coconut,
deep fried to a golden brown
and served with marmalade sauce........ $5.95

Down Under Favorites

Heaps of hearty traditions from the shoreline to deep in the 'never never.' Every one's a beaut! Doo right!

Jackeroo Chops
Two 8-ounce center cut pork chops served with
cinnamon apples and a choice of potato $10.95

Alice Springs Chicken°
Grilled chicken breast and bacon smothered
in mushrooms, melted Monterey Jack
and Cheddar cheeses, with honey-mustard
sauce. Served with Aussie chips $8.95

Queensland Chicken 'N Shrimp°
Seasoned and grilled, over fettuccine
Alfredo, topped with a light lemon sauce..... $9.95

Brisbane Shrimp Sauté
Seasoned and sautéed with mushrooms,
over fettuccine in a light herb butter sauce ...$8.95

House or Caesar Salad with
any Down Under Favorite $1.95

Land Rovers

Our steaks are fair dinkum= absolutely genuine – USDA cuts. It was one of these three dishes that Mad Max was so mad about!

The Outback Special°
A 12-ounce center-cut sirloin, seasoned
and seared to perfection $10.95

Prime Minister's Prime Rib
A tempting, 16-ounce cut, roasted slowly...$14.95
12-ounce cut $12.95
8-ounce cut $10.95

Victoria's Filet°
A 9-ounce tenderloin............................$13.95

The Michael J. "Crocodile" Dundee
A 14-ounce New York Strip $14.95

The Melbourne
A 20-ounce porterhouse –
it's bonzer! $16.95

Rockhampton Rib-Eye
A 12-ounce rib-eye steak.......................$12.95

Land Rover Entrees are served with
a choice of House or Caesar salad, bushman
bread and choice of jacket potato, Aussie
chips, or fresh steamed veggies.

Grilled On The Barbie

Cheers! Get a real taste of the ol' outback, seared to perfection over an open flame!

Chicken On The Barbie
Seasoned and grilled breast served
with BBQ sauce and fresh veggies $7.95

Ribs On The Barbie
Danish baby back ribs, smoked
and grilled, with Aussie chips
and cinnamon apples $10.95

Drover's Platter°
Generous portion of ribs and chicken
breast on the barbie with Aussie
chips and cinnamon apples $10.95

Botany Bay Fish O' The Day
Fresh catch, lightly seasoned and
grilled, with fresh veggies $10.95

House or Caesar Salad with
any Grilled On The Barbie Favorite $1.95

Desserts

No worries, mate. Have a 'bo-peep' at these treats and aye go!

Sydney's Sinful Sundae
Vanilla ice cream rolled in toasted
coconut, covered in chocolate sauce
and topped with whipped cream $2.95

Cheesecake Olivia
New York style with raspberry sauce.......$2.75

Chocolate Thunder From Down Under
Fresh-baked brownie, rich vanilla ice
cream topped with hot homemade
chocolate sauce and chocolate shavings ...$3.95

Joey Menu

You'll jump with joy over this tucker (that's food) special, like, just for you littlies under 12!

Boomerang Burger $2.65
Kookaburra Chicken Fingers............$2.65
Grilled Cheese-A-Roo $2.25
Junior Ribs $3.95
Spotted Dog Sundae $1.75

Sides

Help mates! Keep your tucker in the best o' company with one or more of our bonzer (terrific) accompaniments.

Sautéed 'Shrooms $2.25
Jacket Potato $1.75
Aussie Chips $1.35
Grilled Onions ....$.95
Fresh Veggies $1.75
House or Caesar Salad $3.45

Beverages

Take your pick, mate, from the ol' waterin' hole.

Luzianne Iced Tea   Coca-Cola CLASSIC

O'DOUL'S NON-ALCOHOLIC BREW

FIGURE 8-6. *continued*

FIGURE 8-7

Longhorn Steaks

Another popular steakhouse restaurant is Longhorn Steaks. Headquartered in Atlanta and known for their excellent steaks, Longhorn has recently broadened their menu selections and now offers chicken and salmon to compliment their famous grilled steaks. The menu is printed on specially coated paper and utilizes the two-fold, three-panel format. Red ink is used to call attention to the menu titles. You will also note that Longhorn utilizes the back cover to list their other locations and to advertise gift certificates and group business accommodations (see fig. 8-8).

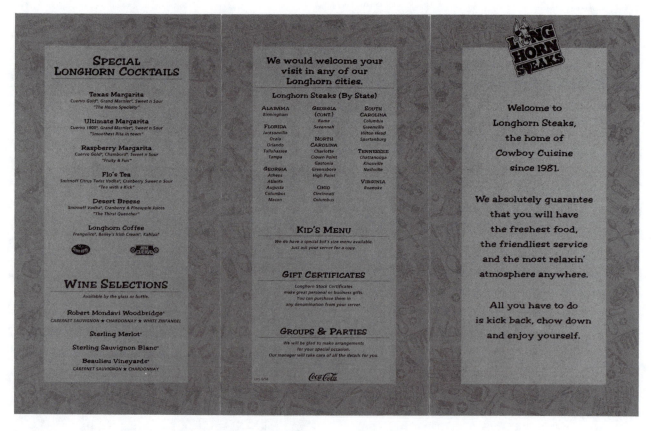

FIGURE 8-8

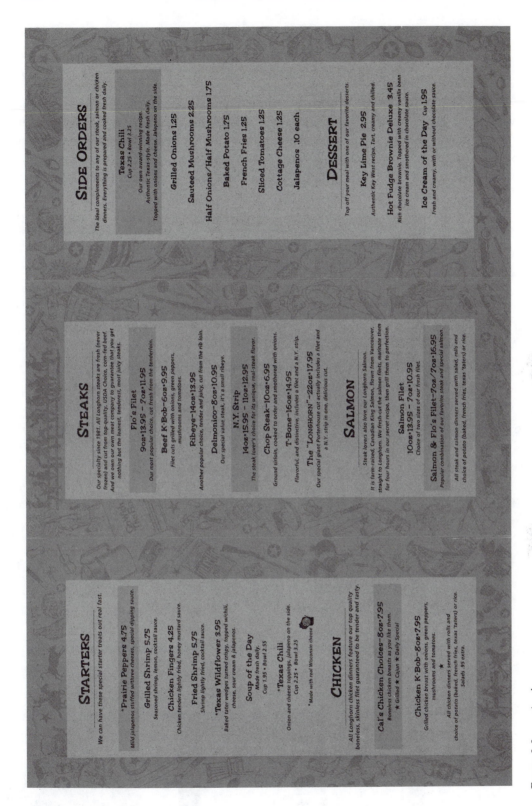

STARTERS

We can have these special starter treats out real fast.

*Prairie Peppers 4.75
Mild jalapenos stuffed w/three cheeses, special dipping sauce.

Grilled Shrimp 5.75
Seasoned shrimp, lemon, cocktail sauce.

Chicken Fingers 4.25
Chicken tenders lightly fried, honey mustard sauce.

Fried Shrimp 5.75
Shrimp lightly fried, cocktail sauce.

*Texas Wildflower 3.95
Baked tater wedges turned crispy, topped w/chili, cheese, sour cream & jalapenos.

Soup of the Day
Made fresh daily.
Cup 1.95 • Bowl 2.55

*Texas Chili
Onion and cheese toppings, jalapeno on the side.
Cup 2.25 • Bowl 3.25
★ Grilled ★ Cajun ★ Daily Special
* Made with real Wisconsin cheese

CHICKEN

All Longhorn chicken dinners feature our top quality boneless, skinless filet guaranteed to be tender and tasty.

Cal's Chicken Choices~8oz~7.95
Boneless chicken breasts as you like them.
★ Grilled ★ Cajun ★ Daily Special

Chicken K·Bob~8oz~7.95
Grilled chicken breast with onions, green peppers, mushrooms and tomatoes.
★
All chicken dinners served with rolls and choice of potato (baked, french fries, texas taters) or rice. Salads .95 extra.

STEAKS

Our specialty since 1981. All Longhorn steaks are fresh (never frozen) and cut from top-quality, USDA Choice, corn-fed beef. And we own our own meat company to guarantee that you get nothing but the leanest, tenderest, most juicy steaks.

Flo's Filet
9oz•13.95 ~ 7oz•11.95
Our most popular choice, cut fresh from the tenderloin.

Beef K·Bob~6oz•9.95
Filet cuts grilled with onions, green peppers, mushrooms and tomatoes.

Ribeye~14oz•13.95
Another popular choice, tender and juicy, cut from the rib loin.

Delmonico~8oz•10.95
Our special value steak, it's a small ribeye.

N.Y. Strip
14oz•15.95 ~ 11oz•12.95
The steak lover's choice for its unique, real-steak flavor.

Chop Steak~10oz•6.95
Ground sirloin, cooked to order and smothered with onions.

T-Bone~16oz•14.95
Flavorful, and distinctive, includes a filet and a N.Y. strip.

The "LONGHORN"~22oz•17.95
Our special giant Porterhouse cut actually includes a filet and a N.Y. strip in one, delicious cut.

SALMON

Steak lovers also love our Longhorn Salmon. It is farm-raised, Canadian King Salmon, flown from Vancouver, straight to Longhorn. We fresh-cut the salmon filets, marinate them for four hours in our secret recipe, then grill them to perfection.

Salmon Filet
10oz•13.95 ~ 7oz•10.95
Choice of two sizes of our fresh filet.

Salmon & Flo's Filet~7oz/7oz•16.95
Popular combination of our favorite steak and special salmon.

All steak and salmon dinners served with salad, rolls and choice of potato (baked, french fries, texas Taters) or rice.

SIDE ORDERS

The ideal complements to any of our steak, salmon or chicken dinners. Everything is prepared and cooked fresh daily.

Texas Chili
Cup 2.25 • Bowl 3.25
Our own award-winning recipe.
Authentic Texas-style. Made fresh daily.
Topped with onions and cheese. Jalapeno on the side.

Grilled Onions 1.25

Sauteed Mushrooms 2.25

Half Onions/Half Mushrooms 1.75

Baked Potato 1.75

French Fries 1.25

Sliced Tomatoes 1.25

Cottage Cheese 1.25

Jalapenos .10 each

DESSERT

Top off your meal with one of our favorite desserts.

Key Lime Pie 2.95
Authentic Key West recipe. tart, creamy and chilled.

Hot Fudge Brownie Deluxe 3.45
Rich chocolate brownie. Topped with creamy vanilla bean ice cream and smothered in chocolate sauce.

Ice Cream of the Day Cup 1.95
Fresh and creamy, with or without chocolate sauce.

FIGURE 8-8. *continued*

9th Street Abbey

The 9th Street Abbey uses a combination of menu items and a wait staff for the service of breakfast/brunch foods, and a self-service buffet line featuring fruits, pastries, and other selected breakfast/brunch items. This menu and method is a combination of the best of both worlds for meals, service, and profit (see fig. 8-9).

FIGURE 8-9

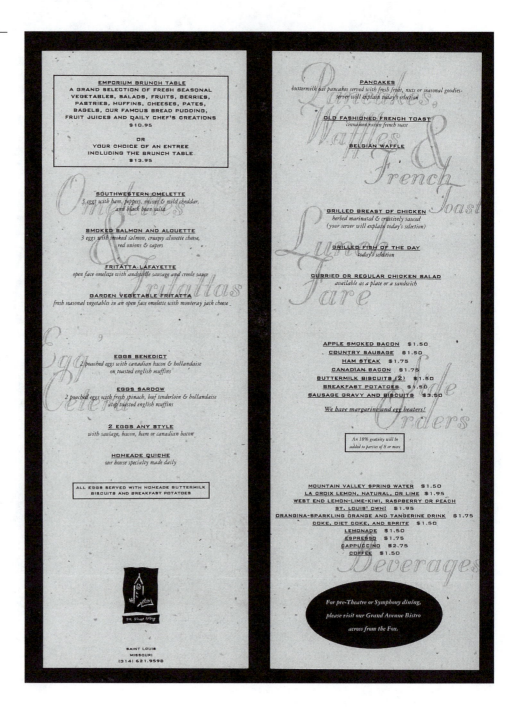

The Trellis

The menu of The Trellis is seasonal and is changed according to the specific time of year. The Trellis also offers a daily luncheon menu (the luncheon menu lists desserts and beverages). On each seasonal menu a prix fixe complete meal is offered. Chef's specials and seasonal specials are offered daily, and the offerings of the menu are changed daily: the selections are based on availability of foods and customer forecasts.

There are obvious differences in the lunch and dinner items offered on the menu. The menu credits the chefs of the restaurant according to their positions (with today's customers' food involvement and knowledge, the recognition is an effective marketing move). Wines and desserts are offered on separate menus during dinner service. The offer of a signed copy of *Death by Chocolate* and other publications by the restaurant's chefs is an outstanding marketing opportunity for the publications and the promotion of menu items listed in the books.

The concern about the menu is that the prices are written in after listing the item. The explanation is that the restaurant management believes this is a better way of price presentation for their menu, and it is most effective on their menu in this market. The penmanship is very good and the price is listed close to the item description. The center art on the menu is representative of the season and the foods of that season, and is very effective: it promotes the ambiance of the restaurant. The menu copy gives a good description of the foods that are offered. With seasonal changes, a good variety of food items are offered on the Trellis menu to maintain guest interest and patronage (see fig. 8-10).

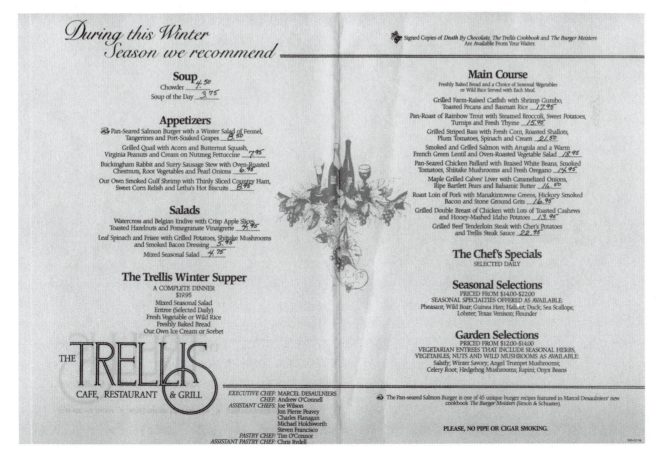

FIGURE 8-10

Hampshire House

Boston, Massachusetts

The Hampshire House in downtown Boston is located above Cheers Bar. It is in an historic area and a tourist "must see" location. The restaurant has gained its own success and reputation through its food and service. The menu focuses on selected healthy choice items and some signature items of the chef. Note the pricing of menu items is done with dollars and in even amounts; there is no odd-cents marketing. All prices are shown near the food descriptions. The location of the restaurant in Boston gives use to the naming of the entrees such as "The Old Merchants Main Courses," a clever marketing name. Appetizers have been designated as "Famous Short Stories." Catering and meeting facilities are covered within the menu copy as well as the special chef's table for special meals. The summer house special offering, a New England market basket, is prominently displayed in the center of the menu, plus a suggestion asking for menu requests from guests. The menu is a one-page static menu with daily specials to give menu variety. Menu size is larger than normal to create an effect and leave an impression with the guest (see fig. 8-11). Hampshire House has large serving rooms, so the menu is in keeping with the dining areas.

FIGURE 8-11

Max & Erma's

This menu continues to be on the cutting edge of what is current in this price category. The menu is printed on panels and is offered to the guest in a plastic covering. The advantage of the current menu presentation is that it gives the restaurant the option to change any section of the menu they wish to emphasize. The menu employs both the front and the back of the plastic cover for their items. They have highlighted some items they wish to promote in various sections of the menu. There is a good variety of combinations of both tastes and preparations listed on this menu. The descriptions of the items on the menu are well done and appropriate (see fig. 8-12).

This menu is typical of what has been described in this book for restaurants offering a value menu with a price range that is appealing to the casual dining ele-

ment. The hamburger continues to be an area of emphasis on Max & Erma's menu, and the panels give this section a prominent sales display. Please note the disclaimer in their luncheon special section, "When it's gone, it's gone." Notations have been made throughout the menu for their add-on menu items, suggesting the purchase at appropriate places on the menu. They have also used an enclosure or box of items they judge to be specialties of the house.

The menu meets the requirements for marketing and sales of the items that are offered in the restaurant. Max & Erma's has always listened to their customers about what they want on the menu with surveys, comment cards, and personal contact with guests. This menu represents a menu based on guests' desires for food items.

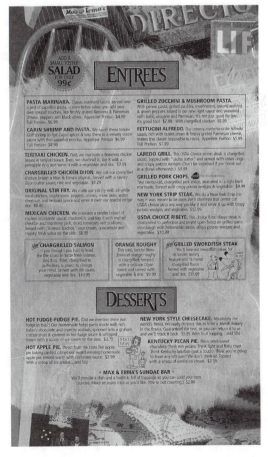

FIGURE 8-12

Harley Davidson Cafe

The Harley Davidson Cafe menu is a static menu with a center fold. It is the equivalent of a vertical one-fold menu (two page menu). The menu is printed in three panels on the page for guest selections. Entrees are at the center top when the menu is opened. Many of the food names, food categories, and drinks are given Harley names for marketing and sales effect. At this printing the menu has no signature items designated. Beverages by their menu location will be given a prime location area for sales and marketing at the guest opening view of the menu. The back of the menu covers the legend of the Harley company.

The guest is offered an opportunity to have a photograph taken on the restaurant's Harley. This is an excellent means for word-of-mouth/past-patron advertising for the restaurant. The current sales success of the Harley company will have a positive sales effect on this restaurant. The oversized menu and plastic covering are for protection because of high customer usage. The large size is for customer impact and to fit the Harley concept of big (see fig. 8-13).

FIGURE 8-13

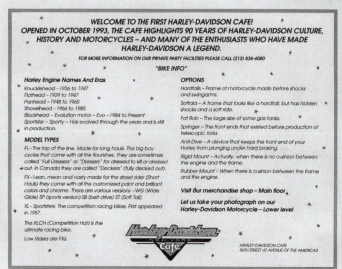

WELCOME TO THE FIRST HARLEY-DAVIDSON CAFE!
OPENED IN OCTOBER 1993, THE CAFE HIGHLIGHTS 90 YEARS OF HARLEY-DAVIDSON CULTURE, HISTORY AND MOTORCYCLES – AND MANY OF THE ENTHUSIASTS WHO HAVE MADE HARLEY-DAVIDSON A LEGEND.

FOR MORE INFORMATION ON OUR PRIVATE PARTY FACILITIES PLEASE CALL (212) 838-6080

"BIKE INFO"

Harley Engine Names And Eras

Knucklehead – 1936 to 1947
Flathead – 1929 to 1947
Panhead – 1948 to 1965
Shovelhead – 1966 to 1985
Blockhead – Evolution motor – Evo – 1984 to Present
Sportster – Sporty – Has evolved through the years and is still in production.

MODEL TYPES

FL – The top of the line. Made for long hauls. The big boy cycles that come with all the flourishes. They are sometimes called "Full Dressers" or "Dressers" for dressed to kill or dressed out. In Canada they are called "Deckers" (fully decked out).

FX – Lean, mean and nasty made for the street rider (Short Hauls) they come with all the customized paint and brilliant colors and chrome. There are various versions – WG (Wide Glide) SP (sports version) SB (belt drive) ST (Soft Tail).

XL – Sportsters. The competition racing bikes. First appeared in 1957.

The XLCH (Competition Hat) is the ultimate racing bike.

Low Riders are FXs.

OPTIONS

Hardtails – Frame of motorcycle made before shocks and swingarms.

Softail – A frame that looks like a hardtail, but has hidden shocks and a soft ride.

Fat Bob – The large size of some gas tanks.

Springer – The front ends that existed before production of telescopic forks.

Anti-Dive – A device that keeps the front end of your Harley from plunging under hard braking.

Rigid Mount – Actually, when there is no cushion between the engine and the frame.

Rubber Mount – When there is cushion between the frame and the engine.

Visit our merchandise shop – Main floor

Let us take your photograph on our Harley-Davidson Motorcycle – Lower level

HARLEY-DAVIDSON CAFE
56TH STREET AT AVENUE OF THE AMERICAS

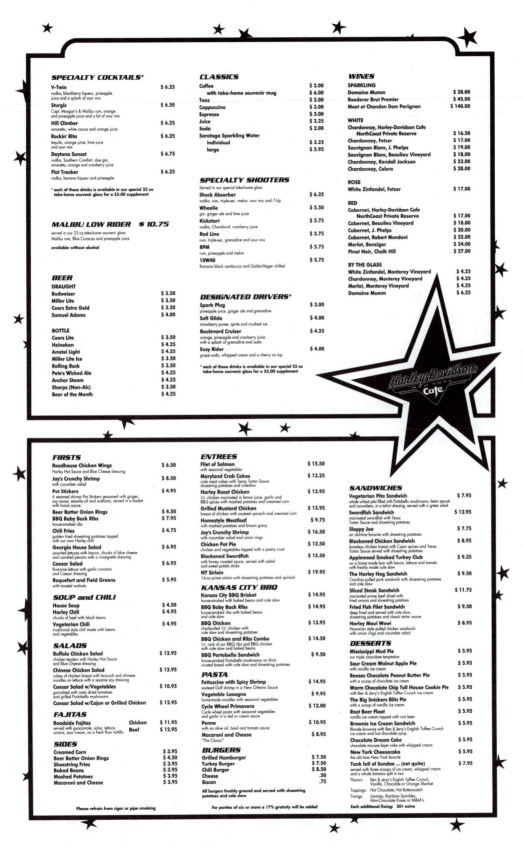

SPECIALTY COCKTAILS*

V-Twin	$ 6.25
vodka, blackberry liqueur, pineapple juice and a splash of sour mix	
Sturgis	$ 6.50
Capt. Morgan's & Malibu rum, orange and pineapple juice and a bit of sour mix	
Hill Climber	$ 6.25
amaretto, white cocoa and orange juice	
Rockin' Rita	$ 6.25
tequila, orange juice, lime juice and sour mix	
Daytona Sunset	$ 6.75
vodka, Southern Comfort, sloe gin, amaretto, orange and cranberry juice	
Flat Tracker	$ 6.25
vodka, banana liqueur and pineapple	

* each of these drinks is available in our special 23 oz take-home souvenir glass for a $5.00 supplement

MALIBU LOW RIDER $ 10.75

served in our 23 oz take-home souvenir glass
Malibu rum, Blue Curacao and pineapple juice

available without alcohol

BEER

DRAUGHT

Budweiser	$ 3.50
Miller Lite	$ 3.50
Coors Extra Gold	$ 3.50
Samuel Adams	$ 4.00

BOTTLE

Coors Lite	$ 3.50
Heineken	$ 4.25
Amstel Light	$ 4.25
Miller Lite Ice	$ 3.50
Rolling Rock	$ 3.50
Pete's Wicked Ale	$ 4.25
Anchor Steam	$ 4.25
Sharps (Non-Alc)	$ 3.50
Beer of the Month	$ 4.25

CLASSICS

Coffee	$ 2.00
with take-home souvenir mug	$ 6.00
Teas	$ 2.00
Cappuccino	$ 3.00
Espresso	$ 3.00
Juice	$ 2.25
Soda	$ 2.00
Saratoga Sparkling Water	
individual	$ 2.25
large	$ 5.95

SPECIALTY SHOOTERS

Served in our special take-home glass

Shock Absorber	$ 6.25
vodka, rum, triple-sec, melon, sour mix and 7-Up	
Wheelie	$ 5.50
gin, ginger ale and lime juice	
Kickstart	$ 5.75
vodka, Chambord, cranberry juice	
Red Line	$ 5.75
rum, triple-sec, grenadine and sour mix	
RPM	$ 5.75
rum, pineapple and melon	
10W40	$ 5.75
Romana black sambucca and Goldschlager chilled	

DESIGNATED DRIVERS*

Spark Plug	$ 3.00
pineapple juice, ginger ale and grenadine	
Soft Glide	$ 4.00
strawberry puree, sprite and crushed ice	
Boulevard Cruiser	$ 4.25
orange, pineapple and cranberry juice with a splash of grenadine and soda	
Easy Rider	$ 4.00
grape soda, whipped cream and a cherry on top	

* each of these drinks is available in our special 23 oz take-home souvenir glass for a $5.00 supplement

WINES

SPARKLING

Domaine Mumm	$ 28.00
Roederer Brut Premier	$ 45.00
Moet et Chandon Dom Perignon	$ 140.00

WHITE

Chardonnay, Harley-Davidson Cafe NorthCoast Private Reserve	$ 16.50
Chardonnay, Fetzer	$ 17.00
Sauvignon Blanc, J. Phelps	$ 19.00
Sauvignon Blanc, Beaulieu Vineyard	$ 18.00
Chardonnay, Kendall Jackson	$ 23.00
Chardonnay, Calera	$ 28.00

ROSE

White Zinfandel, Fetzer	$ 17.00

RED

Cabernet, Harley-Davidson Cafe NorthCoast Private Reserve	$ 17.00
Cabernet, Beaulieu Vineyard	$ 18.00
Cabernet, J. Phelps	$ 20.00
Cabernet, Robert Mondavi	$ 22.00
Merlot, Benziger	$ 24.00
Pinot Noir, Chalk Hill	$ 27.00

BY THE GLASS

White Zinfandel, Monterey Vineyard	$ 4.25
Chardonnay, Monterey Vineyard	$ 4.25
Merlot, Monterey Vineyard	$ 4.25
Domaine Mumm	$ 6.25

FIRSTS

Roadhouse Chicken Wings	$ 6.50
Harley Hot Sauce and Blue Cheese dressing	
Jay's Crunchy Shrimp	$ 8.50
with cucumber salad	
Pot Stickers	$ 4.95
6 steamed shrimp Pot Stickers seasoned with ginger, soy sauce, sesame oil and scallions, served in a basket with hoisin sauce.	
Beer Batter Onion Rings	$ 4.50
BBQ Baby Back Ribs	$ 7.95
house-smoked ribs	
Chili Fries	$ 4.75
golden fried shoestring potatoes topped with our own Harley chili	
Georgia House Salad	$ 6.95
assorted lettuces with bacon, chunks of blue cheese and candied pecans with a vinaigrette dressing	
Caesar Salad	$ 6.95
Romaine lettuce with garlic croutons and Caesar dressing	
Roquefort and Field Greens	$ 5.95
with toasted walnuts	

SOUP and CHILI

House Soup	$ 4.50
Harley Chili	$ 4.95
chunks of beef with black beans	
Vegetarian Chili	$ 4.95
traditional style chili made with beans and vegetables	

SALADS

Buffalo Chicken Salad	$ 12.95
chicken tenders with Harley Hot Sauce and Blue Cheese dressing	
Chinese Chicken Salad	$ 12.95
cubes of chicken breast with broccoli and chinese noodles on lettuce with a sesame soy dressing	
Caesar Salad w/Vegetables	$ 10.95
garnished with oven dried tomatoes and grilled Portobello mushrooms	
Caesar Salad w/Cajun or Grilled Chicken	$ 12.95

FAJITAS

Roadside Fajitas	Chicken	$ 11.95
served with guacamole, salsa, lettuce, onions, sour cream, on a fresh flour tortilla	Beef	$ 12.95

SIDES

Creamed Corn	$ 3.95
Beer Batter Onion Rings	$ 4.50
Shoestring Fries	$ 3.95
Baked Beans	$ 3.95
Mashed Potatoes	$ 3.95
Macaroni and Cheese	$ 3.95

Please refrain from cigar or pipe smoking

ENTREES

Filet of Salmon	$ 15.50
with seasonal vegetables	
Maryland Crab Cakes	$ 13.25
crab meat cakes with Texas Tartar Sauce shoestring potatoes and coleslaw	
Harley Roast Chicken	$ 13.95
1/2 chicken marinated in lemon juice, garlic and BBQ spices with mashed potatoes and creamed corn	
Grilled Mustard Chicken	$ 13.95
breast of chicken with sauteed spinach and creamed corn	
Homestyle Meatloaf	$ 9.75
with mashed potatoes and brown gravy	
Jay's Crunchy Shrimp	$ 16.50
with cucumber salad and onion rings	
Chicken Pot Pie	$ 12.50
chicken and vegetables topped with a pastry crust	
Blackened Swordfish	$ 15.50
with honey roasted sauce, served with salad and sweet potato sticks	
NY Sirloin	$ 19.95
14 oz prime sirloin with shoestring potatoes and spinach	

KANSAS CITY BBQ

Kansas City BBQ Brisket	$ 14.95
house-smoked with baked beans and cole slaw	
BBQ Baby Back Ribs	$ 14.95
house-smoked ribs with baked beans and cole slaw	
BBQ Chicken	$ 13.95
charbroiled 1/2 chicken with cole slaw and shoestring potatoes	
BBQ Chicken and Ribs Combo	$ 14.50
1/2 rack of our BBQ ribs and BBQ chicken with cole slaw and baked beans	
BBQ Portobello Sandwich	$ 9.50
house-smoked Portobello mushrooms on thick crusted bread with cole slaw and shoestring potatoes	

PASTA

Fettuccine with Spicy Shrimp	$ 14.95
sauteed Gulf shrimp in a New Orleans Sauce	
Vegetable Lasagna	$ 9.95
home-made noodles with seasonal vegetables	
Cycle Wheel Primavera	$ 12.00
Cycle wheel pasta with seasonal vegetables and garlic in a red or cream sauce	
Penne	$ 10.95
with an olive oil, basil and tomato sauce	
Macaroni and Cheese	$ 8.95
"The Classic"	

BURGERS

Grilled Hamburger	$ 7.50
Turkey Burger	$ 7.50
Chili Burger	$ 8.50
Cheese	.50
Bacon	.75

All burgers freshly ground and served with shoestring potatoes and cole slaw

For parties of six or more a 17% gratuity will be added

SANDWICHES

Vegetarian Pita Sandwich	$ 7.95
whole wheat pita filled with Portobello mushrooms, bean sprouts and cucumbers, in a tahini dressing, served with a green salad	
Swordfish Sandwich	$ 12.95
marinated swordfish with Texas Tartar Sauce and shoestring potatoes	
Sloppy Joe	$ 7.75
an old-time favorite with shoestring potatoes	
Blackened Chicken Sandwich	$ 8.95
boneless chicken breast with Cajun spices and Texas Tartar Sauce served with shoestring potatoes	
Applewood Smoked Turkey Club	$ 9.25
on a home made bun with bacon, lettuce and tomato with freshly made cole slaw	
The Harley Hog Sandwich	$ 9.50
Carolina pulled pork sandwich with shoestring potatoes and cole slaw	
Sliced Steak Sandwich	$ 11.75
marinated prime beef sliced with fried onions and shoestring potatoes	
Fried Fish Filet Sandwich	$ 9.50
deep fried and served with cole slaw, shoestring potatoes and classic tartar sauce	
Harley Maui Wowi	$ 8.95
Hawaiian style pulled chicken sandwich with onion rings and cucumber salad	

DESSERTS

Mississippi Mud Pie	$ 5.95
our triple chocolate temptation	
Sour Cream Walnut Apple Pie	$ 5.95
with vanilla ice cream	
Reeses Chocolate Peanut Butter Pie	$ 5.95
with a scoop of chocolate ice cream	
Warm Chocolate Chip Toll House Cookie Pie	$ 5.95
with Ben & Jerry's English Toffee Crunch ice cream	
The Big Snickers Blitz Pie	$ 5.95
with a scoop of vanilla ice cream	
Root Beer Float	$ 5.95
vanilla ice cream topped with root beer	
Brownie Ice Cream Sandwich	$ 5.95
Blonde brownie with Ben & Jerry's English Toffee Crunch ice cream and hot chocolate syrup	
Chocolate Dream Cake	$ 5.95
chocolate mousse layer cake with whipped cream	
New York Cheesecake	$ 5.95
the old time New York favorite	
Tank full of Sundae ... (not quite)	$ 7.95
served with three scoops of ice cream, whipped cream and a whole banana split in two	

Flavors:	Ben & Jerry's English Toffee Crunch, Vanilla, Chocolate or Orange Sherbet
Toppings:	Hot Chocolate, Hot Butterscotch
Fixings:	Jimmies, Rainbow Sprinkles, Mini-Chocolate Kisses or M&M's

Each additional fixing: 50¢ extra

FIGURE 8-13. *continued*

Commander's Palace

New Orleans, Louisiana

The menu of Commander's Palace is a combination of many of the menu examples and price-listing methods covered in this text (see chap. 2). The menu is a combination of a static menu and market listings with sections that include a special of the day listing, a la carte menu, and a table d'hôte menu (used only for dinner, not at lunch). Pricing of the various food items is listed according to the serving methods that are used for the food options. At the upper left of the menu, the restaurant offers a prix fixe meal for dinner on a daily basis. Under this are the table d'hôte offerings. A la carte menu selections are listed on the right-hand side of the menu; however, these selections are covered by the printed evening meal offerings. I think a marketing and sales strategy for the restaurant's special or signature foods is why the food items are covered. Items from the printed list on the right column have at least one of the items changed every day, and at week's end the entire list has been changed to all new items.

The menu is printed on a single sheet of plasticized paper. The reverse side has seasonal colors representative of the vegetation and flowers for the garden district location of the restaurant, with scenes of the kitchen and dinning room of the restaurant.

The restaurant has a quarterly menu change program for all the static menu items. A lunch and dinner menu is offered for selections by the guests. Many of the food items that are shown on the menu are representative of classic New Orleans cuisine, a reputation for which Commander's Palace is well known. The variety of price and food selections is broad enough to maintain guest interest and patronage. The range of foods and variety of preparation methods on the menu combined with the daily change of clip-on selections offered gives a wide array of selections for the diners' pleasure (see fig. 8-14).

FIGURE 8-14

Commander's Creole Favorite

TURTLE SOUP AU SHERRY

CHEF SPECIAL SALAD

LYONNAISE GULF FISH

Fresh Gulf fish served with a potato crust in a caper and onion tomato beurre blanc.

BREAD PUDDING SOUFFLE

$32.00

Complete Dinners

Appetizers

TURTLE SOUP AU SHERRY

CREOLE GUMBO DU JOUR

SOUP DU JOUR

SAUTE OF CRAWFISH

COMMANDER'S SMOKED FISH CAKE

PATÉ PLATE

OYSTERS MARINIERE

FRIED OYSTERS

Salads

HEARTS OF ROMAINE

Tossed with thinly sliced onions, garlic croutons, cracked black pepper, anchovy dressing and garnished with shaved parmesan cheese.

SPINACH SALAD

Tossed with andouille vinaigrette, red onions and sliced mushrooms.

Seasonal Specials

GRILLED FISH OF THE DAY — 32.00
Creole seasoned Gulf fish filet with Asian vegetables and lemon grass tamari sauce and finished with pickled ginger and wasabi caviar.
Suggested Wine - Matanzas Creek Sauvignon Blanc - $35.00

GULF SHRIMP
with CREOLE STEWED TOMATOES — 32.00
Jumbo shrimp with stewed tomatoes, linguine, cayenne pepper and garnished with house made garlic bread sticks.
Suggested Wine - Beringer Chardonnay - $28.00

PANEED MISSISSIPPI RABBIT — 29.00
With homemade tasso and mozzarella, served with roasted garlic and eggplant fettuccine and grilled vegetable ratatouille.
Suggested Wine - Ferrari Carano Merlot - $40.00

ROASTED MISSISSIPPI QUAIL — 31.00
Boned and filled with a rock shrimp and corn bread stuffing, touched with a sauce of natural essence and port wine.
Suggested Wine - Saintsbury, Carneros Pinot Noir - $37.00

OSSO BUCCO — 32.00
Served with spring vegetables, rissolé potatoes in a light fond du veau garnished with shaved toasted garlic and rosemary flatbread.
Suggested Wine - Rutherford Hill Merlot - $30.00

Desserts

COMMANDER'S - MADE SORBET WITH FRESH FRUIT

PRALINE PARFAIT

CHOCOLATE FUDGE SHEBA

FRESH COMMANDER'S PECAN PIE A LA MODE

CRÈME BRULÉE WITH SEASONAL FRUIT

LEMON FLAN

DESSERT DU JOUR

CREOLE CREAM CHEESE CHEESECAKE (add $3.00)

BANANAS FOSTER SHORTCAKE (add $3.00)

CREOLE BREAD PUDDING SOUFFLE (add $3.00)

Flaming Desserts With Dinner

LEMON CREPES COMMANDER'S FOR TWO 10.00

BANANAS FOSTER FOR TWO 10.00

Commander's Palace
New Orleans Cookbook
Copies Available from your Captain
$18.95

A la Carte

Soups & Appetizers

TURTLE SOUP AU SHERRY 6.00

CREOLE GUMBO DU JOUR 6.00

SOUP DU JOUR 6.00

SOUPS 1-1-1
A demi serving each of three soups: Gumbo, Turtle, and Soup du Jour. 6.00

SMOKED WILD MUSHROOMS AND TASSO
Sauteed in a light fond du veau mounted with garlic butter over a toasted aioli crouton. 8.50

SAUTE OF CRAWFISH
In a smoked tomato and roasted garlic sauce and tossed with linguine. 7.50

CAVIAR AND GRAVLAX CLUB
Served with homemade bread, grated egg, shallots, capers and Commander's made creme fraiche. 9.00

COMMANDER'S TASSO SHRIMP
Quick seared and coated with a Crystal hot sauce beurre blanc and served with five pepper jelly and pickled okra. 8.50

SHRIMP REMOULADE
A Commander's Specialty. 7.50

COMMANDER'S GULF SMOKED FISH CAKE
Smoked fish cake seasoned with Creole mustard and served with a light caper cream sauce. 7.50

OYSTERS MARINIERE
Gulf oysters lightly poached in their own liquid touched with cream, garlic, shallots and butter. 7.50

CORN FRIED OYSTERS
With shoestring potatoes and a horseradish cream sauce. 7.50

PEPPERCORN SEARED PRIME SIRLOIN CARPACCIO
Sliced thin with a spinach radicchio, julienne marinated pickled cayenne, grilled onion bread and roasted garlic. 8.00

PATÉ PLATE
Garde Manger's daily assortment of paté, bread and chutney. 7.50

Entrees

LYONNAISE GULF FISH
Fresh Gulf fish served with a potato crust in a caper and onion tomato beurre blanc. 22.00

GULF FISH PECAN
Served with lemon thyme infused brown butter, haricot vert and julienne of carrots. 23.00

CRISP SEARED SNAPPER
WITH KOSHER SALT CRUST
Served with creamed potato salad and fresh peas touched with a lemon thyme infused olive oil. 25.00

GRILLED VEAL CHOP TCHOUPITOULAS
Baby Wisconsin veal grilled and presented with a light fond du veau. 27.00

FILET MIGNON ADELAIDE
Filet mignon, done to your taste, served with artichokes, and veal terrine. Touched with bearnaise and homemade Worcestershire demi-glace. 25.00

PRIME SIRLOIN STRIP
16 Ounces of the very best beef on the market, served with Lyonnaise potatoes. 27.00

CHATEAUBRIAND FOR TWO
Melange of fresh vegetables. 23.00 *per person*

TOURNEDOS OF BEEF
Done to your taste with caramelized onions, mushrooms and blue cheese. Potatoes du jour. 23.00

ROAST RACK OF LAMB FOR TWO
Lightly sauced with a mint-Madeira demi-glace. 30.00 *per person*

Side Salads

HEARTS OF ROMAINE
Tossed with thinly sliced onions, garlic croutons, cracked black pepper, anchovy dressing garnished with shaved parmesan cheese. 4.00

GREEN SALAD
Choice of French, Commander's or Blue Cheese Dressing. 3.50

APPLE, WATERCRESS AND PECAN SALAD
With a local goat cheese vinaigrette. 4.50

BIBB LETTUCE AND ONION SALAD
Bibb lettuce, sliced onions and roasted peppers with an extra virgin olive oil balsamic vinaigrette. Sprinkled with crumbled blue cheese. 5.00

WE ASK THAT OUR PATRONS REFRAIN FROM CIGAR AND PIPE SMOKING.

4/95

FIGURE 8-14. *continued*

Accuracy in Menus

The glowing descriptions—*homemade, corn-fed, ground sirloin*, and other similar phrases—are gone from our menus forever unless they are the truth. Several years ago it was said that "if you think consumerism is a gun in your back today, it is going to be a knife at your throat in the future." Accuracy-in-menu legislation has thrust the restaurant industry into that future.

The restaurant industry's attention to truth-in-menu intensified back in the mid 70s. At that time, consumer advocates were calling for uniform standards for labeling and advertising. This naturally spilled over to include restaurant menu wording. Consumer groups claimed that too many liberties were being taken with descriptive copy and misrepresentations were being made. The national chains like McDonald's and Kentucky Fried Chicken were closely monitored for truth-in-menu. Today there is a resurgence of people urging a labeling law for menu items that will list the content and nutritional makeup of the menu items. The National Restaurant Association and many state associations have published guidelines on acceptable menu language and content to guide us.

There is at this time a group of general rules that have been compiled by the NRA and several state restaurant associations to head off increased governmental involvement with new legislation and to assist the restaurant owners in writing menu copy accurately and truthfully. Many suggestions were made in chapters 2 and 3, but all menu copy must remain within the rules and laws of acceptable menu writing. Examples shown in this chapter are taken from NRA guidelines for menu copy. The decade of the 90s has brought increased consumerism and governmental regulation to the restaurant industry.

Do not promise anything you can not do. We have now reached a point of being required to prove and defend what is contained in the menu. The era is one of truth-in-menu and high standards for professionalism. Today's customer is wiser and more knowledgeable about foods and is more discriminating.

THE RESTAURANT OPERATOR'S OBLIGATION

Government regulation at all levels of the restaurant industry is cause for alarm. The industry does not need any additional laws or reviewing agencies to restrict its free-enterprise operations. Without regulations being imposed on us, we have the opportunity to police ourselves and to take actions that will not require laws and inspection agencies. Every restaurant owner or manager and every person involved in developing menus must assume a personal obligation to total accuracy and truthfulness in the copy that describes food offered for sale.

Traditionally the menu has been our vehicle for appealing to our customers' senses with verbal descriptions of menu items. Fortunately there were only a few isolated—and usually unintentional—occasions when menu copy had no relationship to what was prepared and served to a guest. The intent of menu writing always was to stimulate the guest's desire for a specific food by using the most appetizing and appealing words available.

The Missouri Restaurant Association has instituted a major program for education and self-policing of Accuracy In Menu (AIM). A committee of restaurateurs, food vendors, and state officials has been appointed to review menus for accuracy. After a menu is certified as accurate in its description of items, the AIM logo may be affixed to the menu. This alternative to a government regulation and inspection agency is certainly to the advantage of the industry. Based on my own observations, I believe that customers as well as the government are willing, and even anxious, to have the industry achieve this kind of accuracy on its own. Improvement of menus, education in definitions, and prevention of misleading copy are in the best interest of every restaurant, because they give the consumer confidence that the food served is as represented on the menu.

ACCURATE MENU-WRITING GUIDELINES

Inaccuracies do exist in menus. They are not meant to deceive the consumer; they merely result from long-term use of industry terminology. As mentioned earlier, "what you read is what you get" is the guideline for modern menu writing. Poetic license is no longer permissible in menu writing. Basic, simple, honest copy is a must. The menu is a kind of catalog that implies a contract between the foodservice establishment and the consumer.

Representation of Quantity

Proper operational procedures should preclude any problems with misinformation on quantities. Steaks are often merchandised by weight, and the generally accepted practice is to describe the precooked weight.

Representation of Quality

Federal and state grades for standards of quality exist for many restaurant products, including meat, poultry, eggs, dairy products, fruits, and vegetables. Terminology used to describe grades includes *prime, grade A, good, no. 1, choice, fancy, grade AA,* and *extra standard.*

Exercise care in preparing menu descriptions with these words. In certain uses, they can imply certain standards. An item described as *choice sirloin of beef* connotes the United States Department of Agriculture choice grade of sirloin. One recognized exception, however, is the term *prime rib. Prime rib* is a long-established, well-understood, and accepted description for a cut of beef (one of the primal ribs, the sixth to twelfth ribs) and does not represent the grade quality unless the USDA abbreviation is used in conjunction with the description.

Representation of Price

If your pricing structure includes a cover charge, service charge, or gratuity, these must be brought to the attention of customers. If extra charges are made for requests such as "all-white meat" or "no ice drinks," these must be stated to the customer at the time of ordering.

Any restrictions placed on the use of a coupon or premium promotion must be defined clearly. If a price promotion involves a multiunit company, the units that are participating must be indicated clearly.

All menus should accurately state the total price of menu items.

Representation of Brand Names

Any brand of product that you advertise must be the one served. A registered or copyrighted trademark or brand name must not be used generically to refer to a product. (For example, do not advertise Coca-Cola and then serve other cola drinks instead.)

Your own house brand of a product may be so labeled even if it is prepared by an outside source, as long as it was manufactured to your specifications. Containers of condiments and sauces placed on a table must hold the product that appears on the container label.

Representation of Product Identification

Because of the similarity of many food products, substitutions often are necessary because of nondelivery, nonavailability, merchandising considerations, or price. When such substitutions are effected, be certain the changes are reflected on your menu.

Representation of Points of Origin

Potential errors can occur in the description of the point of origin of a menu offering. Be sure you can substantiate claims by packaging labels, invoices, or other documentation provided by your supplier. Of course, mistakes are possible due to shifting sources of supply and availability of product.

Many geographic names are used in a generic sense to describe a method of preparation or presentation. Such terminology is readily understood and accepted by the customer, and no restrictions are necessary on the use of these names.

Representation of Merchandising Claims

A difficult area for making a distinction between right and wrong is the use of merchandising claims. "We serve the best gumbo in town" is understood for what it is—boasting for advertising's sake. However, "We use only the finest beef" implies that USDA prime beef is used. Advertising exaggerations are tolerated if they do not mislead.

Mistakes are possible in properly identifying steak cuts. Use the industry standards that are provided in the National Association of Meat Purveyors' *Meat Buyer's Guide*.

Home-style, homemade-style, or *our own* are accepted terminology—rather than *homemade*—to describe menu offerings prepared according to a home recipe. Most foodservice sanitation ordinances prohibit the preparation of foods in home facilities.

Use of any of the following claims should be verifiable: *fresh daily, flown in daily, kosher meat, aged steaks, finest quality, own special sauce,* and *low calorie.*

Representation of Means of Preservation

The accepted means of preserving foods are numerous, including canned, chilled, bottled, frozen, and dehydrated. If you choose to describe your menu se-

lections with these terms, be sure they are accurate. Frozen orange juice is not fresh, canned peas are not frozen, and bottled applesauce is not canned.

Representation of Food Preparation

The means of food preparation is often the determining factor in the customer's selection of a menu entree. Here absolute accuracy is a must.

Customers will readily comprehend if you specify that items are charcoal-broiled, deep-fried, smoked, prepared from scratch, roasted, mesquite-grilled, grilled, or barbecued.

Representation of Visual and Verbal Presentation

When your menu, wall placards, or other advertising contains a pictorial representation of a meal or a platter, the picture must accurately portray the actual contents. Examples of visual misrepresentations include whole strawberries pictured on a shortcake when sliced strawberries are used; a single thick slice of meat pictured when numerous thin slices are served; six shrimp pictured when five shrimp are served; vegetables or other extras pictured with a meal when they are not included.

Servers must also provide accurate descriptions of menu items. Verbal misrepresentation occurs when a service person asks, "Would you like sour cream or butter with your potatoes?" when an imitation sour cream or margarine is served. It is also wrong to say, "The pies are baked in our kitchen," when in fact they were baked elsewhere.

Representation of Dietary or Nutritional Claims

Accuracy is essential when representing the dietary or nutritional content of food. Foods listed as salt-free or sugar-free must be exactly that to protect customers who are under particular dietary restraints. When using terms such as *high fiber, low fat, low sodium,* or *low cholesterol,* be prepared to answer questions and to quantify *high* and *low.* Low-calorie claims must be backed by specific data.

The importance of accuracy in this area should be stressed to all restaurant employees. All employees should have a thorough knowledge of ingredients and preparation of foods so that they can respond intelligently and accurately to patrons' questions.

STANDARDS OF BUSINESS PRACTICES

The following is a position statement by the National Restaurant Association that was adopted in 1985.

As a member of the National Restaurant Association and in keeping with the spirit of the highest standards of public service and business responsibility, we pledge to:

Food   Provide the optimal value of wholesome food to our customers.

Service   Maintain courteous, attentive, and efficient service in a pleasant atmosphere.

Health   Protect everyone's health by operating clean, safe, and sanitary premises.

Employment standards   Establish performance standards for personnel, based on education and training, and provide equitable wages and attractive working conditions.

Citizenship   Contribute to community life by participation in civic and business development through association and cooperation with responsible authorities.

Fair competition   Engage in fair and open competition, based on truthful representation of product and services offered.

Competitive purchasing   Purchase goods and services only from reputable purveyors on a competitive basis.

Industry development   Contribute through service to the public toward the growth and development of the foodservice industry.

Reasonable profit   Maintain the ability to earn a reasonable profit for service rendered.

The "truth in dining" movement is not confined to the proposition that restaurant menus be absolutely accurate in the representations. Legislation and ordinances have been proposed that would require identification of a specific means of preservation, method of preparation, or statement of food origin. Such requirements could unjustly imply that certain foods, processes, or places of origin are unwholesome or inferior.

Government action must be confined to problems where its intervention can be effective and at a cost commensurate with the benefits to be gained.

Note. These statements are reprinted with the permission of the National Restaurant Association.

ACCURACY IN MENU LANGUAGE (U.S. GOVERNMENT GUIDELINES)

Menu Listing	Accurate Description	Improper Usage
FRESH	Denotes timeliness or recency of production as in freshly baked bread. A product which has not been frozen. A product as grown or harvested which is not canned, dried or processed. Contains no preservatives to extend shelf life.	Serving a commercially baked or processed food product. Substituting a frozen juice, seafood, and vegetable. Salads made with commercially packed fruit sections which contain a preservative to extend shelf life.
HOMEMADE	A product which is prepared on the premises.	Serving products which have been commercially baked, cooked or processed.
OUR OWN or HOUSE BRAND	Food which is prepared on the premises. Food which is commercially prepared to exclusive recipe or specification. A product which bears your label or name.	Substitution of commercially prepared (baked, cooked or processed) foods or brand name products.
IN SEASON	A product which is readily available in the fresh state.	Substitution of a frozen or processed food product.
GEOGRAPHIC ORIGIN	A product which is grown, harvested, processed or packed at the location specified on the menu.	Serving a product from a different geographic origin than stated on the menu.

ACCURACY IN MENU LANGUAGE (U.S. GOVERNMENT GUIDELINES)

Menu Listing	Accurate Description	Improper Usage
GEOGRAPHIC ORIGIN (*continued*)	Recommend the word *imported* be used in lieu of a specific country unless there is an assurance of continued availability of the product from a specified country. Further recommend the use of geographic area designation for domestic products in lieu of listing a specific state, e.g., "Gulf Coast Shrimp" in lieu of "Louisiana Shrimp." This provides a degree of flexibility and assures menu accuracy if the product should originate from Florida. *Note:* Since the consumer perceives products advertised by geographic origin may represent a desired quality and value, it is essential that the product served be as advertised.	
CREAM	A product derived from milk and contains a minimum of 18% milkfat.	The substitution of half-and-half (contains approximately 12% milkfat) or nondairy coffee blends.
FRENCH ICE CREAM	Ice cream that contains egg yolks and which meets the D.C. standard of identity for frozen custard.	Serving ice cream to include a premium or high quality line which is not labeled French.
MAPLE SYRUP	A natural product obtained from the sap of the maple tree.	The serving of imitation flavored maple syrup or blends known as table syrup.
ROQUEFORT CHEESE	A semi-hard cheese which derives its name from the village of Roquefort, France. Usually made from sheep's milk but goat's milk may be used. Looks like blue cheese but has a stronger flavor.	Making a substitution with blue cheese or serving a product which is not labeled Roquefort.
KOSHER STYLE	A product flavored or seasoned in a particular manner which has no religious significance.	
KOSHER	Those products which have been prepared or processed to meet the requirements of the orthodox Jewish religion. They are usually identified by the presence of Hebrew lettering or symbols on the tag, label or product wrapping.	Substitution of a non-kosher or kosher *style* product.
AGED MEAT (TRADITIONAL METHOD)	Storage of select primal cuts of meat for a period of 3 to 6 weeks under controlled temperature and humidity. Meat is tenderized through enzymatic action and it acquires a characteristic flavor as a result of this aging.	Substitution of meats which have not been aged by the traditional method.
PRIME	A product which is first in quality excellence or value. Highest quality grade assigned to meat products by the USDA.	Serving choice, "house grades" or ungraded meats for prime.

ACCURACY IN MENU LANGUAGE (U.S. GOVERNMENT GUIDELINES)

Menu Listing	Accurate Description	Improper Usage
PRIME (*continued*)	Prime denotes a USDA grade of meat *except when it precedes the word* rib.	
CHOICE	The second highest quality grade assigned to meat products by the USDA.	Serving "house grade" or ungraded meats as choice.
PRIME RIB	A primal cut from the forequarter which contains 7 ribs (6th through 12th inclusive). This beef cut adjoins the anterior portion of the loin in a side of beef. When the word *prime* precedes *rib* on the menu, it denotes the generic name of the cut and not the USDA grade.	Advertising Rib of Prime Beef and serving USDA choice or an ungraded beef rib.
BEEF LOIN	That portion of a hindquarter remaining after removal of the round. It is comprised of the short loin and the sirloin.	
SIRLOIN	The posterior of the beef loin. It is comprised of the sirloin butt (top and bottom) and the butt tenderloin.	Serving roasts or cuts derived from the beef round.
CLUB STEAK	A steak cut which is obtained from the anterior portion of the short loin. It precedes the T-bone and is noted by lack of a tenderloin. May also be a boneless cut from the strip loin.	Substitution of steaks from the top of bottom sirloin butt.
TENDERLOIN (FILET)	The most tender boneless meat cut obtained from the loin of animals.	Serving miscellaneous boneless meat cuts as tenderloin or filet.
GROUND BEEF	A product comprised of small pieces of meat from boning and trimming operations or non-specific cuts and combinations thereof which is ground. Product may be prepared to varying degrees of leanness. There is no USDA quality grade associated with this product unless the product is so labeled or is prepared exclusively from graded (USDA) meats. This product may be advertised as chopped beefsteak (nondescript).	Representing the product as being obtained from specific cuts, steaks or a USDA quality grade, i.e., chopped sirloin, ground sirloin, sirloin steak, chopped round, prime chopped sirloin etc.
CHOPPED/GROUND SIRLOIN	A product labeled in this manner or derived from grinding of trimmings/ portions of meat from the beef loin.	Product labeled ground beef or derived by grinding meat which is not from the loin.
CHOPPED/GROUND ROUND STEAK	The product labeled in this manner or prepared by the exclusive grinding of a cut of round steak.	Using a product which is not ground round steak.
VEAL	The product of a bovine animal which is slaughtered between 3 and 6 weeks of age and seldom over 3 months. The USDA designates whether product is veal when the product is graded.	
CALF	Mature veal slaughtered between 3 and 10 months of age. Identified as calf by USDA on graded product.	Serving this product as milk-fed veal.

ACCURACY IN MENU LANGUAGE (U.S. GOVERNMENT GUIDELINES)

Menu Listing	Accurate Description	Improper Usage
VEAL CUTLET	A single slice of veal obtained from the veal round.	Substitution with veal steaks or patties.
VEAL STEAK	A slice or slices of veal obtained from other areas of the carcass. It may consist of slices which have been formed.	Substitution with veal patties.
VEAL PATTIES	This is a ground formed product which primarily consists of veal.	Serving this product as a veal cutlet or veal steak.
BAKED HAM	A ham which has been heated in an oven for a specified time. The product may exhibit a crust and have a residue of syrup or a caramelization of sugar apparent on the surface.	Serving ham which is not labeled "baked," or a product which has not been oven baked.
COUNTRY HAM	A dry cure ham prepared in the country.	Serving "canned," "smoked," or "fully cooked" hams.
VIRGINIA HAM	A dry salt cured ham from Virginia which is cured from 1 month to over a year. This product is not smoked.	Making a substitution with "Virginia style" or "country ham."
VIRGINIA STYLE HAM	Ham which is cured in the same manner as a Virginia ham but it is not from Virginia.	
SMITHFIELD TYPE VIRGINIA HAM	A dry cure ham which has been smoked.	Serving "Virginia style" or "country ham."
SPRING LAMB	Those lambs born during early winter and slaughtered between March and early October. These carcasses are identified and stamped "Spring Lamb" by the USDA when they are graded.	Lamb not identified as "Spring Lamb" by the USDA.
CAPON	A surgically unsexed male chicken usually under 18 months of age. It is tender meated and has soft, pliable, smooth-textured skin.	Serving other classes of chicken as capon.
CHICKEN SALAD	A mixture containing chicken as the primary ingredient with spices, dressing and possible inclusion of vegetable(s).	Prepared from turkey in lieu of chicken.
FISH FILLET	Fillets are the sides of the fish cut lengthwise away from the backbone. Usually they are boneless.	Representation of other than this market form as a fillet.
FISH PORTION	Are uniform shaped (generally square) pieces cut from frozen fish blocks made from fillets (not minced fish). Portions must weigh more than 1 ½ ounces a piece and are at least ⅜ of an inch thick.	Representation of portions as fish fillets is economic fraud.
SALMON	Members of the family Salmonidae are found in many waters of the world. The U.S. fisheries is centered in the Pacific Northwest and utilizes the following species:	
Chinook, King, Spring	This species, *Oncorhynchus tshawytscha*, is usually sold as canned and steaks.	Substitution of any species or market form for a more expensive species or market form would be considered fraudulent.

ACCURACY IN MENU LANGUAGE (U.S. GOVERNMENT GUIDELINES)

Menu Listing	Accurate Description	Improper Usage
SALMON (*continued*)		
Blueback, Red, Sockeye	This species, *Oncorhynchus perka*, is usually sold as canned.	
Coho, Cohoe, Medium red, Silver	This species, *Oncorhynchus kisutch*, is usually sold as steaks, dressed, and some canned.	
Pink	This species, *Oncorhynchus gorbuscha*, is usually sold as canned.	
Chum, Keta	The flesh of this species, *Oncorhynchus keta*, ranges from pink to almost white. They are sold as canned and as steaks.	
Masou, Cherry	This species, *Oncorhynchus masou*, is found only around the Asian coast. It closely resembles the Chum in appearance, but is generally considered superior. Seldom canned, sold in the Orient as fresh, frozen or salted.	
SOLE and FLOUNDER	This category includes a number of species of flatfish. Flatfish are those that have both eyes on one side of the head. They are found in waters around the world and most species are considered very edible. The following are some of the most common commercial species:	Inaccurately representing specific species of sole or flounder would be a misrepresentation.
Sole	*Parophrys vetulus*—English sole *Glyptocephalus cynoglossus*—Gray sole *Eopsella jordani*—Petrale sole *Pseudopleuronectes americanus*—Lemon sole *Lepidopsetta bilinesta*—Rock sole *Psettichthys melanostictus*—Sand sole	
Dover Sole	A flatfish of the species *Microstomus pacificus* that can reach 10 pounds. It is found in waters off of Washington, Oregon, California and Alaska. Approximately sixteen million pounds of fillets per year are produced by the U.S. fisheries.	The representation of lesser value sole, domestic or imported, as the very popular "Dover Sole" would be a serious misrepresentation.
Flounder	*Pseudopleuronectes americanus*—Black back flounder *Limanda ferruginea*—Yellowtail flounder *Hippoglossoides platesscides*—Dab, Plaice *Paralichthys dentatus*—Fluke *Platichthys stellatus*—Starry flounder	
TROUT		
Rainbow	A fresh water relative of the Salmon. The species, *Salmo gairdnetii*, is found naturally in rivers and streams throughout the United States, but wild rainbows are *not commercially fished*.	The representation of hatchery reared trout as "wild" or "naturally occurring" would be considered fraudulent. Imported trout listed as native would also be a misrepresentation.

ACCURACY IN MENU LANGUAGE (U.S. GOVERNMENT GUIDELINES)

Menu Listing	Accurate Description	Improper Usage
TROUT (*continued*) Rainbow (*continued*)	Those found in the market are hatchery reared and many are imported from Denmark and Japan and should be marketed as such.	
Brook	This fresh water fish, *Salvelinas fontinalis* is found naturally in Maine, Labrador to the Saskatchewan, South in the Alleghenies and has been introduced into waters west of the Mississippi. It is dark gray or olive with small round gray or red spots. It is *not fished commercially*. The brook trout found in the market are hatchery raised. Some are imported from foreign countries.	
CRUSTACEANS Blue Crab	Crustaceans of the species *Callinectes sapidus*, which is about 7 inches across the back. Found in the waters off the Atlantic and Gulf Coasts. Marketed whole and as picked meat (flaked, lump and claw). It is usually more marketable on the east coast than Dungeness Crab.	Substituting a lesser value crab or crab meat for a more expensive one.
Dungeness Crab	Crustaceans of the species *Cancer magister* (9 inches across the shell) fished in the Pacific from northern California to Alaska. Marketed whole and picked meat (body and leg meat). It is usually more marketable in the west coast than Blue Crab.	
King Crab	Crustaceans of the species *Paralithodes camtschatica*, *Paralithodes brevipes*, and *Paralithodes piatypus* found in the waters of Alaska as well as north and south of the Aleutian Islands. They are 3 ½ to 4 feet from the tip of the leg to tip of the leg. King Crab meat is sold both picked body meat and leg sections. It is usually more expensive than Snow Crab.	Substitution of the Snow Crab for the usually more expensive King Crab. Substitution of picked or body meat of either species for legs.
Snow Crab	Any crustacean of the species *Chinoecetes* spp, which is 2 ½ feet from tip of leg to tip of leg. Fished in the Pacific Coast waters off Oregon, Washington, Alaska, Bering Sea and the Aleutian Islands. Snow Crab meat is sold as picked body meat and leg sections.	
North Atlantic Lobster	Crustacean of the species *Homarus americanus* found off the coasts of New England and Canada. It has pincers and is usually sold live and sometimes as picked canned meat.	Substitution with picked meat of a lesser economic value.

ACCURACY IN MENU LANGUAGE (U.S. GOVERNMENT GUIDELINES)

Menu Listing	Accurate Description	Improper Usage
CRUSTACEANS (*continued*)		
Spiny or Sea Crayfish Lobster	This lobster has no pincers and is usually sold only as frozen tails. The tails are sold by size with larger ones less expensive per pound than the medium size. This crustacean, *Panularis argus*, is found in waters from Beaufort, North Carolina, to Brazil and is a close relative to *Panularis interuptus*, which is found on the West Coast of Africa, New Zealand and Australia.	Substituting a warm water tail for the more expensive cold water tail.
Danish or Dublin Bay Prawn Lobster	This crustacean is of the species *Nephrops norvegicus* and is the size of a large U.S. shrimp. They are found off the coasts of Britain, France, Iceland, Spain, Ireland and Denmark.	Representation of Danish lobster tail as a spiny lobster tail.
Breaded Shrimp	The tail portion of shrimp of accepted commercial species, i.e., *Pineaus*. These crustaceans complete their life cycle in brackish and salt water. The tail portion of shrimp of commercial species must comprise 50% of the total weight of the finished product labeled "breaded shrimp."	
Lightly Breaded Shrimp	The shrimp content is 65% by weight of the finished product.	Any misrepresentation of the various market forms.
Imitation Shrimp	The shrimp content is less than 50% by weight of the finished product.	
Round Shrimp	Round peeled shrimp with tail segment attached.	
Fantail or Butterflied Shrimp	Prepared by peeling the shrimp except the tail fins remain attached, then splitting the shrimp meat on its long axis.	Any representation of a lesser value size as a more expensive size.
Shrimp Pieces	Pieces or parts of peeled shrimp without tail segments.	
Shrimp Size	Usually the smaller the size shrimp the less the cost.	
Prawns	Applied to a number of shrimp-like crustaceans which complete their life cycle in fresh water.	Representing prawns as shrimp.
MOLLUSKS		
Soft Shell Clams (Long Neck, Mananose, etc.)	Bivalves of the species *Mya arenaria* are taken from the Atlantic Coast waters of North America from South Carolina to the Arctic Ocean. Size determines cost and use (large-chowder, medium-fryers, and small-steamers).	Substitution with clams of lesser market value.
Hard Clams (quahog, quahoug)	Bivalves of the species *Venus mercenaria* taken from the Atlantic Coast waters of	Substitution of large sizes for more expensive smaller sizes.

ACCURACY IN MENU LANGUAGE (U.S. GOVERNMENT GUIDELINES)

Menu Listing	Accurate Description	Improper Usage
MOLLUSKS		
Hard Clams (quahog, quahoug) (*continued*)	North America from Cape Cod to Texas. The smaller the size the more expensive. "Chowders" are often chopped up for wholesale marketing. Shell size determines cost and use (chowders 4″ and larger, medium 3″ to 4″, cherry stone 2.25″ to 3″, little necks 2″ to 2.25″).	
East Coast or Cove Oysters	Mollusks of the species *Ostrea virginica* found in the waters off the eastern U.S. and Gulf Coast. Oysters of this species are often given names which include the area in which they are cultured. These specially identified oysters have some market characteristic which demands a high price, i.e., size, shape, flavor, or color.	
Bluepoint Oysters	Planted and cultivated at 4 months in the waters of Great South Bay on Long Island. Brings a higher price than the common oyster.	
Chincoteague Oysters	Planted and cultivated in Chincoteague Bay waters located on the seaside of the Eastern shore of Maryland and Virginia. Brings a higher price than common oysters.	Substitution of common East Coast oysters.
Maurice Cove	Planted and cultivated in the waters of Maurice Cove in the Delaware Bay off the New Jersey coast. Brings a higher price than common oysters.	
Cotuit Oyster	Planted and cultivated in the waters of Cotuit Bay off Nantucket Sound in Massachusetts. Brings a higher price than common oysters.	
Lynnhaven Oyster	Planted and cultivated in Lynnhaven Bay waters off Lynnhaven, Virginia. They have a larger size and elongated shape—brings a higher price than common oysters.	
Count sizes for East Coast Oysters		
Extra Large	This size commands the higher price, with the smaller sizes varying proportionate to size. One gallon contains not more than 160 oysters. One quart of the smallest oysters from the gallon contains not more than 44 oysters.	The substitution of smaller sizes for larger.
Large (Extra Selects)	One gallon contains from 160 to 210 oysters per gallon.	

ACCURACY IN MENU LANGUAGE (U.S. GOVERNMENT GUIDELINES)

Menu Listing	Accurate Description	Improper Usage
Count sizes for East Coast Oysters (*continued*)		
Medium (Selects)	One gallon contains from 210 to 300 oysters.	
Small (Standards)	One gallon contains from 300 to 500 oysters.	
Very Small	One gallon contains more than 500 oysters. The least expensive size.	
Olympia Oysters	Mollusks of the species *Ostrea lurida* which are only from the waters of Puget Sound. These tiny oysters number 2,200 meats per gallon and demand a very high price.	The substitution with small oysters of any other species.
Pacific Coast Oysters	Mollusks of the species *Ostrea gigas* which are found in the waters off the West Coast of the U.S. These oysters are larger than the East Coast variety, but are not usually marketed on the East Coast.	
Count sizes for Pacific Coast Oysters		
Large	One gallon contains not more than 64 oysters and the largest is not more than twice the weight of the smallest oyster therein.	Substitution with smaller sizes for larger.
Medium	One gallon contains from 64 oysters to 96 oysters.	
Small	One gallon contains from 96 to 144 oysters.	
Extra Small	One gallon contains more than 144 oysters.	
Bay Scallops	A ridge shelled bivalve mollusk *Pectin irradians*, taken from the bays and the sounds from Massachusetts to the Gulf of Mexico. They are ½ to ¾ inch in diameter (much smaller than sea scallops), and run 500 to 850 meats per gallon. Bay Scallops are usually more expensive than Sea Scallops.	Substitution with Sea Scallops.
Sea Scallops	A smooth shelled bivalve mollusk, *Placopecten grandis*, taken from depths of 1 to 150 fathoms. Much larger than Bay Scallops with 110 to 170 scallops per gallon—found from New Jersey to Labrador.	Advertising the product as fresh or from domestic sources when they are imported.
FROG LEGS	Are the skinless hind legs of any of the members of the family Ranidae. Those mostly marketed are *Rana catesbiana* or common bullfrogs. Few commercial frog farms exist in the U.S. Most frog legs on the market are imported from India, Indonesia, Bangladesh, and Japan as frozen products.	
STATED PORTION	Product listed on the menu by size or weight.	Serving portions smaller than stated.

Reprinted by permission of the Environmental Health Administration—Government of the District of Columbia, from *Accuracy in Menu Language Guidelines for the Food Service Industry*.

APPENDIX I

Nutrition and Healthy Menus

Nutritional considerations are very important in planning and writing a menu for a commercial restaurant. Customers today are very conscious of calories and fat in food, and they are seeking alternatives to fried and high-fat foods. In this section the objective is to offer suggestions that will be helpful and easy to follow when you are writing and planning your menu. The commercial restaurant menu does not need to be as strict nutrition and diet wise as a hospital or healthcare facility foodservice, but it does need to reflect the dietary requirements of your clientele. This is not easy, because your customers' dietary requirements will vary depending on age, gender, and activity levels. The restaurant should offer selections from all five levels of the food pyramid. By pricing certain items a la carte, guests can choose those items that will provide them with a healthful and nutritious meal. The accompanying guidelines in this section will be of assistance in preparing healthy menus for a commercial restaurant.

The following material is adapted from Karen Drummond-Eich *Nutrition for the Foodservice Professional*, 2d ed., New York: Van Nostrand Reinhold, 1994.

NUTRITION IN A NUTSHELL

Nutrition is the science of food (and the substances found in food) and how it relates to health and disease. Nutrition also examines the processes by which you choose different kinds and amounts of foods and the balance of foods and nutrients in your diet. A balanced diet is one with a variety of foods that does not emphasize certain foods at the expense of others.

Nutrients are substances in food that provide energy and promote the growth and maintenance of your body. Nutrients also regulate the many body processes going on, such as heartbeat and digestion, and support the optimum health of your body. There are about fifty nutrients that can be arranged into six groups as follows.

1. Carbohydrate
2. Fat
3. Protein
4. Vitamins
5. Minerals
6. Water

Most foods are a mixture of carbohydrate, fat, and protein. Carbohydrate, fat, and protein all provide energy for the body as well as promote growth and maintenance and regulate body processes. Vitamins and minerals also regulate body processes, and minerals also promote growth and maintenance.

It's been said many times, "You are what you eat." This is certainly true. The nutrients you eat are found in the body. Water is the most plentiful nutrient in the body and accounts for about 55 percent of your weight. Protein and fat each account for about 20 percent of your weight, while carbohydrate is only 0.5 percent of your weight. The remainder of your weight includes minerals, such as calcium in bones, and traces of vitamins.

Certain nutrients provide energy. The energy in food or the energy needs of the body are measured in units called *calories*. Of the nutrients, only carbohydrate, fat, and protein provide energy.

RECOMMENDED DIETARY ALLOWANCES

The Recommended Dietary Allowances have been prepared by the Food and Nutrition Board of the National Academy of Sciences/National Research Council in Washington, D.C., since 1941. They include recommendations on nutrient intakes for Americans (Canada has its own set of recommendations) and are revised about every five years to keep them up to date. RDAs are defined as the levels of intake of essential nutrients that, on the basis of scientific knowledge, are judged by the Food and Nutrition Board to be adequate to meet the known nutrient needs of practically all healthy persons in the United States (*Recommended Dietary Allowances*, 10th ed., Washington, D.C.: National Research Council, 1989).

SO WHAT SHOULD WE BE SERVING?

Dietary recommendations have been published for the healthy American public for almost one hundred years. The most recent set of U.S. dietary recommendations are the Dietary Guidelines for Americans (third edition), which were published in 1990. These guidelines are for healthy Americans ages two years and over—not for younger children and infants, whose dietary needs differ. They reflect recommendations of nutrition authorities who agree that enough is known about diet's effect on health to encourage certain dietary practices.

1. Eat a variety of foods.
2. Maintain a healthy weight.
3. Choose a diet low in fat, saturated fat, and cholesterol.
4. Choose a diet with plenty of vegetables, fruits, and grain products.
5. Use sugars only in moderation.
6. Use salt and sodium only in moderation.
7. If you drink alcoholic beverages, do so in moderation.

Of these seven recommendations, if you follow number 3 (eat less fat, saturated fat, and cholesterol), most of the other recommendations will fall into place. In other words, the less meat, cookies, and other fatty foods you eat, the more fruits, vegetables, and grains (sources of natural sugar, starch, and fiber) you will have to consume to take their place. With less fat, your intake of sugar will probably be lower, as well as your caloric intake, enhancing the possibility of maintaining a healthy weight. Of course, you will still need to eat a variety of foods and use sodium and alcohol in moderation.

The Food Guide Pyramid published by the United States Department of Agriculture is an outline of what to eat each day based on the Dietary Guidelines. It's not a rigid prescription but a general guide that lets you choose a healthful diet that's right for you. The pyramid calls for eating a variety of foods to get the nutrients you need and at the same time the right amount of calories to maintain healthy weight. There are five food groups in the pyramid.

1. Breads, cereals, and other grain products
2. Fruits
3. Vegetables
4. Meat, poultry, fish, and alternates (eggs, dry beans and peas, nuts, and seeds)
5. Milk, cheese, and yogurt

DESIGNING NUTRITIOUS MENUS

Marketing healthy alternatives on restaurant menus is increasing. The American Heart Association has its "Heart-wise" endorsement program. Consumer surveys show that perhaps more than half of all consumers order healthful dishes when eating out. The first step to designing nutritious and healthy menu selections is to utilize healthy ingredients and preparation methods into the recipes of regular menu items.

1. Use existing items on your menu. Certain menu selections, such as fresh vegetable salads or roasted chicken, may already meet U.S. Dietary Guidelines.
2. Modify existing items to make them more nutritious. For example, offer fish broiled with a small amount of vegetable oil or margarine rather than butter, or use herbs and spices to season vegetables instead of salt. In general, modification centers

around decreasing fat (which also decreases calories), cholesterol, and sodium.

3. Create new selections. There are currently many healthy and nutritious cookbooks on the market, many for consumers and some for foodservices.

Karen Drummond-Eich's *Nutrition for the Foodservice Professional* gives specific information on foods that can be used to meet such dietary goals as increasing fiber, decreasing sugar, decreasing fat and cholesterol, and decreasing sodium.

The following should be considered when developing a health-wise menu program.

1. Menu items need to be delicious and attractive as well as nutritious. In other words, if the food does not taste delicious and have eye appeal, it is not going to sell.

2. Nutritious selections need to blend with and complement the menu concept. For example, a self-service salad bar with plenty of fresh vegetables and reduced calorie salad dressings may be appropriate for a fast-food restaurant, family restaurant, or institutional cafeteria, but probably not for a white-tablecloth operation. Nutritious items should not dominate a menu, as only a minority of customers will order from it.

3. Menu items need to be creative and convey a desirable image. The old-fashioned diet plate of a hamburger with no roll, cottage cheese, and a canned pear is not novel, desirable, or nutritious!

4. A successful nutrition program starts with only two to four entrees and one to two appetizers and desserts. Start off simple, with only a few quality items, and then evaluate the success of the program to see if it is worth expanding. Keep in mind that on the average, 15 to 20 percent of orders come from this section of the menu; also bear in mind that selection of rich desserts has been increasing.

5. Quite often a nutrition program is of interest to lunch customers who are likely to be businesspeople who eat out more frequently. Dinner customers may be out for social reasons and want to indulge in a heavier meal.

6. All new recipes need to be tested and evaluated by staff and management.

7. Last, but certainly not least, nutritious menu selections need to be profitable, just like every other selection on the menu. A thorough cost analysis should be done on each item, and prices set accordingly.

COMPUTERIZED NUTRIENT ANALYSIS

Computers are becoming a very popular tool for analyzing and amounts of nutrients in a recipe. Little wonder when a task that used to take half an hour or more can be done in less than a few minutes by a computer. The computer has done a lot to speed up this process and increase its accuracy. Computerized nutrient-analysis programs contain the nutrient information of many different resources.

By typing in the name of an ingredient, the computer lists similar ingredients so that you can choose exactly which one is appropriate. You then type in how much of that ingredient you want to be used in the analysis, such as 1 cup. After inputting all the ingredients, you can ask the computer to divide the results by the yield, such as 12 portions. Then the computer will tell you exactly how much of each nutrient (and the percent of the RDA) is contained in 1 portion.

Most computer analysis programs can also give you a percentage breakdown of calories from protein, fat, carbohydrate, and alcohol. These figures are all printed out and/or stored in the computer's memory. Restaurateurs may find this information useful to provide to customers and also to determine which recipes might fit into a nutritious dining program.

Nutrition calculations of daily requirements are easily determined within the cycle of the menu. Variations of the items on the menu can be accomplished within the menu. Significant changes can be made to improve the combinations of colors, flavorings, shapes, and textures by changing selected menu items. The menu can be planned or adjusted within the cycles to reflect the typical seasonal foods and holidays within the time frame of the cycle. Computer programs are now on the market that can write the entire cycle and check item repeats for the number of times a specific item is offered during the cycle.

These programs will also calculate and do arithmetic and accounting functions for the item's serving cost, nutritional value of the food, inventory calculation, and ordering amounts based on menus and recipes. The program will also calculate the inventory cost based upon the recipe cost and usage control input.

APPENDIX 2

Americans with Disabilities Act Resources and Information

This information concerning the Americans with Disabilities Act is an information source as opposed to a knowledge source as well as a resource for additional information.

The ADA became effective July 26, 1994, and at that time all restaurants were required to offer barrier-free access and service to all disabled persons. The material here is a general guide for managers, owners, and builders for providing the service and facilities that are required by this act. The access that is required includes entry, table seating, service, and rest rooms within the restaurant. This law opens a new market group to the restaurant industry; the disabled are people who may not have been in your customer pool prior to this date.

The law requires compliance for all new construction and requires modification of existing restaurants to make them accessible to all persons. You may be required to give the employees additional training on how to deal with and respond to individuals with a disability. Sensitivity to the needs of the disabled by the staff is a most critical area for compliance with the service of disabled persons. Most of the access require-

ments can be met by retrofitting the existing facility with a minimum amount of expense.

The information that is included in this section gives basic requirements of the act for access only and is a reproduction from material published by the National Restaurant Association. You may need to meet additional requirements of the total act to comply with the requirements for hearing impaired persons or persons who are sightless, depending on what level you will attain in your point of compliance with the requirements of the legislation.

HOW THE ADA AFFECTS YOUR RESTAURANT

All areas of the restaurant used by the public are places of public accommodation under the ADA and thus are subject to the requirements of Title III. That title regulates access to both a restaurant's physical facilities and to the services it offers. In terms of access to physical facilities, new construction designed for first occupancy after January 26, 1993, is required to meet the ADA Accessibility Guidelines (ADAAG). ADAAG provides technical design requirements to assure that the newly constructed facilities are accessible to individuals with disabilities. Alterations undertaken after January 26, 1992, that affect the usability of the facility must also meet the guidelines. **Existing facilities are not required to be retrofitted to provide full accessibility. However, barrier removal that is readily achievable, defined as easily accomplishable without significant difficulty or expense, is required in all existing buildings.** The factors for determining what is readily achievable in removing barriers are listed in the NRA booklet *Americans with Disabilities Act—Answers for Foodservice Operators.* Details are shown on how to identify barriers. Examples of readily achievable barrier removal include rearranging tables, installing grab bars in rest room stalls, adding signage to direct a customer to an existing accessible entrance or to demarcate men's and women's rest rooms in Braille or raised letters, and providing a ramp over a few steps. A checklist is included in chapter 2 of the booklet to help identify barriers and to suggest solutions. When barrier removal is not readily achievable, alternative methods involving service should be used as long as those alternative methods are readily achievable.

Title III also has a significant impact in terms of how services are delivered to customers and requires that such services be delivered in a nondiscriminatory manner. There are three important requirements for nondiscrimination in relation to services.

1. Eligibility Criteria. A foodservice operator cannot impose criteria that might screen out individuals with disabilities. Legitimate safety concerns and standard policies that relate to all customers are permitted. For example, if an individual is disturbing other patrons with noisy outbursts, management may ask the individual to leave even if the outburst is related to mental illness; it is not discriminatory as long as the same standard of asking disruptive individuals to leave applies to all patrons.

2. Modifications in Policies. This requires that changes be made to accommodate patrons with disabilities. Modifying the restaurant's policy concerning pets to permit access by a person accompanied by a service animal is a good example.

3. Auxiliary Aids and Services. This is a very new concept and requirement under the ADA. It calls for effective communication with patrons who may

have vision, hearing, speech, or cognitive disabilities. Expensive equipment is not required. The idea is to offer a means to exchange information. Examples include reading a menu to a patron who is visually impaired, or providing volume control devices for public telephones and note paper and pencils for patrons with hearing disabilities. When providing an auxiliary aid or service requires significant difficulty or expense, then it may be considered an undue burden and need not be provided. However, although the criteria for determining undue burden are identical to those for readily achievable barrier removal, there is a higher standard for providing auxiliary aids and services. This higher standard in a sense acknowledges that people with communication disabilities have been discriminated against with minimal legal recourse until the ADA. While architectural access has been a requirement for many years, increased communications access is expanded under ADA.

WHAT DO OTHER TITLES COVER?

Title II contains the requirements that apply to all units of state and local government including public sector dining facilities. Generally, all public entities must comply with the requirements of Titles I and II and assure that facilities and services are accessible to individuals with disabilities. Accessibility requirements for transportation facilities and services are covered under both Title II and III. Title IV requires the establishment of interstate telecommunications relay services to provide national telephone communication access to individuals who have hearing or speech disabilities. A relay system enables an individual who has a hearing or speech disability to communicate over the telephone through the use of a communications assistant who is trained to convey conversations between an individual who uses a text telephone (such as a Telecommunications Device for the Deaf, or TDD) and one who does not use such a device. Through use of the relay service, people who have hearing or speech disabilities will be able to call a restaurant to make a reservation.

The Council of the Better Business Bureaus Foundation provides the following guidelines as their guide for compliance with the ADA. Shown below are the general requirements concerning compliance to the act according to the Better Business Bureaus' Foundation. The requirements are shown to provide a measure of the similarity between the NRA and the foundation requirements. Additional and more detailed information can be obtained by contacting the foundation at the address listed below.

WHO IS PROTECTED?

Under the ADA, a person with a disability is someone with a physical or mental impairment that substantially limits one or more major life activities, or someone with a record of such an impairment or who is regarded as having such an impairment.

Examples of disabilities include orthopedic, visual, speech, and hearing impairments; cerebral palsy; epilepsy; muscular dystrophy; multiple sclerosis; cancer; heart disease; diabetes; mental retardation; psychiatric disability; specific learning disabilities; HIV disease (whether symptomatic or asymptomatic); tuberculosis; drug addiction (although people who are currently illegally using drugs are not covered); and alcoholism.

WHAT ARE "PUBLIC ACCOMMODATIONS" UNDER THE ADA?

Title III of the ADA specifies twelve types of business entities that, regardless of size, are considered *public accommodations* and are covered by the law. They are (1) places of lodging, (2) places of exhibition, (3) places of entertainment, (4) places of public gathering, (5) places of public display or collection, (6) places of recreation and exercise, (7) private educational institutions, (8) establishments serving food or drink, (9) sales or rental establishments, (10) service establishments, (11) stations used for specific public transportation, and (12) social service center establishments.

WHEN MUST PUBLIC ACCOMMODATIONS COMPLY WITH THE ADA?

Title III went into effect on January 26, 1992, for all covered businesses, including small ones. However, small businesses have been given a grace period before legal action can be taken against them. For businesses with ten or fewer employees and gross annual receipts of less than $500,000, the grace period extends until January 26, 1993. This grace period does not apply to violations of the ADA's requirements for new construction or alterations.

ACTIONS THAT ARE DISCRIMINATORY

The ADA identifies actions that discriminate against people with disabilities. In general, denial of the right to participate and unequal or separate treatment are prohibited by the ADA. For example, a business cannot ask a person with a disability to leave because an employee or another customer is uncomfortable with that person's disability or because its insurance company's conditions of coverage or rates depend on the absence of people with disabilities. Nor, for example, can people with disabilities be limited to attending only certain performances at a theater.

SERVICES IN AN INTEGRATED SETTING

Title III requires that public accommodations provide their services to people with disabilities in the most integrated setting possible. For example, restaurants may not seat an individual with a disability in a segregated or separate section solely because she or he has a disability.

REASONABLE MODIFICATIONS TO POLICIES, PRACTICES, AND PROCEDURES

Public accommodations are required to make reasonable modifications to their policies, practices, and procedures in order to make their goods and services available to people with disabilities unless the business can demonstrate that a modification would fundamentally alter the nature of the goods or services provided. For example, a restaurant or bar with a blanket "no pets allowed" policy must modify the policy by making an exception for service animals used by persons with disabilities.

ELIGIBILITY CRITERIA

A public accommodation is not allowed to apply eligibility criteria for its goods or services that tend to, or that actually do, screen out people with disabilities except when the criteria are necessary to provide the goods or services that are being offered. For example, a restaurant or bar cannot accept only a driver's license as valid proof of age for serving alcohol because people with disabilities such as vision impairments are ineligible to obtain a license.

The ADA also requires that any criteria used be applied fairly and equally to all members of the public. It prohibits public accommodations from basing their eligibility criteria on assumptions that would unnecessarily exclude individuals with disabilities who, in fact, are eligible to participate in an activity.

EFFECTIVE COMMUNICATION WITH THE PUBLIC

Public accommodations are required to communicate effectively with customers or clients who are deaf or hard of hearing or who have speech or vision impairments by whatever means are appropriate. In the ADA, the term *auxiliary aids and services* refers to the means for achieving effective communication. This term includes sign language interpreters; written materials; assistive listening devices; Telecommunication Device(s) for the Deaf (TDD); taped, brailled, or large print materials; readers; and other communication tools.

The auxiliary aid requirement is a flexible one. The goal is to find an effective means of communication that is appropriate for the particular circumstance. For example, jotting down a restaurant's daily specials on a note pad for a deaf customer may suffice, but this means of communication might not be appropriate in complex consumer transactions such as planning a banquet.

A business is not required to provide any particular auxiliary aid or service that it can demonstrate would fundamentally alter the nature of the goods or services being provided or would result in an undue burden on the business. It must, however, provide those needed auxiliary aids and services that would not result in an undue burden. Undue burden is defined as significant difficulty or expense when considered in light of a variety of factors including the nature and cost of the auxiliary aid or service and the overall financial and other resources of the business. The undue burden standard is intended to be applied on a case-by-case basis.

REMOVAL OF ARCHITECTURAL BARRIERS IN EXISTING FACILITIES— WHAT IS "READILY ACHIEVABLE"?

Public accommodations are required to remove architectural barriers—those elements of a facility that impede access by people with disabilities—to ensure access for customers, clients, or patrons where it is possible to do so in a readily achievable manner. Examples of barriers are curbs and steps; narrow exterior and interior doorways and aisles; rest room doorways and stalls that are too narrow for use by a person who uses a wheelchair; and inaccessible drinking fountains and telephones.

The ADA defines readily achievable as "easily accomplishable and able to be carried out without much difficulty or expense." Examples of barrier removal possibilities include providing a ramp for one or even several steps, widening doorways, reconfiguring display shelves to increase aisle width, widening bathroom doorways, moving toilet stall partitions, and installing grab bars.

The readily achievable standard does not require barrier removal that involves extensive restructuring or burdensome expense. Required barrier removal for a particular public accommodation will depend on its financial and other resources. The readily achievable standard is intended to be a flexible one that is applied on a case-by-case basis.

The Department of Justice has recommended an order of priorities for barrier removal that it urges businesses to follow. First, provide access from parking areas, sidewalks, and entrances to the public accommodation so a person with a disability can "get through the door." Second, provide access to those areas where goods and services are provided. Third, provide access to rest room facilities when they are open to the public. Fourth, take other measures to provide access to the goods, services, or facilities.

If you should need or want additional information about the ADA compliance requirements, the following is a resource list of addresses where information can be obtained concerning the law. The list is not complete but it is a starting source for information.

National Restaurant Association
1200 Seventeenth Street NW
Washington, DC 20036-3097

National Center for Access Unlimited
1522 K Street NW, Suite 1112
Washington, DC 20005

Council of Better Business Bureaus Foundation
4200 Wilson Boulevard
Arlington, VA 22203

Architectural & Transportation Barriers
    Compliance Board
1111 18th Street NW, Suite 501
Washington, DC 20036

Equal Employment Opportunity Commission
1801 L Street NW, Room 9024
Washington, DC 20507

President's Committee on Employment of Persons
    with Disabilities
1111 20th Street NW, Suite 636
Washington, DC 20036-3470

Every State has a human rights commission as well as a commission on the employment of people with disabilities. These offices are generally located at the state capital and will make information available to you at your request. Call or write for information.

APPENDIX 3

Attracting Solo Diners

The solo diner has been around for years. We have chosen for some unknown reason to neglect catering to this market, but it is a very large one that, if cultivated, could offer many returns to our operations. A recent book by Marya Charles Alexander titled *Solo Diners* addresses this market. In it Alexander states that a large number of unmarried adults, people on business trips, and singles who choose to vacation alone make up the bulk of this market. Below are excerpts from Alexander's book on how to cater to the solo diner. We would be wise to follow her recommendations and improve our skills in dealing with and attracting this market.*

SEVENTY-THREE THINGS YOU CAN DO TODAY TO ATTRACT SOLO DINING DOLLARS

1. Honor reservations for one.
2. Suggest dining at the bar to a patron who seems reluctant to sit alone in the dining room.
3. Present the menu immediately upon seating a solo so he or she will have something to do.
4. Encourage staff to converse briefly if the diner wants to talk.
5. Don't force cheerful chatter on a diner who really wants to be alone!
6. Learn (and use) the customer's name.
7. Suggest menu specialties that lend themselves to preparation for one.
8. Seat solos where they can observe their fellow diners.
9. If patrons seat themselves, provide a few large tables for customers to share.
10. In busy times, ask solos if they'll share a table.
11. Cluster small tables in one area of the room so solos don't feel lost in a sea of large parties.
12. Encourage solos to dine where they feel most comfortable.
13. Display full meal setups in a certain area of your bar to encourage dining there.
14. Never greet a solo with "Only one?"
15. Provide reading material, especially newspapers at breakfast.
16. Set up one or more tables for just one diner.
17. Offer a communal table—and advertise it!
18. Don't be patronizing toward solos.
19. Encourage serving staff to get to know the customer, to make him or her feel "at home."
20. Have staff point out dishes that lend themselves to half portions to make solos aware of the array of choices.
21. Seat solos on the perimeter of the room so they don't feel surrounded.
22. Don't assume that silver hair means the diner wants the senior citizen's menu or discount—ask!
23. Use hand signals to alert staff to prepare a table for one; don't announce it to the whole room.
24. Treat a solo the same as you would a party of two or more.
25. Set the pace of the service to the wishes of the solo. Don't rush and don't drag.

26. Share "insider" comments—about the food, other diners, etc. (But don't gossip!)
27. Seat a solo carrying reading material at a table with good light.
28. Invite a solo to make a reservation next time.
29. Seat solos away from heavy traffic patterns.
30. Never permit a general cleanup of the area around a solo diner, who will think he or she is being asked to leave.
31. Help the diner have a good time!
32. Hire a woman bartender to make women feel less threatened.
33. Seat a solo in the dining room if he or she seems reluctant to dine at the bar.
34. Provide a wine list, even if one is not requested. Looking at it gives the solo something to do.
35. If a solo wants just a salad or something light, don't impose a complete menu unless it is requested.
36. Learn exactly how your solo diners want things done—and do them!
37. Be alert for men harassing solo women diners, and discourage them.
38. View the solo diner as an advance scout; next time he or she may bring a whole group along!
39. Encourage local solos to view your establishment as a second home.
40. Encourage traveling solos to view your establishment as a home away from home.
41. Encourage the female hostesses to chat with the male solos for a few minutes.
42. Encourage the male hosts to chat with the female solos for a few minutes.
43. Share information about the food items as they are ordered.
44. Explain the food items as they are presented.
45. Don't seat solos in the middle of a room unless they request it.
46. Offer a sign-up sheet for individuals who are amenable to sharing a table with another.
47. Offer a large, round table that solos and couples are welcome to join.
48. Try to avoid seating solos by the kitchen (or in a dark place, or by the rest rooms, or near the telephone).
49. If you must offer a less than ideal seat, apologize profusely!
50. Train your staff to be especially hospitable and courteous to solo diners.

51. Educate the staff to the idea that many diners enjoy dining solo and do so by choice.
52. Comp the solo with an appetizer (or an after-dinner drink, or dessert).
53. Let the solo know that solos really are welcome in your restaurant.
54. Ask your solo diners for suggestions on how to better serve them on future visits.
55. Offer a long table where singles or couples can sit together.
56. Greet solos so they feel welcome rather than discriminated against.
57. Offer smaller portions of entrees.
58. When a solo makes a reservation, offer the option of seating him or her with another solo diner.
59. Seat solo diners where they can see what's going on inside and/or outside of the restaurant.
60. Provide ample space between solos and larger parties.
61. Provide tables large enough to accommodate reading materials and the meal.
62. Encourage breakfast solos to bring in their own coffee mugs.
63. Encourage staff to share information about the neighborhood or city with customers visiting the area.
64. Be certain not to discriminate by seating men solos who are behind women solos in line.
65. Suggest that the staff encourage solos to read if they so please.
66. Don't segregate solo diners if by doing so it calls attention to them.
67. Don't seat solos next to romantic couples.
68. Counsel staff not to check in with solo diners every five minutes. Allow a certain amount of private time.
69. Ask what the restaurant can do to make the solo's meal more comfortable and enjoyable.
70. Solos enjoy being briefly joined by the owner or maitre d' for a welcoming chat.
71. Stock good wines in splits.
72. Offer a variety of wines by the glass.
73. Offer special service to solos who dine ahead of the crowd (or after it).

* Reprinted by permission of Rockbridge Publishing.

APPENDIX 4

Restaurants and Institutions Forum

In chapter 3 some reasons were given for the failure of guests to return to an establishment. The last mentioned, and one I believe to be one of the principal reasons, is that some individual at the restaurant was totally unconcerned about the guest during his or her dining time, leaving the impression that nobody cared. The psychological impact of this type of feeling can magnify so greatly in a guest's mind that he or she will simply say, "I'll never go there again." Some of the minor infractions that can build up in this way are listed below.*

1. Anything that makes the guest feel wrong, stupid or clumsy.
2. Salads that aren't chilled.
3. Water glasses and coffee cups not automatically refilled.
4. Hot food on cold plates or hot beverages in cold cups.
5. Hot food that's not hot or cold food at room temperature.
6. Being put on "hold" for more than 30 seconds.
7. Chipped dishes or glasses.
8. Spotted or tarnished silverware.
9. Streaked glasses. (Hold them up to the light to check.)
10. Menus or place mats that are ripped, stained, or smudged.
11. Bread or rolls stale around the edges.
12. Not enough menus for all guests.
13. Boring salad bars or buffets (no "razzle dazzle").
14. Waiting for three minutes without having a drink order taken.
15. Food sitting visibly in the pickup window without being picked up.
16. Running out of china, silver, or glassware.
17. Silverware set crooked on the tables.
18. Tabletops that are not picture perfect.
19. Sugar bowls that are dirty inside (remove packets and check).
20. Salt and pepper shakers that are greasy to the touch or half empty.
21. Ketchup bottles that are coated at the neck.
22. Running out of any item in the bar or restaurant—any time.
23. Service staff with an "I'm doing you a favor" attitude.
24. Banquets, receptions, or coffee breaks that start late.
25. "Flat" soft drinks.
26. Debris, bits of paper and food not immediately picked up.
27. Opening late or closing early contrary to posted hours.
28. Paying top dollar for quality food and beverage and not getting it.
29. Ordering a dish and getting something else.
30. Not being acknowledged with eye contact, a smile, and a hello immediately upon entering the restaurant.
31. Waiting in line when empty tables are visible.

32. Chairs or booths that are dirty, stained, or have crumbs.
33. Not getting free coffee at breakfast if the wait for coffee is more than 3 minutes.
34. Dried-out fruit garnish at the bar.
35. Buffet tables or salad bars not supervised or promptly replenished.
36. Not getting breakfast coffee immediately upon seating.
37. Orders that arrive incomplete.
38. Service staff asking "Who gets what?"
39. Stained coffee cups (check inside).
40. Murky water in the bud vase or wilted flowers on the table.
41. Coffee that's not steaming hot, especially at banquets.
42. Table linen with small holes, rips, or burns.
43. Wobbly tables and chairs.
44. Greasy, dirty rags used to wipe down tables or countertops.
45. Service staff who talk to their order pads.
46. Frozen desserts served too hard to get a spoon into, especially at banquets.
47. Not being sincerely thanked before leaving the restaurant.
48. Managers and staff who aren't listening when spoken to.
49. Being on a tight schedule and not being able to get through breakfast in 25 minutes.
50. Food checks that are sloppy, wet, stained, or calculated wrong.
51. Service staff who avoid eye contact and a smile.
52. Drinking with nothing to nibble on.
53. Butter so hard it rips the bread.
54. Dirty or disorderly kitchens (yes, the guests can see into the kitchen!).
55. The feeling of being "processed" rather than being served.
56. Failure to promptly resolve a complaint (in favor of the guest!).
57. Seating smokers beside nonsmokers.
58. Lighting that's too dim to read the menu easily.
59. Long dissertations of the restaurant's specials (keep it short).
60. "Background" music that intrudes on conversation.
61. Restrooms that are not spotless, clean smelling, and well stocked.
62. Unclear (or absent) signage.
63. Staff eating or drinking at work stations, especially in view of the guest.
64. Poor personal hygiene and sanitation practices (like sneezing, then handling food without washing hands).
65. Soiled or ill-fitting uniforms.
66. Sitting at the table for more than one minute without being acknowledged.
67. Staff who can't answer basic questions about the menu items.
68. Service not provided to guests in the order of their arrival or seating.
69. Grossly inaccurate estimates of waiting time or lost reservations.
70. Wiping seats and table tops with the same cloth.
71. Wet or sticky tabletops.

---

* Reprinted by permission of *Restaurants and Institutions* magazine.

Glossary

Acceptable Sales Factor: A percentage of sales in relationship to total sales to judge the market acceptability of a menu product.

Accuracy in Menu: Menu terms to insure that the food listed is what is served.

A La Carte Pricing: An item priced by itself without normal accompaniments of salad, potato, etc.

Analysis Ratio: A mathematical relationship between any items of operational cost or revenue.

As Purchased (AP): Foods as they are received from the vendor.

Average Check (AC): Dollar food sales or beverage divided by total number of checks.

Beverage Cost: Money spent to purchase alcoholic beverages.

Break-Even: Income from sales equals the total cost of operations, so there is no profit and no loss.

Catering: Food served on site or off premise to a group for a special event.

Check Distribution: The number of persons that purchase at specific levels of price.

Chinese Menu Syndrome: A variety of menu item offerings by the combination of two or more items currently on the menu.

Clip-On: A small card or piece of paper attached to the menu to promote items not on the menu.

Closing Point: The point at which a restaurant would save money by closing its doors rather than remaining open because sales do not cover the costs of opening (e.g., labor, utilities, food, etc.).

Contribution Margin (CM or Gross Profit): The profit or margin after the product cost is subtracted from its selling price.

Controllable Cost: Any cost that is decreased or increased by management actions.

Cost (Expense): The reduction of an asset for the benefit of the company.

Cost/Margin Sales Analysis: A technique to identify menu items that are popular, low in food cost, and that have a high weighted contribution to margin. Combines criteria of Menu Engineering and Miller matrix techniques of analysis.

Cost of Food Consumed: The dollar value of food consumed for all purposes (sold, wasted, stolen, eaten by employees).

Cost of Food Sold: The dollar value of the food sold at menu price to only the customers of the establishment; equals cost of food consumed minus all uses for which no revenue was received.

Cuisine: Type of cooking and food common to a specific group.

Customer-Service Attitude: The natural attribute of genuine friendliness and conviviality that is openly displayed and demonstrated by management and staff.

Daily Actual Food Cost: The food cost determined on a day-to-day basis using one of several different methods.

Demographics: Specific characteristics of your customer base (e.g., age, sex, income, education, number of children, etc.).

Demography: A study of population and its characteristics.

Destination Restaurant: A restaurant where people go to "dine." The social, recreational, and entertainment motives are part of the decision. Budget restraints are relaxed; distance traveled is not a criteria of choice.

Direct Labor Cost: Labor cost spent directly on the preparation of a food item from scratch on the premises (e.g., cutting steaks, baking pies and breads, etc.).

Discount Coupon: A promotion that allows the operator to monitor the number of patrons who come in as a result of the discount promotion. Customer must present a coupon to get the discount.

Discount Promotion: Any promotion where price is lowered in an attempt to increase customer traffic.

Edible Portion (EP): Food items ready to serve after preparation and cooking is done.

Entree: Primary food item on a menu.

Eye Magnets: The use of graphics, type fonts, color, and illustrations to direct or divert the gaze motion or draw the eyes to a specific area or section of the menu to promote item selection for ordering.

Fad Menu Items: Any menu item that attains rapid popularity over a short time span but does not retain popularity for the long run.

Fixed Cost: Any cost not responsive to volume.

Focus Sale: Selection of one item or menu group for a concentrated sales effort or promotion.

Food Cost: Cost of food purchased to serve in the restaurant.

Food Trend: Any menu item that over time becomes accepted as a standard on menu listings.

Forecast: A measure of estimated or expected volume or income.

Gaze Motion: The movement and focus of the eyes across the menu page.

Goal Value: A factor to measure the individual item meeting food cost percentage and profit goal of the operation.

Gross Profit: The amount that remains after food cost has been deducted from the menu price; see Contribution Margin.

Indirect Competition: Any sales effort not restaurant related that competes with the restaurant for the consumers spendable income.

Internal Sales: Any sales promotion based on point-of-sale advertising or done by the service personnel.

Logo: Emblem that identifies restaurant or operation.

Loss Leader Price: Price cuts or special price to attract customers to the restaurant.

Market Plan: A systematic program to make a penetration into a market with the products offered on the menu.

Market Share: That portion of the business done in relationship to the total amount of business done for a market segment.

Menu: The most important marketing, cost-control, and communication tool the restaurant has.

Menu Engineering: A system for evaluating and pricing the menu based on contribution to margin and item popularity.

Menu Mix (or Sales Mix): The total of the individual sales of each of the menu items in relation to total sales.

Menu Objective: A formal statement of the expectations that you have of the operation based on the market plan and menu policy.

Menu Policy: A statement of the number of items and types of food that will be offered for sale.

Menu Psychology: The techniques utilized by menu designers and printers to make the menu a marketing, cost-control, and communication tool.

Merchandising: Whatever is done in the operation to promote sales.

Miller Matrix: A system for evaluating a menu sales mix focusing on low food and popularity.

Overhead: All costs over and above food and labor.

Percentage Cost: The cost of any profit-and-loss item expressed as a percentage of sales:

$$\text{Percentage Cost} = \frac{\text{Cost}}{\text{Sales}} \times 100\%$$

Price-Value: The customer's perception of value based on the relationship between price paid and the customer's expectations in terms of quantity and quality.

Prix Fixe Menu: A meal at a set price as opposed to individually priced items, usually including gratuity.

Pricing: The method of establishing the menu prices to be charged to the customers.

Primacy and Recency: The placing of menu items first or last position on the menu where the item will be most likely to be seen and remembered by the guest when reading the menu.

Profit: The resultant income after all expenses have been deducted from income.

Profit-and-Loss Statement: A listing of all income less all expenses, with the resultant profit.

Profit Objective: The amount of profit that is desired to be earned on sales.

Promotion: Any sales or marketing plan used to promote the selling of product or service.

Raw Food Cost: The edible portion cost of each ingredient in a recipe.

Sales Mix: Sales of each menu item in relationship to total sales of all items.

Secondary Sales: The sales of additional items; i.e., appetizers, drinks, and desserts, in addition to the entree items.

Shrinkage: Loss of weight or volume during cooking or preparation of a food item.

Signature Food: A menu item with local or national recognition as the best of its kind for uniqueness or quality.

Standard: Established quality and performance as a basis for comparison of an operation's performance.

Standard Food Cost: The potential food cost that should exist, provided that all established standards are adhered to and there is minimal food waste in the operation.

Standardized Recipe: Amounts of ingredients to prepare a food item of a known quality at a known cost.

Suggestive Selling: Recommending appetizers, entrees, and desserts to the guest to increase their enjoyment and satisfaction of the entire dining experience.

Table d'hôte Pricing: The pricing of a complete meal at one price including appetizer, salad, entree, vegetable, and dessert; may even include wine.

Table d'hôte Pricing (Modified): The pricing of an entree with salad, bread, and potato.

Trigger Point: A term used to describe the sales level customer count needed for a coupon promotion to break even.

Uncontrollable Cost: Costs that operations management does not influence (e.g., rent, depreciation, interest, taxes, and insurance).

Unit Cost: The cost of each recipe portion.

Upselling: A suggestion made by a server when a customer is ordering that will enhance the food or beverage item, such as using premium liquor in a drink or suggesting a side order of sautéed mushrooms with a steak. In the process the average check is increased.

Value Meal: The combining of a la carte items into a "bundle" priced lower than the same items could be purchased separately.

Value Perceived: A belief by the customer that there is a value to the items that they purchase.

Variable Cost: Any cost that is responsive to volume.

Variances: Differences between the actual and the established standard.

Yield: The usable quantity or edible portion after processing the AP or raw product used to produce the item.

Bibliography

Conducting a Feasibility Study for a New Restaurant. Chicago: National Restaurant Association, 1983.

Great Menu Graphics. Glen Cove, N.Y.: PBC International, 1989.

Recommended Dietary Allowances. 10th ed. Washington, D.C.: National Research Council, 1989.

Uniform System of Accounts for Restaurants. Chicago: National Restaurant Association, 1983.

Alejandro, Reynaldo. *Classic Menu Design, from the Collection of The New York Public Library.* Glen Cove, N.Y.: PBC International, 1988.

Alexander, Mayra Charles. *Solo Diners.* N.p.: Rockridge Publishers, 1990.

Barrows, Clayton W. "Pricing and Profits: Marketing for Maximization." *Journal of Foodservice Marketing,* vol. 1, no. 1 (1994):75–88.

Bell, Donald A. *Food and Beverage Cost Control.* Berkeley: McCutchan Publishing Corp., 1984.

Bove, Tony, Cheryl Rhodes, and Wes Thomas. *The Art of Desktop Publishing.* 2d ed. New York: Bantam Books, Inc., 1987.

Carlson, Harold M., Joseph Brodner, and Henry T. Maschal. *Profitable Food & Beverage Operation.* 4th ed. New York: Ahrens Publishing, 1962.

Dittmer, Paul R., and Gerald C. Griffin. *Principles of Food, Beverage, and Labor Cost Controls for Hotels and Restaurants.* 4th ed. New York: Van Nostrand Reinhold, 1989.

Doerfler, William. "Menu Design for Effective Merchandising." *Cornell Hotel and Restaurant Administration Quarterly,* vol. 3, no. 19 (1978):38–46.

Dreis, Timothy E. *A Survivor's Guide to Effective Restaurant Pricing Strategy.* New York: Lebhar-Friedman Books, 1982.

Drysdale, John A. *Profitable Menu Planning.* Englewood Cliffs, N.J.: Prentice Hall, 1994.

Dukas, Peter, and Donald Lundberg. *How to Plan and Operate a Restaurant,* 2d ed. rev. New York: Hayden, 1972.

Eckstein, Eleanor. *Menu Planning.* 3d ed. Westport, Conn.: AVI, 1983.

Eich, Karen Drummond. *Nutrition for the Foodservice Professional.* 2d. ed. New York: Van Nostrand Reinhold, 1994.

Fay, Clifford T., Richard C. Rhoads, and Robert L. Rosenblatt. *Managerial Accounting for the Hospitality Service Industries.* 2d ed. Dubuque, Iowa: Wm. C. Brown Company, 1976.

Fellman, Leonard F. *Merchandising by Design: Developing Effective Menus and Wine Lists.* New York: Lebhar-Friedman Books, 1981.

Ferguson, Dennis H. "Hidden Agendas in Consumer Purchase Decisions." *Cornell Hotel and Restaurant Administration Quarterly,* vol. 28, no. 1 (1987): 31–39.

Gilleran, Susan. *Kids Dine Out: Attracting the Family Foodservice Market with Children's Menus and Pint-Sized Promotions.* New York: John Wiley & Sons, 1993.

Hayes, David K., and Lynn Huffman. "Menu Analysis: A Better Way." *Cornell Hotel and Restaurant Administration Quarterly,* vol. 25, no. 4 (1985):64–70.

Henderson, B.D. "The Experience Curve Reviewed: The Growth Share Matrix of the Product Portfolio." *Perspectives,* no. 135 (1973).

Hess, Alan. *Googie: Fifties Coffee Shop Architecture.* San Francisco: Chronicle Books, 1985.

Hug, Richard J., and M.C. Warfel. *Menu Planning and Merchandising.* Berkeley: McCutchan Publishing Co., 1991.

James, Robert W. "Decision Points in Developing New Product." U.S. Small Business Management Series, No. 39. Washington, D.C.: U.S. Small Business Administration, Department of Commerce, n.d.

Kasavana, Michael L., and Donald I. Smith. *Menu Engineering: A Practical Guide to Menu Analysis.*

Rev. ed. Lansing, Mich.: Hospitality Publications, 1990.

Keiser, Ralph J., and Elmer Kallio. *Controlling and Analyzing Costs in Food Service Operations.* 2d ed. New York: John Wiley & Sons, 1989.

Keister, Douglas C. *Food and Beverage Control.* 2d ed. Englewood Cliffs, N.J.: Prentice Hall, 1990.

———. *How to Use the Uniform System of Accounts for Hotels and Restaurants.* Chicago: National Restaurant Association, 1977.

Kotschevar, Lendal H. *Management by Menu.* 2d ed. Chicago: National Institute for the Foodservice Industry, 1987.

Kotschevar, Lendal H., and John B. Knight. *Quantity Food Production: Planning & Management.* 2d ed. New York: Van Nostrand Reinhold, 1988.

Kreck, Lothar A. *Menu: Analysis & Planning.* 2d ed. New York: Van Nostrand Reinhold, 1984.

Kreul, Lee M. "Magic Numbers: Psychological Aspects of Menu Pricing." *Cornell Hotel and Restaurant Administration Quarterly,* vol. 23, no. 3 (1982): 70–75.

Krohn, Norman O. *The Menu Mystique: The Diner's Guide to Fine Food and Drink.* Middle Village, N.Y.: Jonathan David Publishers, 1983.

Langdon, Philip. *Orange Roofs, Golden Arches: The Architecture of American Chain Restaurants.* New York: Alfred A. Knopf, 1986.

Lundberg, Donald E. *The Restaurant from Concept to Operations.* New York: John Wiley & Sons, 1985.

Mariani, John. *America Eats Out.* New York: William Morrow and Co., 1991.

McVety, Paul J., and Bradley J. Ware. *Fundamentals of Menu Planning.* New York: Van Nostrand Reinhold, 1989.

Miller, Jack E. *Menu Pricing and Strategy.* Boston: CBI Publishers, 1980.

Miller, Jack E., and David K. Hayes. *Basic Food and Beverage Cost Controls.* New York: John Wiley & Sons, 1994.

Morrison, Alastair M. *Hospitality & Travel Marketing.* Albany, N.Y.: Delmar Publishing, Inc., 1989.

Ninemeier, J. *Planning and Control for Food and Beverage Operations.* 3d ed. East Lansing, Mich.: Educational Institute of American Hotel & Motel Assoc., 1991.

Pavesic, David V. "Cost-Margin Analysis: A Third Approach to Menu Pricing and Design." *International Journal of Hospitality Management,* vol. 2, no. 3 (1983):127–134.

———. "Indirect Cost Factors in Menu Pricing." *The Bottom Line,* vol. 5, no. 5, (1990):22–26.

Pavesic, David V., By-the-Ounce Pricing of Salad and Food Bars, *Journal of College and University Foodservice,* vol. 1, no. 4 (1994):3–11.

———. "Psychological Aspects of Menu Pricing." *The Bottom Line,* vol. 15, no. 6 (1990–91): 22–26.

———. "Taking the Anxiety Out of Menu Price Increases." *Restaurant Management,* vol. 2, no. 2 (1988): 56–57.

———. "The Restaurant Menu." In *An Introduction to Hotel and Restaurant Management,* 5th ed., edited by Robert Brymer, 97–101. Dubuque, Iowa: Kendall-Hunt Publishers, 1988.

———. "The Myth of Discount Promotions." *International Journal of Hospitality Management,* vol. 4, no. 2 (1985):67–73.

———. "Prime Numbers: Finding Your Menu's Strengths." *Cornell Hotel and Restaurant Administration Quarterly,* vol. 26, no. 3 (1986):71–77.

———. "Cost/Margin Analysis: A Third Approach to Menu Pricing and Design." In *The Practice of Hospitality Management,* 291–305. Westport, Conn.: AVI, 1986.

PBC International. *Great Menu Graphics.* Glen Cove, N.Y.: PBC International, 1989.

Pillsbury, Richard. *From Boarding House to Bistro: The American Restaurant Then and Now.* Boston: Unwin Hyman Publishers, 1990.

Radice, Judi. *Menu Design: Marketing the Restaurant Through Graphics.* Glen Cove, N.Y.: PBC International, 1985.

Radice, Judi, and the National Restaurant Association. *Menu Design 2.* Glen Cove, N.Y.: PBC International, 1987.

———. *Menu Design 3.* Glen Cove, N.Y.: PBC International, 1988.

———. *Menu Design 4.* Glen Cove, N.Y.: PBC International, 1990.

Riely, Elizabeth. *The Chef Companion: A Concise Dictionary of Culinary Terms.* New York: Van Nostrand Reinhold, 1986.

Samuelson, Paul A., and Will D. Nordhaus. *Economics.* 13th ed. New York: McGraw-Hill, 1989.

Scanlon, Nancy L. *Marketing by Menu.* New York: Van Nostrand Reinhold, 1990.

Scanlon, Nancy L. *Catering Menu Management.* New York: John Wiley & Sons, 1992.

Schewe, Charles, and Reuben Smith. *Marketing Concepts and Applications*, 2d ed. New York: McGraw-Hill, 1983.

Seaberg, Albin G. *Menu Design: Merchandising and Marketing.* 4th ed. New York: Van Nostrand Reinhold, 1991.

Shaw, Margaret. "Positioning and Price: Merging Theory, Strategy and Tactics." *Hospitality Research Journal*, vol. 15, no. 2, (1992): 31–39.

Shoemaker, Stowe. "A Proposal to Improve the Overall Price Value Perceptions of a Product Line." *Journal of Restaurant and Foodservice Marketing*, vol. 1, no. 1 (1994):89–101.

Shugart, Grace S., and Mary Molt. *Food for Fifty.* 9th ed. New York: Macmillan, 1993.

Stanton, William J. *Fundamentals of Marketing.* 8th ed. New York: McGraw-Hill, 1987.

Stokes, John W. *How to Manage a Restaurant: Or Industrial Food Service.* 4th ed. Dubuque, Iowa: Wm. C. Brown Co., 1982.

West, Bessie B. *Food Service in Institutions.* 6th ed. New York: Macmillan, 1988.

Witzky, Herbert K. *Practical Hotel-Motel Cost Reduction Handbook.* New York: Ahrens Book Co., 1970.

INDEX